W9-BKV-358

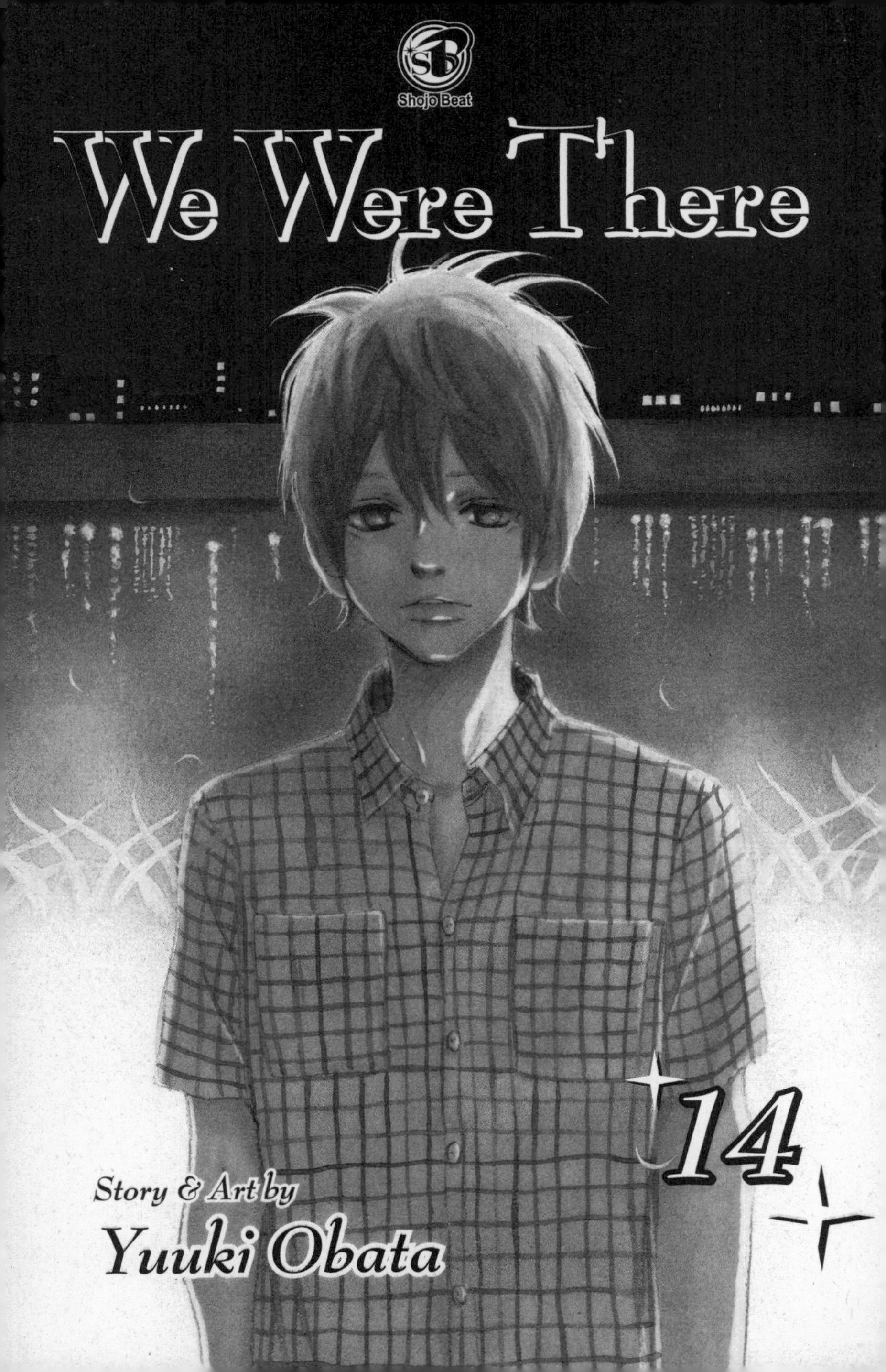
Shojo Beat
We Were There
14
Story & Art by
Yuuki Obata

Contents

Characters

Masafumi Takeuchi
Yano's best friend. He works for a foreign finance company. He used to date Nanami, but...

Nanami Takahashi
Nanami works at a publishing company in Tokyo. She is unable to forget her feelings for Yano.

Motoharu Yano
Nanami's ex-boyfriend. He works for an architecture and design firm. He is currently living with Yuri.

Story

After Takeuchi proposes, Nanami realizes her true feelings, and she meets Yano after six years. But their reunion ends with the two of them having to part. Then Takeuchi meets with Yano, but Takeuchi is unable to hold back his anger after hearing Yano's comments about his relationship with Nanami...

Chapter 54

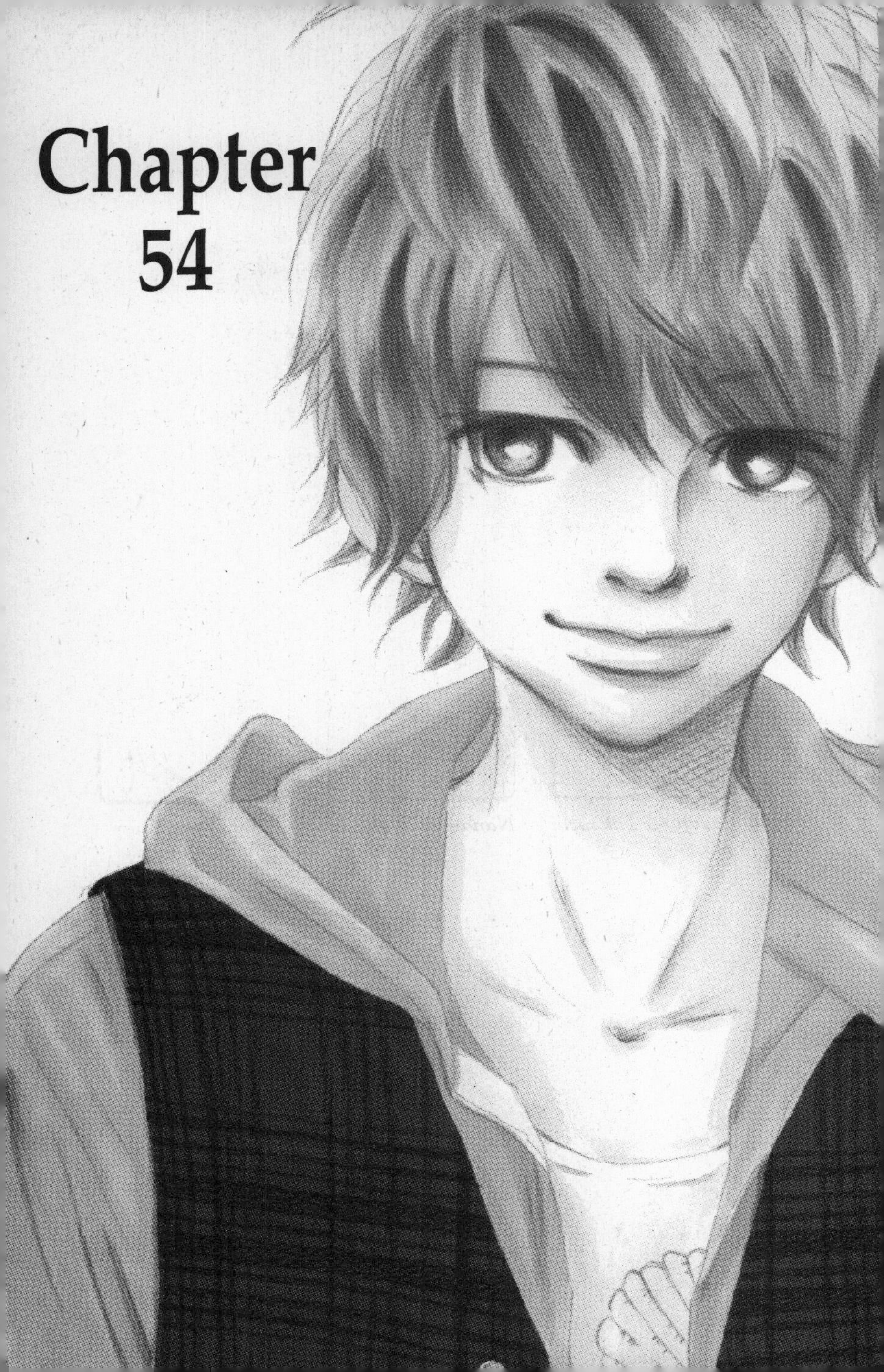

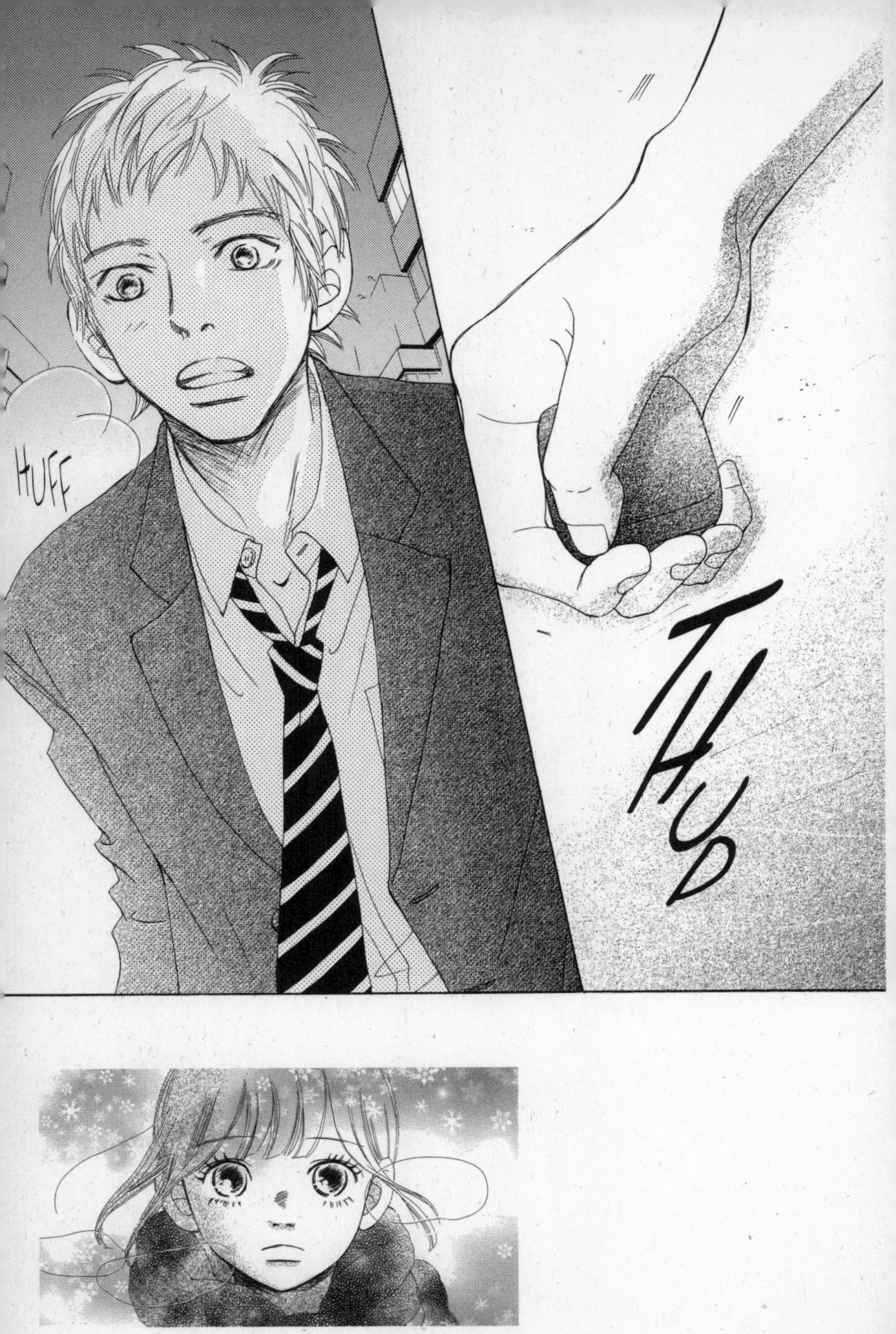
THUD
HUFF

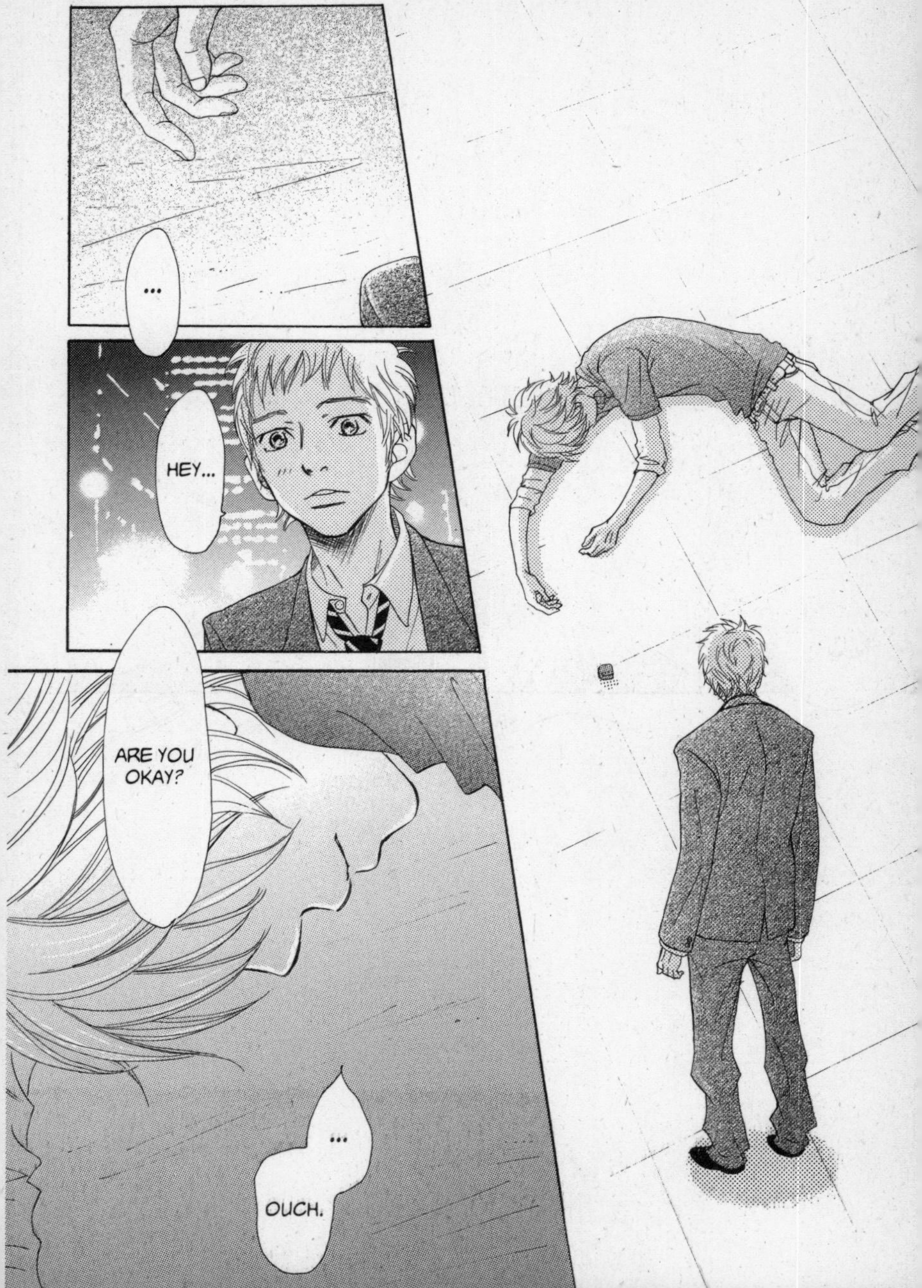
...
HEY...
ARE YOU OKAY?
... OUCH.

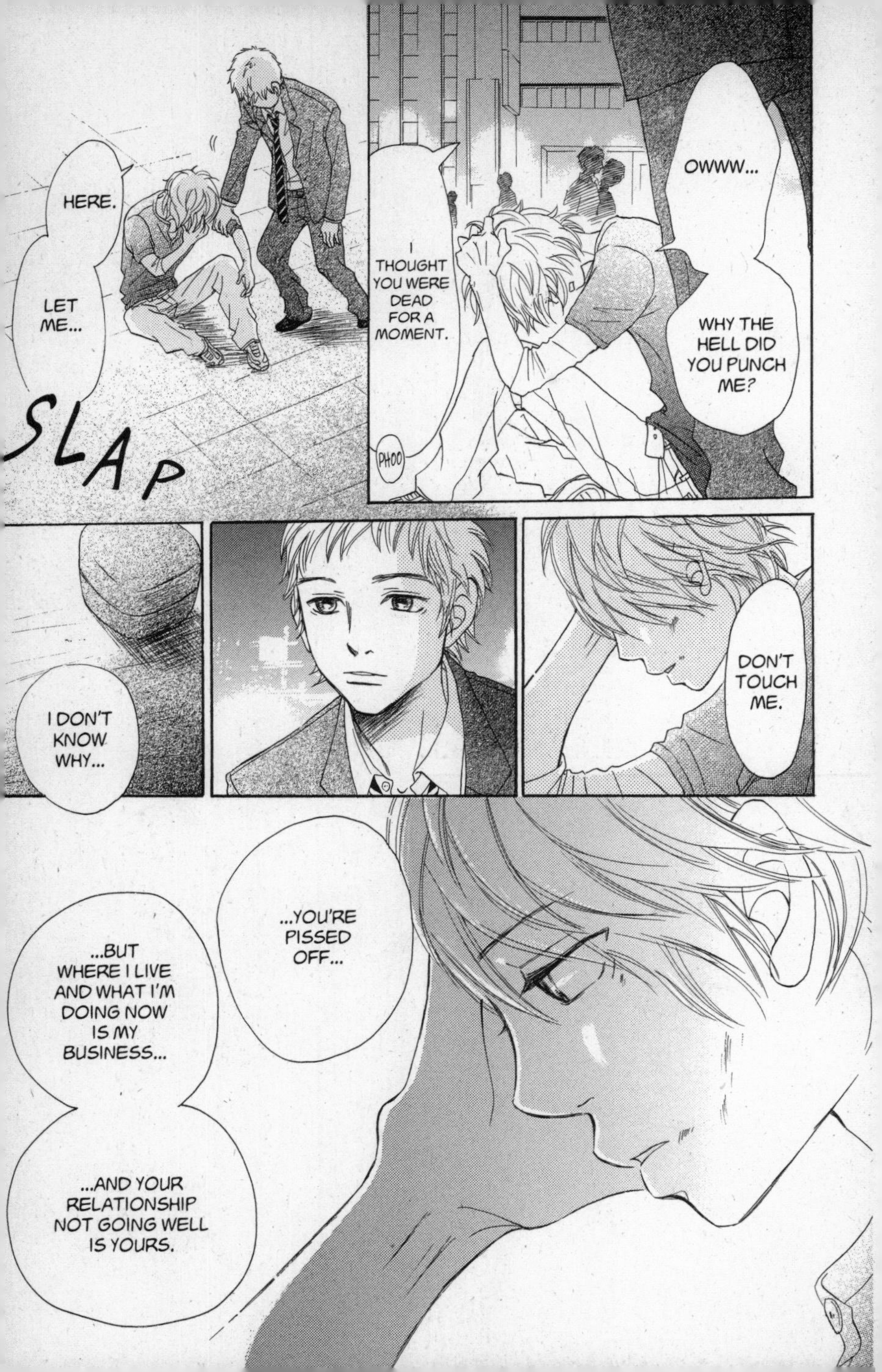
OWWW...
WHY THE HELL DID YOU PUNCH ME?
I THOUGHT YOU WERE DEAD FOR A MOMENT.
PHOO
HERE.
LET ME...
SLAP
DON'T TOUCH ME.
I DON'T KNOW WHY...
...YOU'RE PISSED OFF...
...BUT WHERE I LIVE AND WHAT I'M DOING NOW IS MY BUSINESS...
...AND YOUR RELATIONSHIP NOT GOING WELL IS YOURS.

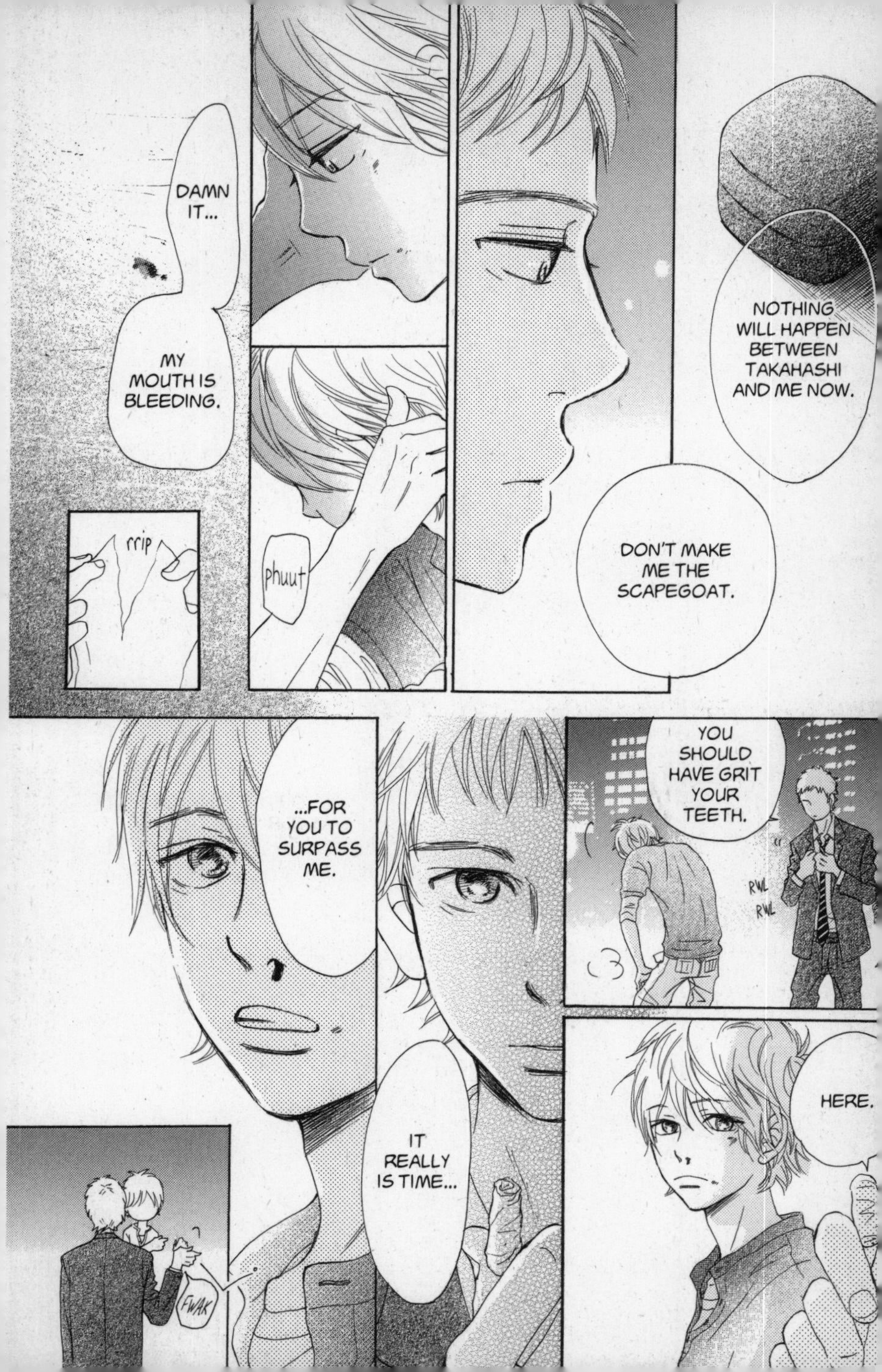
NOTHING WILL HAPPEN BETWEEN TAKAHASHI AND ME NOW.
DON'T MAKE ME THE SCAPEGOAT.
phuut
DAMN IT...
MY MOUTH IS BLEEDING.
rrip
YOU SHOULD HAVE GRIT YOUR TEETH.
RWL RWL
HERE.
IT REALLY IS TIME...
...FOR YOU TO SURPASS ME.
FWAK

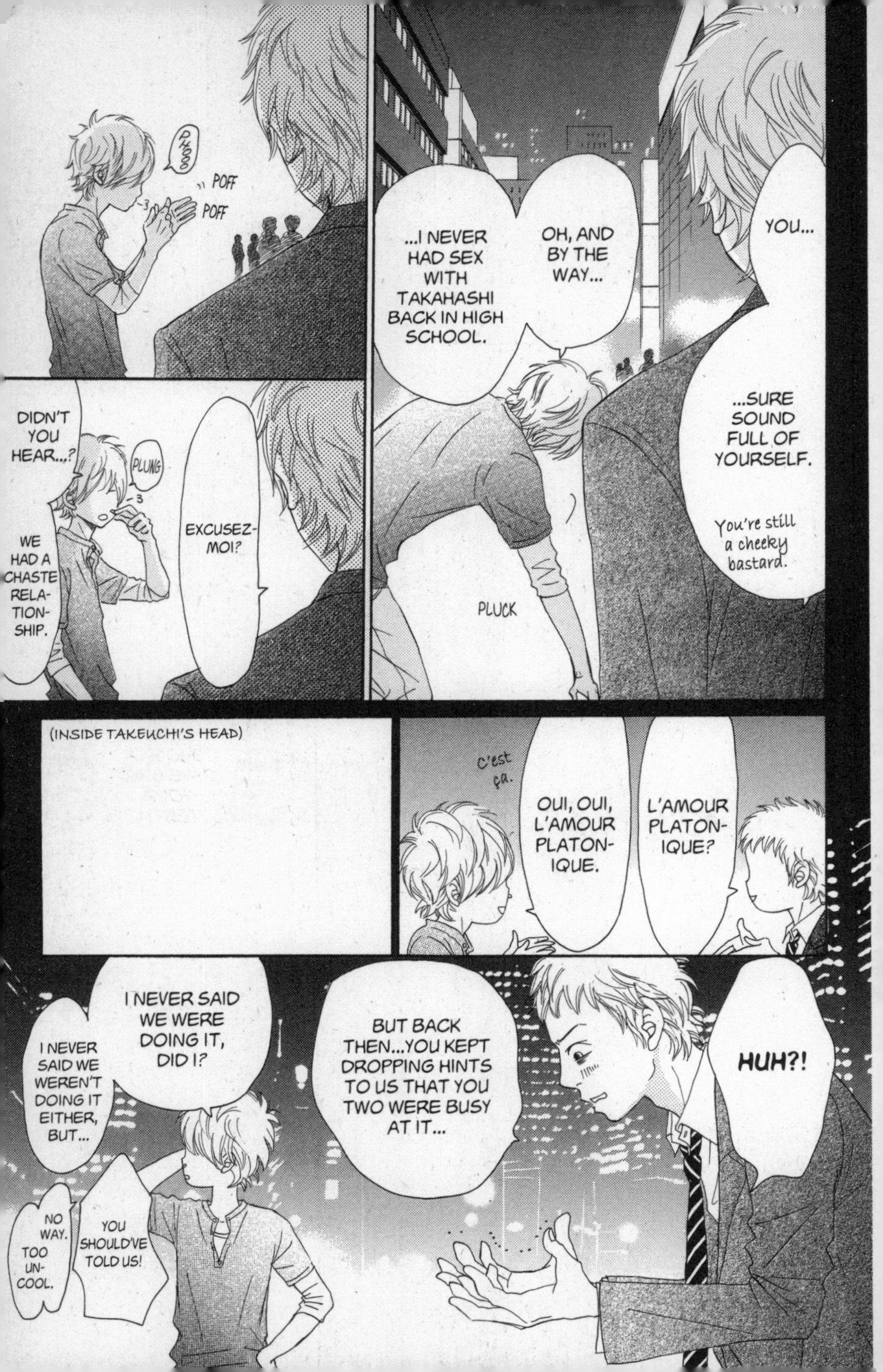
OH, AND BY THE WAY...
...I NEVER HAD SEX WITH TAKAHASHI BACK IN HIGH SCHOOL.
YOU... ...SURE SOUND FULL OF YOURSELF.
You're still a cheeky bastard.
PLUCK
POFF
POFF
EXCUSEZ-MOI?
PLUNG
DIDN'T YOU HEAR...?
WE HAD A CHASTE RELATIONSHIP.
L'AMOUR PLATONIQUE?
OUI, OUI, L'AMOUR PLATONIQUE.
C'est ça.
(INSIDE TAKEUCHI'S HEAD)
HUH?!
BUT BACK THEN...YOU KEPT DROPPING HINTS TO US THAT YOU TWO WERE BUSY AT IT...
I NEVER SAID WE WERE DOING IT, DID I?
I NEVER SAID WE WEREN'T DOING IT EITHER, BUT...
YOU SHOULD'VE TOLD US!
NO WAY. TOO UNCOOL.

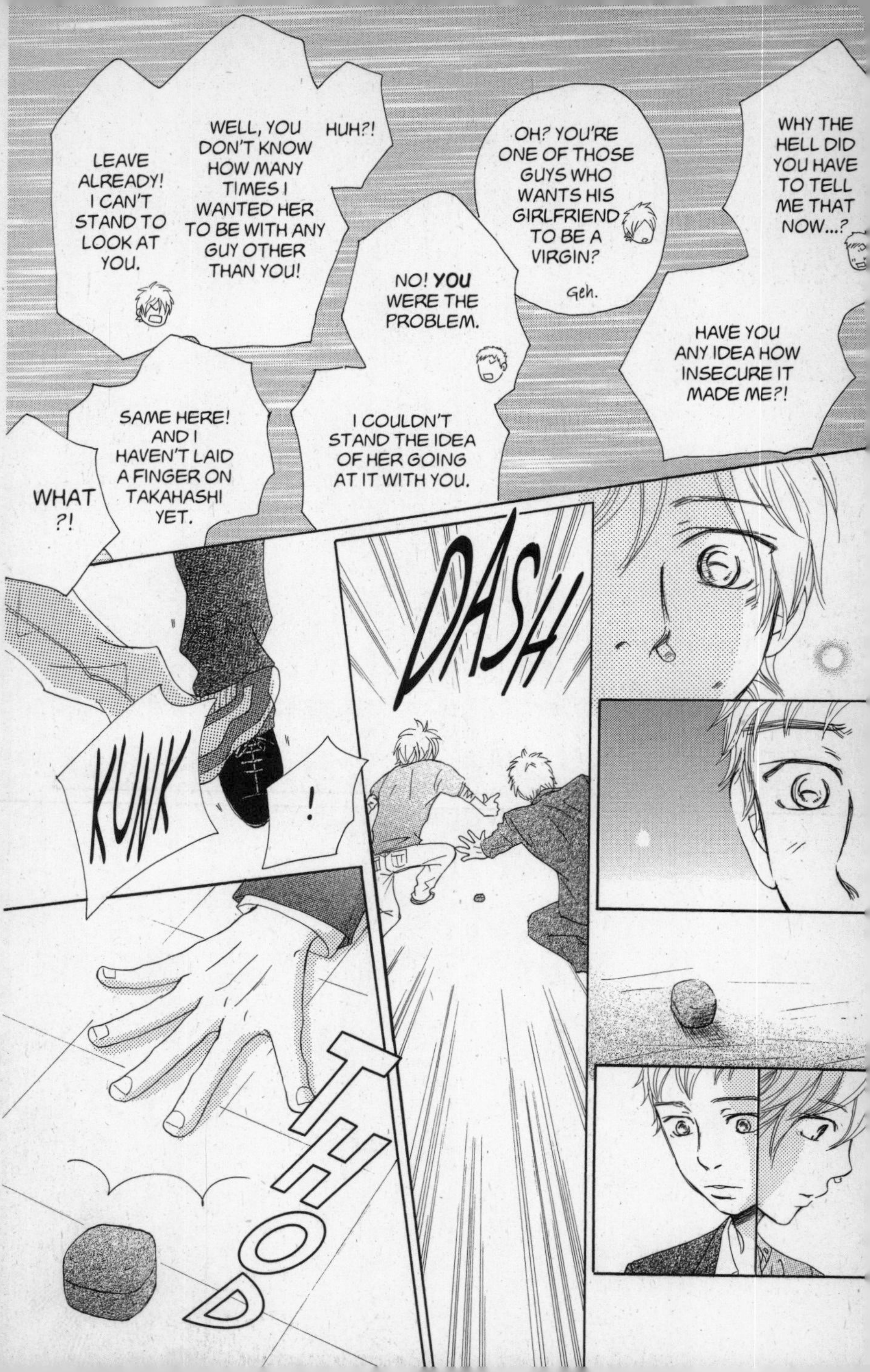
WHY THE HELL DID YOU HAVE TO TELL ME THAT NOW...?
HAVE YOU ANY IDEA HOW INSECURE IT MADE ME?!
OH? YOU'RE ONE OF THOSE GUYS WHO WANTS HIS GIRLFRIEND TO BE A VIRGIN?
Geh.
NO! YOU WERE THE PROBLEM.
I COULDN'T STAND THE IDEA OF HER GOING AT IT WITH YOU.
HUH?!
WELL, YOU DON'T KNOW HOW MANY TIMES I WANTED HER TO BE WITH ANY GUY OTHER THAN YOU!
LEAVE ALREADY! I CAN'T STAND TO LOOK AT YOU.
SAME HERE! AND I HAVEN'T LAID A FINGER ON TAKAHASHI YET.
WHAT ?!
DASH
!
KUNK
THOOD

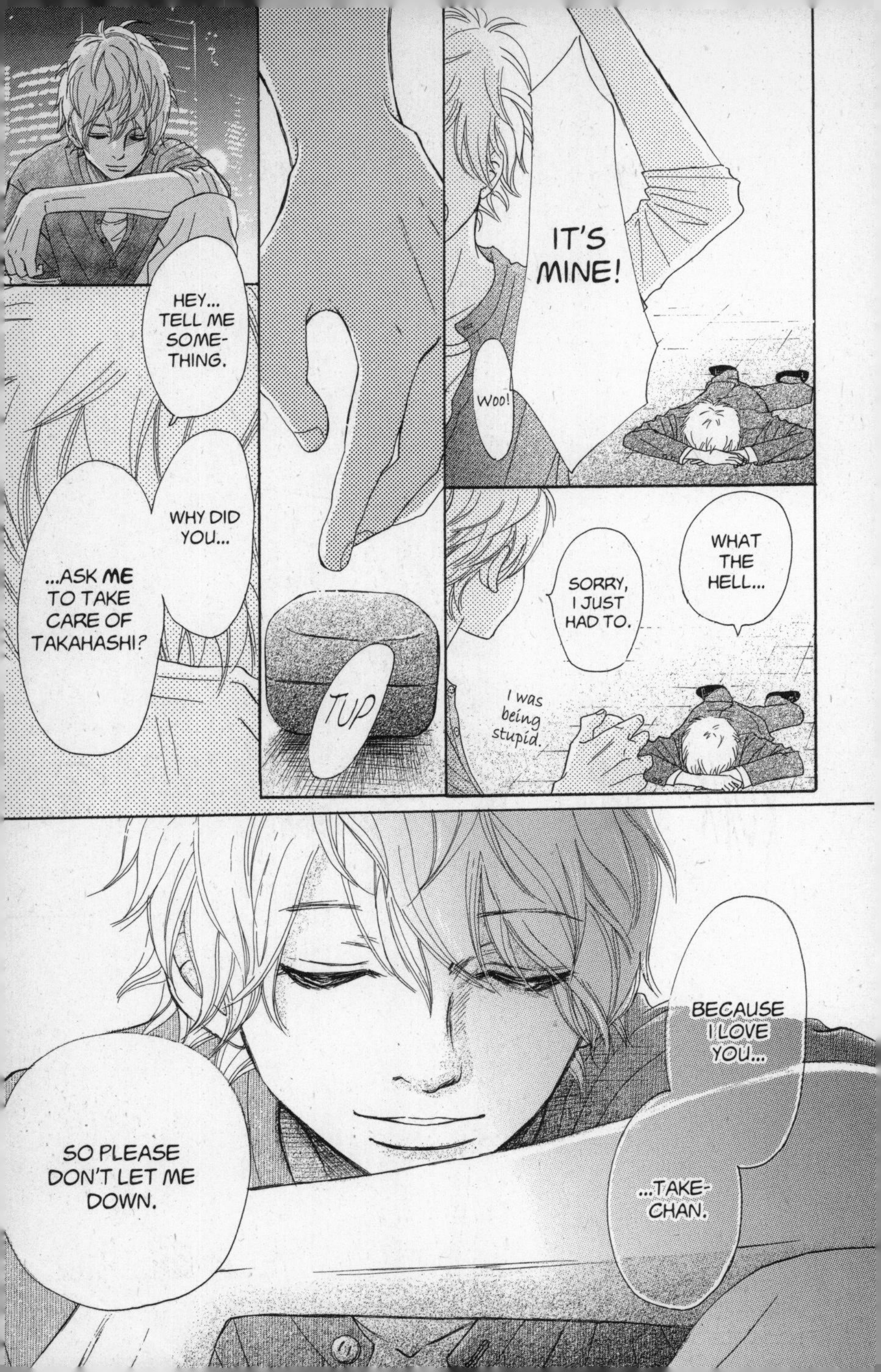
IT'S MINE!
Woo!
WHAT THE HELL...
SORRY, I JUST HAD TO.
I was being stupid.
TUP
HEY... TELL ME SOMETHING.
WHY DID YOU...
...ASK ME TO TAKE CARE OF TAKAHASHI?
BECAUSE I LOVE YOU...
...TAKE-CHAN.
SO PLEASE DON'T LET ME DOWN.

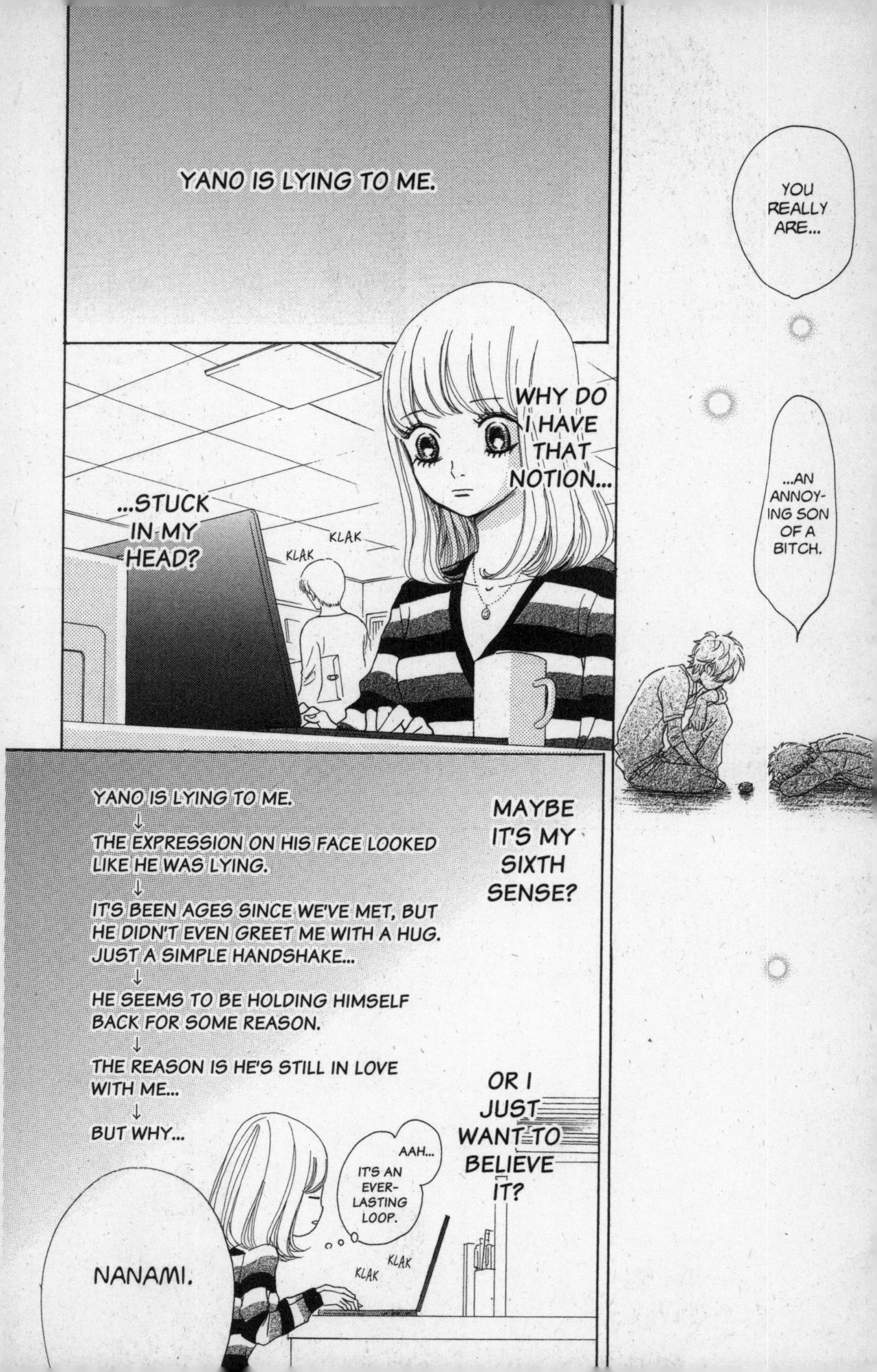
YOU REALLY ARE...
...AN ANNOYING SON OF A BITCH.
YANO IS LYING TO ME.
WHY DO I HAVE THAT NOTION...
KLAK
KLAK
...STUCK IN MY HEAD?
MAYBE IT'S MY SIXTH SENSE?
OR I JUST WANT TO BELIEVE IT?
YANO IS LYING TO ME.
↓
THE EXPRESSION ON HIS FACE LOOKED LIKE HE WAS LYING.
↓
IT'S BEEN AGES SINCE WE'VE MET, BUT HE DIDN'T EVEN GREET ME WITH A HUG. JUST A SIMPLE HANDSHAKE...
↓
HE SEEMS TO BE HOLDING HIMSELF BACK FOR SOME REASON.
↓
THE REASON IS HE'S STILL IN LOVE WITH ME...
↓
BUT WHY...
AAH... IT'S AN EVERLASTING LOOP.
KLAK
KLAK
NANAMI.

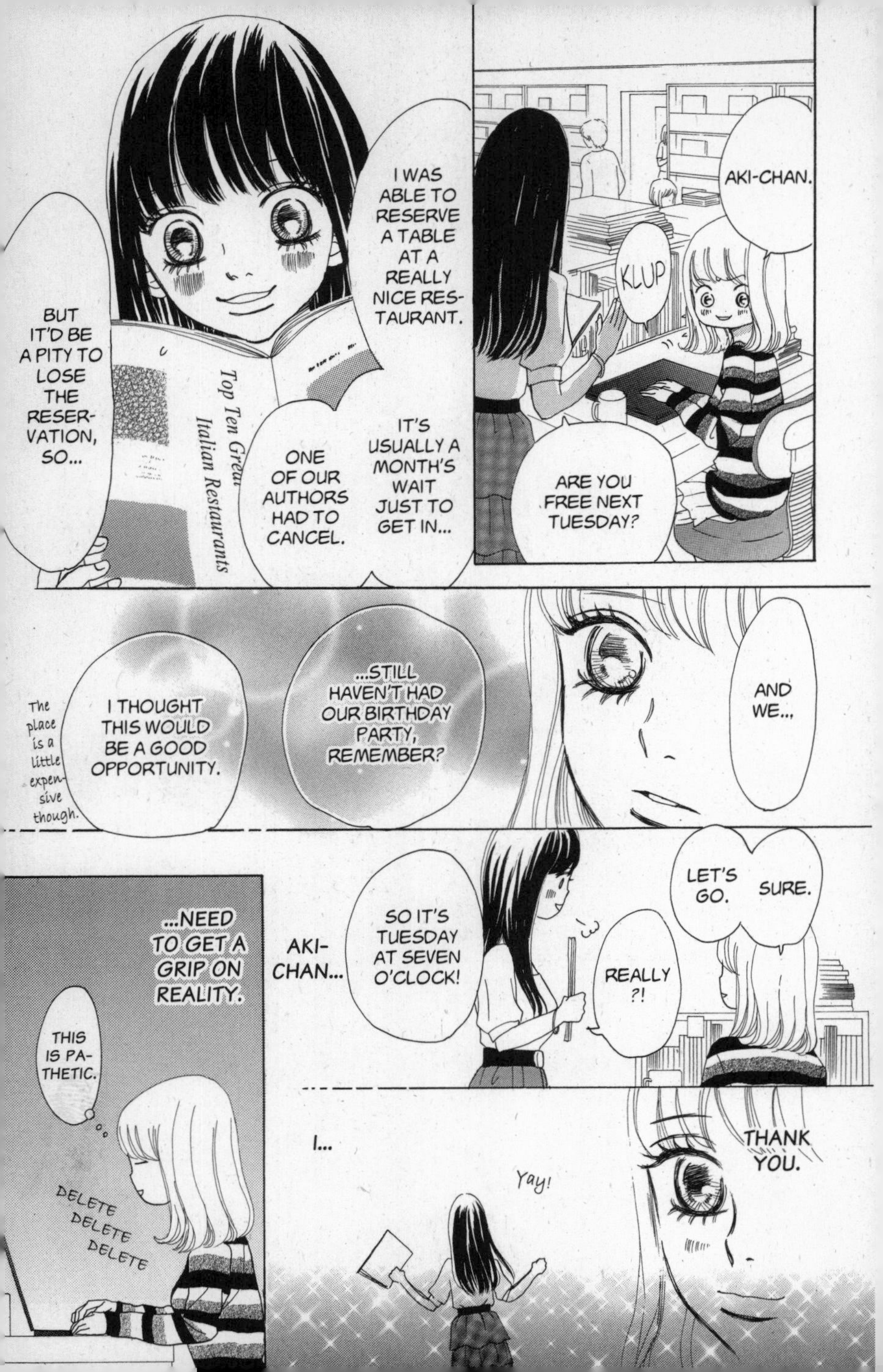
AKI-CHAN.
KLUP
ARE YOU FREE NEXT TUESDAY?
I WAS ABLE TO RESERVE A TABLE AT A REALLY NICE RESTAURANT.
IT'S USUALLY A MONTH'S WAIT JUST TO GET IN...
ONE OF OUR AUTHORS HAD TO CANCEL.
Top Ten Great Italian Restaurants
BUT IT'D BE A PITY TO LOSE THE RESERVATION, SO...
AND WE...,
...STILL HAVEN'T HAD OUR BIRTHDAY PARTY, REMEMBER?
I THOUGHT THIS WOULD BE A GOOD OPPORTUNITY.
The place is a little expensive though.
SURE.
LET'S GO.
REALLY?!
SO IT'S TUESDAY AT SEVEN O'CLOCK!
AKI-CHAN...
THANK YOU.
Yay!
I...
...NEED TO GET A GRIP ON REALITY.
THIS IS PATHETIC.
DELETE DELETE DELETE

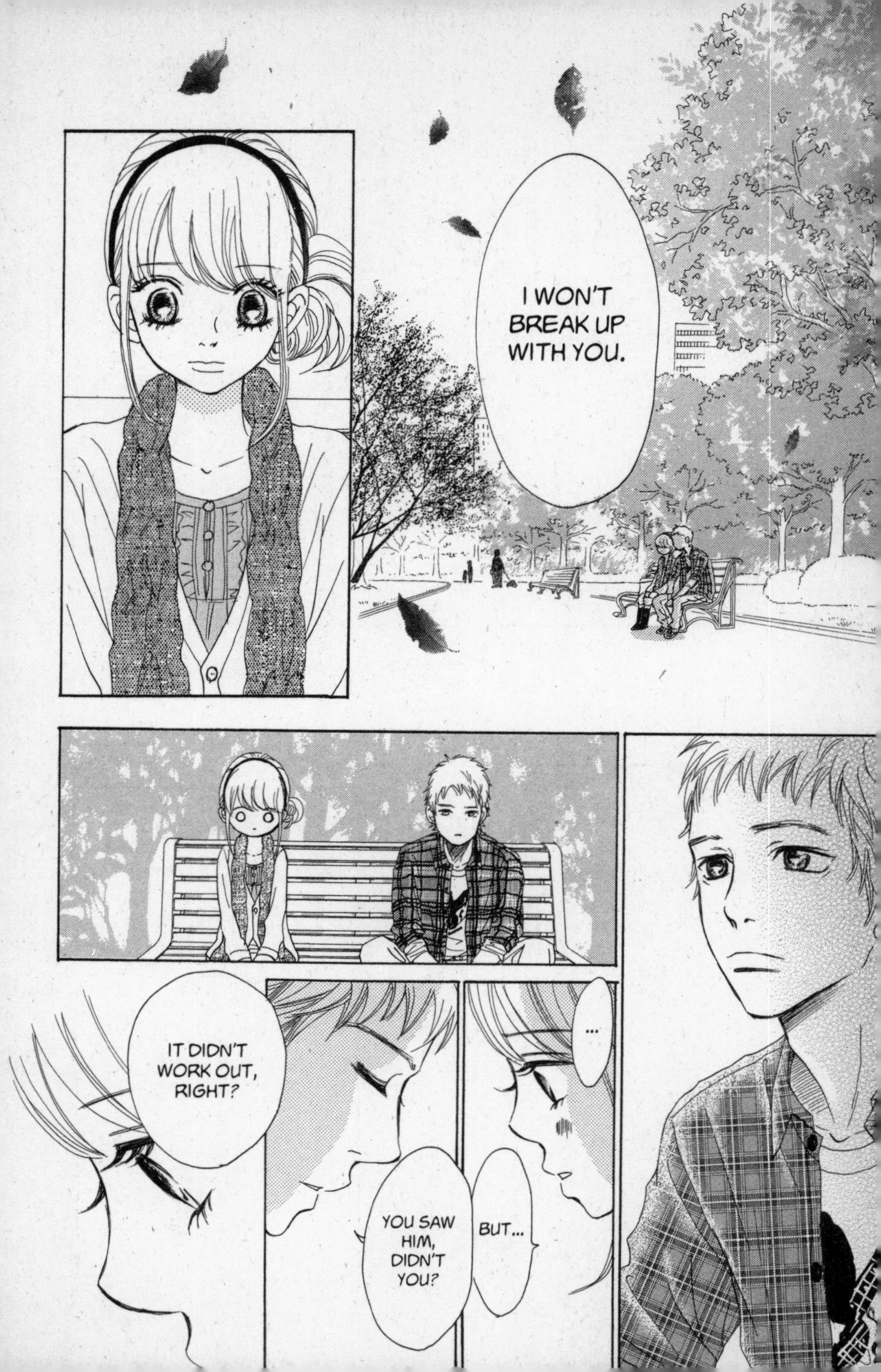
I WON'T BREAK UP WITH YOU.
...
BUT...
YOU SAW HIM, DIDN'T YOU?
IT DIDN'T WORK OUT, RIGHT?

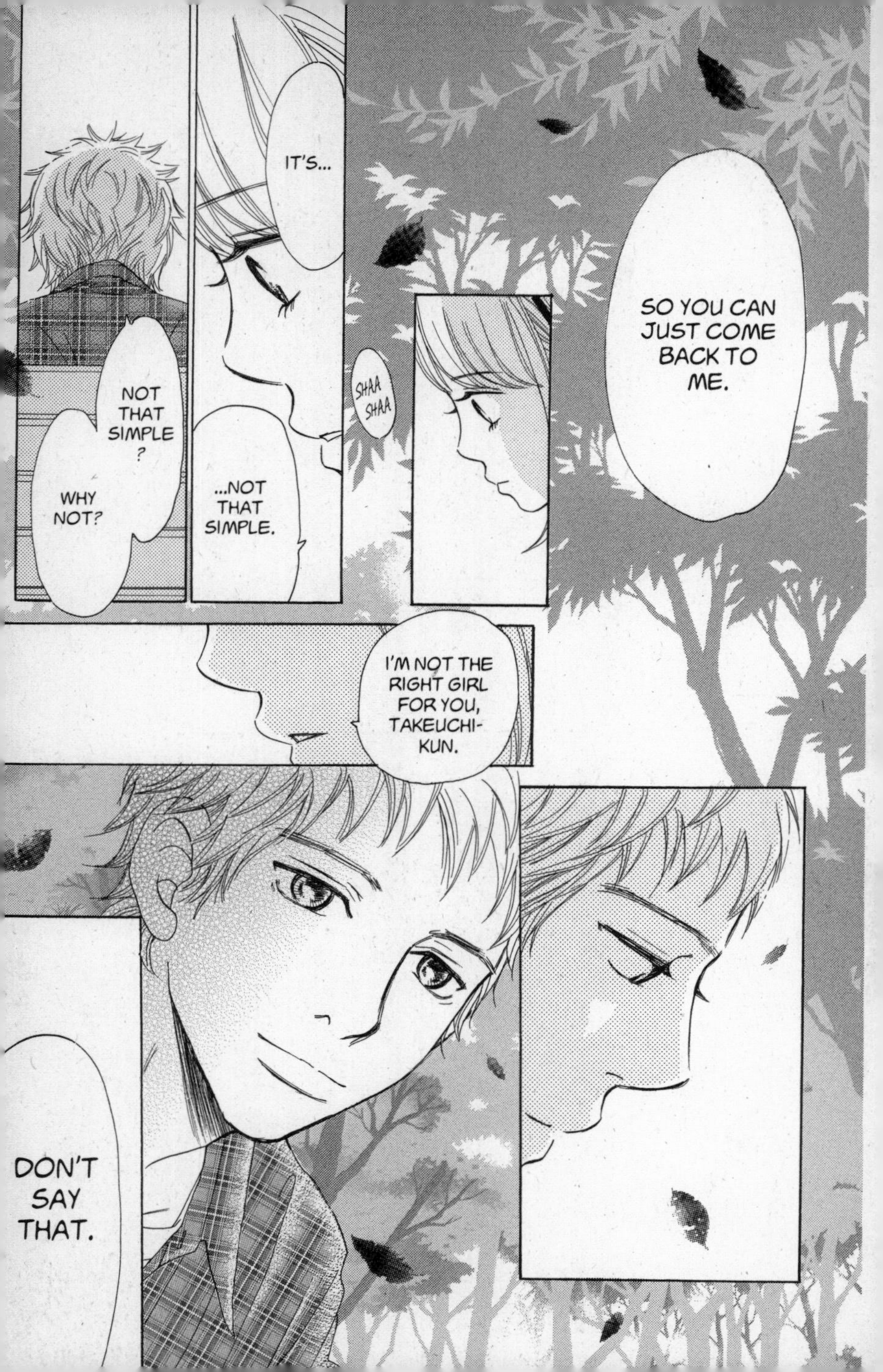
SO YOU CAN JUST COME BACK TO ME.
SHAA SHAA
IT'S...
...NOT THAT SIMPLE.
NOT THAT SIMPLE?
WHY NOT?
I'M NOT THE RIGHT GIRL FOR YOU, TAKEUCHI-KUN.
DON'T SAY THAT.

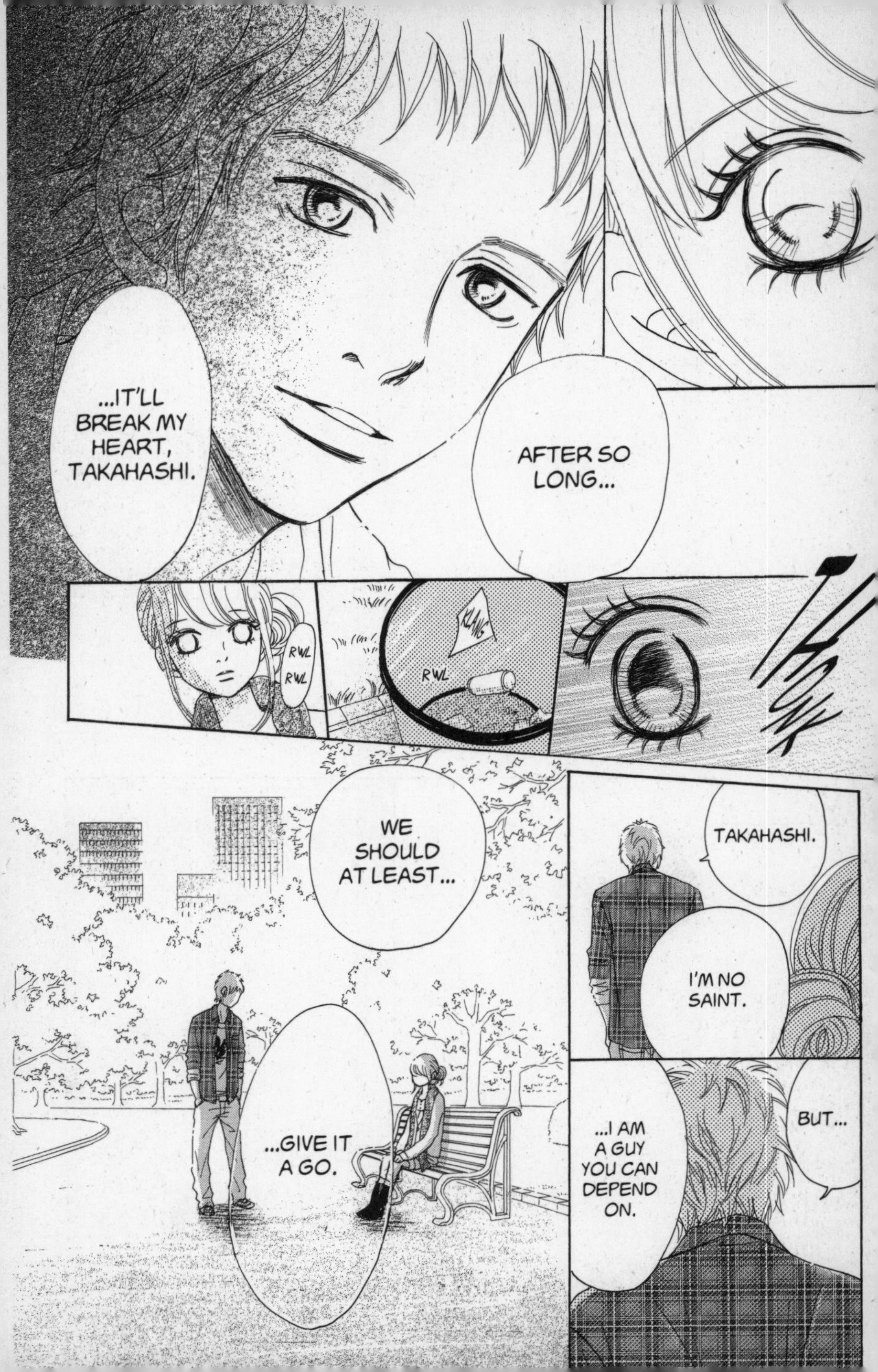
AFTER SO LONG...
...IT'LL BREAK MY HEART, TAKAHASHI.
HONK
KLANG
RWL
RWL
RWL
TAKAHASHI.
I'M NO SAINT.
BUT...
...I AM A GUY YOU CAN DEPEND ON.
WE SHOULD AT LEAST...
...GIVE IT A GO.

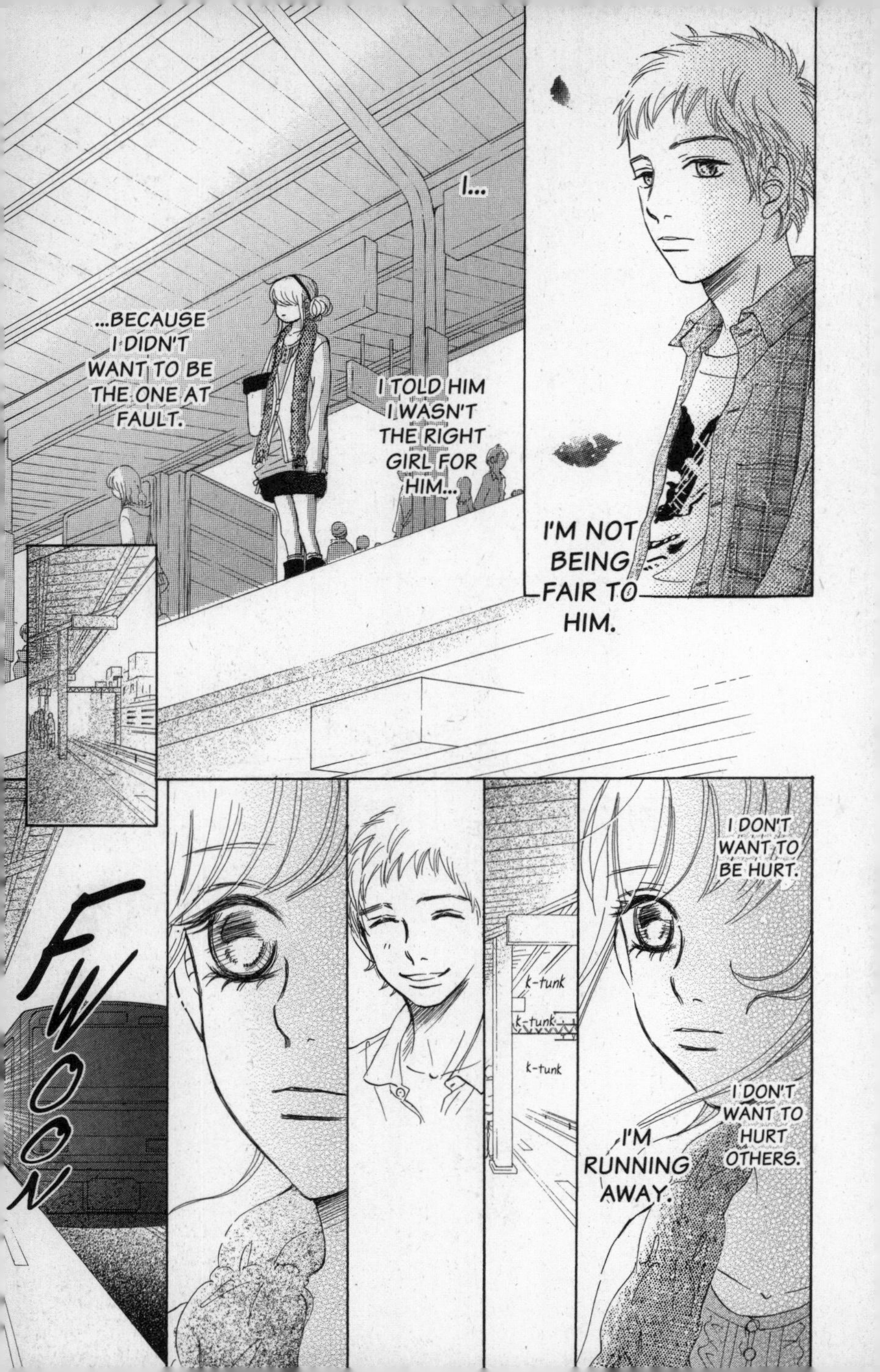
I'M NOT BEING FAIR TO HIM.
I...
I TOLD HIM I WASN'T THE RIGHT GIRL FOR HIM...
...BECAUSE I DIDN'T WANT TO BE THE ONE AT FAULT.
I DON'T WANT TO BE HURT.
I DON'T WANT TO HURT OTHERS.
I'M RUNNING AWAY.
k-tunk
k-tunk
k-tunk
FWOON

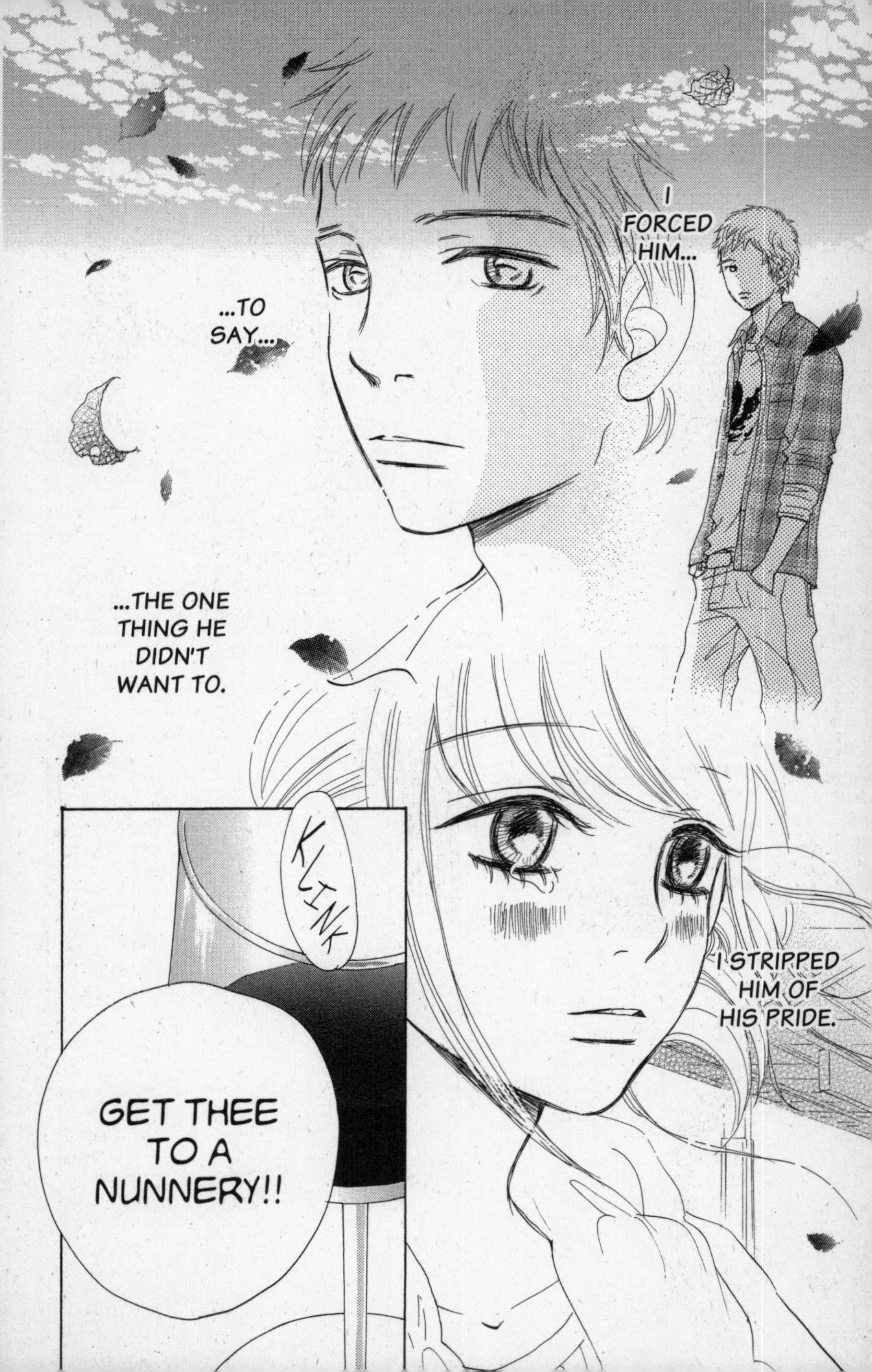
I FORCED HIM...
...TO SAY...
...THE ONE THING HE DIDN'T WANT TO.
I STRIPPED HIM OF HIS PRIDE.
KLINK
GET THEE TO A NUNNERY!!

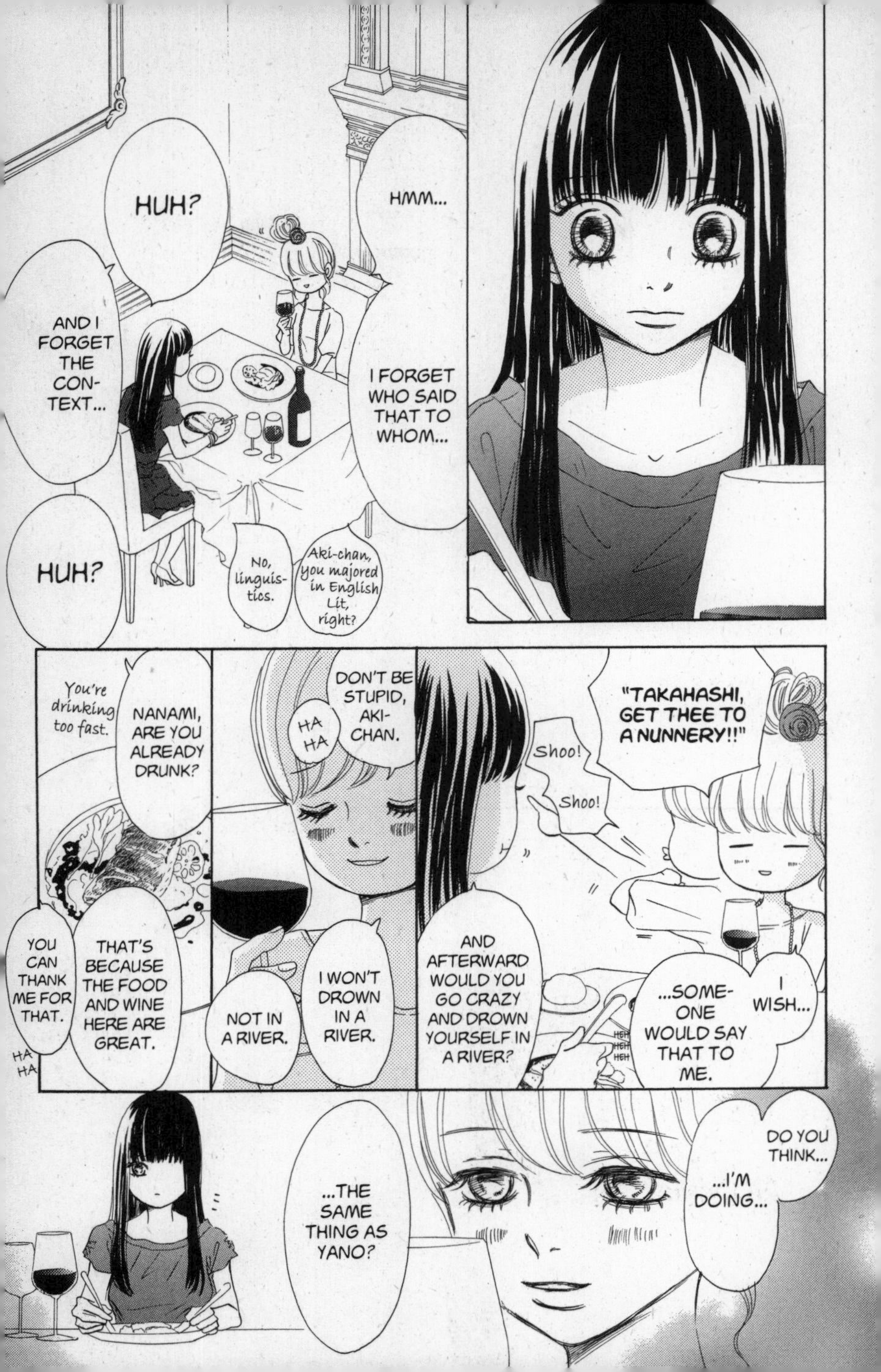
HMM...
I FORGET WHO SAID THAT TO WHOM...
HUH?
AND I FORGET THE CONTEXT...
Aki-chan, you majored in English Lit, right?
No, linguistics.
HUH?
"TAKAHASHI, GET THEE TO A NUNNERY!!"
Shoo!
Shoo!
I WISH...
...SOMEONE WOULD SAY THAT TO ME.
HEH HEH HEH
AND AFTERWARD WOULD YOU GO CRAZY AND DROWN YOURSELF IN A RIVER?
DON'T BE STUPID, AKI-CHAN.
HA HA
I WON'T DROWN IN A RIVER.
NOT IN A RIVER.
NANAMI, ARE YOU ALREADY DRUNK?
You're drinking too fast.
THAT'S BECAUSE THE FOOD AND WINE HERE ARE GREAT.
YOU CAN THANK ME FOR THAT.
HA HA
DO YOU THINK...
...I'M DOING...
...THE SAME THING AS YANO?

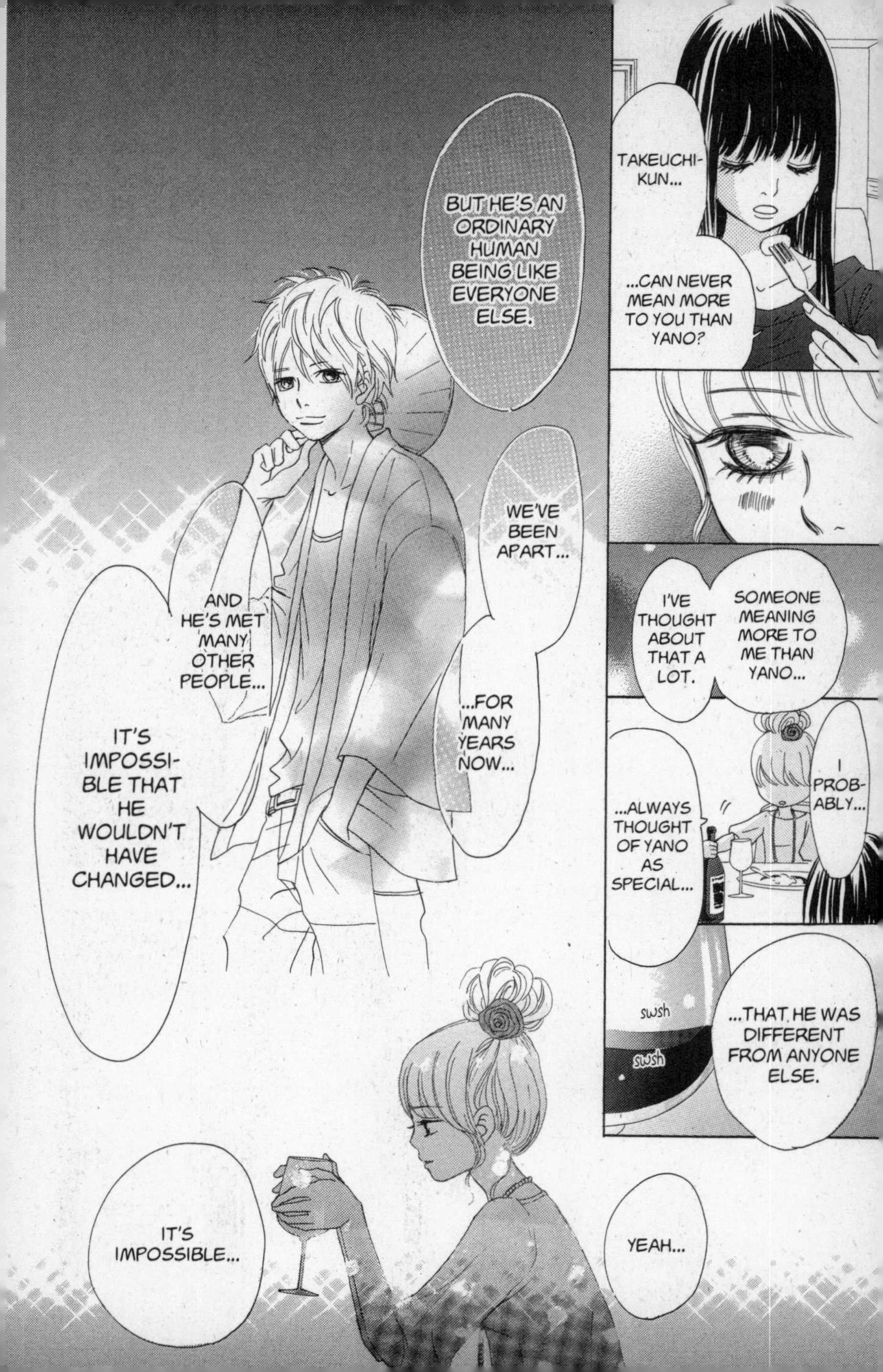
TAKEUCHI-KUN...
...CAN NEVER MEAN MORE TO YOU THAN YANO?
SOMEONE MEANING MORE TO ME THAN YANO...
I'VE THOUGHT ABOUT THAT A LOT.
I PROBABLY...
...ALWAYS THOUGHT OF YANO AS SPECIAL...
swsh
swsh
...THAT HE WAS DIFFERENT FROM ANYONE ELSE.
BUT HE'S AN ORDINARY HUMAN BEING LIKE EVERYONE ELSE.
WE'VE BEEN APART...
...FOR MANY YEARS NOW...
AND HE'S MET MANY OTHER PEOPLE...
IT'S IMPOSSIBLE THAT HE WOULDN'T HAVE CHANGED...
YEAH...
IT'S IMPOSSIBLE...

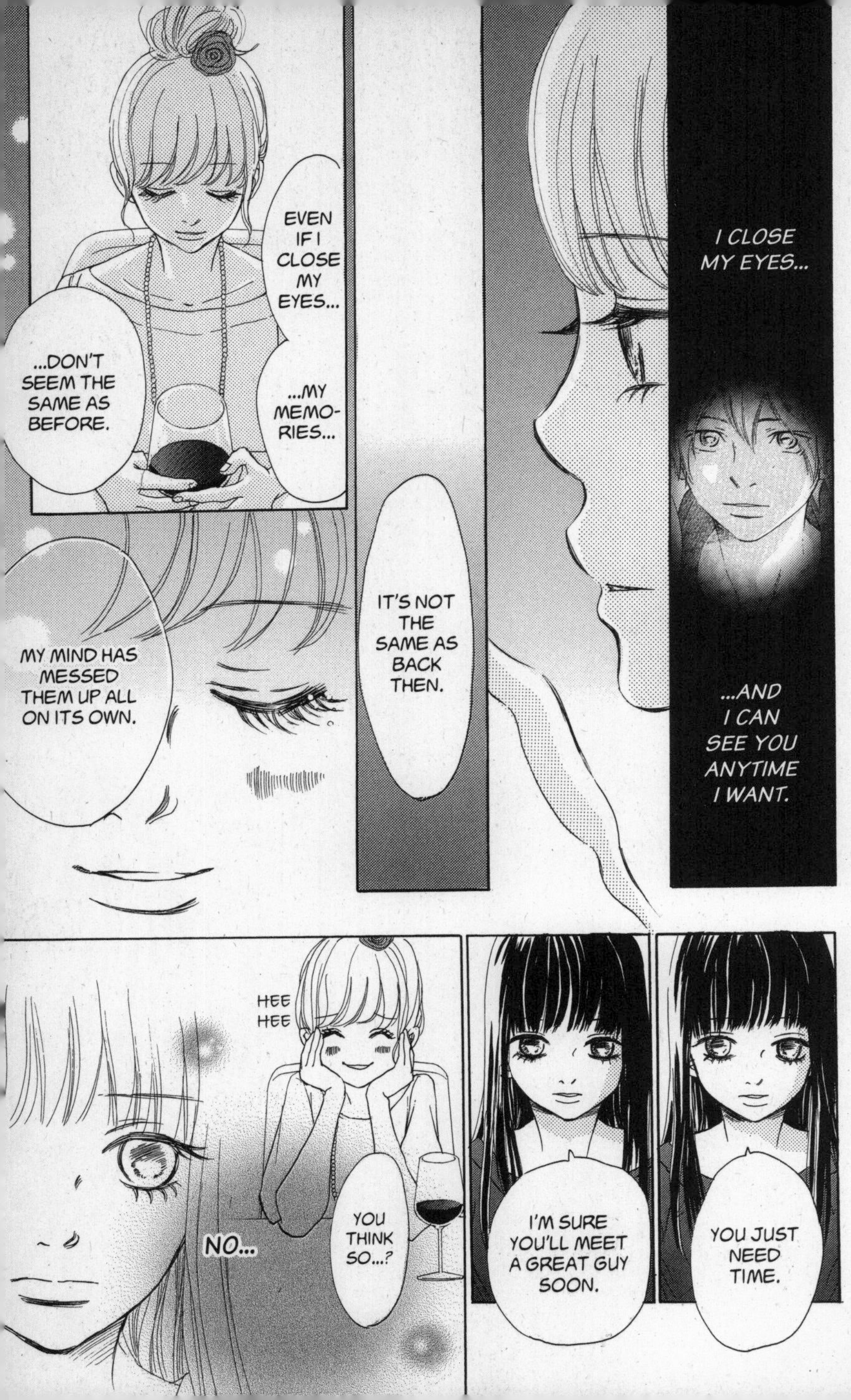
I CLOSE MY EYES...
...AND I CAN SEE YOU ANYTIME I WANT.
IT'S NOT THE SAME AS BACK THEN.
EVEN IF I CLOSE MY EYES...
...MY MEMORIES...
...DON'T SEEM THE SAME AS BEFORE.
MY MIND HAS MESSED THEM UP ALL ON ITS OWN.
YOU JUST NEED TIME.
I'M SURE YOU'LL MEET A GREAT GUY SOON.
HEE HEE
YOU THINK SO...?
NO...

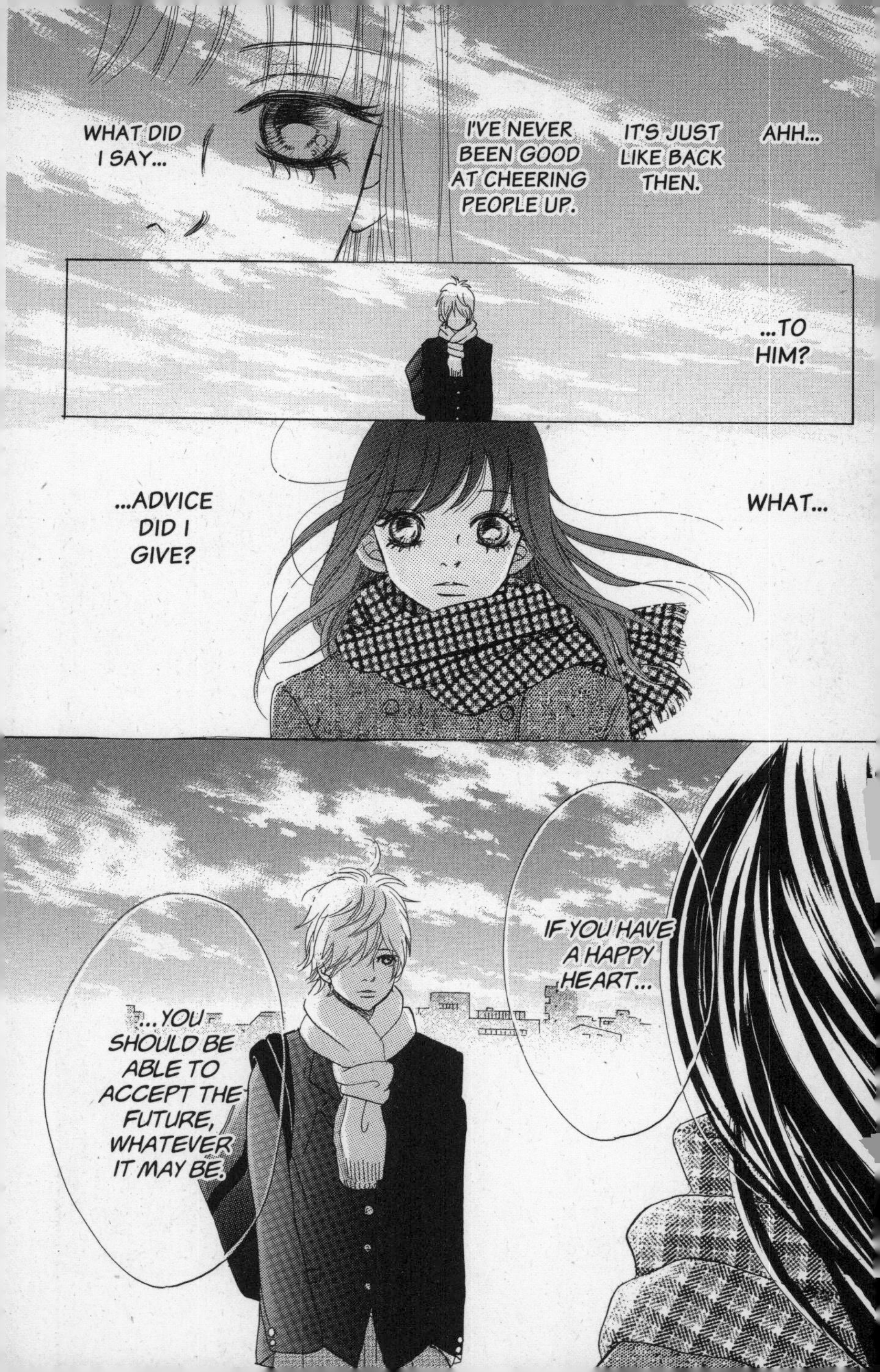
AHH...
IT'S JUST LIKE BACK THEN.
I'VE NEVER BEEN GOOD AT CHEERING PEOPLE UP.
WHAT DID I SAY...
...TO HIM?
WHAT...
...ADVICE DID I GIVE?
IF YOU HAVE A HAPPY HEART...
...YOU SHOULD BE ABLE TO ACCEPT THE FUTURE, WHATEVER IT MAY BE.

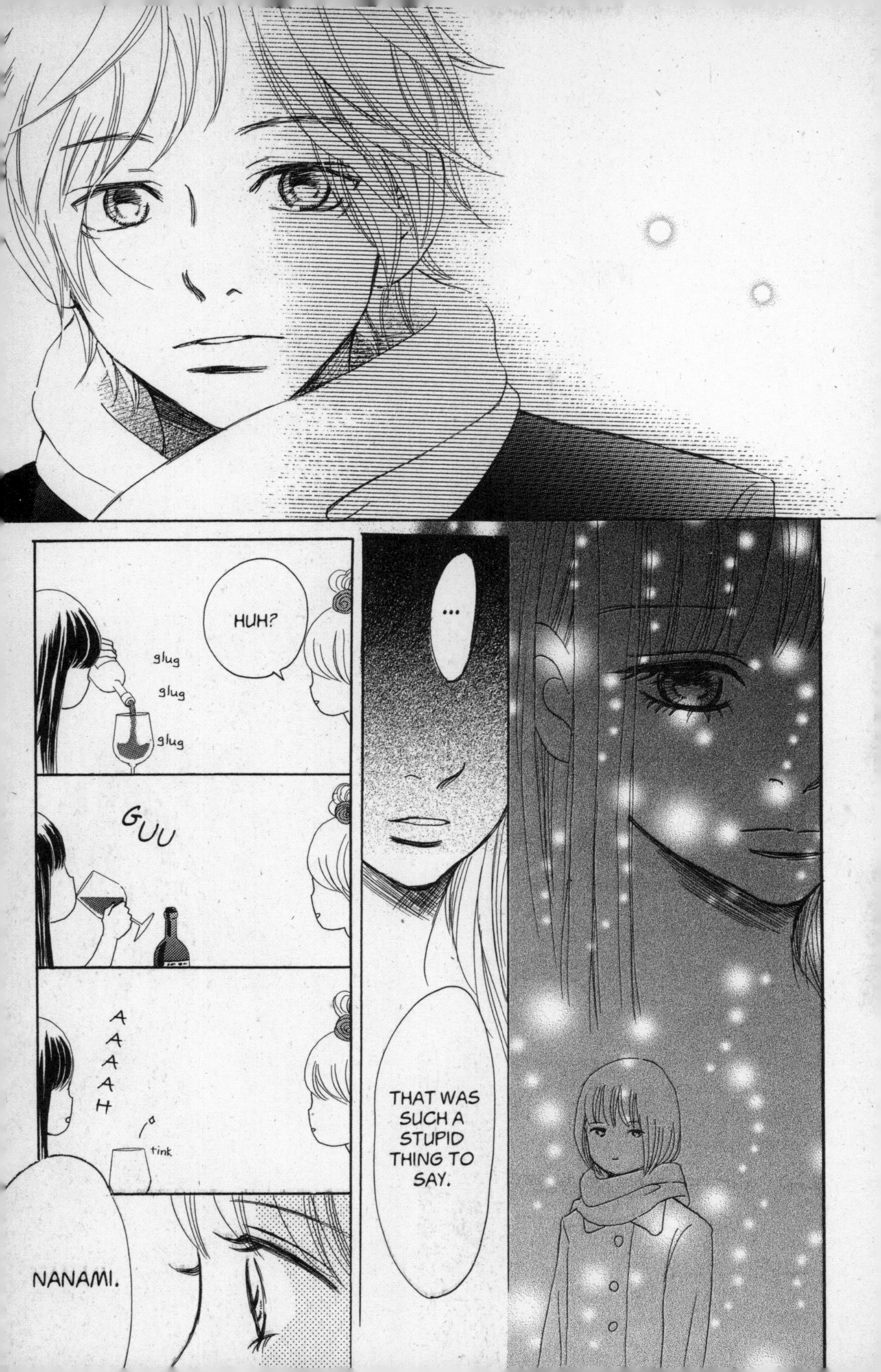
...
THAT WAS SUCH A STUPID THING TO SAY.
HUH?
glug
glug
glug
GUU
AAAAH
tink
NANAMI.

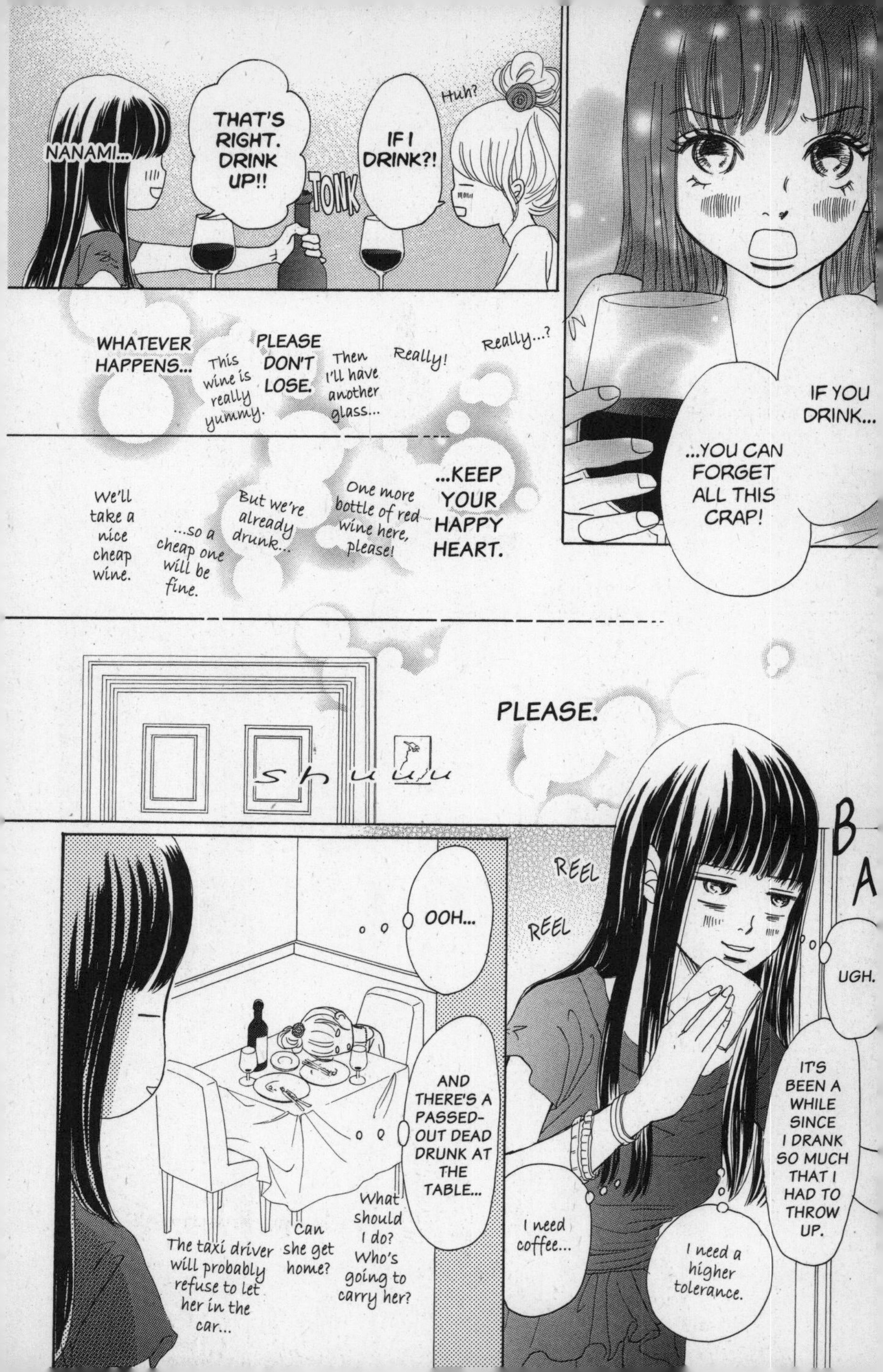
IF YOU DRINK...
...YOU CAN FORGET ALL THIS CRAP!
Huh?
IF I DRINK?!
TONK
THAT'S RIGHT. DRINK UP!!
NANAMI...
Really...?
Really!
Then I'll have another glass...
PLEASE DON'T LOSE.
This wine is really yummy.
WHATEVER HAPPENS...
...KEEP YOUR HAPPY HEART.
One more bottle of red wine here, please!
But we're already drunk...
...so a cheap one will be fine.
We'll take a nice cheap wine.
PLEASE.
shuuu
BA
UGH.
REEL
REEL
IT'S BEEN A WHILE SINCE I DRANK SO MUCH THAT I HAD TO THROW UP.
I need a higher tolerance.
I need coffee...
OOH...
AND THERE'S A PASSED-OUT DEAD DRUNK AT THE TABLE...
What should I do? Who's going to carry her?
Can she get home?
The taxi driver will probably refuse to let her in the car...

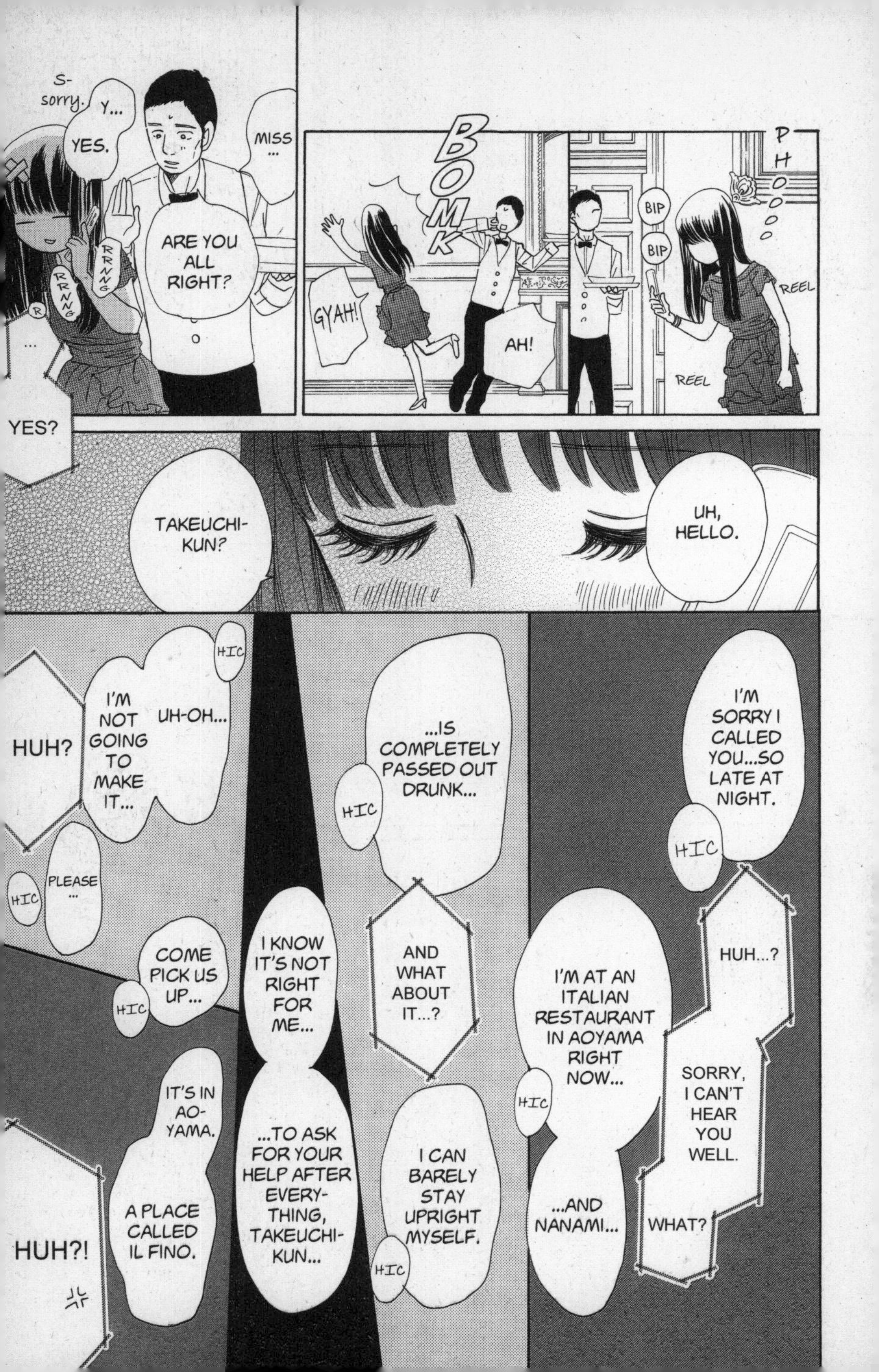
PHOOOOO
BIP
BIP
REEL
REEL
BOMK
GYAH!
AH!
MISS...
ARE YOU ALL RIGHT?
S-sorry.
Y...
YES.
RRNNG
RRNNG
R
...
YES?
UH, HELLO.
TAKEUCHI-KUN?
I'M SORRY I CALLED YOU...SO LATE AT NIGHT.
HIC
HUH...?
SORRY, I CAN'T HEAR YOU WELL.
WHAT?
I'M AT AN ITALIAN RESTAURANT IN AOYAMA RIGHT NOW...
HIC
...AND NANAMI...
...IS COMPLETELY PASSED OUT DRUNK...
HIC
AND WHAT ABOUT IT...?
I CAN BARELY STAY UPRIGHT MYSELF.
HIC
I KNOW IT'S NOT RIGHT FOR ME...
...TO ASK FOR YOUR HELP AFTER EVERYTHING, TAKEUCHI-KUN...
HIC
UH-OH...
I'M NOT GOING TO MAKE IT...
HUH?
PLEASE...
HIC
COME PICK US UP...
HIC
IT'S IN AO-YAMA.
A PLACE CALLED IL FINO.
HUH?!

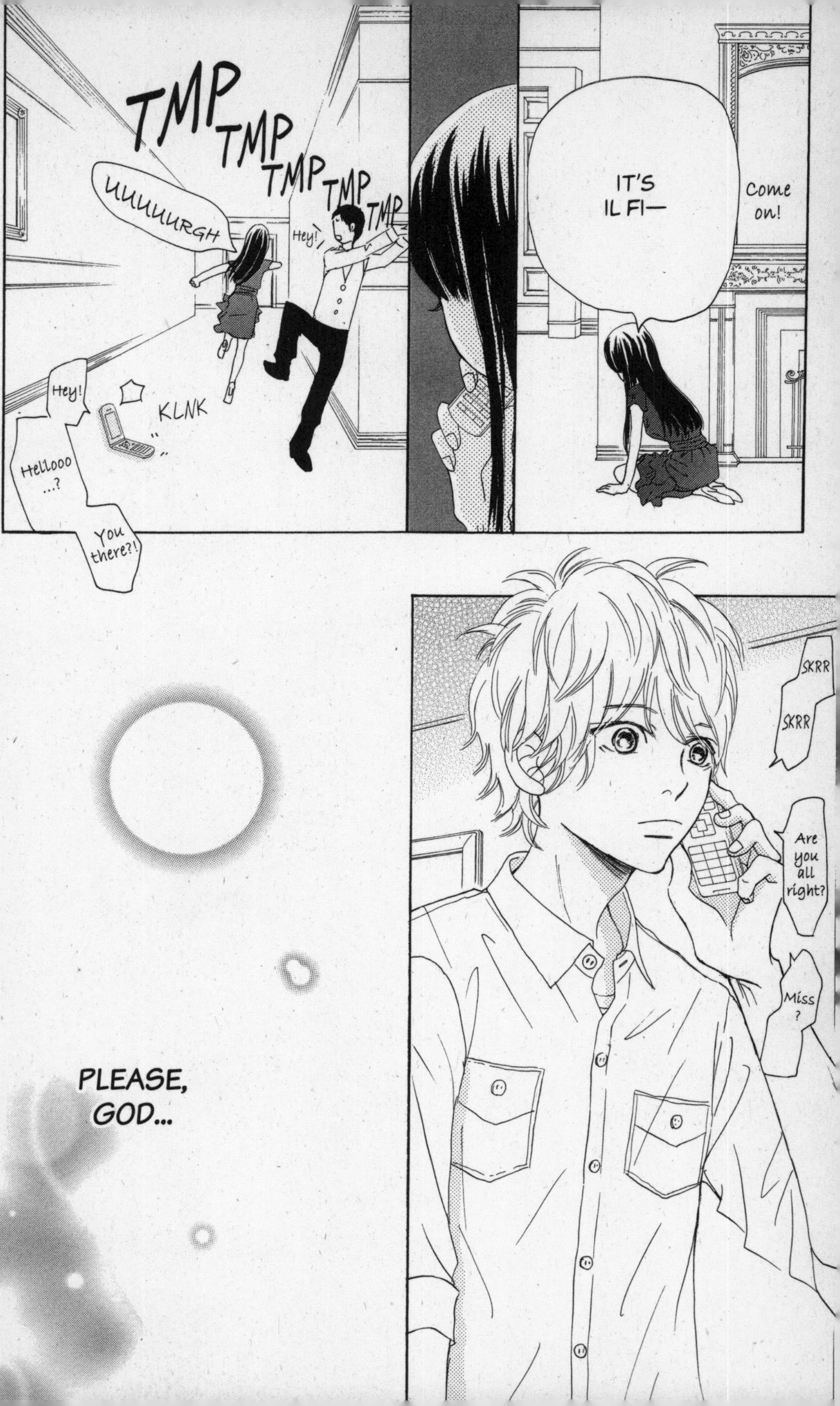

Come on!
IT'S IL FI—
TMP TMP TMP TMP TMP
UUUUURGH
Hey!
Hey!
KLNK
Hellooo ...?
You there?!
SKRR
SKRR
Are you all right?
Miss?
PLEASE, GOD...

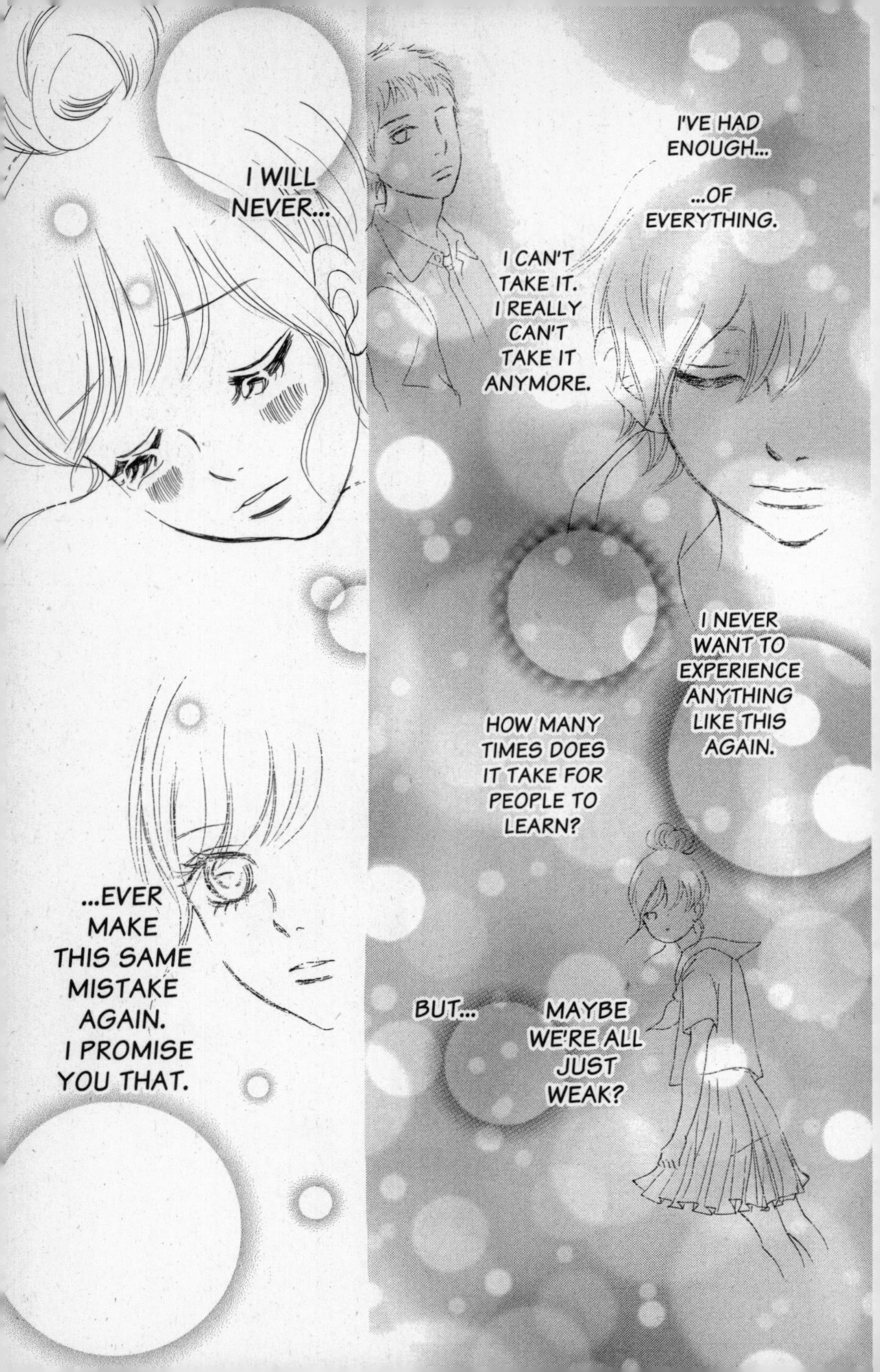
I'VE HAD ENOUGH...
...OF EVERYTHING.
I CAN'T TAKE IT. I REALLY CAN'T TAKE IT ANYMORE.
I NEVER WANT TO EXPERIENCE ANYTHING LIKE THIS AGAIN.
HOW MANY TIMES DOES IT TAKE FOR PEOPLE TO LEARN?
MAYBE WE'RE ALL JUST WEAK?
BUT...
I WILL NEVER...
...EVER MAKE THIS SAME MISTAKE AGAIN. I PROMISE YOU THAT.

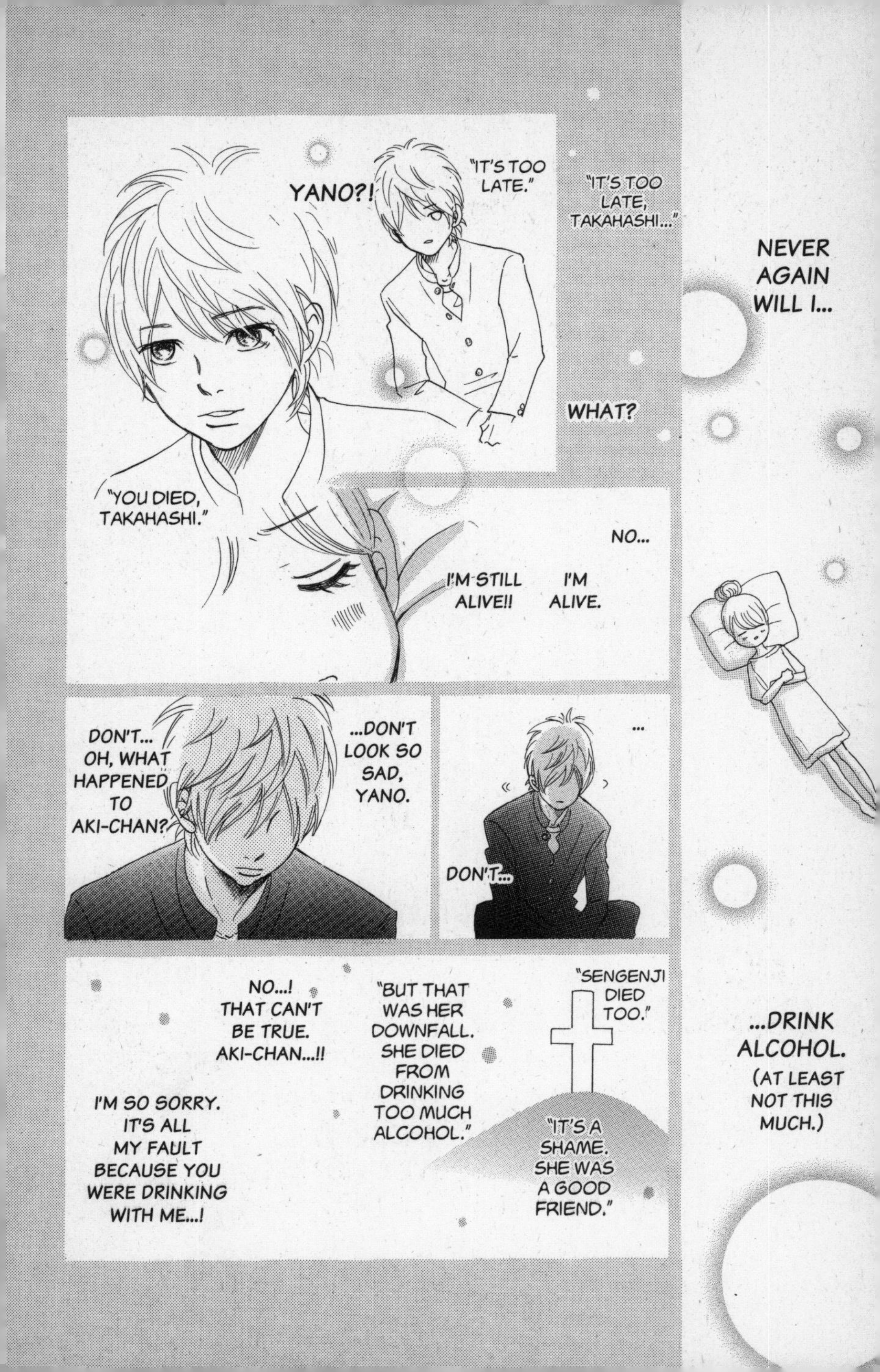
NEVER AGAIN WILL I...
...DRINK ALCOHOL.
(AT LEAST NOT THIS MUCH.)
"IT'S TOO LATE, TAKAHASHI..."
"IT'S TOO LATE."
YANO?!
WHAT?
"YOU DIED, TAKAHASHI."
NO...
I'M ALIVE.
I'M STILL ALIVE!!
...
DON'T...
...DON'T LOOK SO SAD, YANO.
DON'T... OH, WHAT HAPPENED TO AKI-CHAN?
"SENGENJI DIED TOO."
"IT'S A SHAME. SHE WAS A GOOD FRIEND."
"BUT THAT WAS HER DOWNFALL. SHE DIED FROM DRINKING TOO MUCH ALCOHOL."
NO...! THAT CAN'T BE TRUE. AKI-CHAN...!!
I'M SO SORRY. IT'S ALL MY FAULT BECAUSE YOU WERE DRINKING WITH ME...!

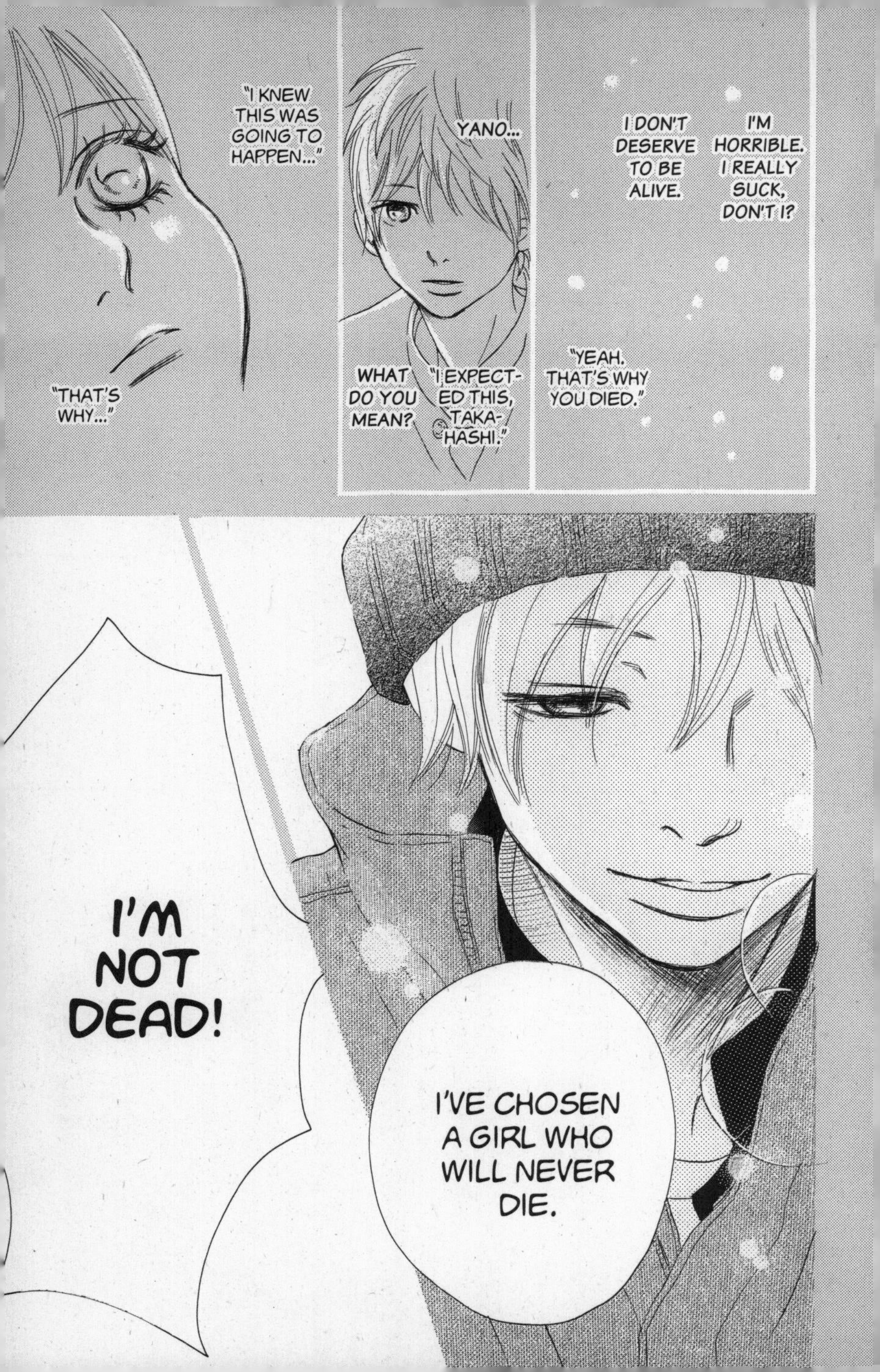
I'M HORRIBLE. I REALLY SUCK, DON'T I?
I DON'T DESERVE TO BE ALIVE.
"YEAH. THAT'S WHY YOU DIED."
YANO...
"I EXPECTED THIS, TAKAHASHI."
WHAT DO YOU MEAN?
"I KNEW THIS WAS GOING TO HAPPEN..."
"THAT'S WHY..."
I'VE CHOSEN A GIRL WHO WILL NEVER DIE.
I'M NOT DEAD!

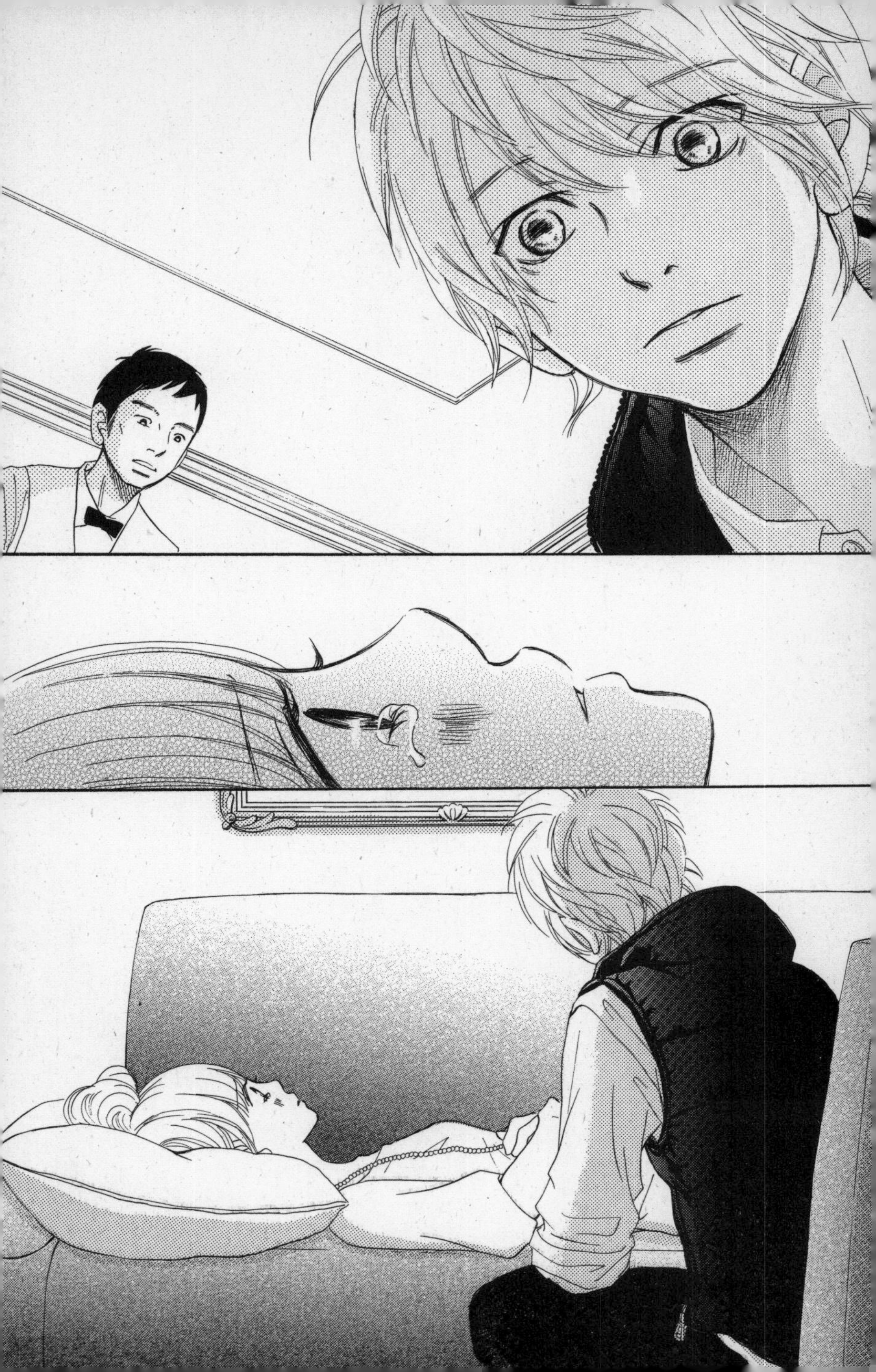

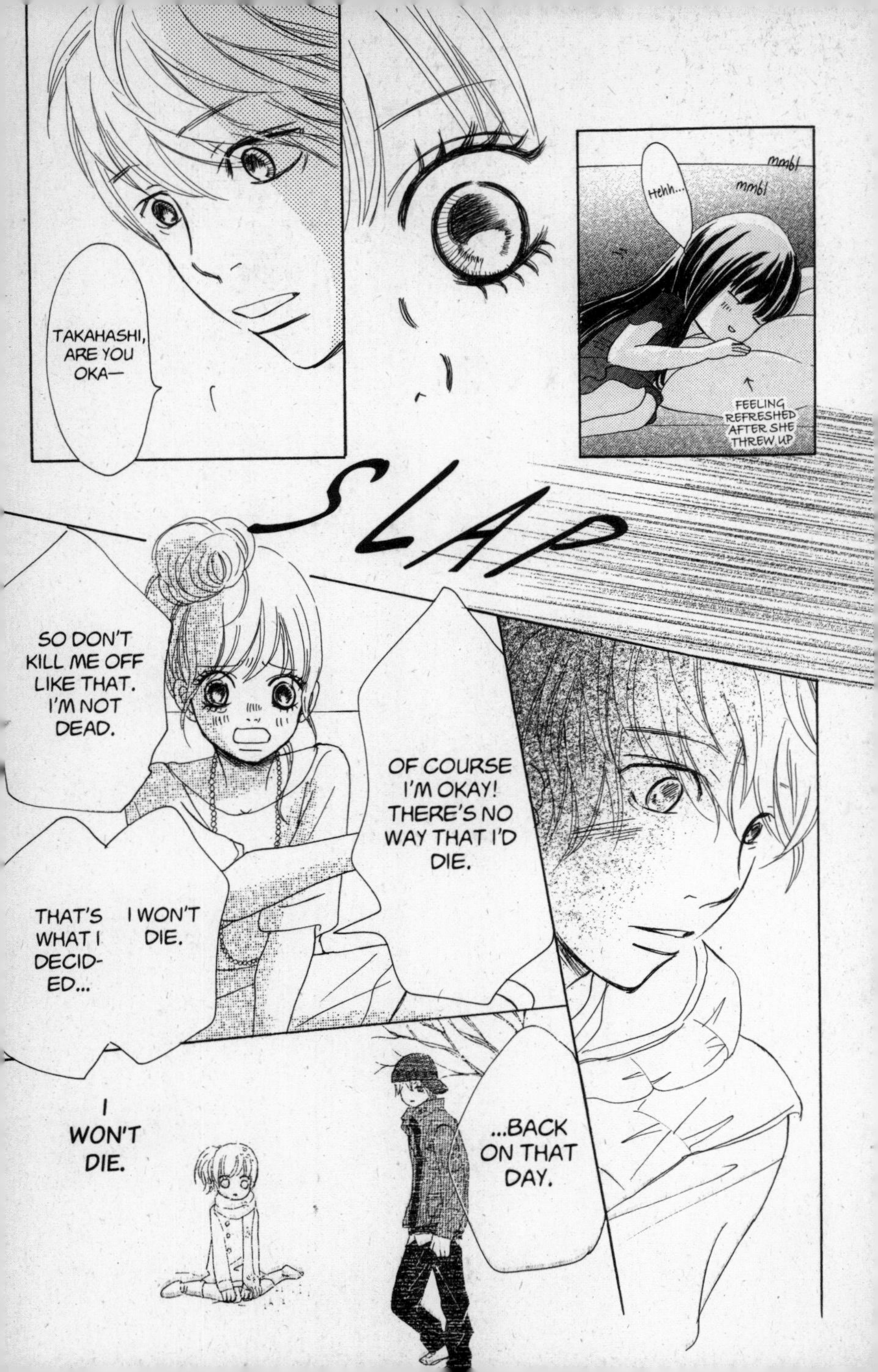
mmbl
mmbl
Hehh...
FEELING REFRESHED AFTER SHE THREW UP
TAKAHASHI, ARE YOU OKA—
SLAP
OF COURSE I'M OKAY! THERE'S NO WAY THAT I'D DIE.
SO DON'T KILL ME OFF LIKE THAT. I'M NOT DEAD.
I WON'T DIE.
THAT'S WHAT I DECIDED...
...BACK ON THAT DAY.
I WON'T DIE.

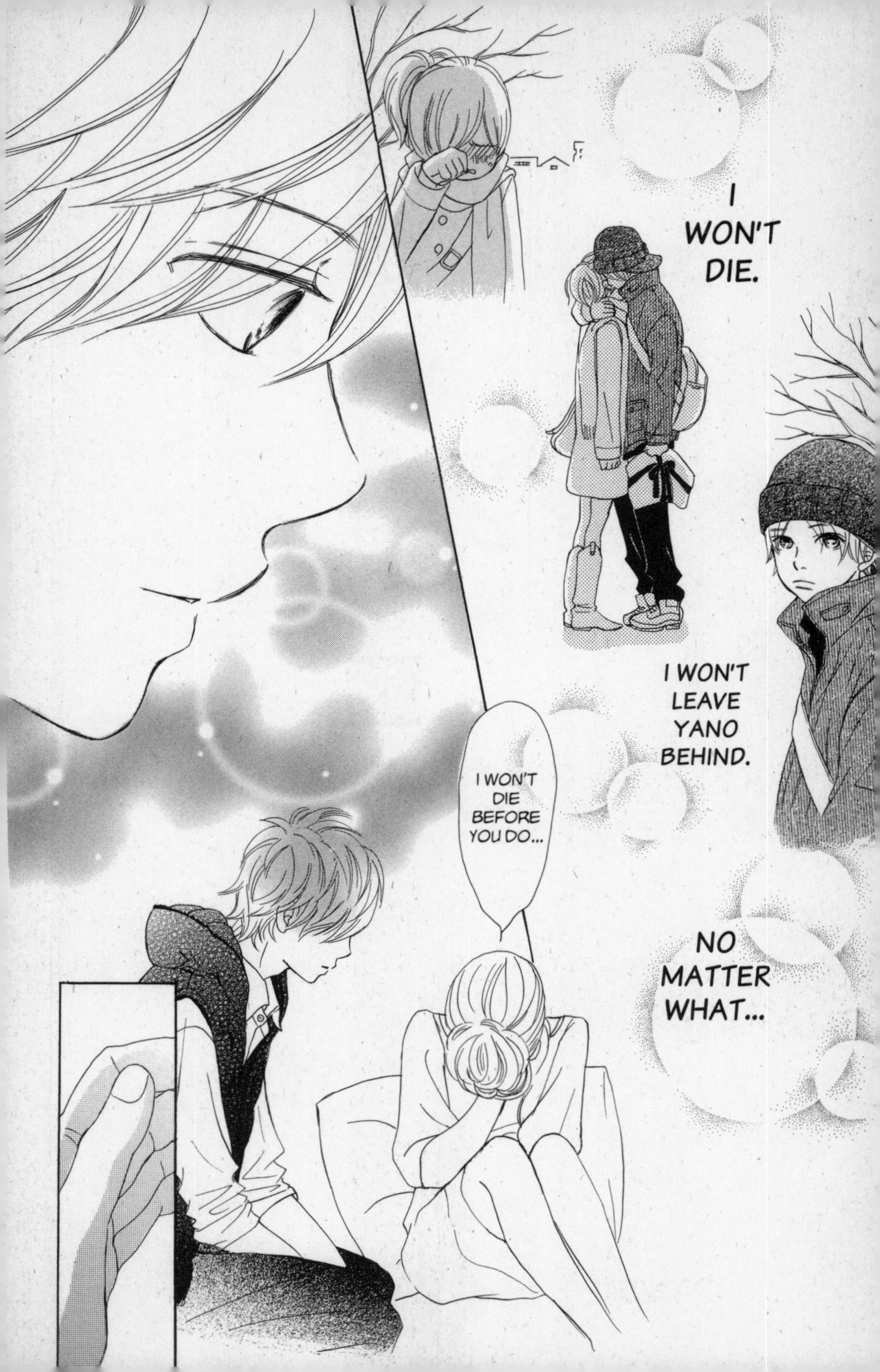
I WON'T DIE.
I WON'T LEAVE YANO BEHIND.
I WON'T DIE BEFORE YOU DO...
NO MATTER WHAT...

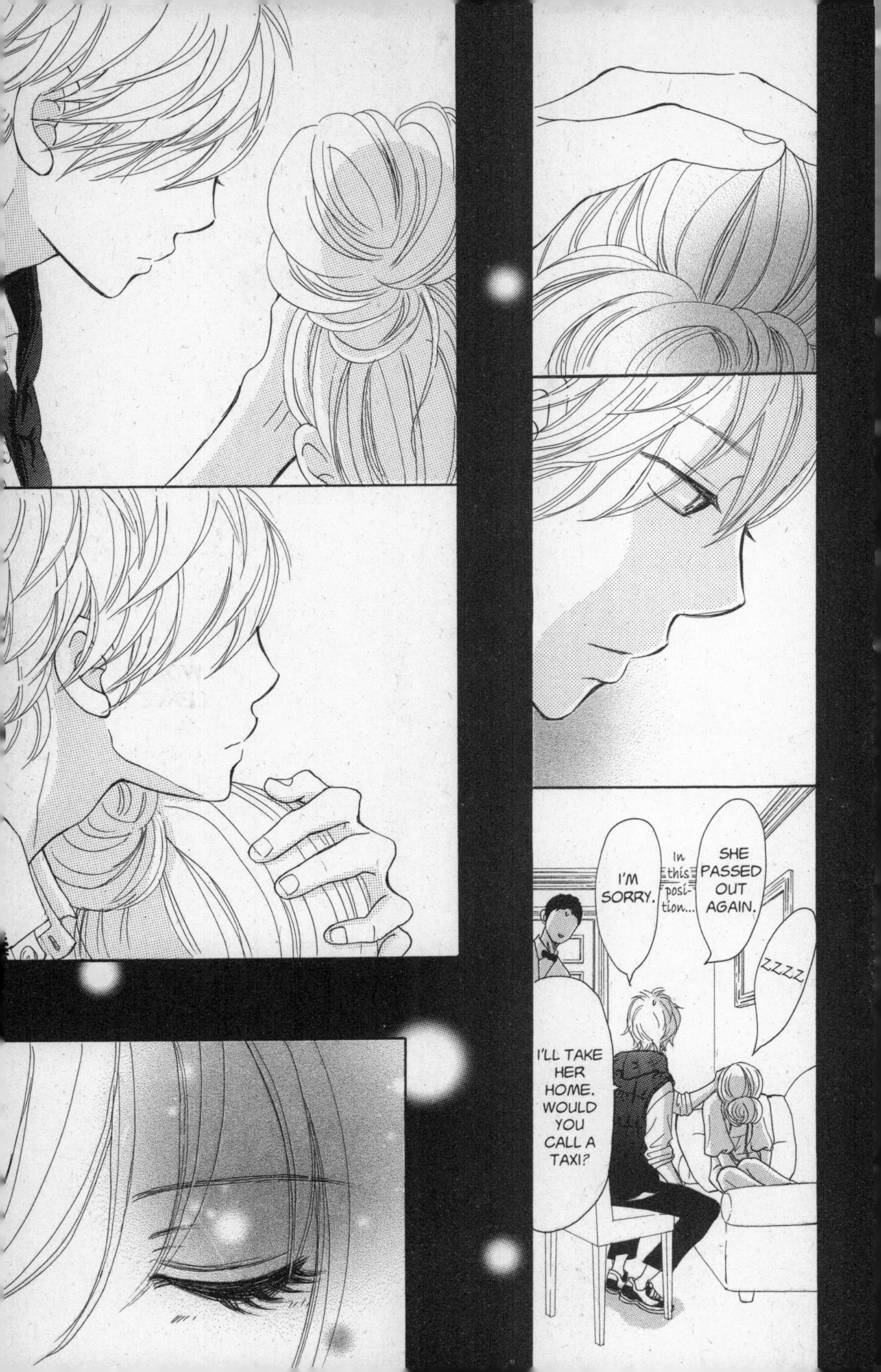
SHE PASSED OUT AGAIN.
In this posi-tion...
I'M SORRY.
ZZZZ
I'LL TAKE HER HOME. WOULD YOU CALL A TAXI?

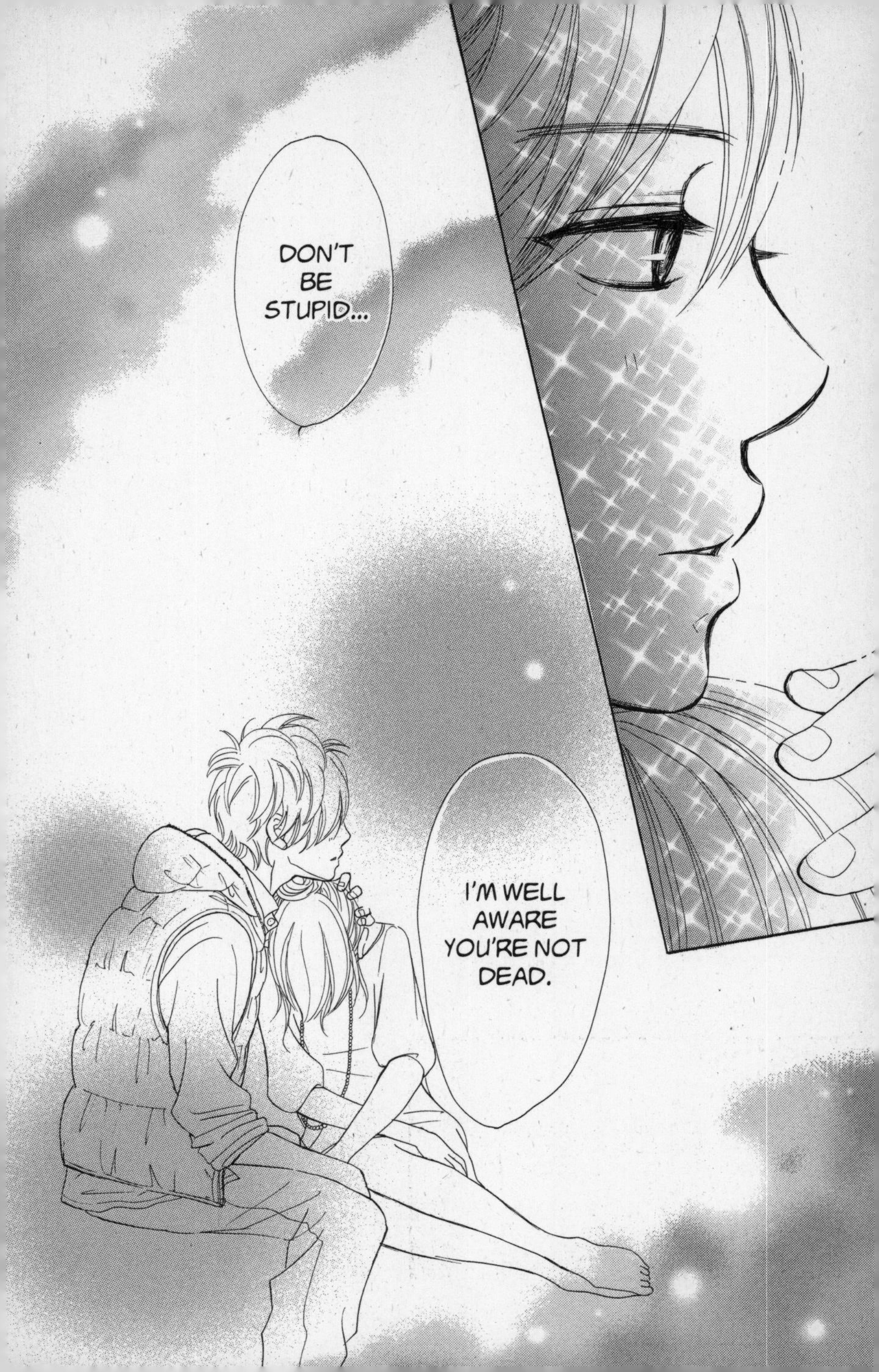
DON'T BE STUPID...
I'M WELL AWARE YOU'RE NOT DEAD.

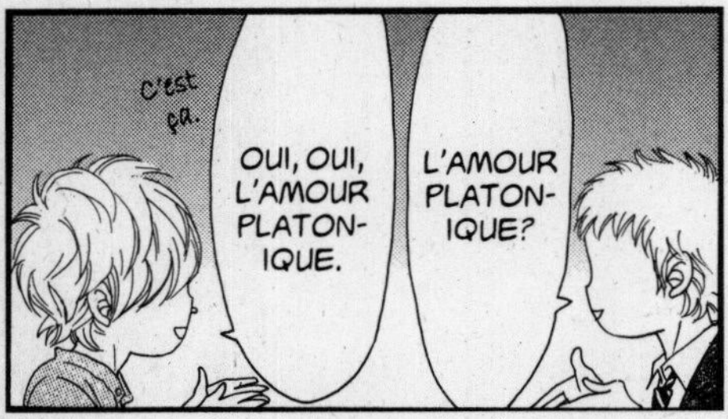
L'AMOUR PLATON-IQUE?
OUI, OUI, L'AMOUR PLATON-IQUE.
C'est ça.

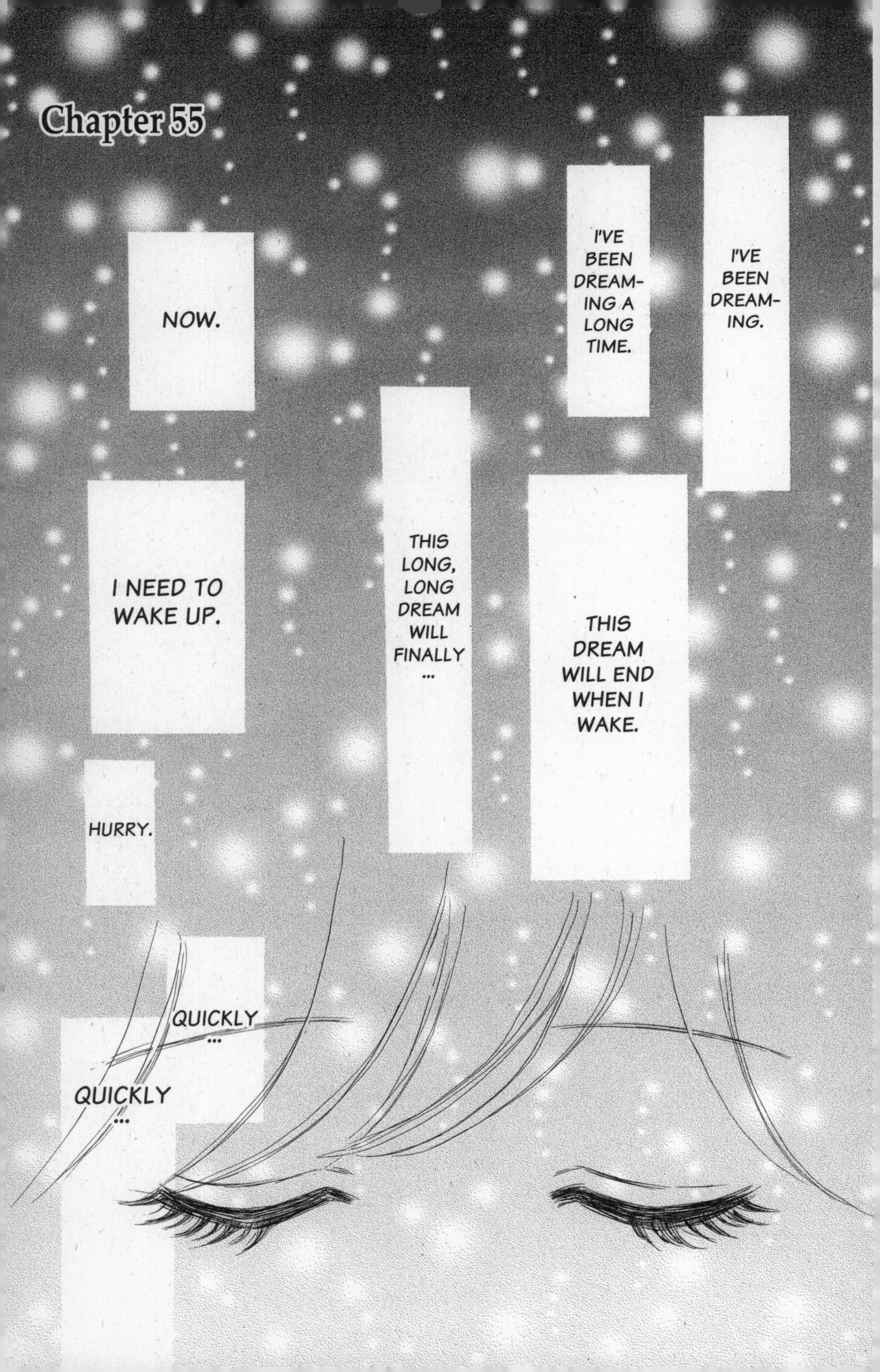
Chapter 55
I'VE BEEN DREAMING.
I'VE BEEN DREAMING A LONG TIME.
NOW.
THIS DREAM WILL END WHEN I WAKE.
THIS LONG, LONG DREAM WILL FINALLY ...
I NEED TO WAKE UP.
HURRY.
QUICKLY ...
QUICKLY ...

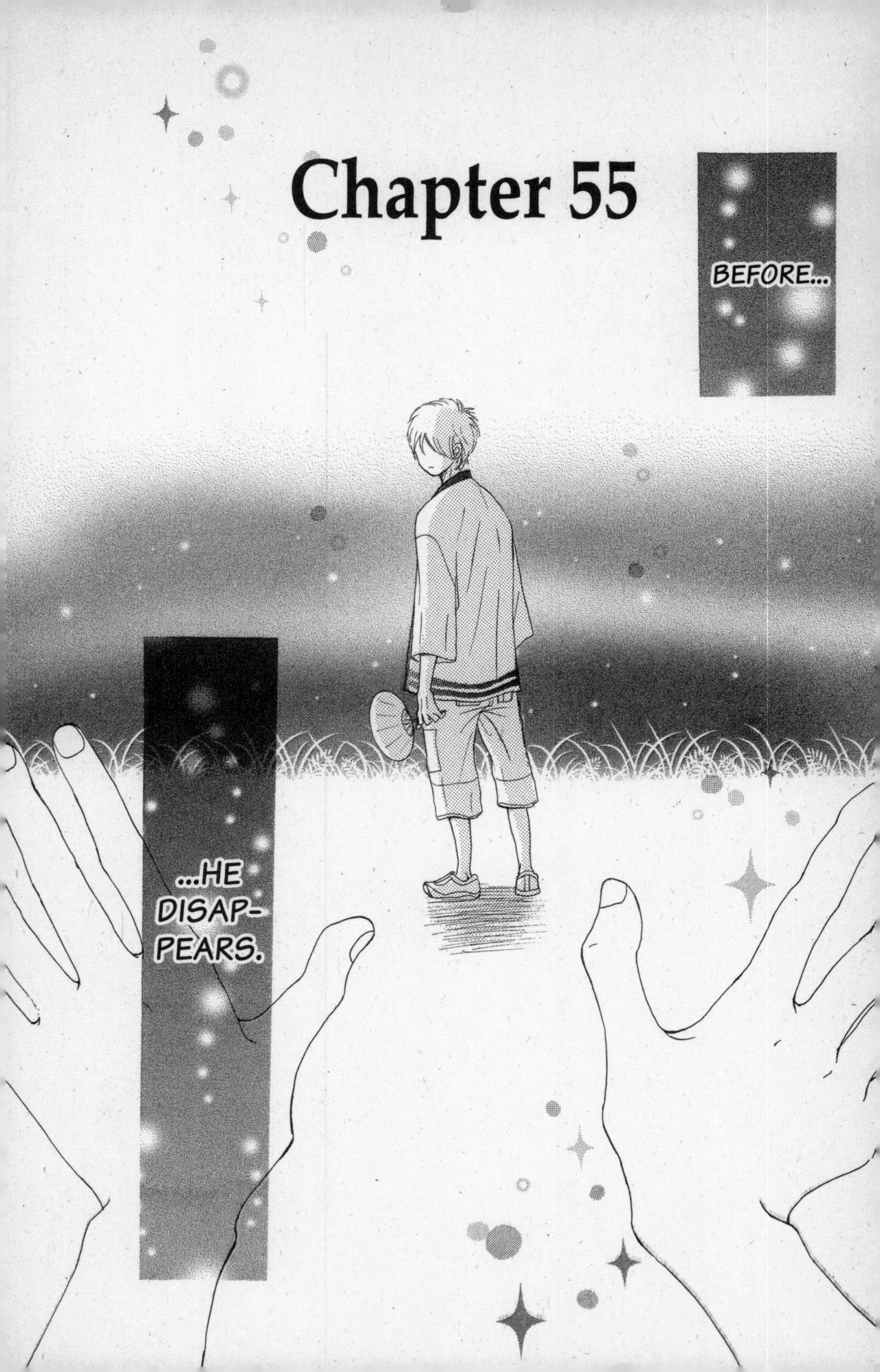
Chapter 55
BEFORE...
...HE DISAP-PEARS.

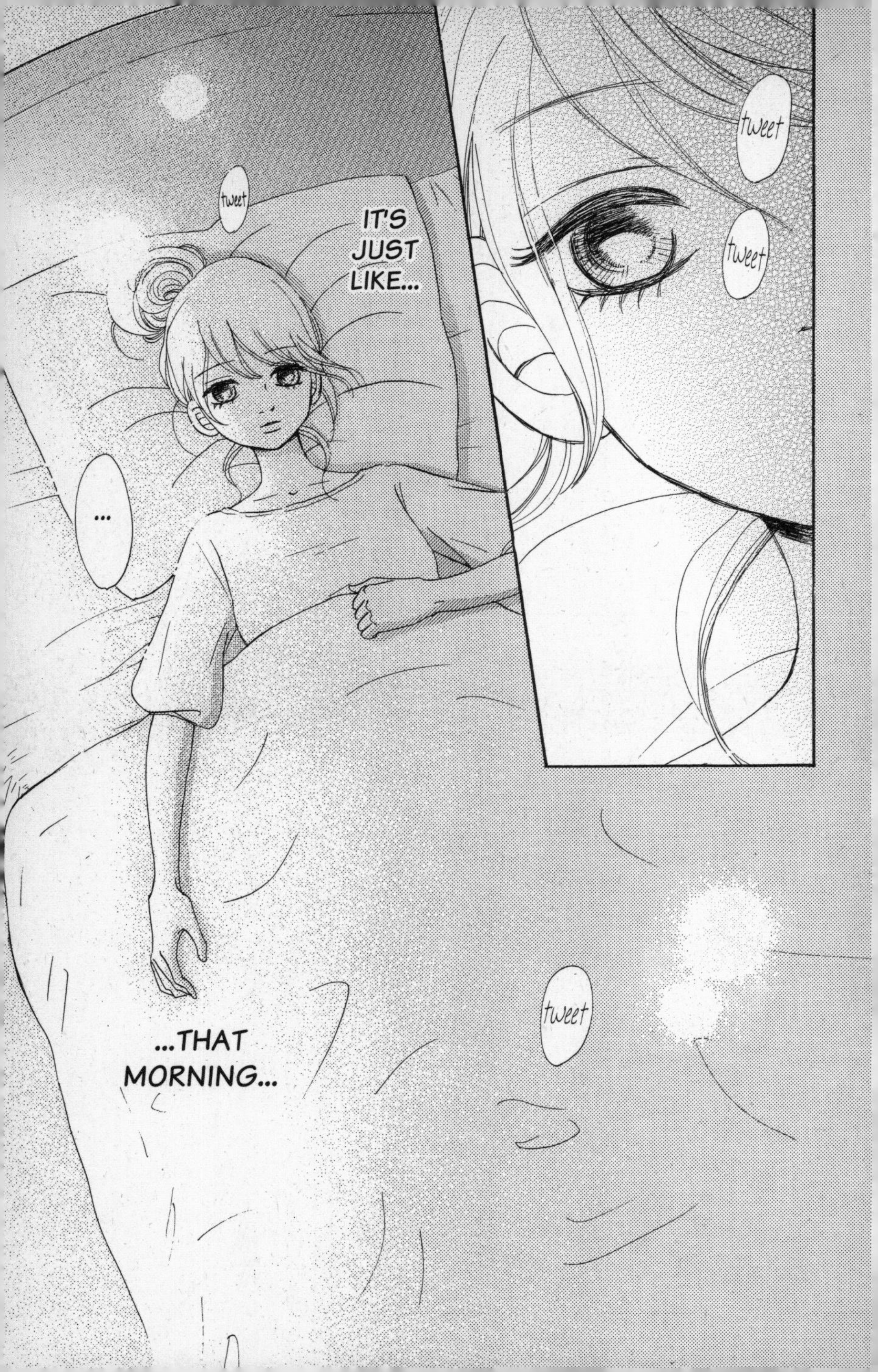
tweet
tweet
IT'S JUST LIKE...
tweet
...
tweet
...THAT MORNING...

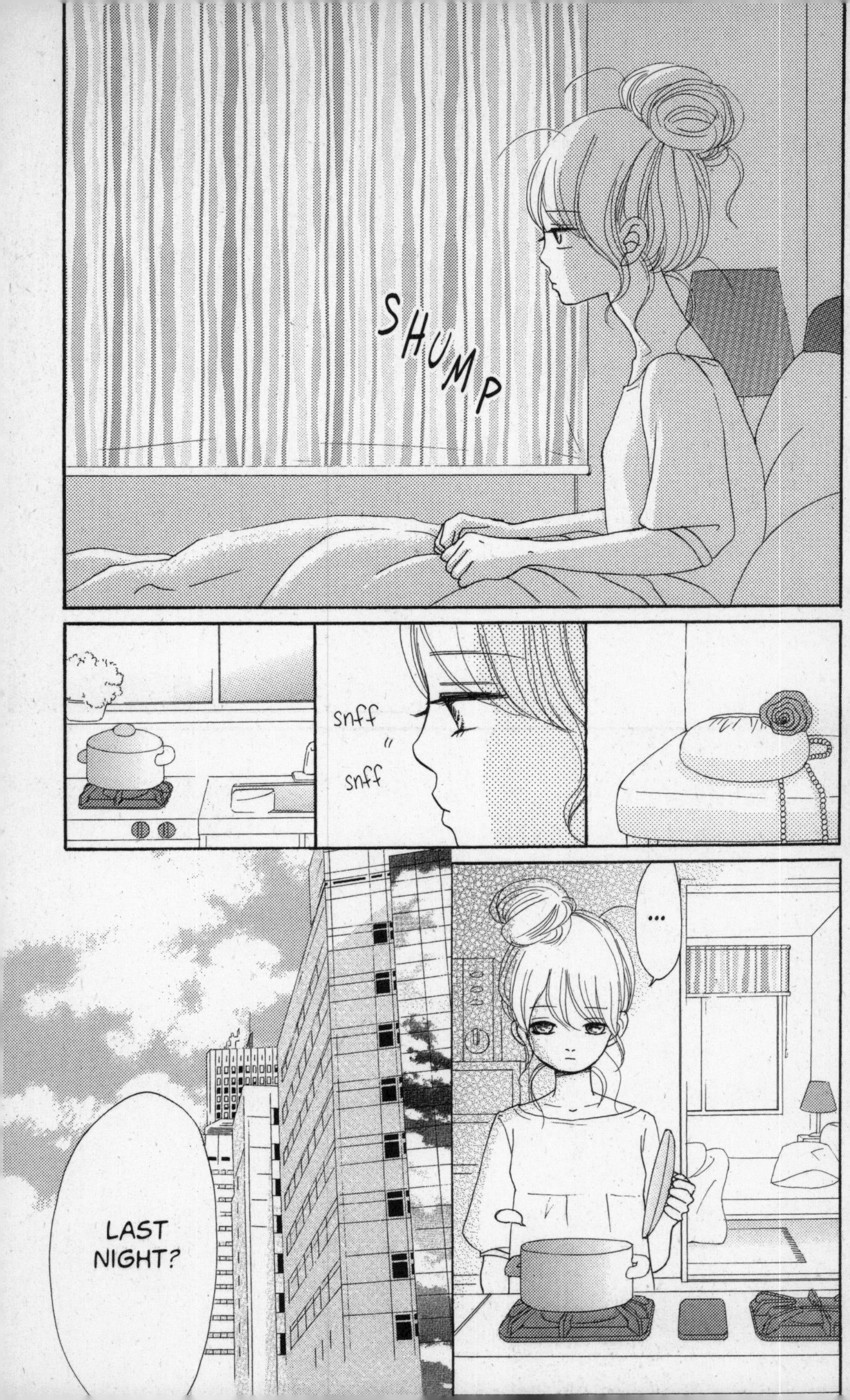
SHUMP
snff " snff
...
LAST NIGHT?

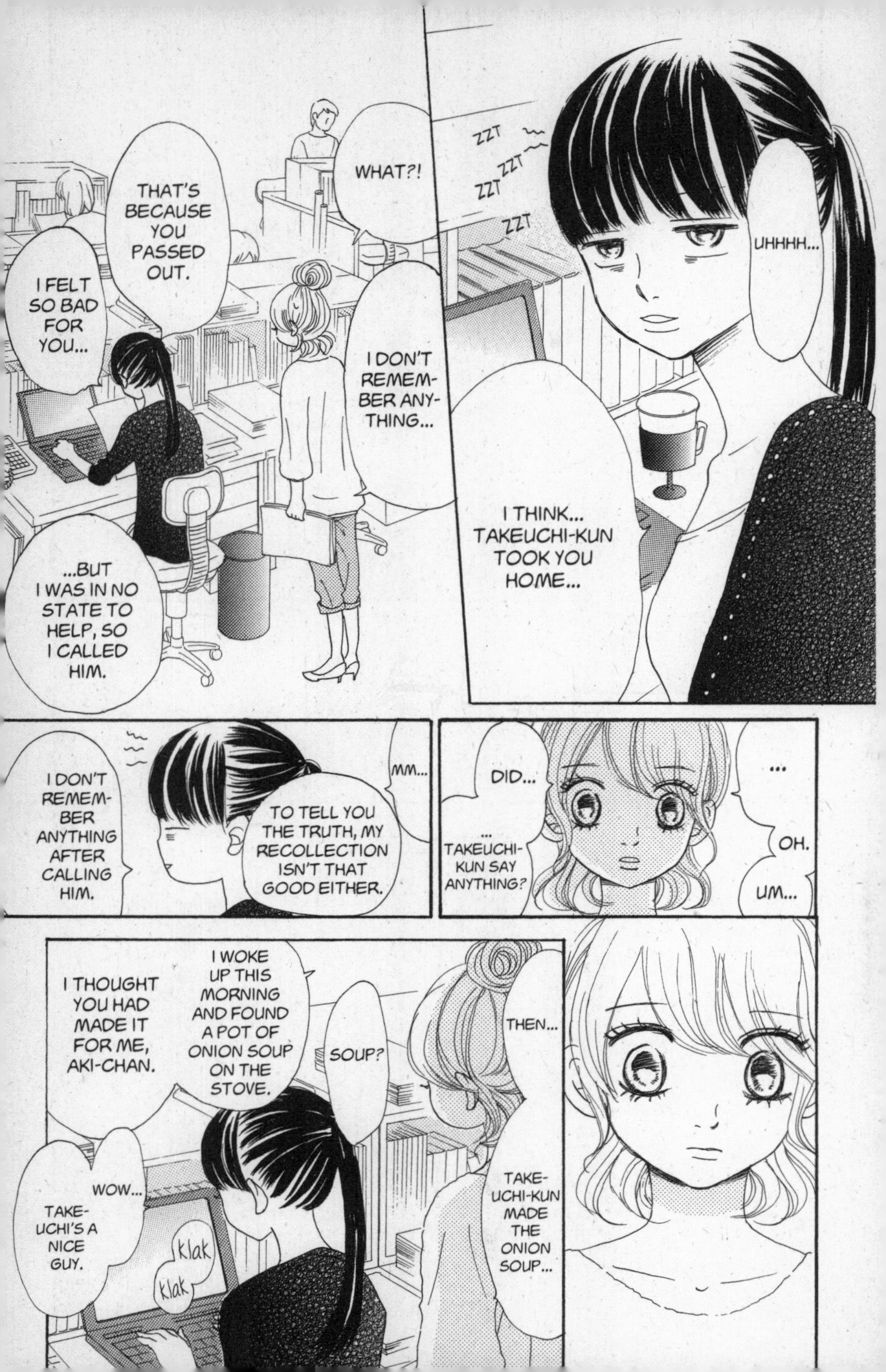
ZZT ZZT ZZT ZZT
UHHHH...
I THINK... TAKEUCHI-KUN TOOK YOU HOME...
WHAT?!
THAT'S BECAUSE YOU PASSED OUT.
I DON'T REMEMBER ANYTHING...
I FELT SO BAD FOR YOU...
...BUT I WAS IN NO STATE TO HELP, SO I CALLED HIM.
...
DID... ...TAKEUCHI-KUN SAY ANYTHING?
OH.
UM...
MM...
TO TELL YOU THE TRUTH, MY RECOLLECTION ISN'T THAT GOOD EITHER.
I DON'T REMEMBER ANYTHING AFTER CALLING HIM.
I WOKE UP THIS MORNING AND FOUND A POT OF ONION SOUP ON THE STOVE.
SOUP?
I THOUGHT YOU HAD MADE IT FOR ME, AKI-CHAN.
WOW... TAKEUCHI'S A NICE GUY.
klak klak
THEN...
TAKEUCHI-KUN MADE THE ONION SOUP...

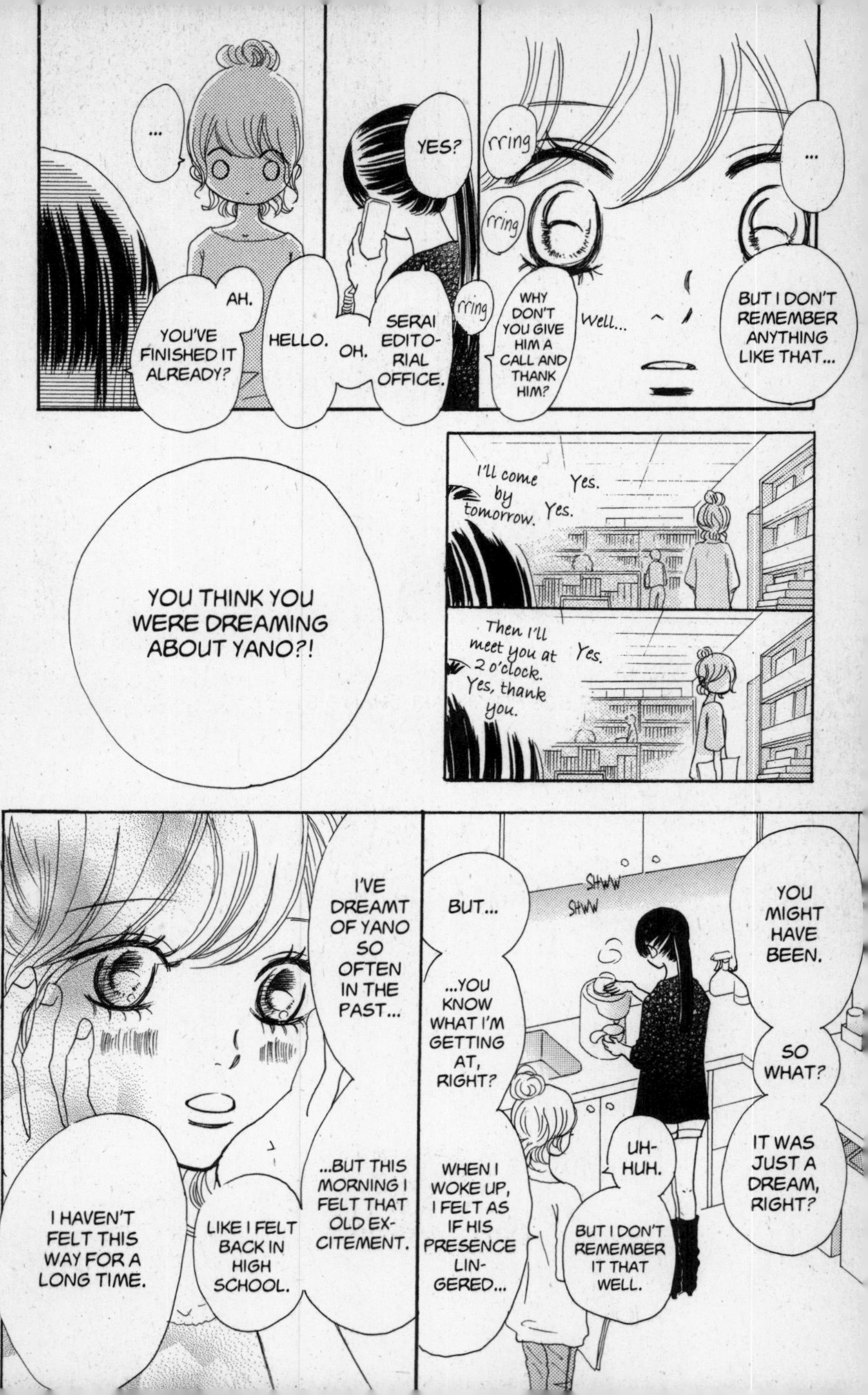
...
BUT I DON'T REMEMBER ANYTHING LIKE THAT...
rring
rring
Well...
WHY DON'T YOU GIVE HIM A CALL AND THANK HIM?
rring
YES?
SERAI EDITORIAL OFFICE.
OH.
HELLO.
...
AH.
YOU'VE FINISHED IT ALREADY?
I'll come by tomorrow.
Yes.
Yes.
Then I'll meet you at 2 o'clock. Yes, thank you.
Yes.
YOU THINK YOU WERE DREAMING ABOUT YANO?!
YOU MIGHT HAVE BEEN.
SO WHAT?
IT WAS JUST A DREAM, RIGHT?
SHWW
SHWW
UH-HUH.
BUT I DON'T REMEMBER IT THAT WELL.
BUT...
...YOU KNOW WHAT I'M GETTING AT, RIGHT?
WHEN I WOKE UP, I FELT AS IF HIS PRESENCE LINGERED...
I'VE DREAMT OF YANO SO OFTEN IN THE PAST...
...BUT THIS MORNING I FELT THAT OLD EXCITEMENT.
LIKE I FELT BACK IN HIGH SCHOOL.
I HAVEN'T FELT THIS WAY FOR A LONG TIME.

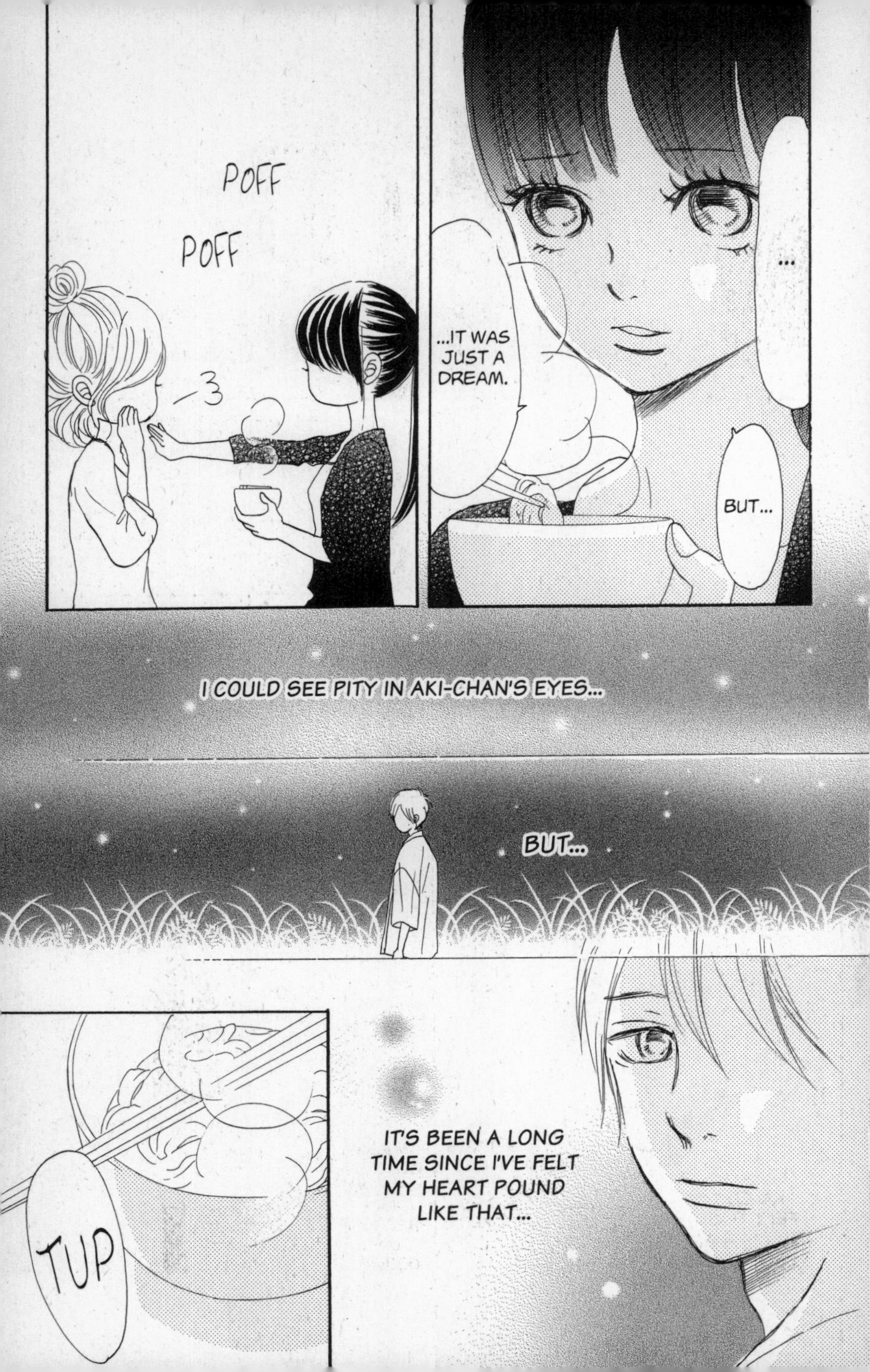
...
...IT WAS JUST A DREAM.
BUT...
POFF
POFF
I COULD SEE PITY IN AKI-CHAN'S EYES...
BUT...
IT'S BEEN A LONG TIME SINCE I'VE FELT MY HEART POUND LIKE THAT...
TUP

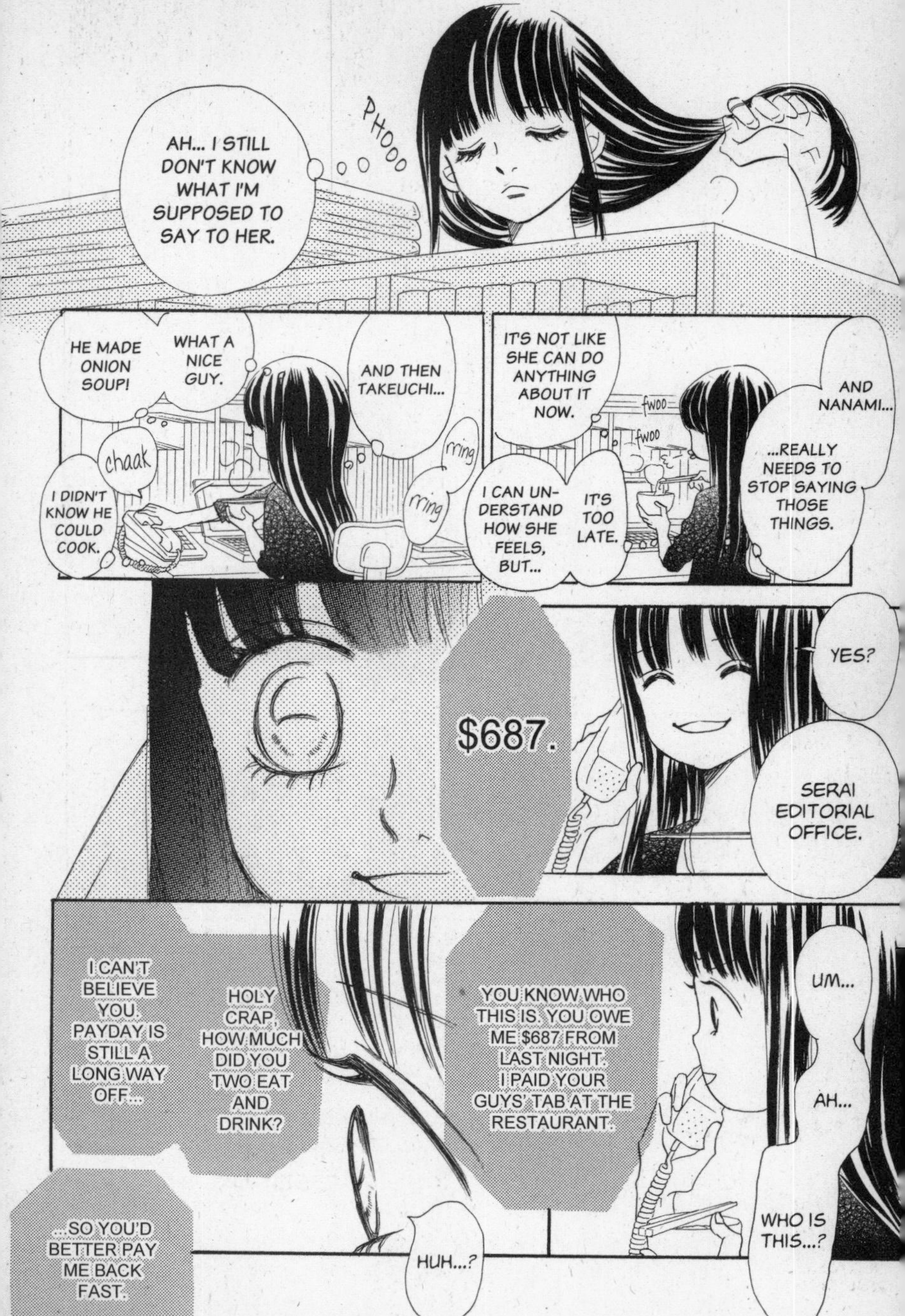
PHOOO
AH... I STILL DON'T KNOW WHAT I'M SUPPOSED TO SAY TO HER.
AND NANAMI...
...REALLY NEEDS TO STOP SAYING THOSE THINGS.
IT'S NOT LIKE SHE CAN DO ANYTHING ABOUT IT NOW.
fwoo
fwoo
IT'S TOO LATE.
I CAN UN-DERSTAND HOW SHE FEELS, BUT...
AND THEN TAKEUCHI...
rring
rring
WHAT A NICE GUY.
HE MADE ONION SOUP!
chaak
I DIDN'T KNOW HE COULD COOK.
YES?
SERAI EDITORIAL OFFICE.
$687.
UM...
AH...
WHO IS THIS...?
YOU KNOW WHO THIS IS. YOU OWE ME $687 FROM LAST NIGHT. I PAID YOUR GUYS' TAB AT THE RESTAURANT.
HOLY CRAP, HOW MUCH DID YOU TWO EAT AND DRINK?
I CAN'T BELIEVE YOU. PAYDAY IS STILL A LONG WAY OFF...
HUH...?
...SO YOU'D BETTER PAY ME BACK FAST.

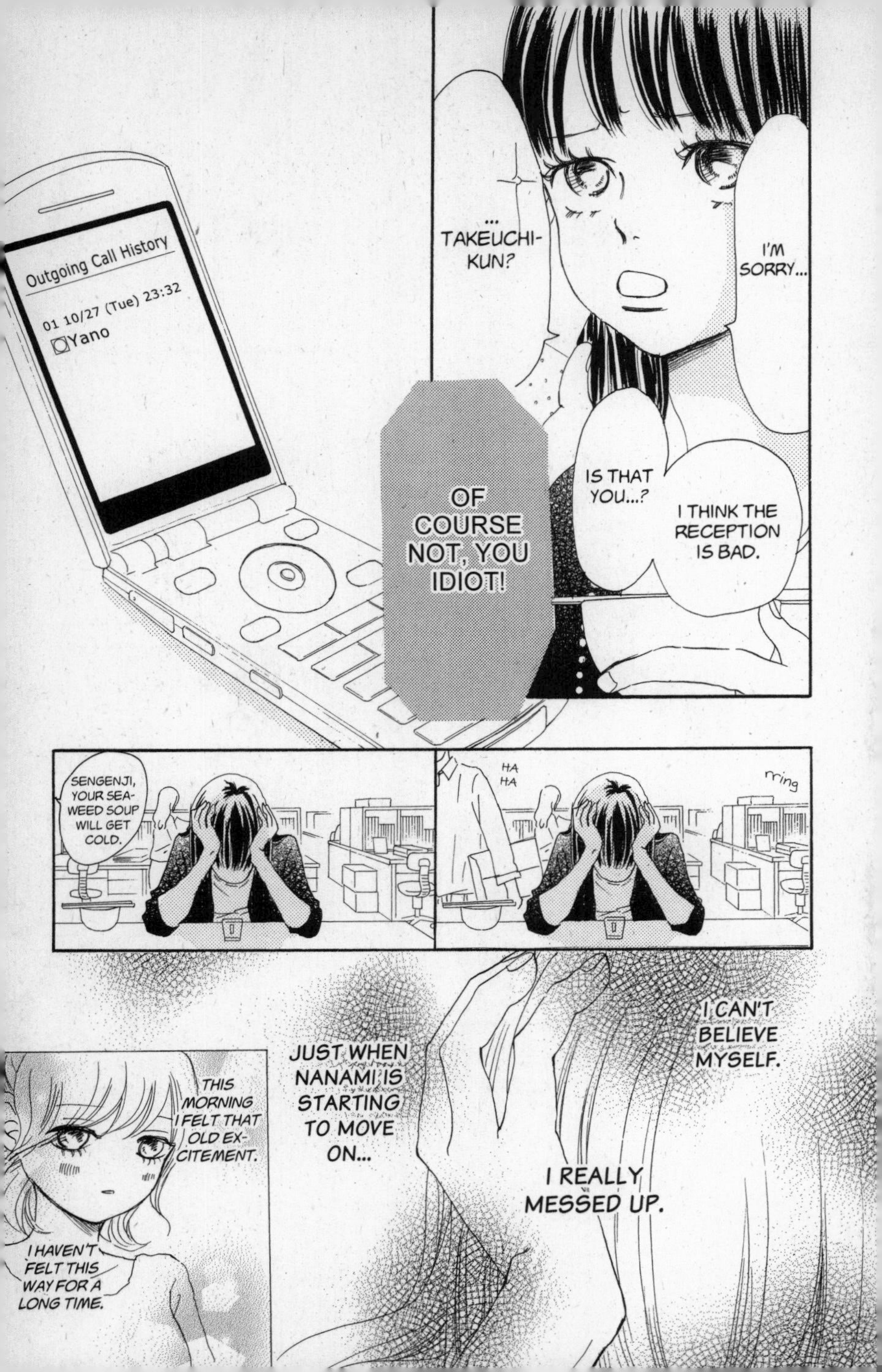
...TAKEUCHI-KUN?
IS THAT YOU...?
I'M SORRY...
I THINK THE RECEPTION IS BAD.
Outgoing Call History
01 10/27 (Tue) 23:32
Yano
OF COURSE NOT, YOU IDIOT!
HA HA
rring
SENGENJI, YOUR SEA-WEED SOUP WILL GET COLD.
I CAN'T BELIEVE MYSELF.
I REALLY MESSED UP.
JUST WHEN NANAMI IS STARTING TO MOVE ON...
THIS MORNING I FELT THAT OLD EX-CITEMENT.
I HAVEN'T FELT THIS WAY FOR A LONG TIME.

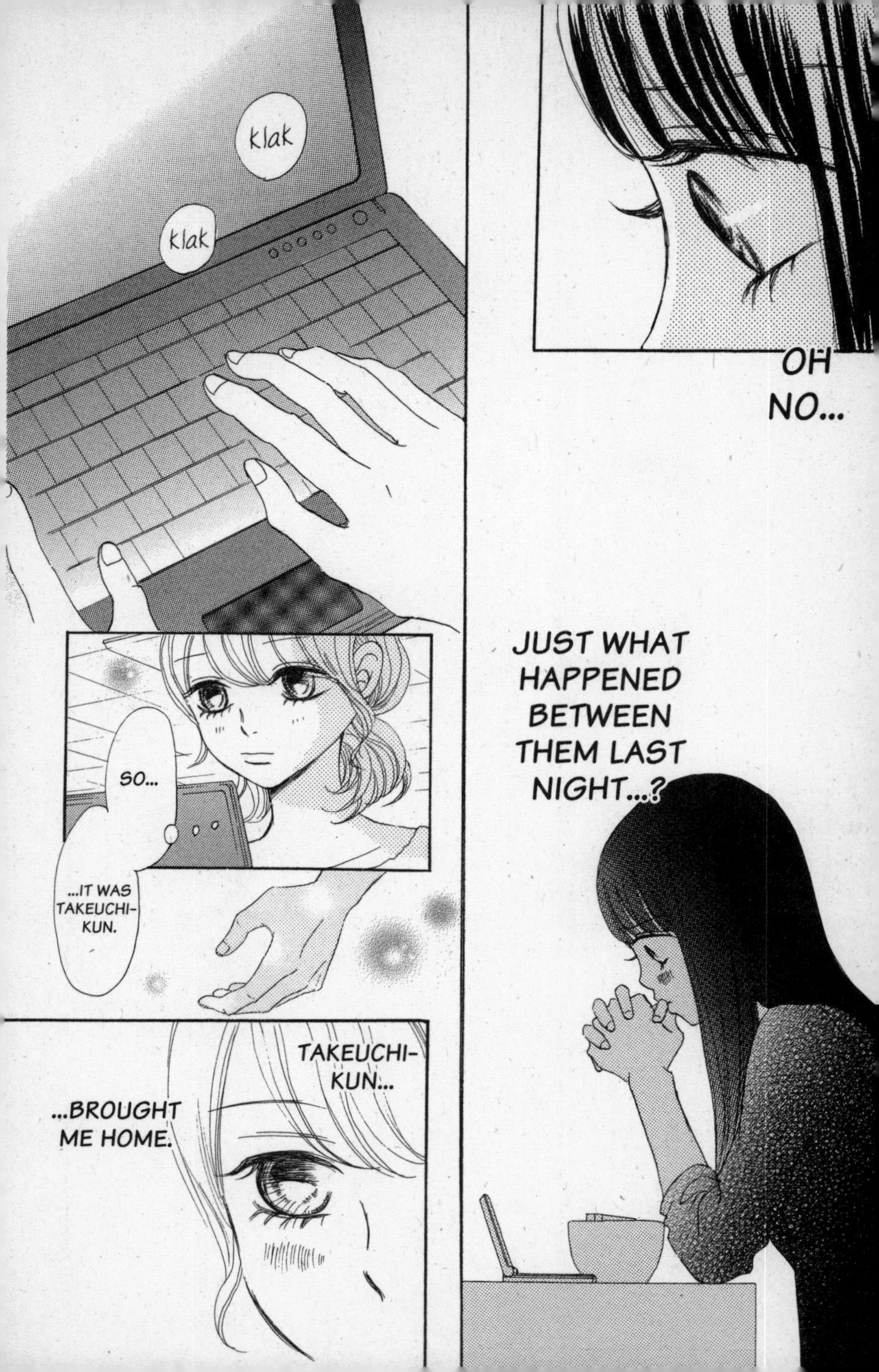
OH NO...
JUST WHAT HAPPENED BETWEEN THEM LAST NIGHT...?
klak
klak
SO...
...IT WAS TAKEUCHI-KUN.
TAKEUCHI-KUN...
...BROUGHT ME HOME.

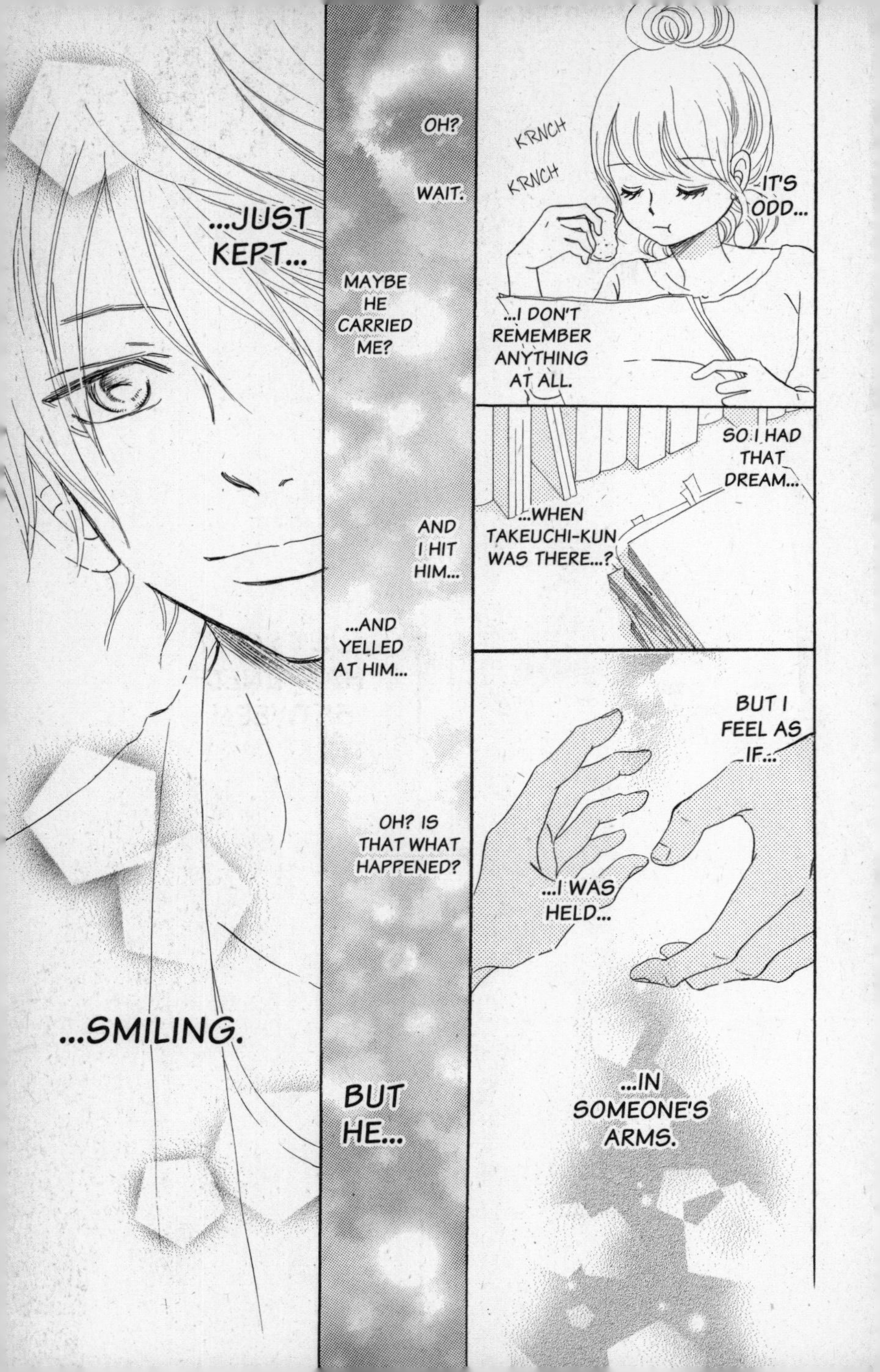
KRNCH
KRNCH
IT'S ODD...
...I DON'T REMEMBER ANYTHING AT ALL.
SO I HAD THAT DREAM...
...WHEN TAKEUCHI-KUN WAS THERE...?
BUT I FEEL AS IF...
...I WAS HELD...
...IN SOMEONE'S ARMS.
OH?
WAIT.
MAYBE HE CARRIED ME?
AND I HIT HIM...
...AND YELLED AT HIM...
OH? IS THAT WHAT HAPPENED?
BUT HE...
...JUST KEPT...
...SMILING.

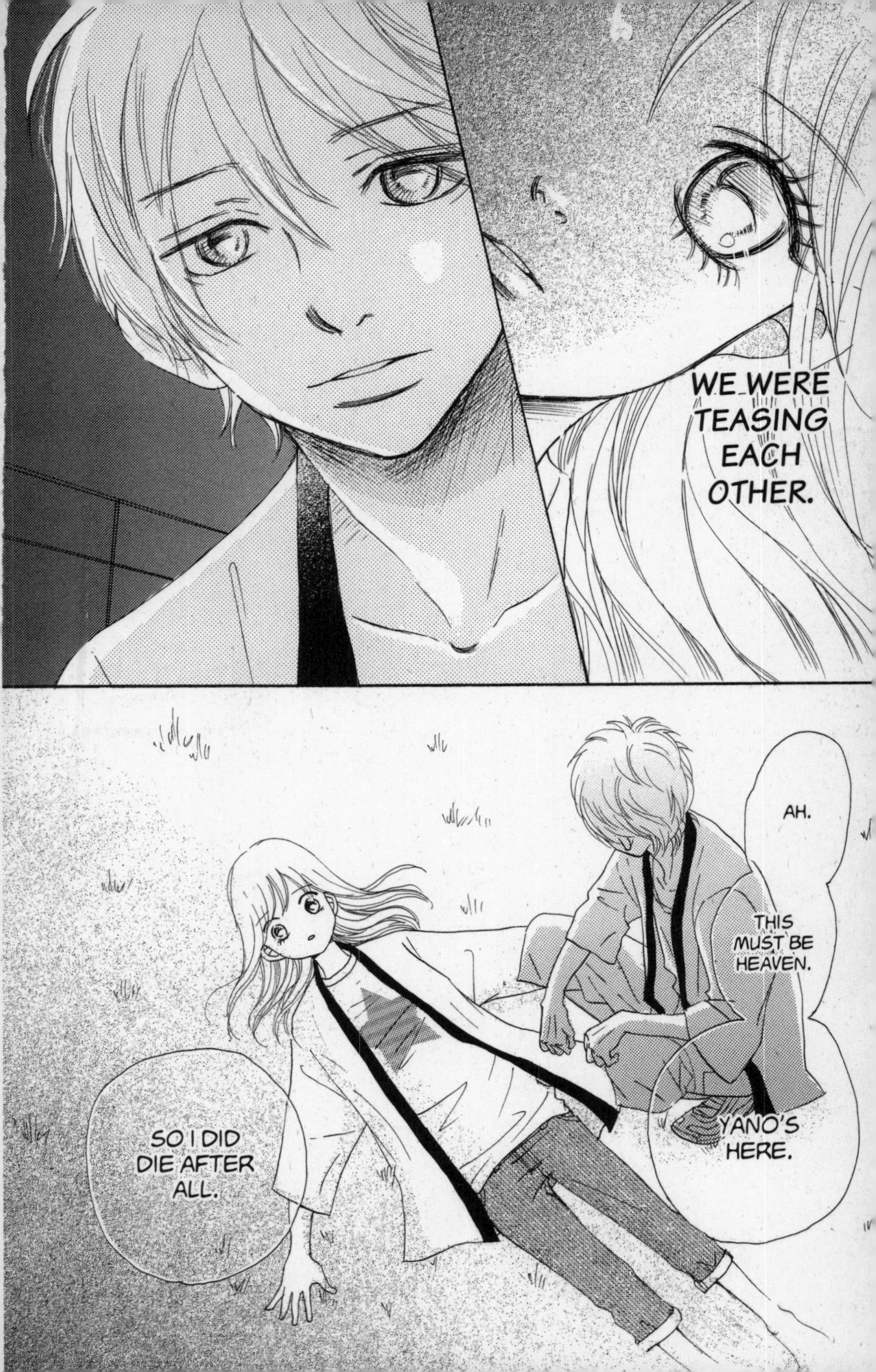
WE WERE TEASING EACH OTHER.
AH.
THIS MUST BE HEAVEN.
YANO'S HERE.
SO I DID DIE AFTER ALL.

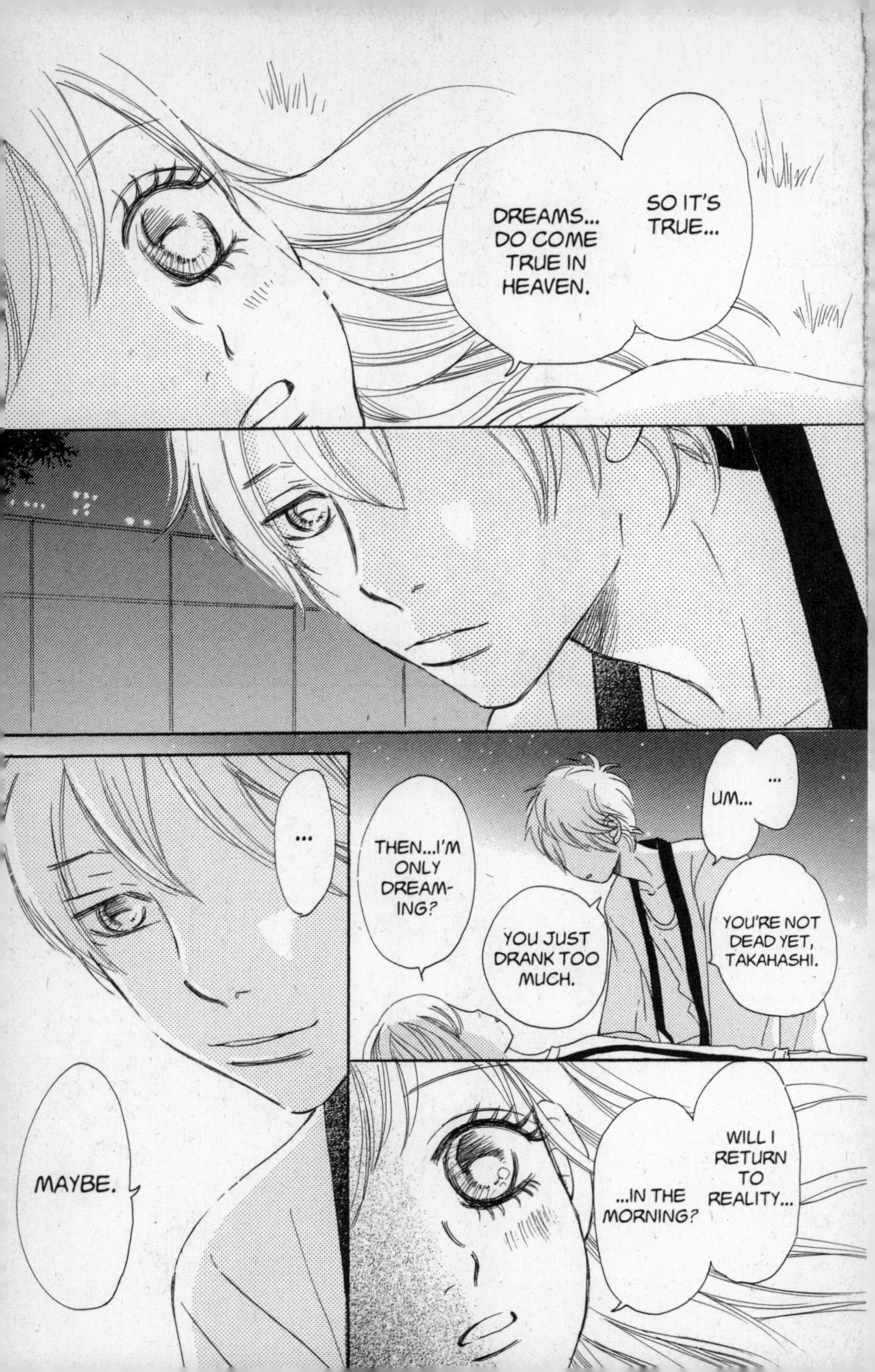
SO IT'S TRUE...
DREAMS... DO COME TRUE IN HEAVEN.
... UM...
YOU'RE NOT DEAD YET, TAKAHASHI.
YOU JUST DRANK TOO MUCH.
THEN...I'M ONLY DREAMING?
WILL I RETURN TO REALITY...
...IN THE MORNING?
...
MAYBE.

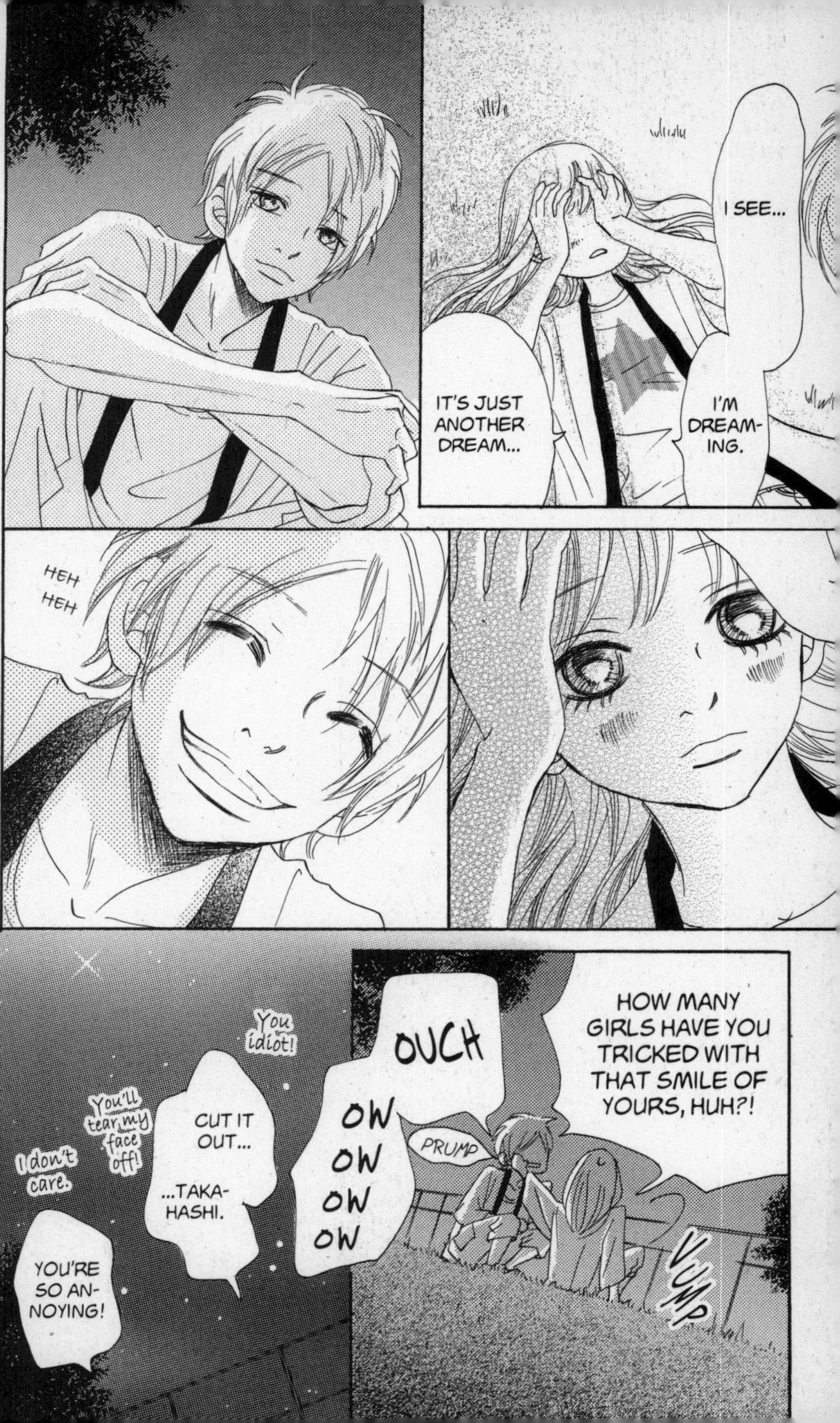
I SEE...
I'M DREAM-ING.
IT'S JUST ANOTHER DREAM...
HEH HEH
HOW MANY GIRLS HAVE YOU TRICKED WITH THAT SMILE OF YOURS, HUH?!
VUMP
PRUMP
OUCH
OW OW OW OW
You idiot!
CUT IT OUT...
...TAKA-HASHI.
You'll tear my face off!
I don't care.
YOU'RE SO AN-NOYING!

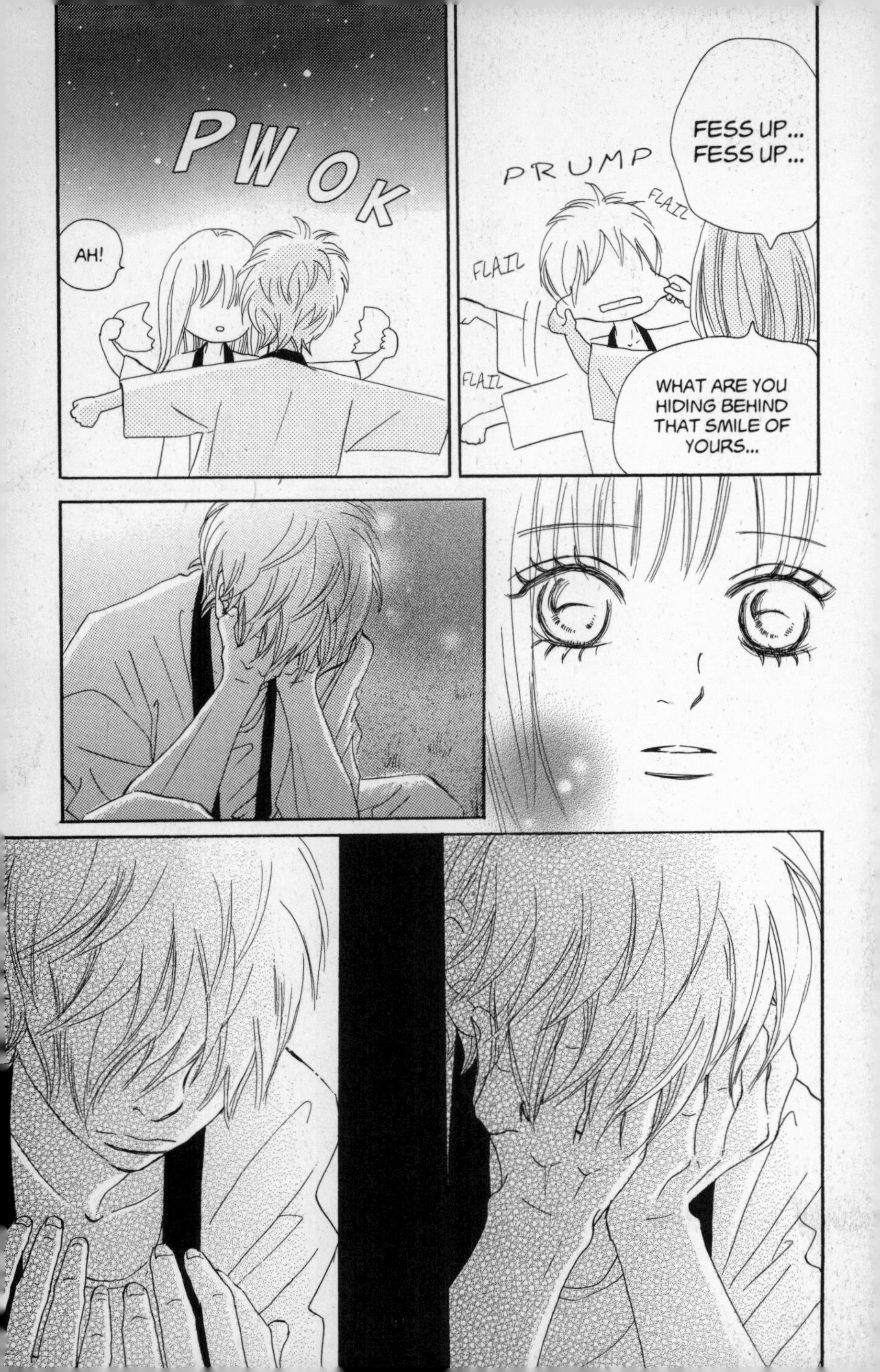
FESS UP... FESS UP...
PRUMP
FLAIL
FLAIL
FLAIL
WHAT ARE YOU HIDING BEHIND THAT SMILE OF YOURS...
PWOK
AH!

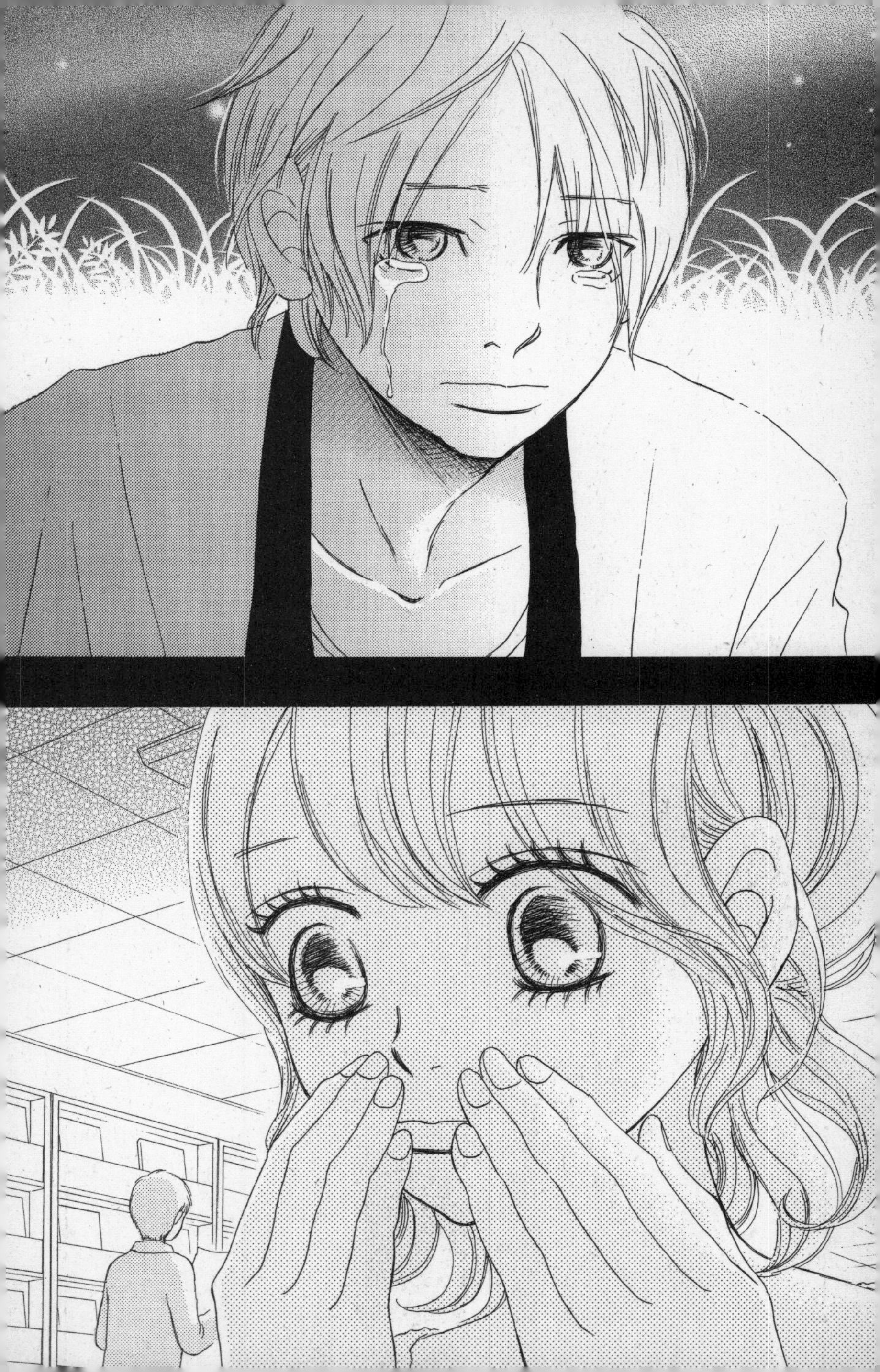

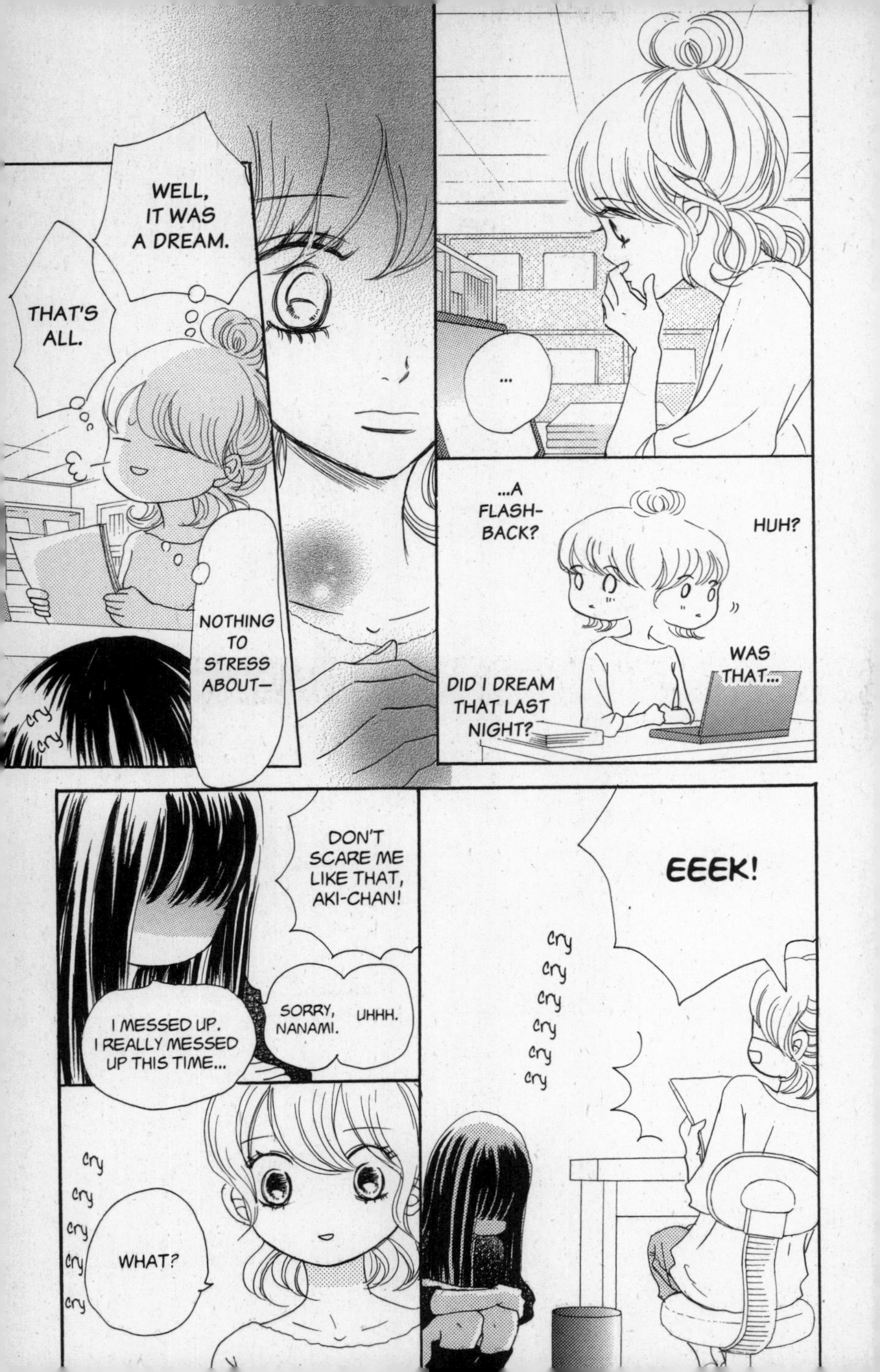
...
HUH?
...A FLASH-BACK?
WAS THAT...
DID I DREAM THAT LAST NIGHT?
WELL, IT WAS A DREAM.
THAT'S ALL.
NOTHING TO STRESS ABOUT—
cry cry
EEEK!
cry cry cry cry cry cry
DON'T SCARE ME LIKE THAT, AKI-CHAN!
UHHH.
SORRY, NANAMI.
I MESSED UP. I REALLY MESSED UP THIS TIME...
cry cry cry cry cry
WHAT?

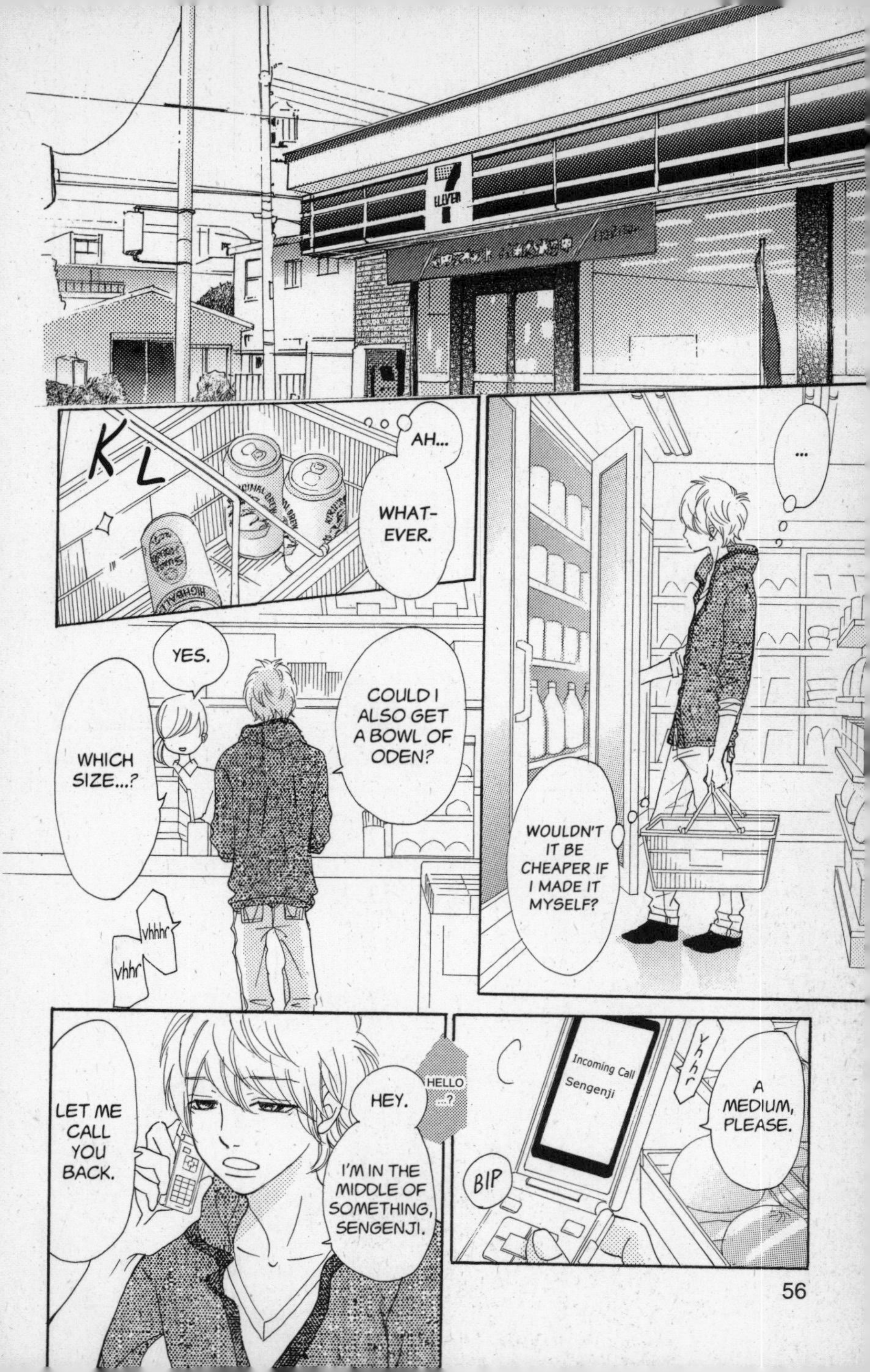
...
WOULDN'T IT BE CHEAPER IF I MADE IT MYSELF?
KL
AH...
WHATEVER.
COULD I ALSO GET A BOWL OF ODEN?
YES.
WHICH SIZE...?
vhhhr
vhhr
vhhr
A MEDIUM, PLEASE.
Incoming Call
Sengenji
BIP
HELLO ...?
HEY.
I'M IN THE MIDDLE OF SOMETHING, SENGENJI.
LET ME CALL YOU BACK.

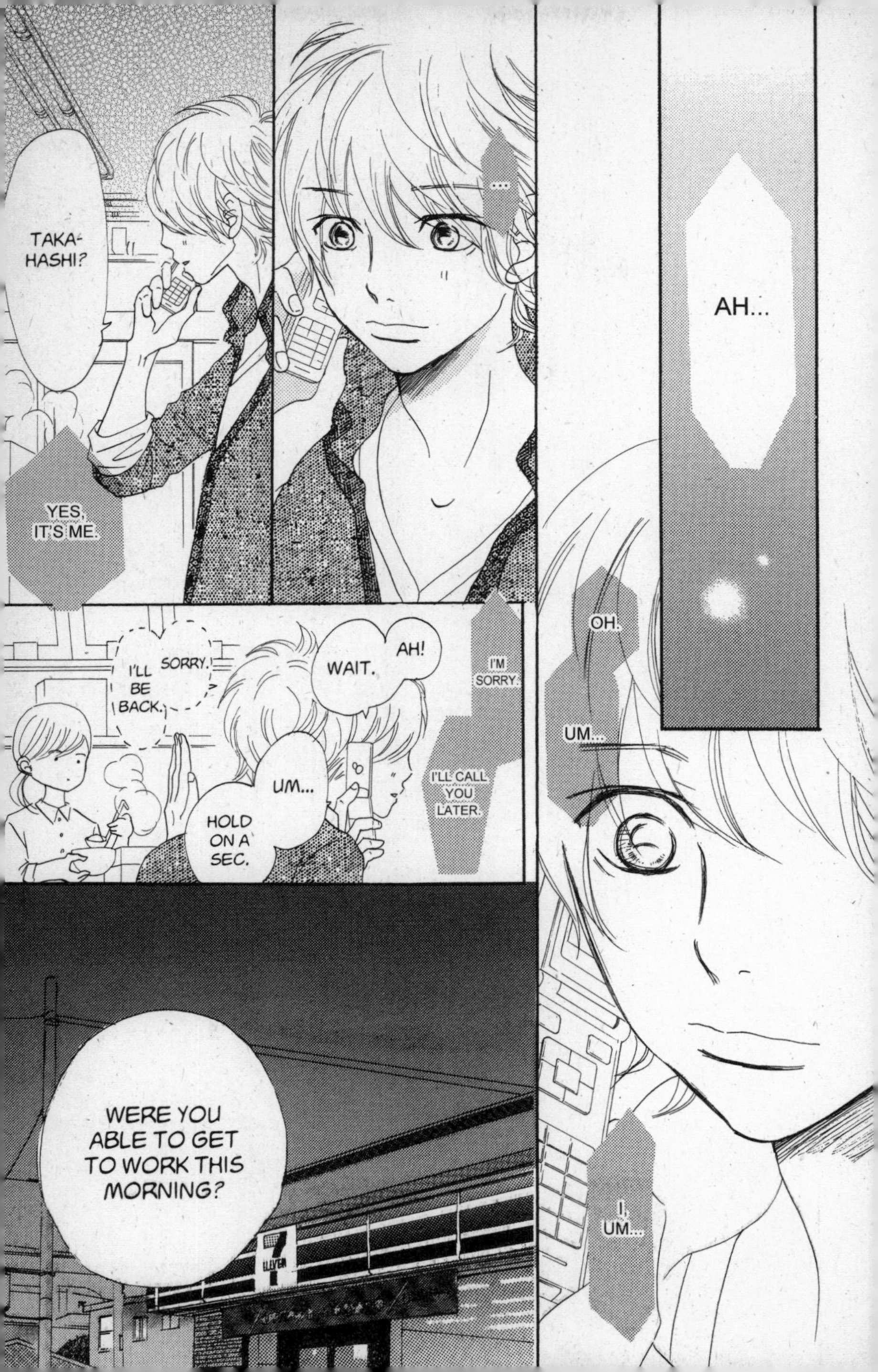
AH...
OH.
UM...
I, UM...
...
TAKA-HASHI?
YES, IT'S ME.
I'M SORRY.
I'LL CALL YOU LATER.
AH!
WAIT.
UM...
HOLD ON A SEC.
SORRY.
I'LL BE BACK.
WERE YOU ABLE TO GET TO WORK THIS MORNING?

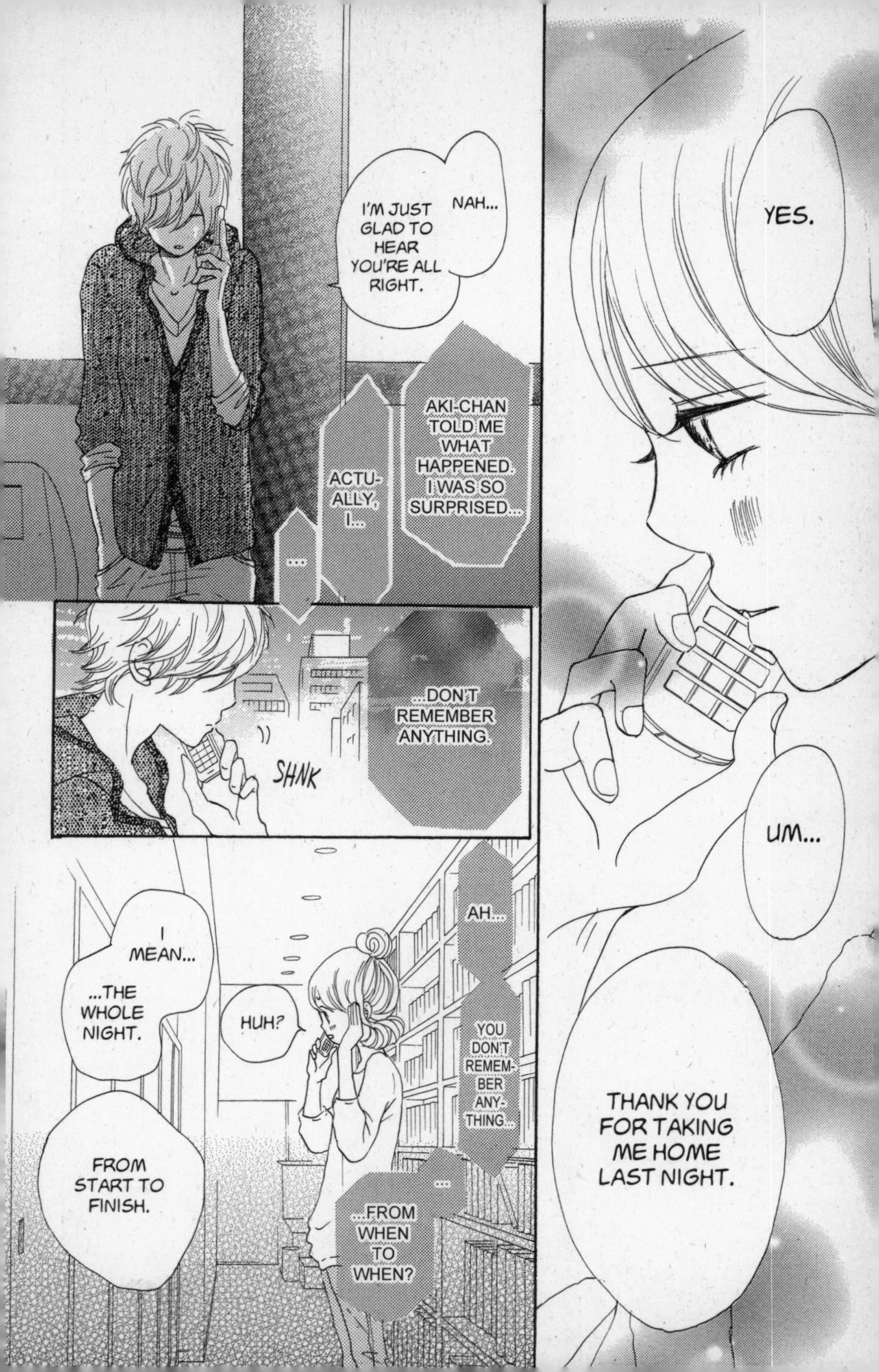
YES.
UM...
THANK YOU FOR TAKING ME HOME LAST NIGHT.
NAH... I'M JUST GLAD TO HEAR YOU'RE ALL RIGHT.
AKI-CHAN TOLD ME WHAT HAPPENED. I WAS SO SURPRISED...
ACTU-ALLY, I...
...
...DON'T REMEMBER ANYTHING.
SHNK
AH...
YOU DON'T REMEM-BER ANY-THING...
...
...FROM WHEN TO WHEN?
HUH?
I MEAN... ...THE WHOLE NIGHT.
FROM START TO FINISH.

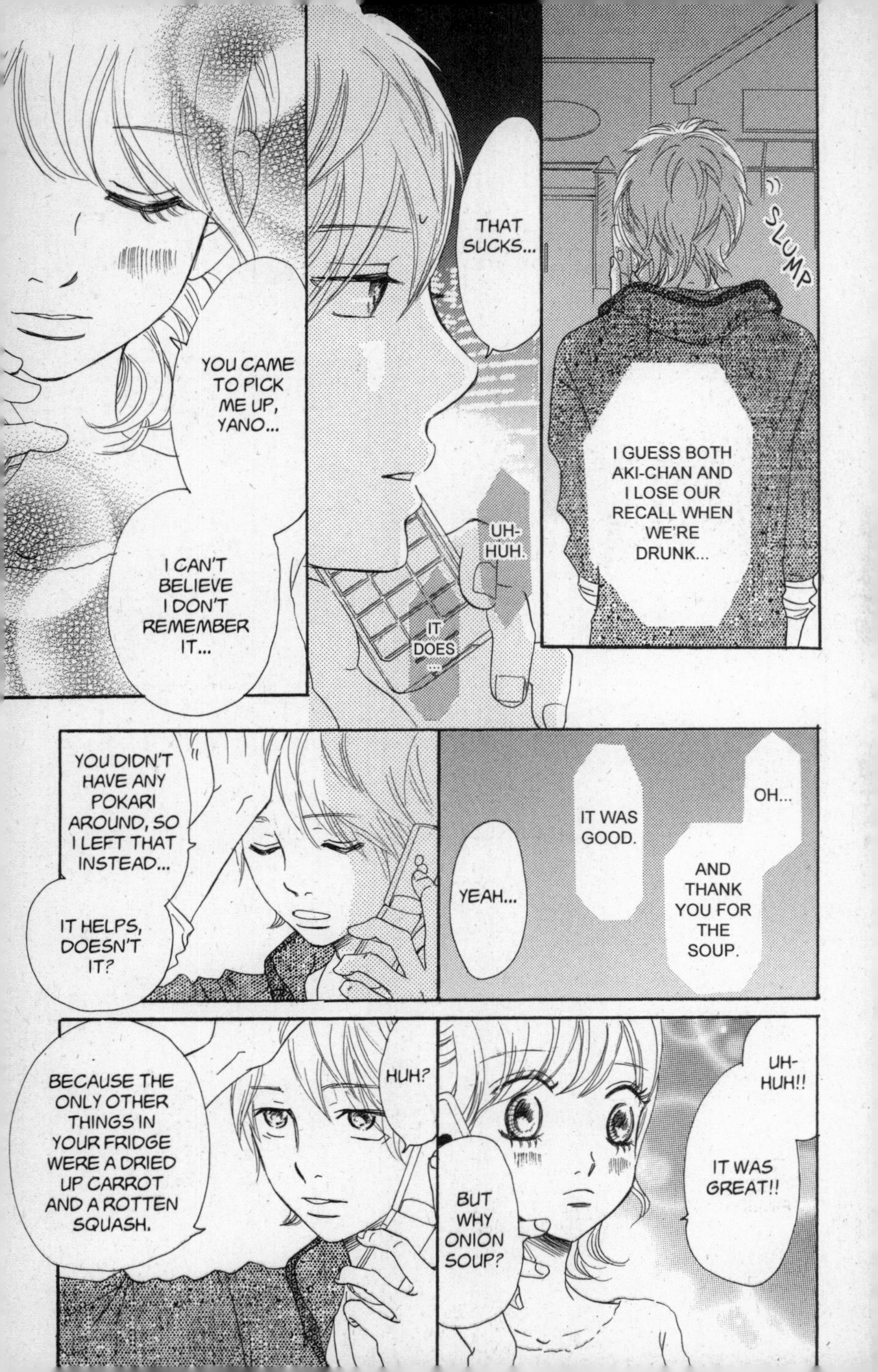
SLUMP
I GUESS BOTH AKI-CHAN AND I LOSE OUR RECALL WHEN WE'RE DRUNK...
THAT SUCKS...
UH-HUH.
IT DOES...
YOU CAME TO PICK ME UP, YANO...
I CAN'T BELIEVE I DON'T REMEMBER IT...
OH...
AND THANK YOU FOR THE SOUP.
IT WAS GOOD.
YEAH...
YOU DIDN'T HAVE ANY POKARI AROUND, SO I LEFT THAT INSTEAD...
IT HELPS, DOESN'T IT?
UH-HUH!!
IT WAS GREAT!!
BUT WHY ONION SOUP?
HUH?
BECAUSE THE ONLY OTHER THINGS IN YOUR FRIDGE WERE A DRIED UP CARROT AND A ROTTEN SQUASH.

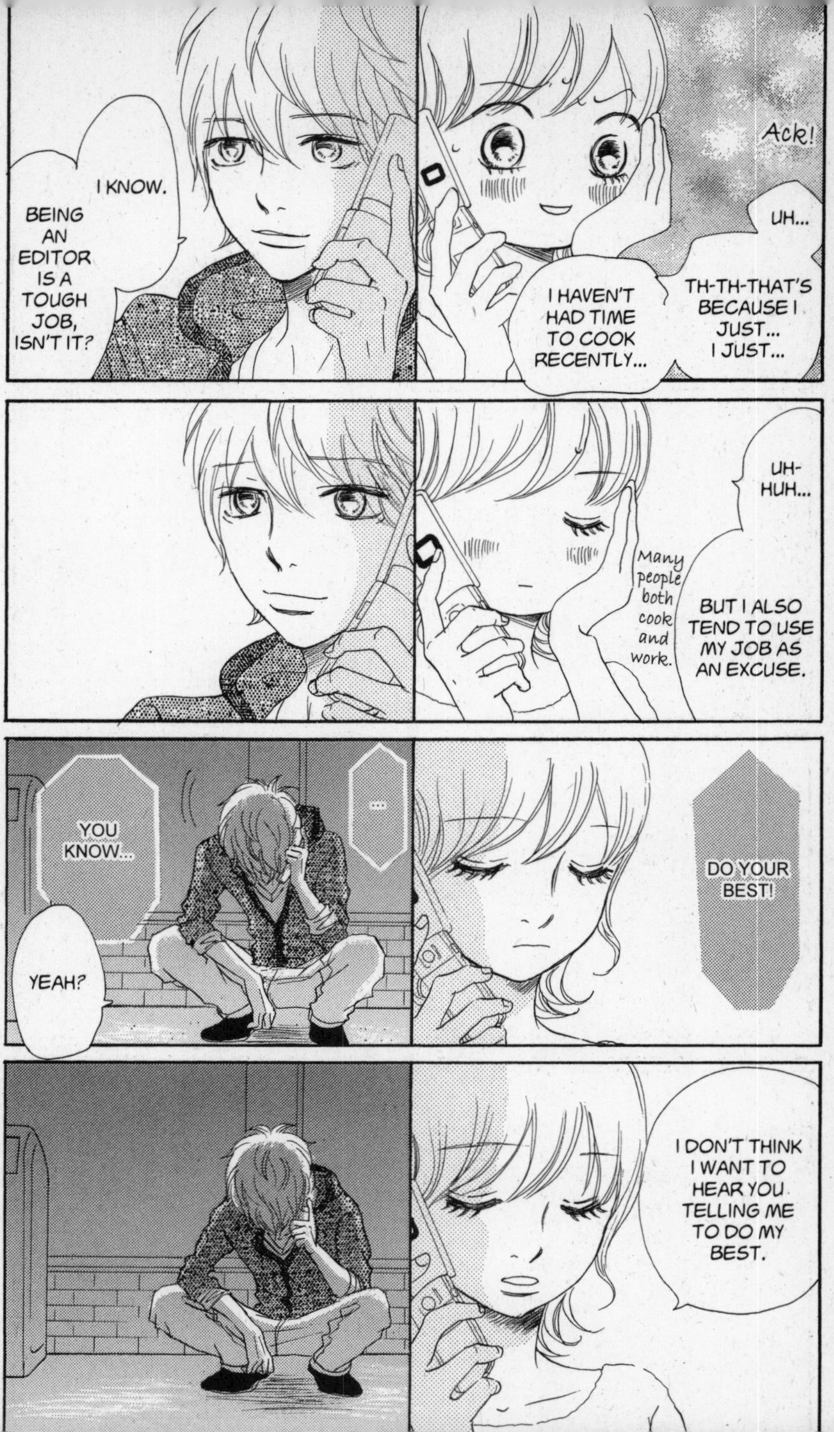
Ack!
UH...
TH-TH-THAT'S BECAUSE I JUST... I JUST...
I HAVEN'T HAD TIME TO COOK RECENTLY...
I KNOW.
BEING AN EDITOR IS A TOUGH JOB, ISN'T IT?
UH-HUH...
BUT I ALSO TEND TO USE MY JOB AS AN EXCUSE.
Many people both cook and work.
DO YOUR BEST!
...
YOU KNOW...
YEAH?
I DON'T THINK I WANT TO HEAR YOU TELLING ME TO DO MY BEST.

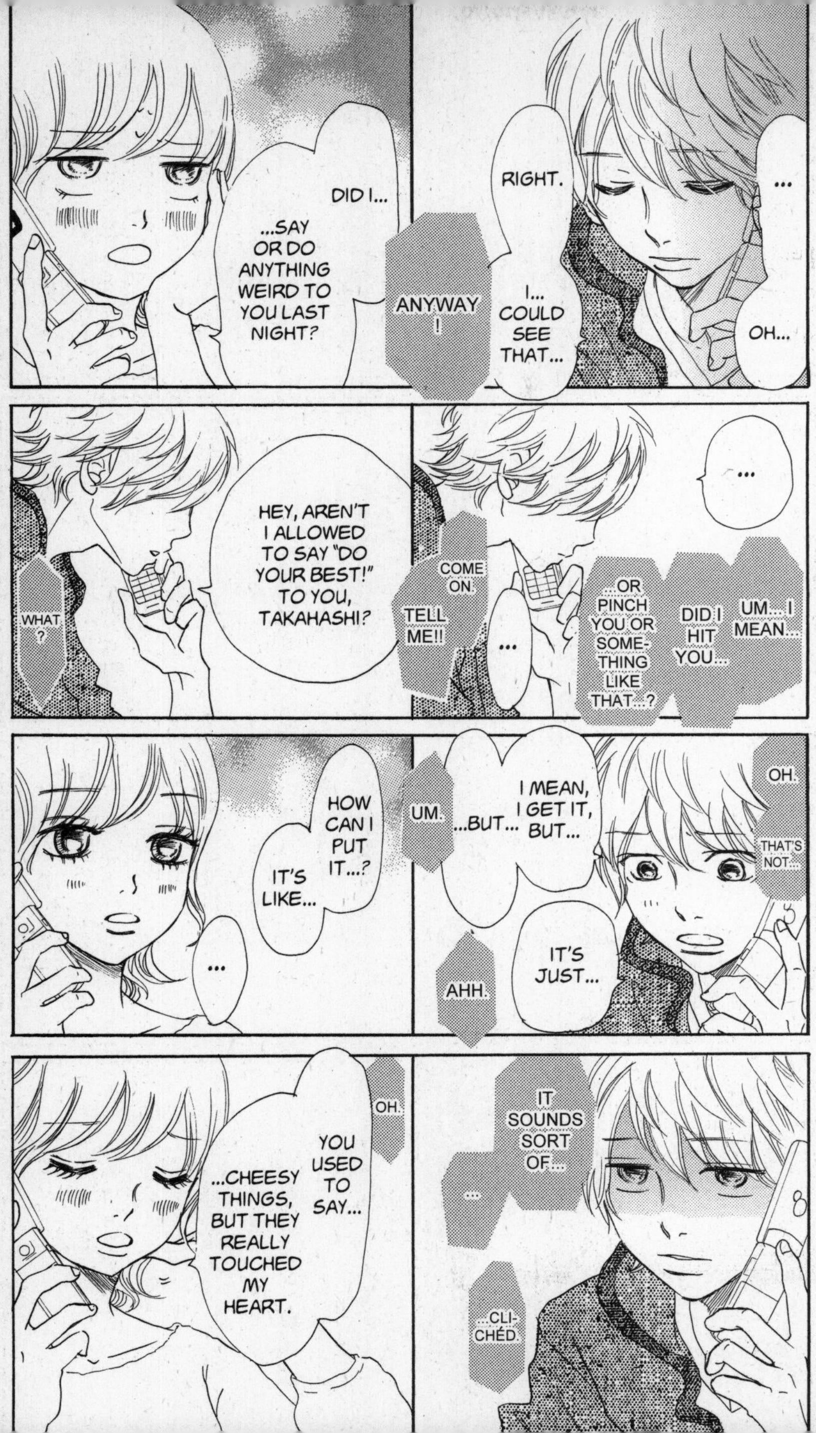
...
RIGHT.
OH...
I... COULD SEE THAT...
ANYWAY!
DID I...
...SAY OR DO ANYTHING WEIRD TO YOU LAST NIGHT?
...
UM... I MEAN...
DID I HIT YOU...
...OR PINCH YOU OR SOMETHING LIKE THAT...?
...
COME ON. TELL ME!!
HEY, AREN'T I ALLOWED TO SAY "DO YOUR BEST!" TO YOU, TAKAHASHI?
WHAT?
OH. THAT'S NOT...
I MEAN, I GET IT, BUT...
...BUT...
UM.
IT'S JUST...
AHH.
HOW CAN I PUT IT...?
IT'S LIKE...
...
IT SOUNDS SORT OF...
...
...CLICHÉD.
OH.
YOU USED TO SAY...
...CHEESY THINGS, BUT THEY REALLY TOUCHED MY HEART.

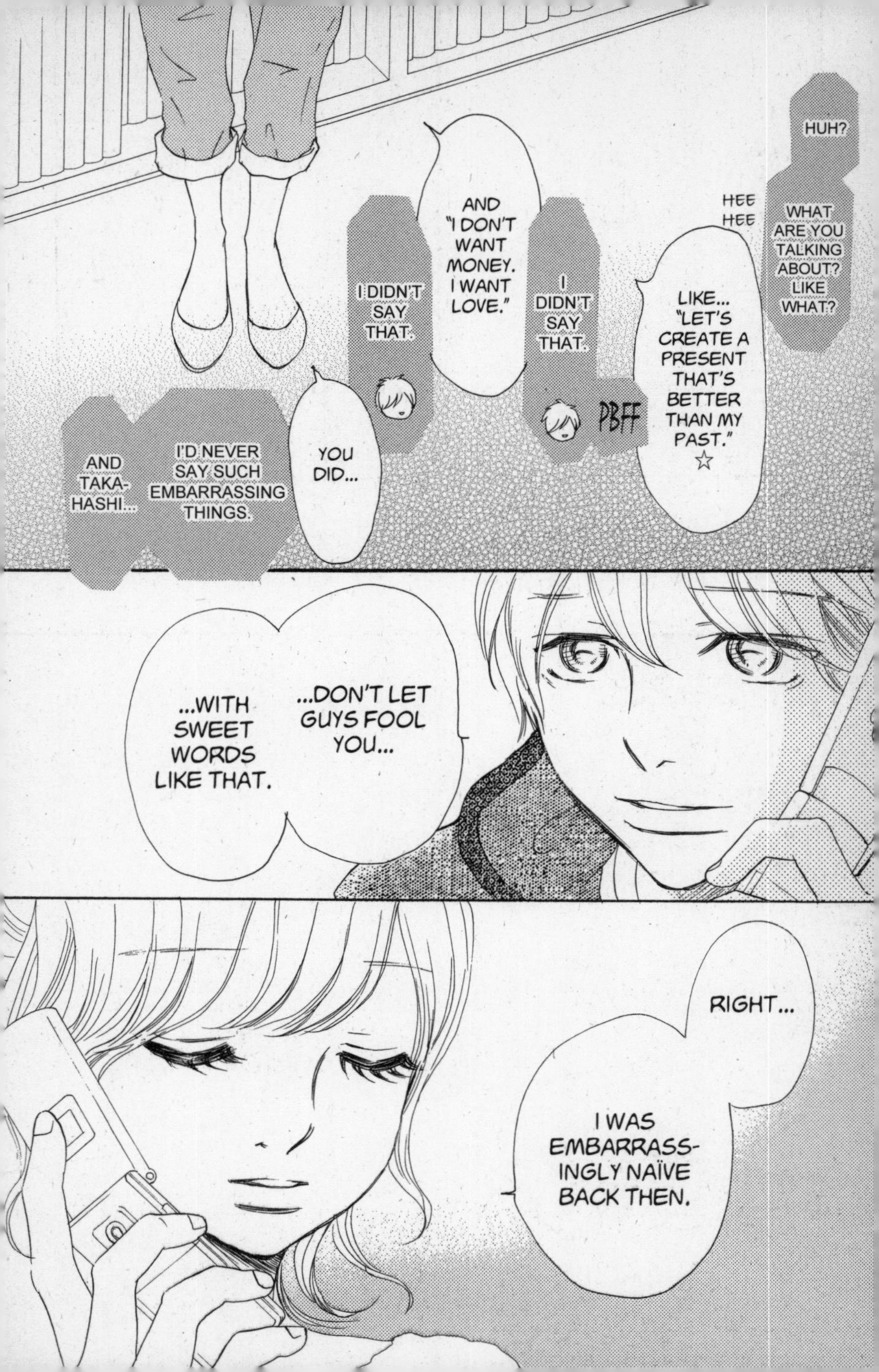
HUH?
WHAT ARE YOU TALKING ABOUT? LIKE WHAT?
HEE HEE
LIKE... "LET'S CREATE A PRESENT THAT'S BETTER THAN MY PAST." ☆
PBFF
I DIDN'T SAY THAT.
AND "I DON'T WANT MONEY. I WANT LOVE."
I DIDN'T SAY THAT.
YOU DID...
I'D NEVER SAY SUCH EMBARRASSING THINGS.
AND TAKA-HASHI...
...DON'T LET GUYS FOOL YOU...
...WITH SWEET WORDS LIKE THAT.
RIGHT...
I WAS EMBARRASS-INGLY NAÏVE BACK THEN.

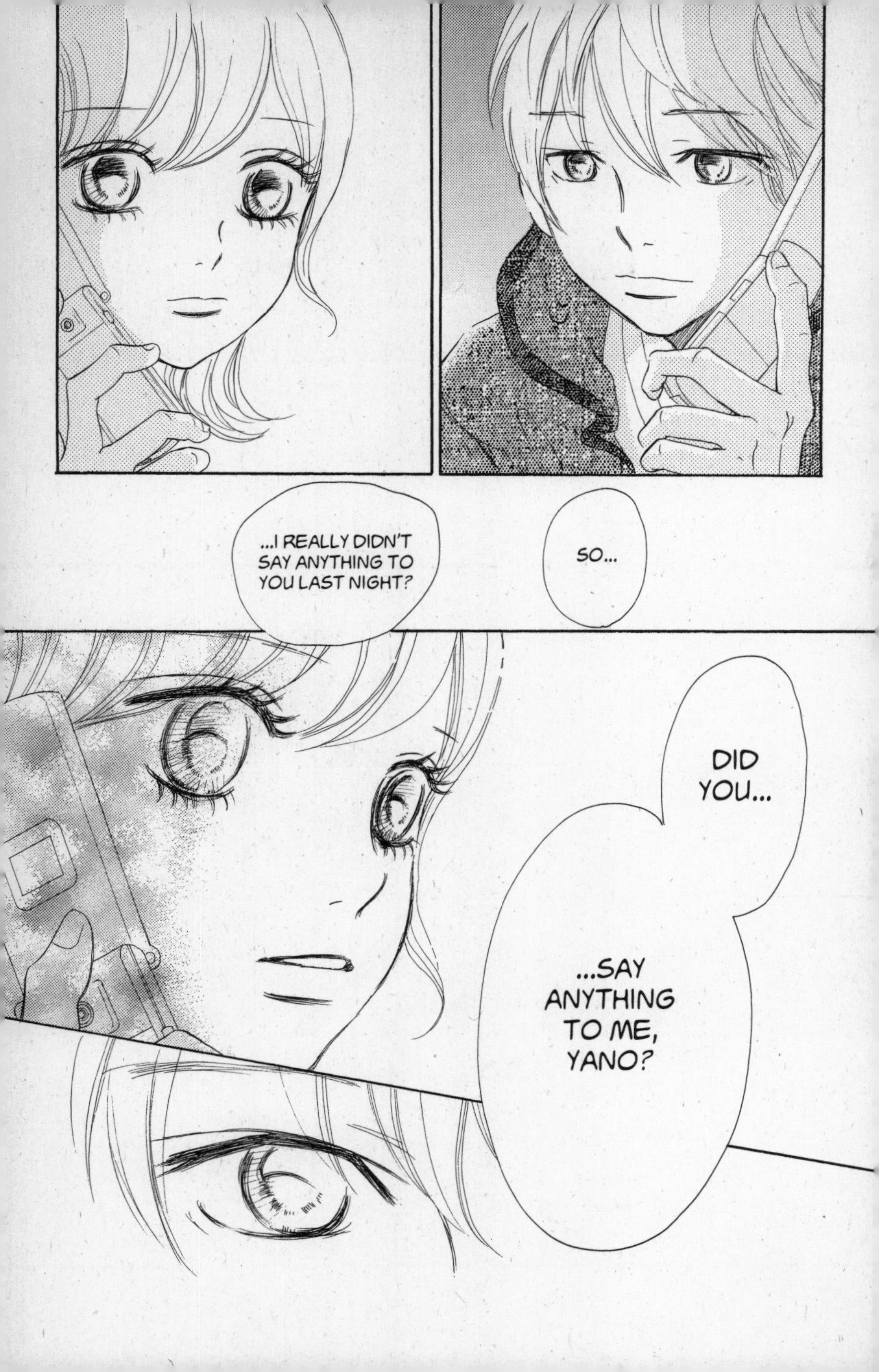
SO...
...I REALLY DIDN'T SAY ANYTHING TO YOU LAST NIGHT?
DID YOU...
...SAY ANYTHING TO ME, YANO?

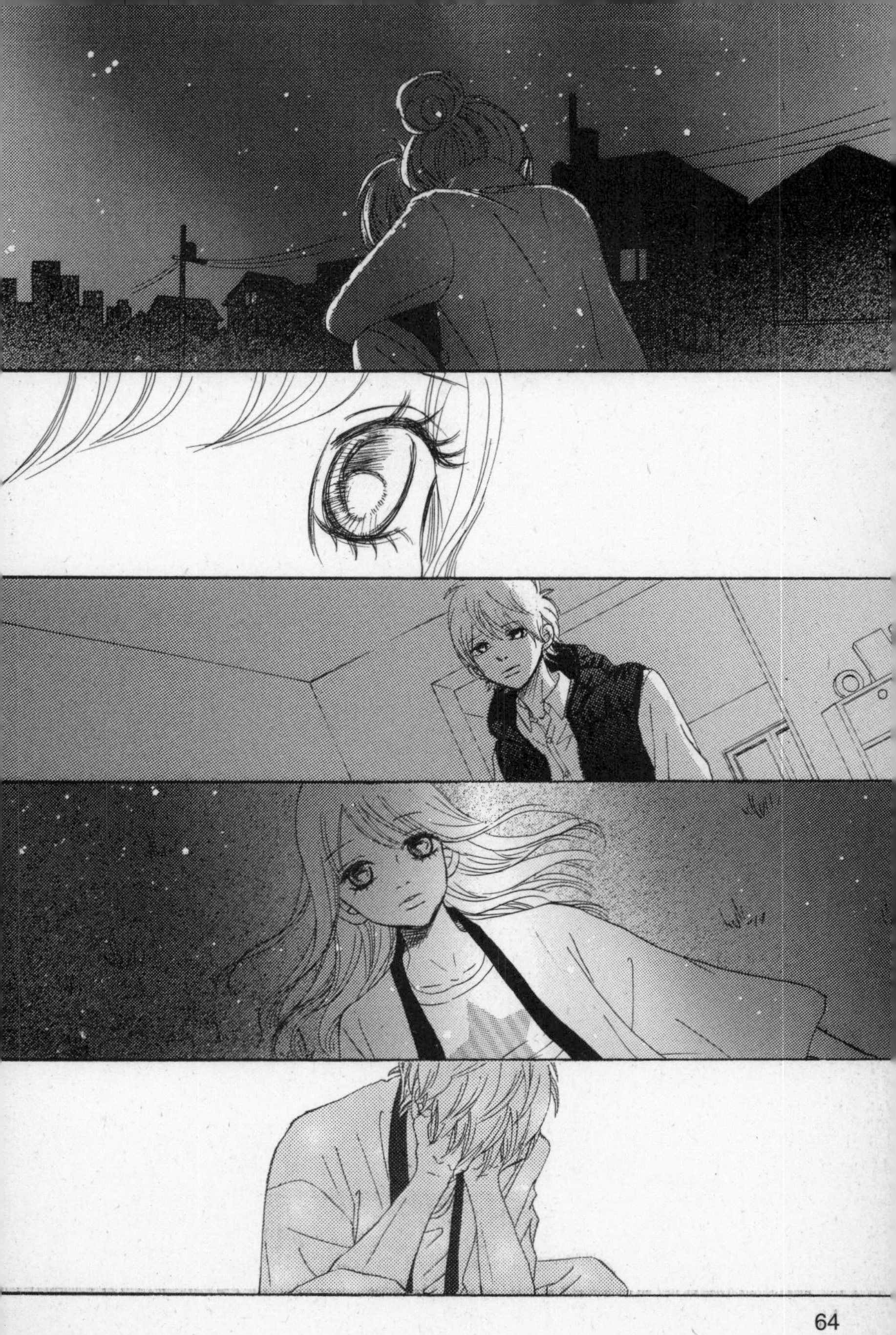

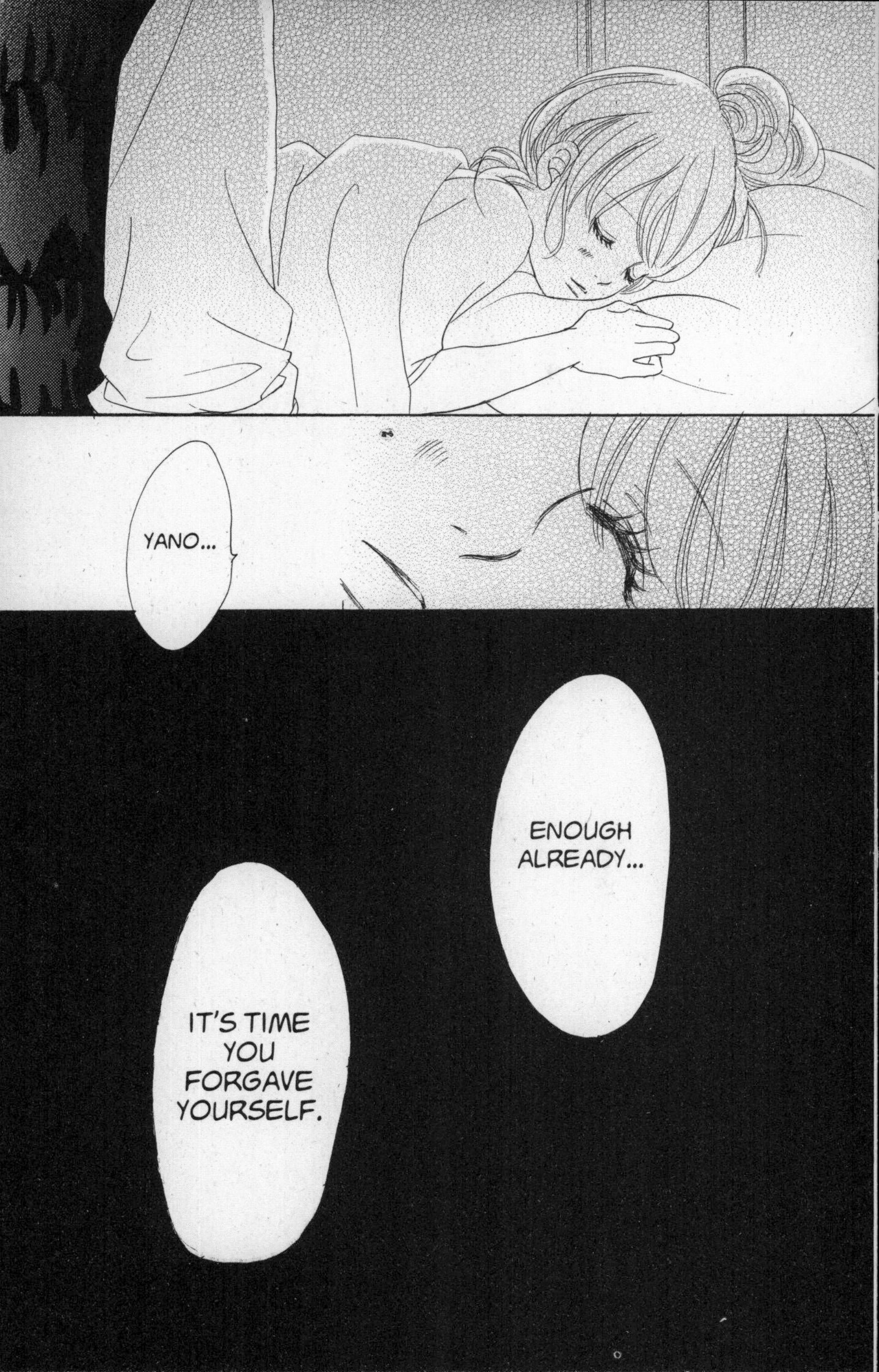
YANO...
ENOUGH ALREADY...
IT'S TIME YOU FORGAVE YOURSELF.

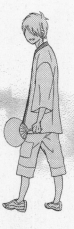

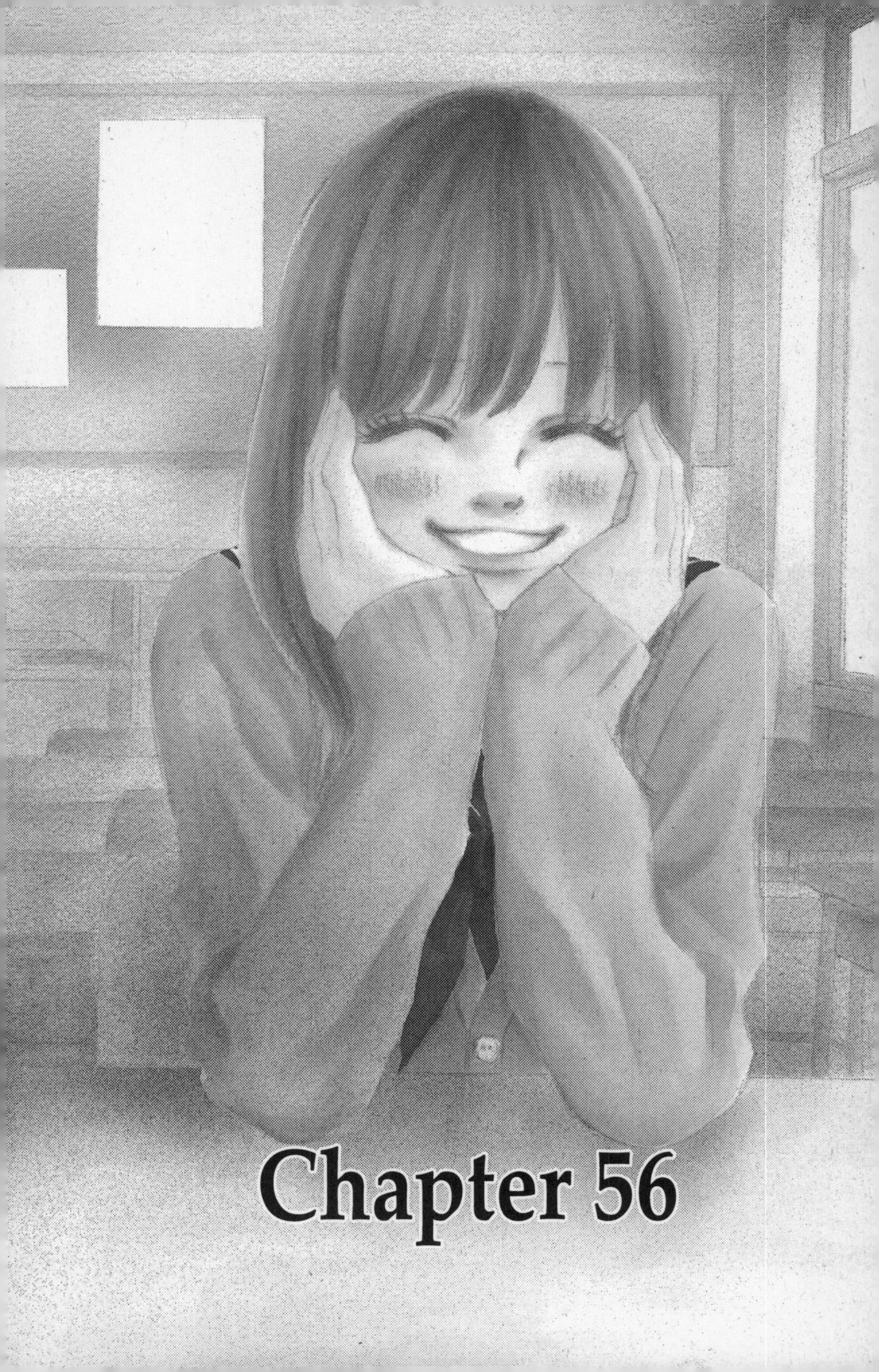
Chapter 56

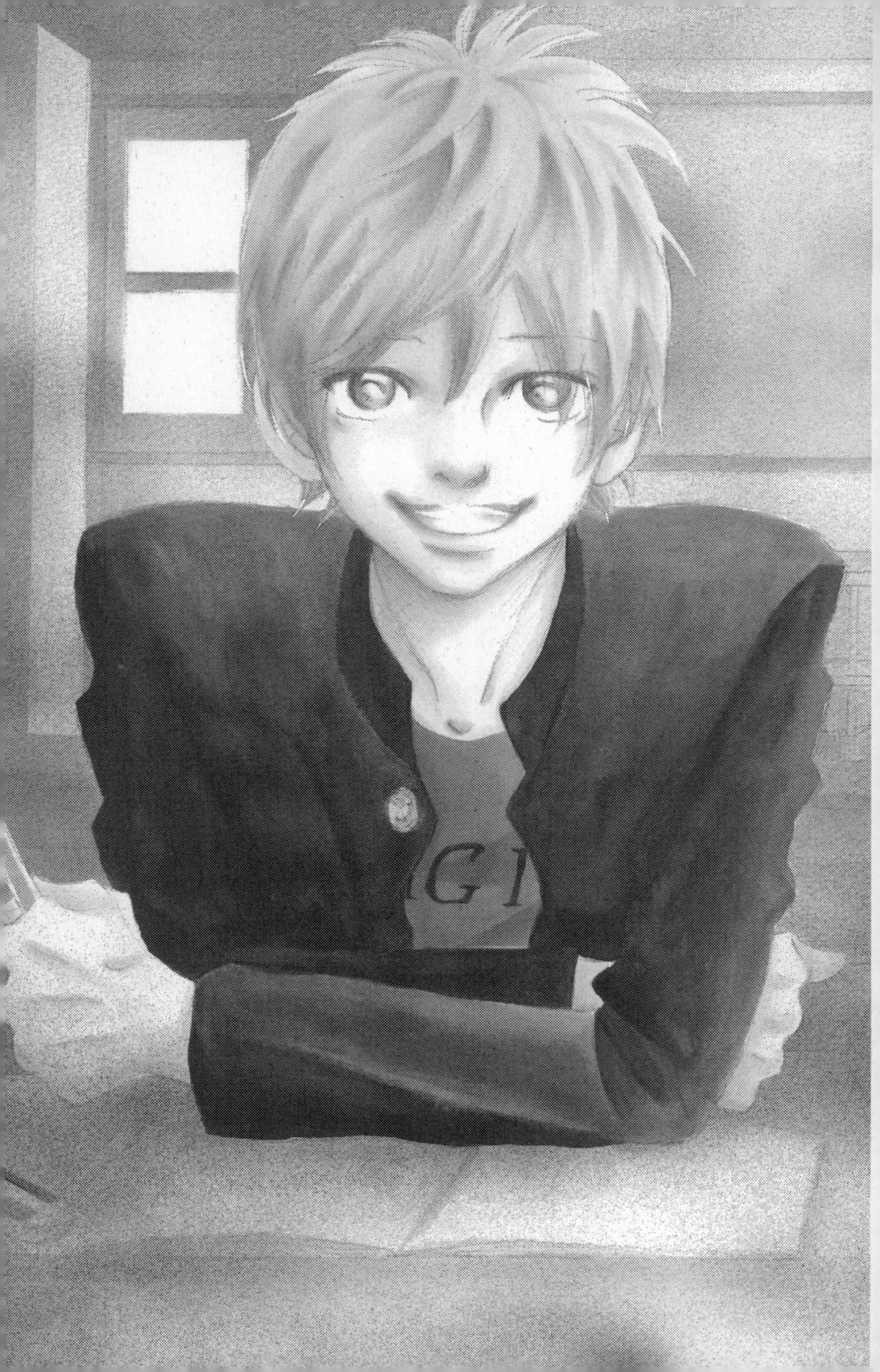

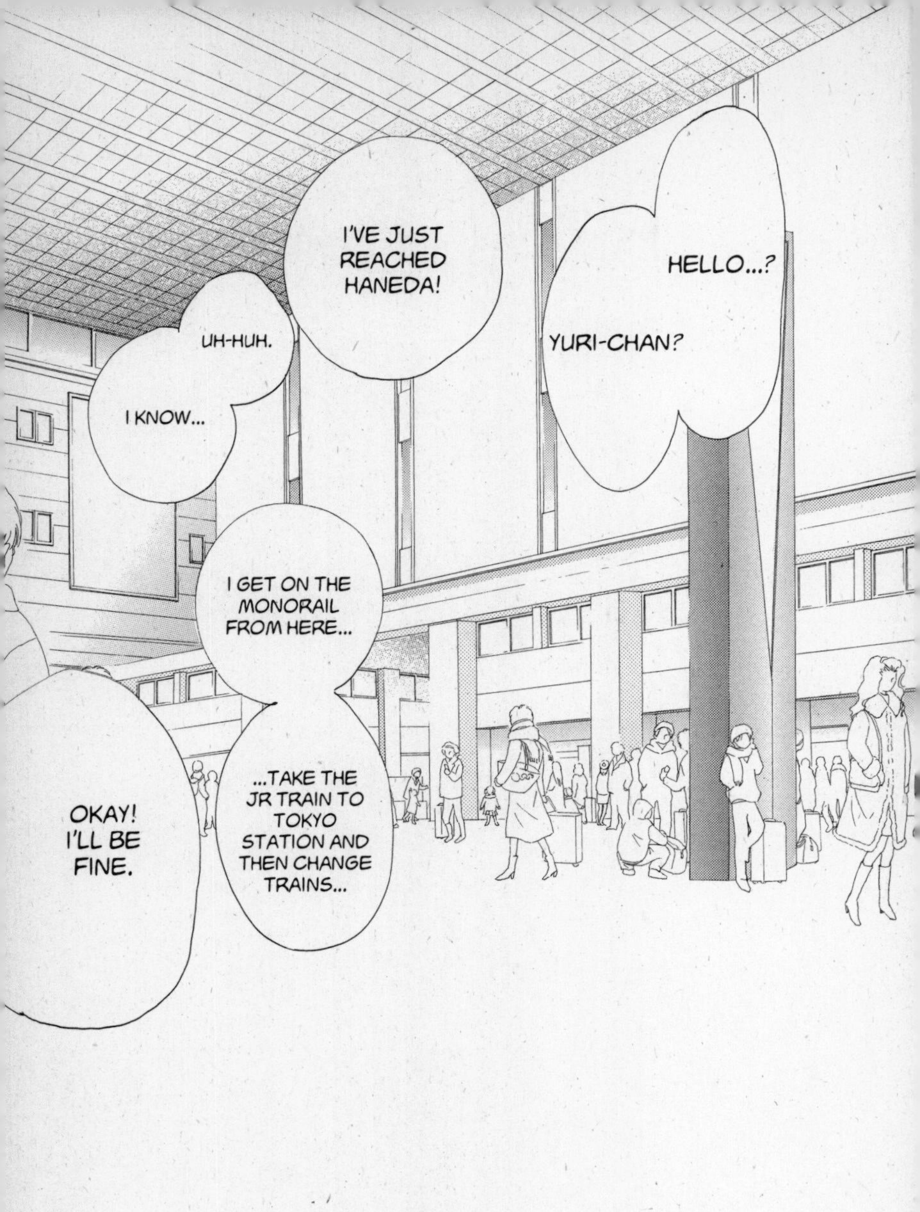
HELLO...? YURI-CHAN?
I'VE JUST REACHED HANEDA!
UH-HUH. I KNOW...
I GET ON THE MONORAIL FROM HERE...
...TAKE THE JR TRAIN TO TOKYO STATION AND THEN CHANGE TRAINS...
OKAY! I'LL BE FINE.

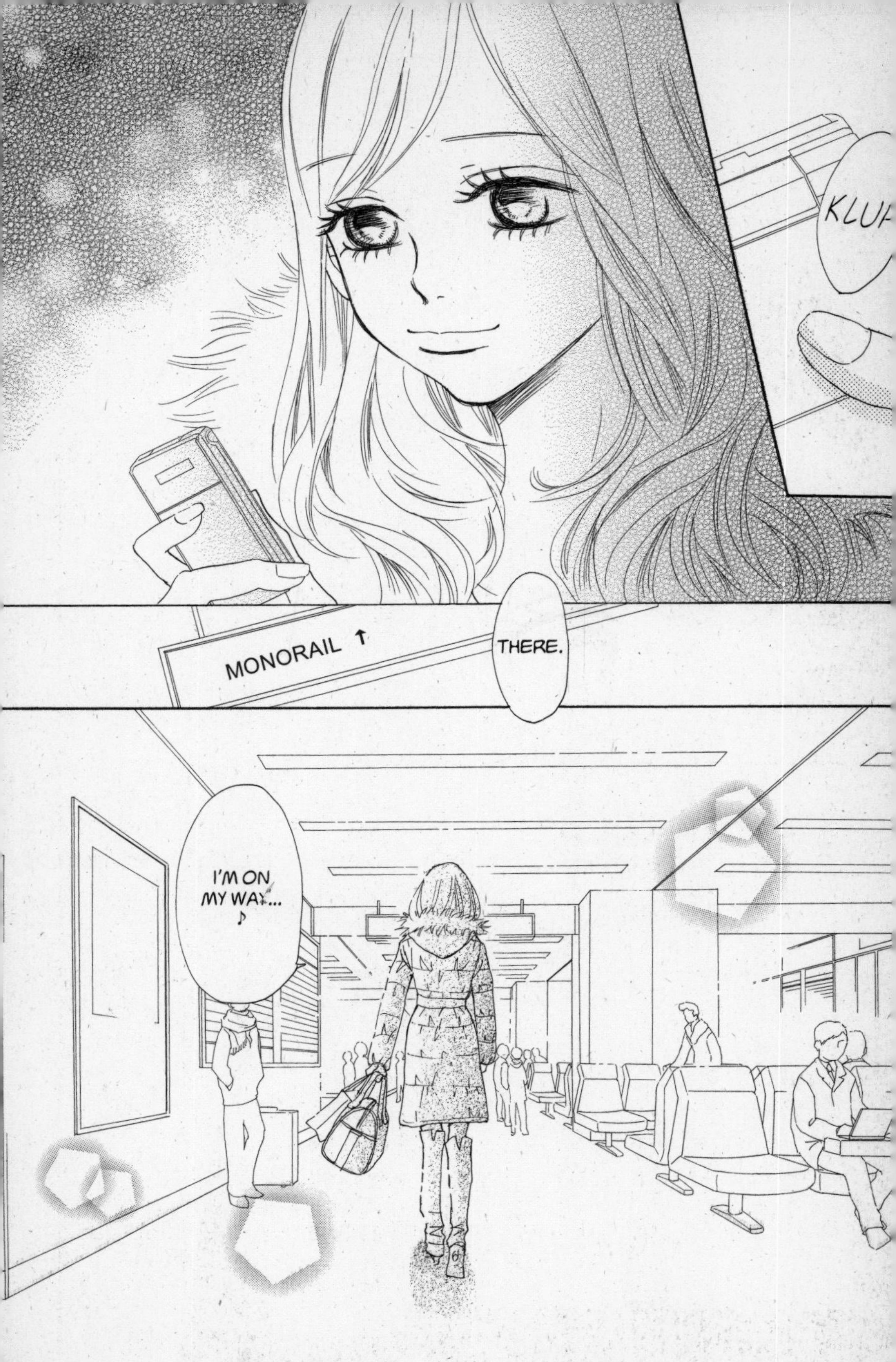
KLUP
THERE.
MONORAIL ↑
I'M ON MY WAY... ♪

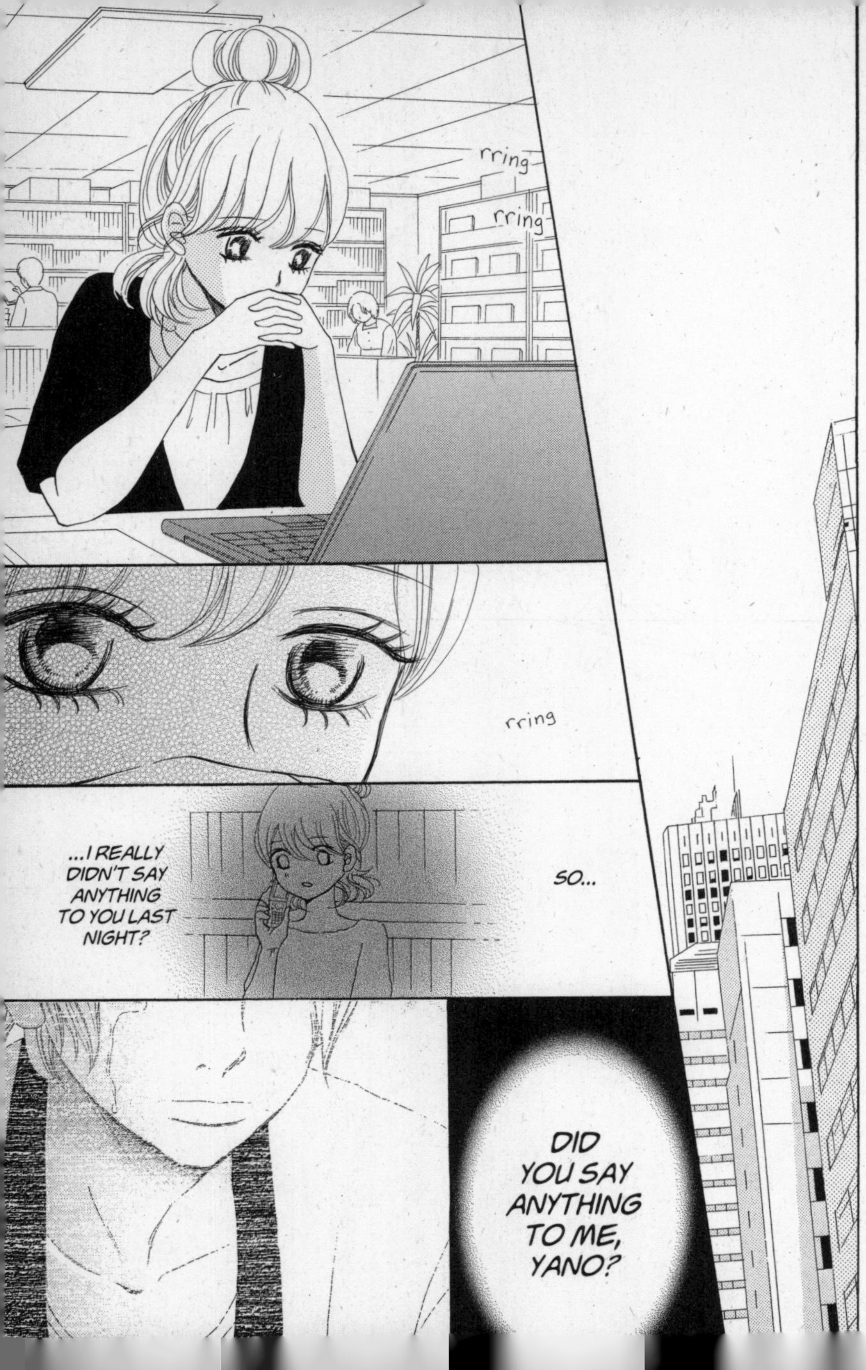
rring
rring
rring
SO...
...I REALLY DIDN'T SAY ANYTHING TO YOU LAST NIGHT?
DID YOU SAY ANYTHING TO ME, YANO?

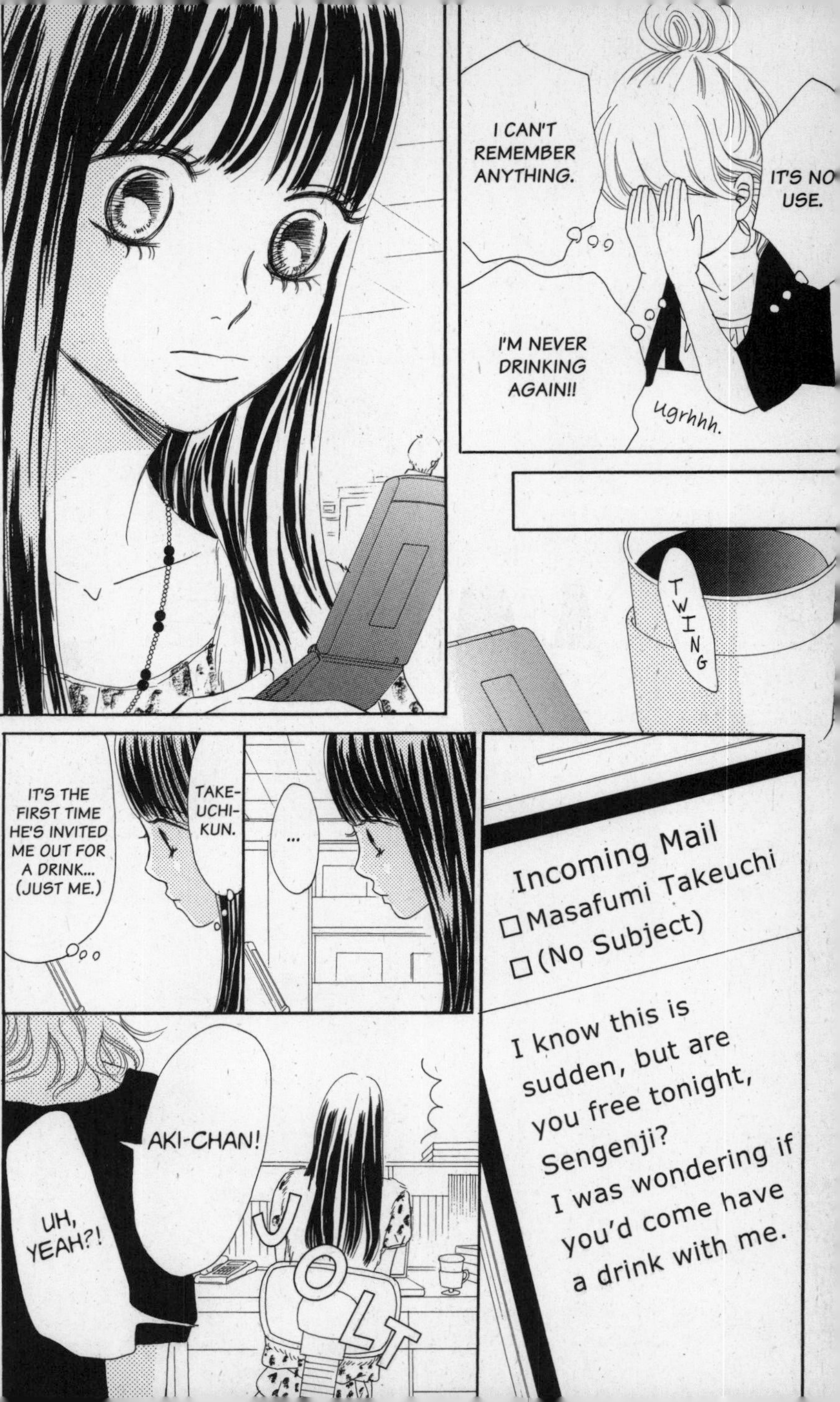
IT'S NO USE.
I CAN'T REMEMBER ANYTHING.
I'M NEVER DRINKING AGAIN!!
ugrhhh.
TWING
Incoming Mail
Masafumi Takeuchi
(No Subject)
I know this is sudden, but are you free tonight, Sengenji?
I was wondering if you'd come have a drink with me.
...
TAKE-UCHI-KUN.
IT'S THE FIRST TIME HE'S INVITED ME OUT FOR A DRINK... (JUST ME.)
AKI-CHAN!
JOLT
UH, YEAH?!

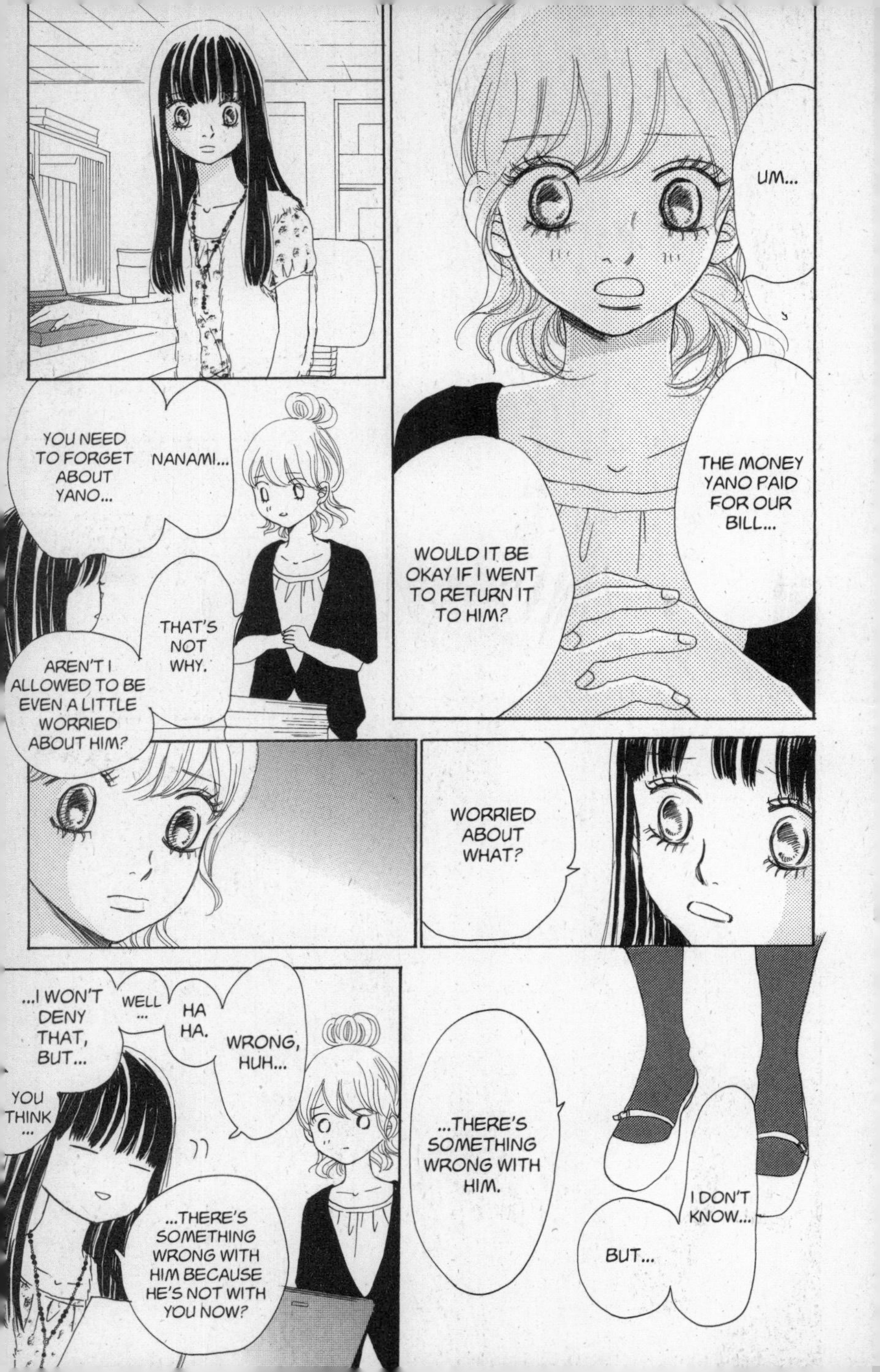
UM...
THE MONEY YANO PAID FOR OUR BILL...
WOULD IT BE OKAY IF I WENT TO RETURN IT TO HIM?
NANAMI...
YOU NEED TO FORGET ABOUT YANO...
THAT'S NOT WHY.
AREN'T I ALLOWED TO BE EVEN A LITTLE WORRIED ABOUT HIM?
WORRIED ABOUT WHAT?
I DON'T KNOW...
BUT...
...THERE'S SOMETHING WRONG WITH HIM.
WRONG, HUH...
HA HA.
WELL...
...I WON'T DENY THAT, BUT...
YOU THINK...
...THERE'S SOMETHING WRONG WITH HIM BECAUSE HE'S NOT WITH YOU NOW?

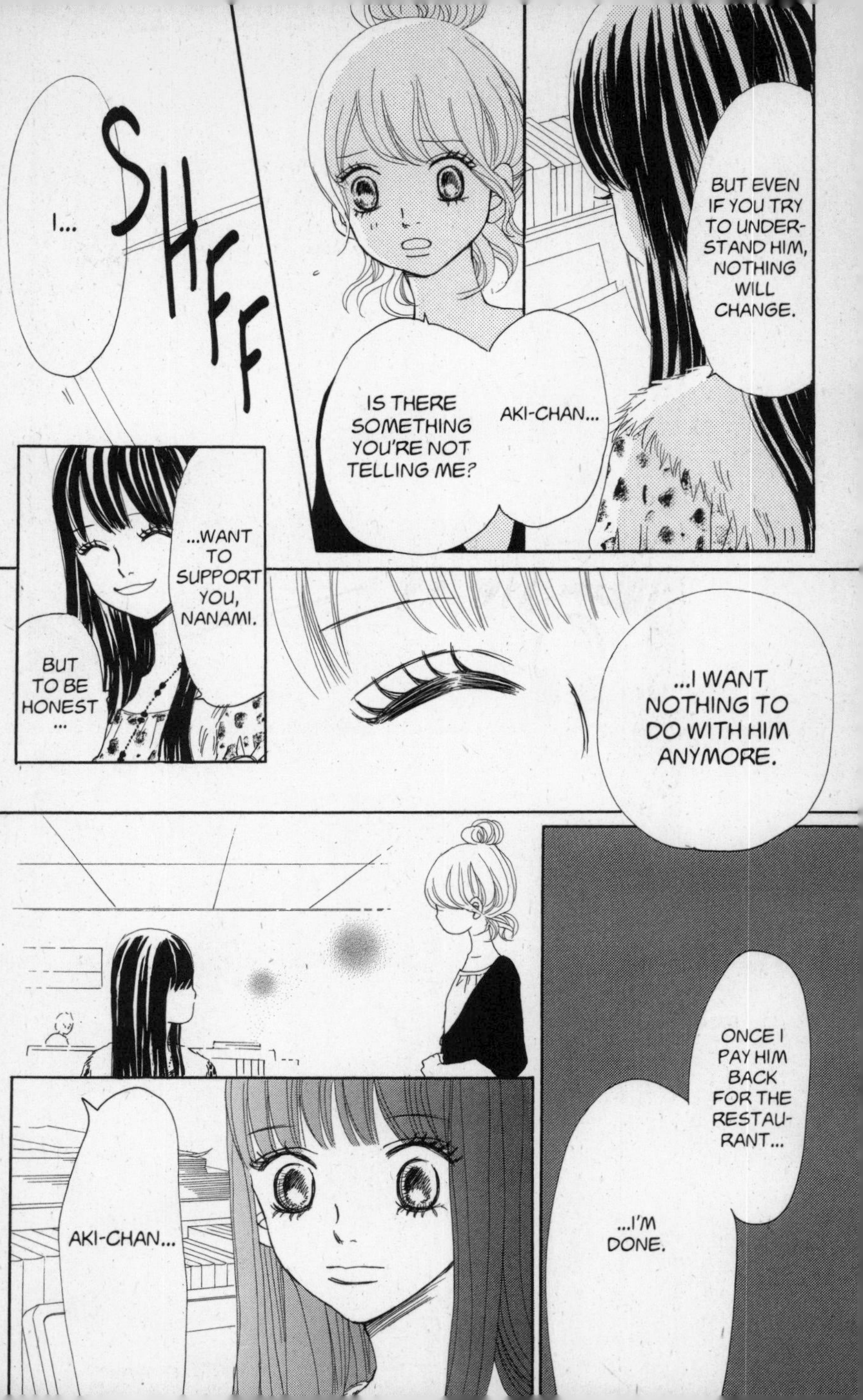
BUT EVEN IF YOU TRY TO UNDERSTAND HIM, NOTHING WILL CHANGE.
AKI-CHAN...
IS THERE SOMETHING YOU'RE NOT TELLING ME?
SHFF
I...
...WANT TO SUPPORT YOU, NANAMI.
BUT TO BE HONEST...
...I WANT NOTHING TO DO WITH HIM ANYMORE.
ONCE I PAY HIM BACK FOR THE RESTAURANT...
...I'M DONE.
AKI-CHAN...

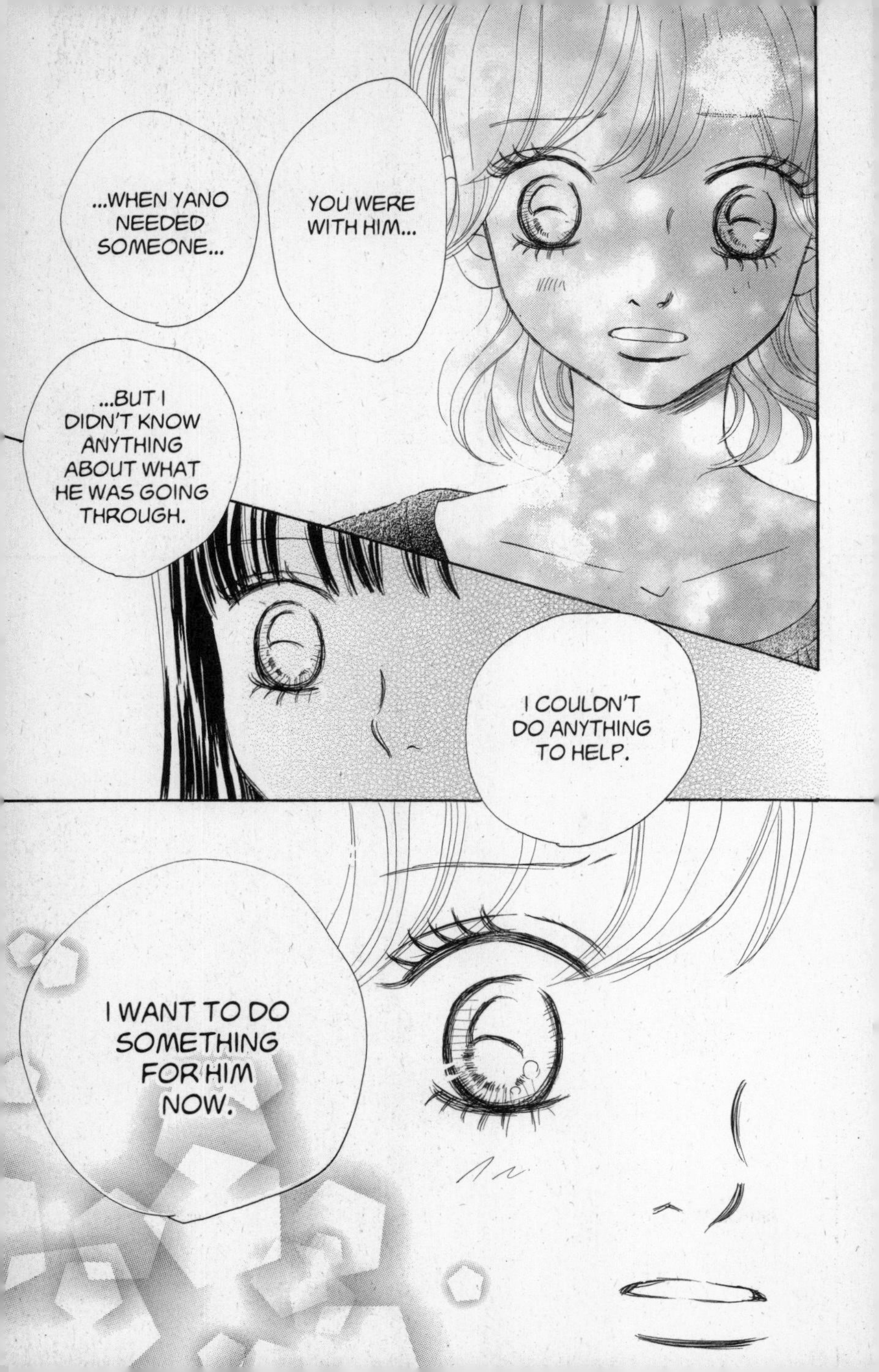
YOU WERE WITH HIM...
...WHEN YANO NEEDED SOMEONE...
...BUT I DIDN'T KNOW ANYTHING ABOUT WHAT HE WAS GOING THROUGH.
I COULDN'T DO ANYTHING TO HELP.
I WANT TO DO SOMETHING FOR HIM NOW.

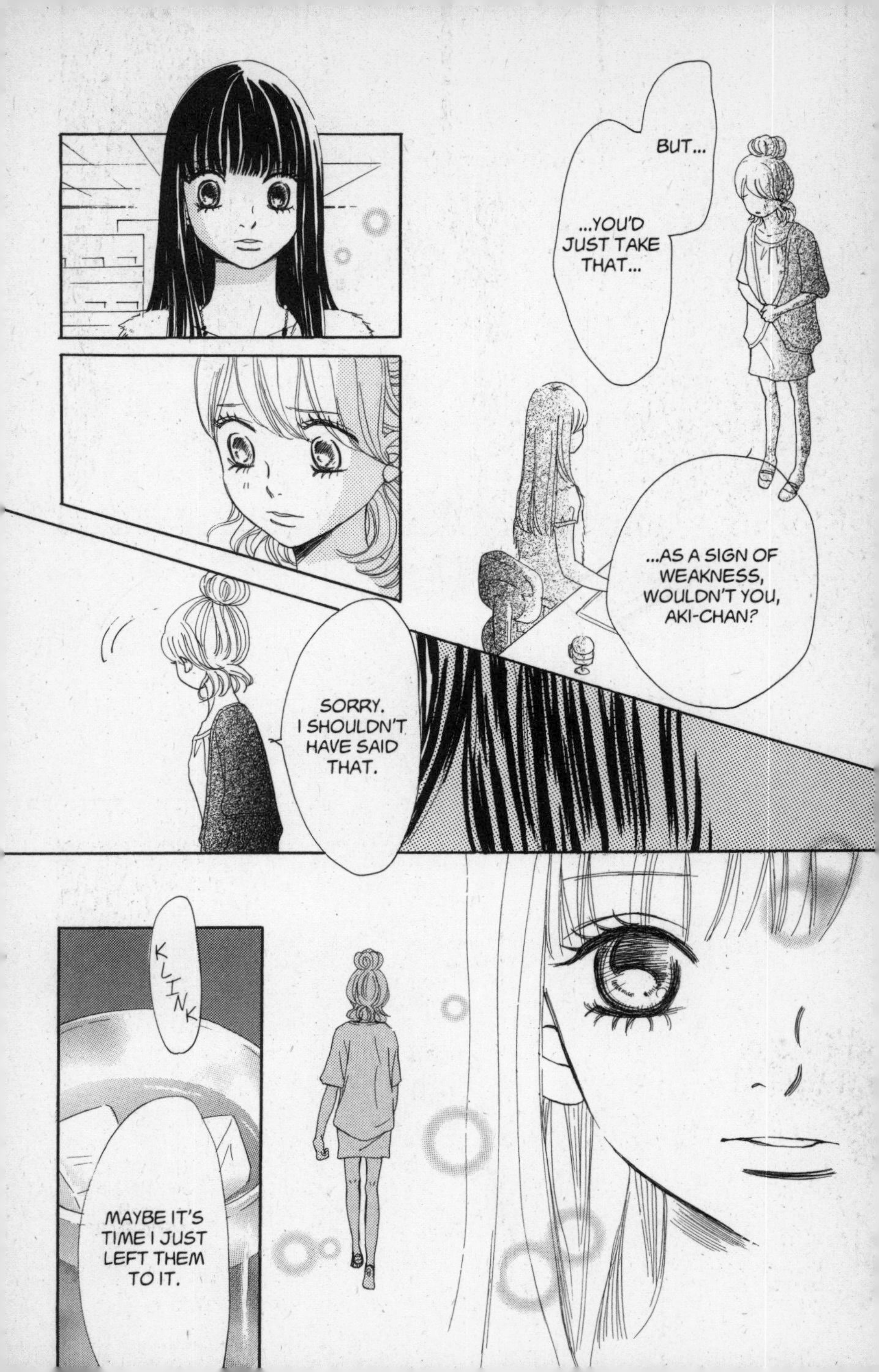
BUT...
...YOU'D JUST TAKE THAT...
...AS A SIGN OF WEAKNESS, WOULDN'T YOU, AKI-CHAN?
SORRY. I SHOULDN'T HAVE SAID THAT.
KLINK
MAYBE IT'S TIME I JUST LEFT THEM TO IT.

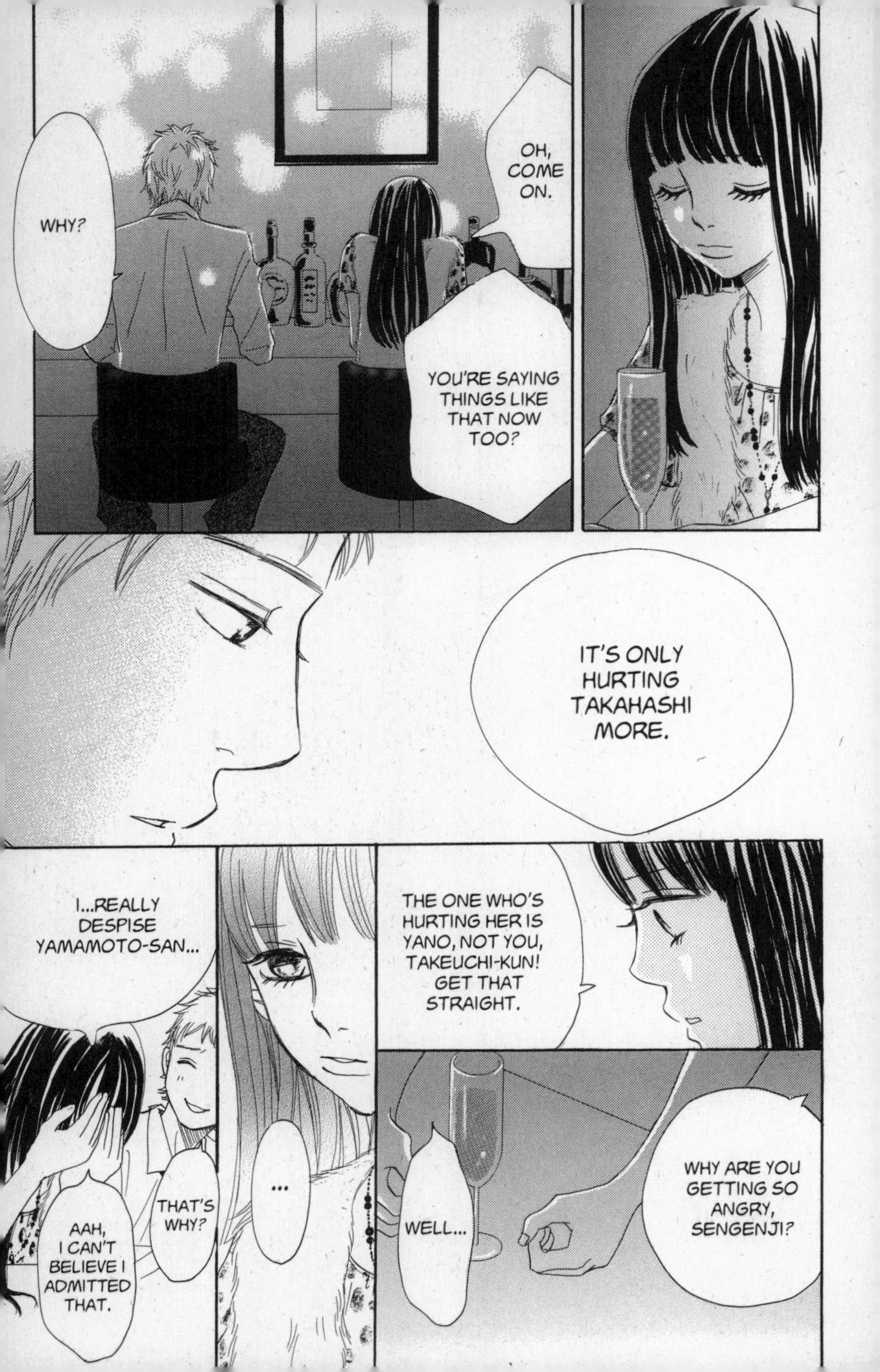
OH, COME ON.
YOU'RE SAYING THINGS LIKE THAT NOW TOO?
WHY?
IT'S ONLY HURTING TAKAHASHI MORE.
THE ONE WHO'S HURTING HER IS YANO, NOT YOU, TAKEUCHI-KUN! GET THAT STRAIGHT.
WHY ARE YOU GETTING SO ANGRY, SENGENJI?
WELL...
...
I...REALLY DESPISE YAMAMOTO-SAN...
THAT'S WHY?
AAH, I CAN'T BELIEVE I ADMITTED THAT.

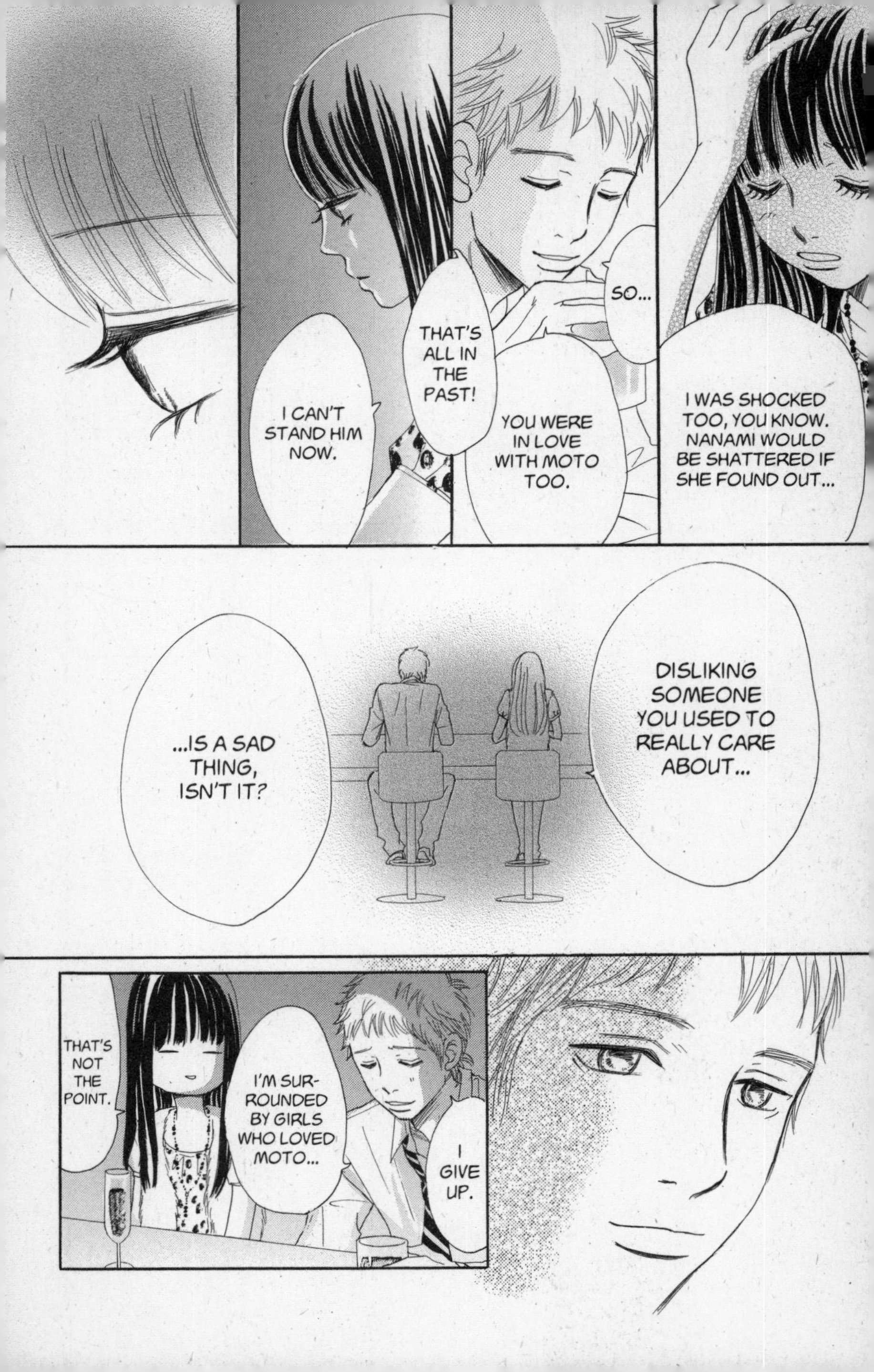
I WAS SHOCKED TOO, YOU KNOW. NANAMI WOULD BE SHATTERED IF SHE FOUND OUT...
SO...
YOU WERE IN LOVE WITH MOTO TOO.
THAT'S ALL IN THE PAST!
I CAN'T STAND HIM NOW.
DISLIKING SOMEONE YOU USED TO REALLY CARE ABOUT...
...IS A SAD THING, ISN'T IT?
I GIVE UP.
I'M SUR-ROUNDED BY GIRLS WHO LOVED MOTO...
THAT'S NOT THE POINT.

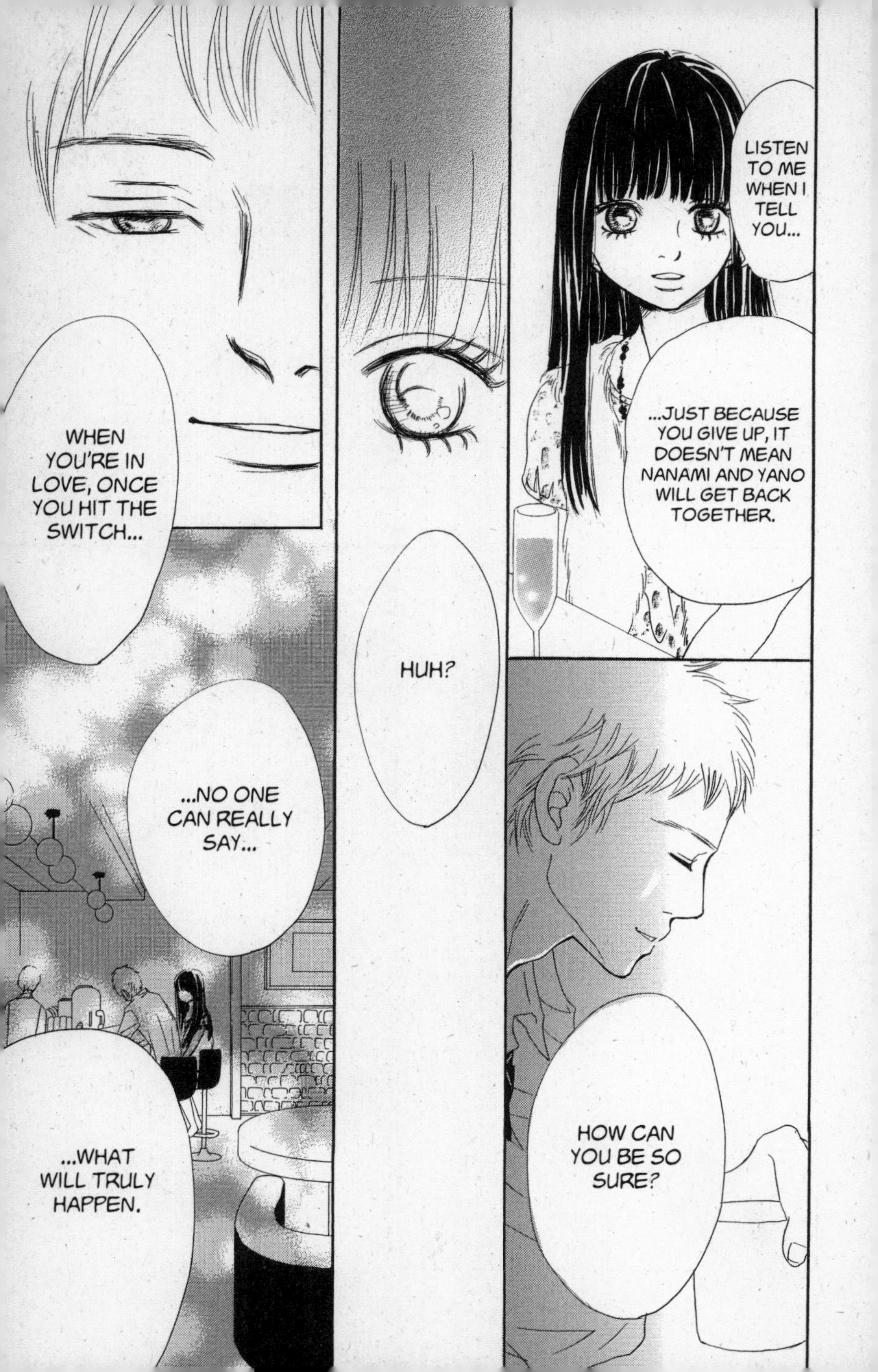
LISTEN TO ME WHEN I TELL YOU...
...JUST BECAUSE YOU GIVE UP, IT DOESN'T MEAN NANAMI AND YANO WILL GET BACK TOGETHER.
HOW CAN YOU BE SO SURE?
HUH?
WHEN YOU'RE IN LOVE, ONCE YOU HIT THE SWITCH...
...NO ONE CAN REALLY SAY...
...WHAT WILL TRULY HAPPEN.

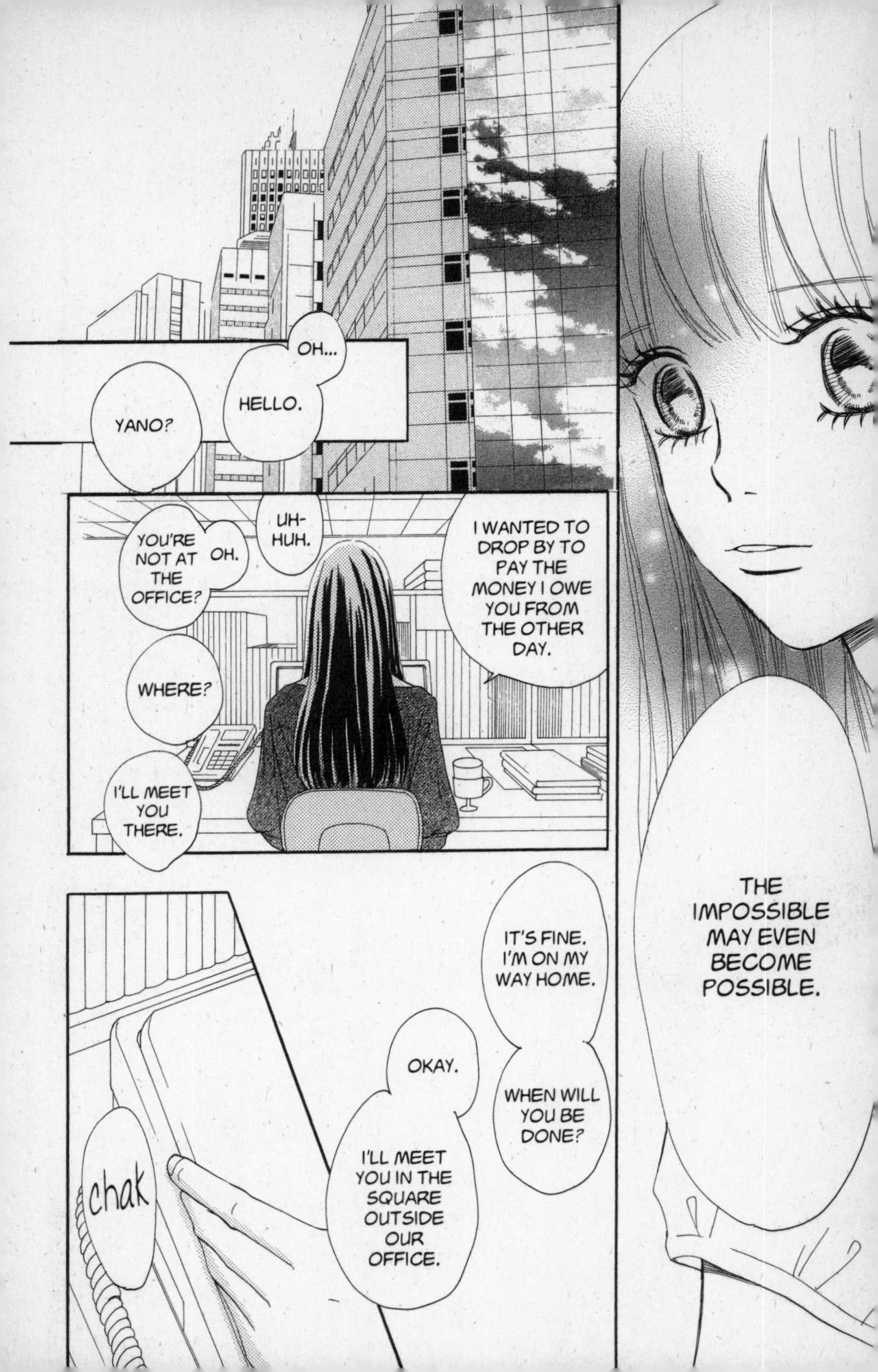
THE IMPOSSIBLE MAY EVEN BECOME POSSIBLE.
OH...
HELLO.
YANO?
I WANTED TO DROP BY TO PAY THE MONEY I OWE YOU FROM THE OTHER DAY.
UH-HUH.
OH.
YOU'RE NOT AT THE OFFICE?
WHERE?
I'LL MEET YOU THERE.
IT'S FINE. I'M ON MY WAY HOME.
WHEN WILL YOU BE DONE?
OKAY.
I'LL MEET YOU IN THE SQUARE OUTSIDE OUR OFFICE.
chak

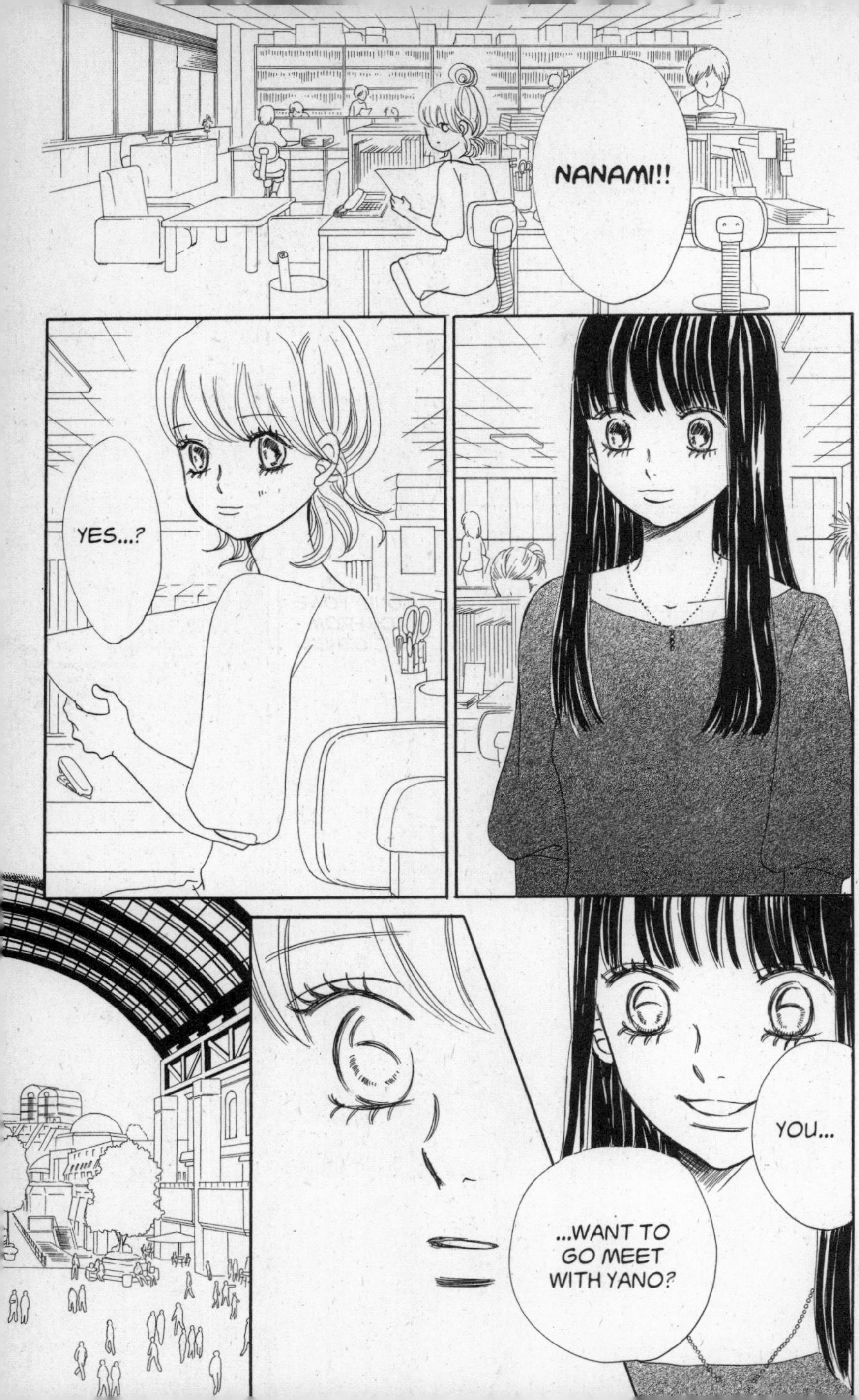
NANAMI!!
YES...?
YOU...
...WANT TO GO MEET WITH YANO?

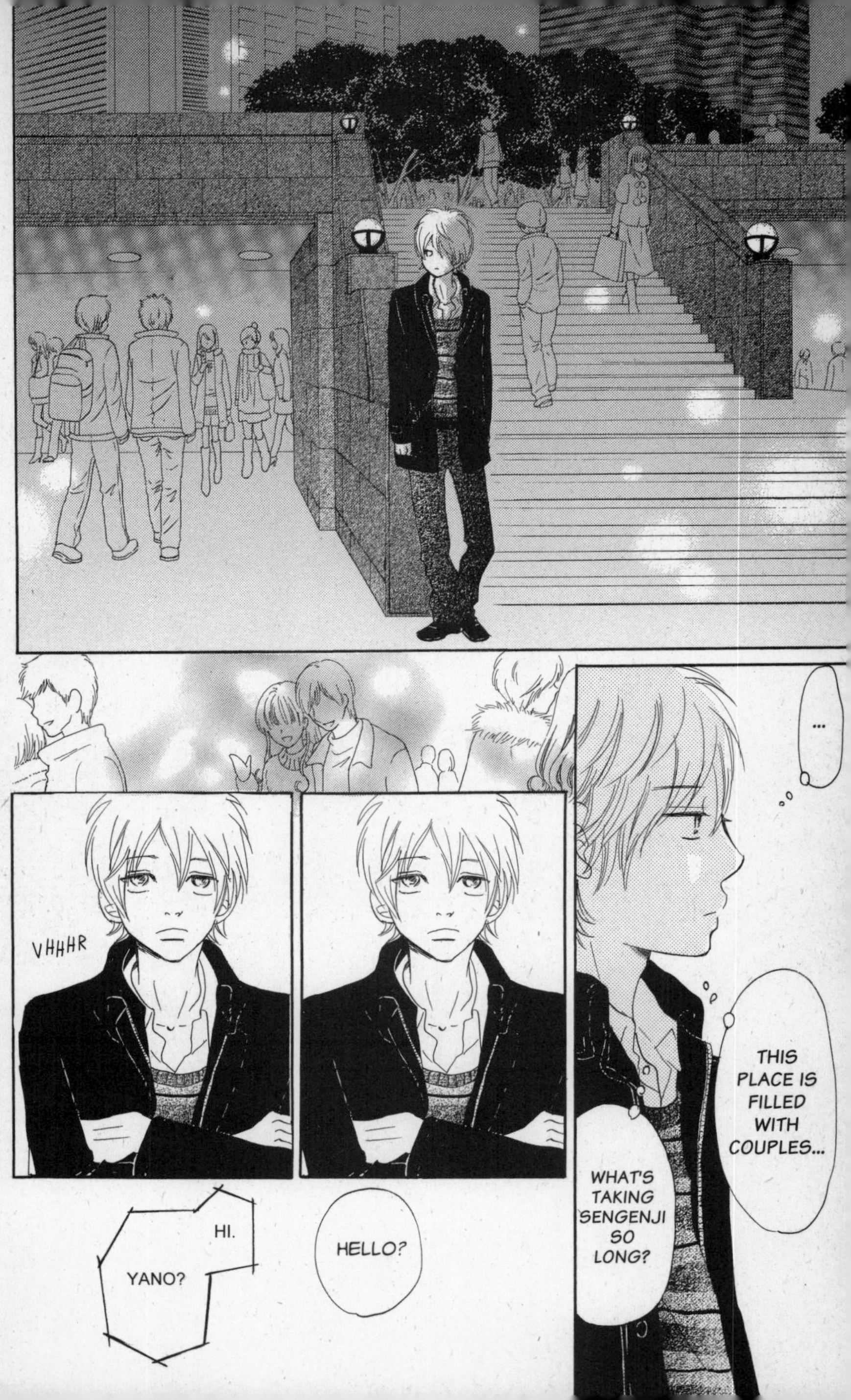
...
THIS PLACE IS FILLED WITH COUPLES...
WHAT'S TAKING SENGENJI SO LONG?
HELLO?
VHHHR
HI. YANO?

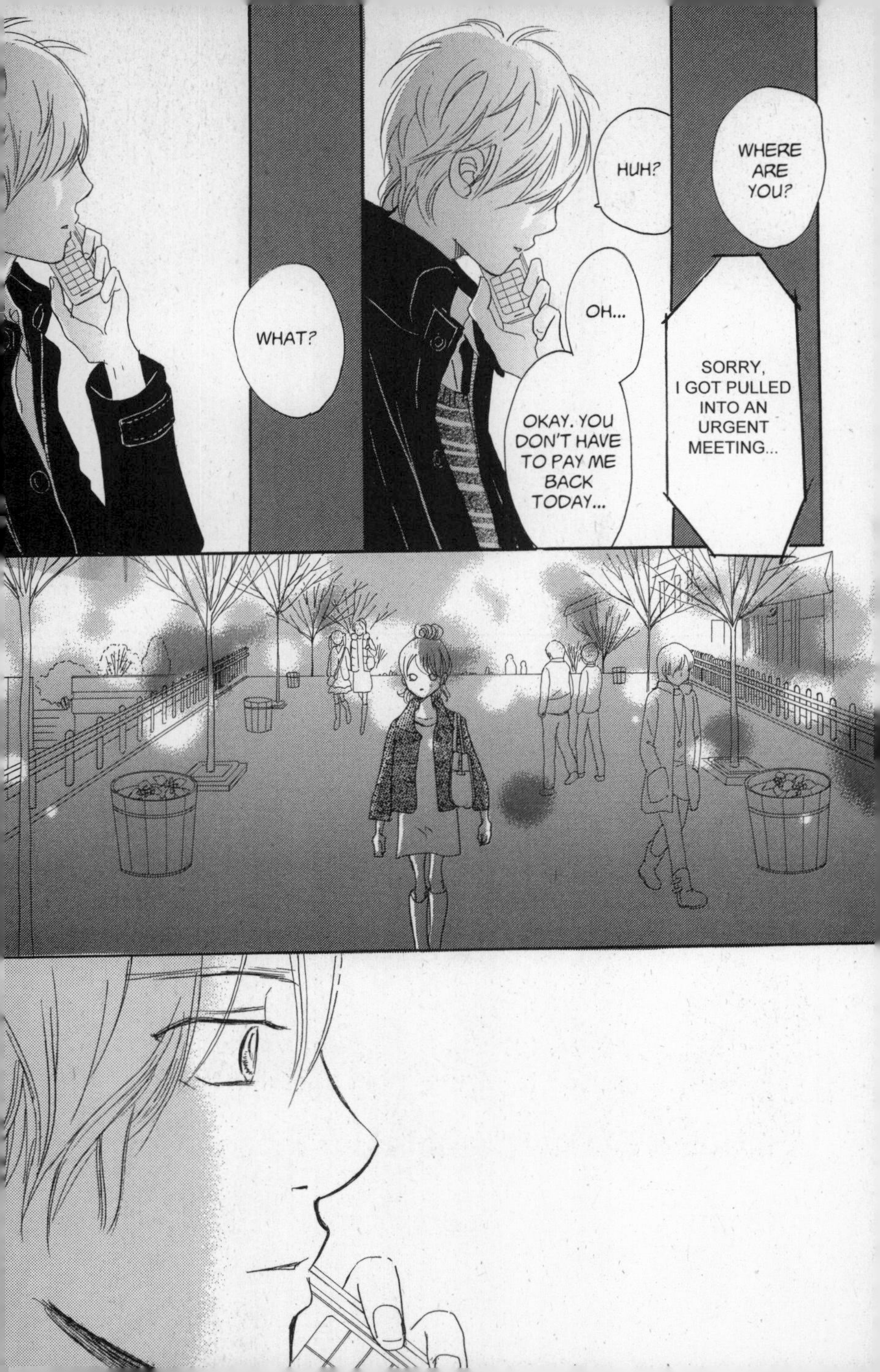
WHERE ARE YOU?
SORRY, I GOT PULLED INTO AN URGENT MEETING...
HUH?
OH...
OKAY. YOU DON'T HAVE TO PAY ME BACK TODAY...
WHAT?

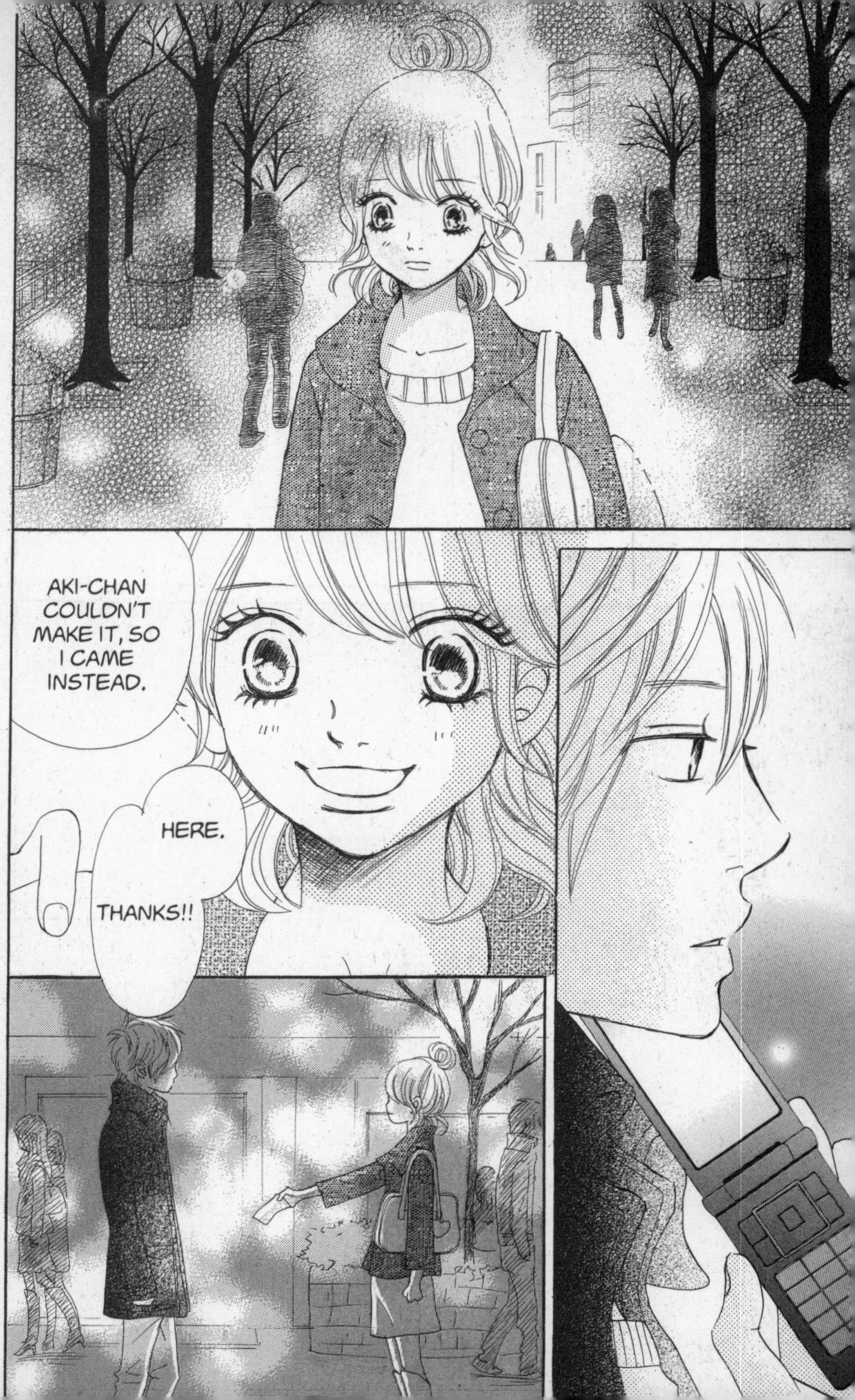
AKI-CHAN COULDN'T MAKE IT, SO I CAME INSTEAD.
HERE.
THANKS!!

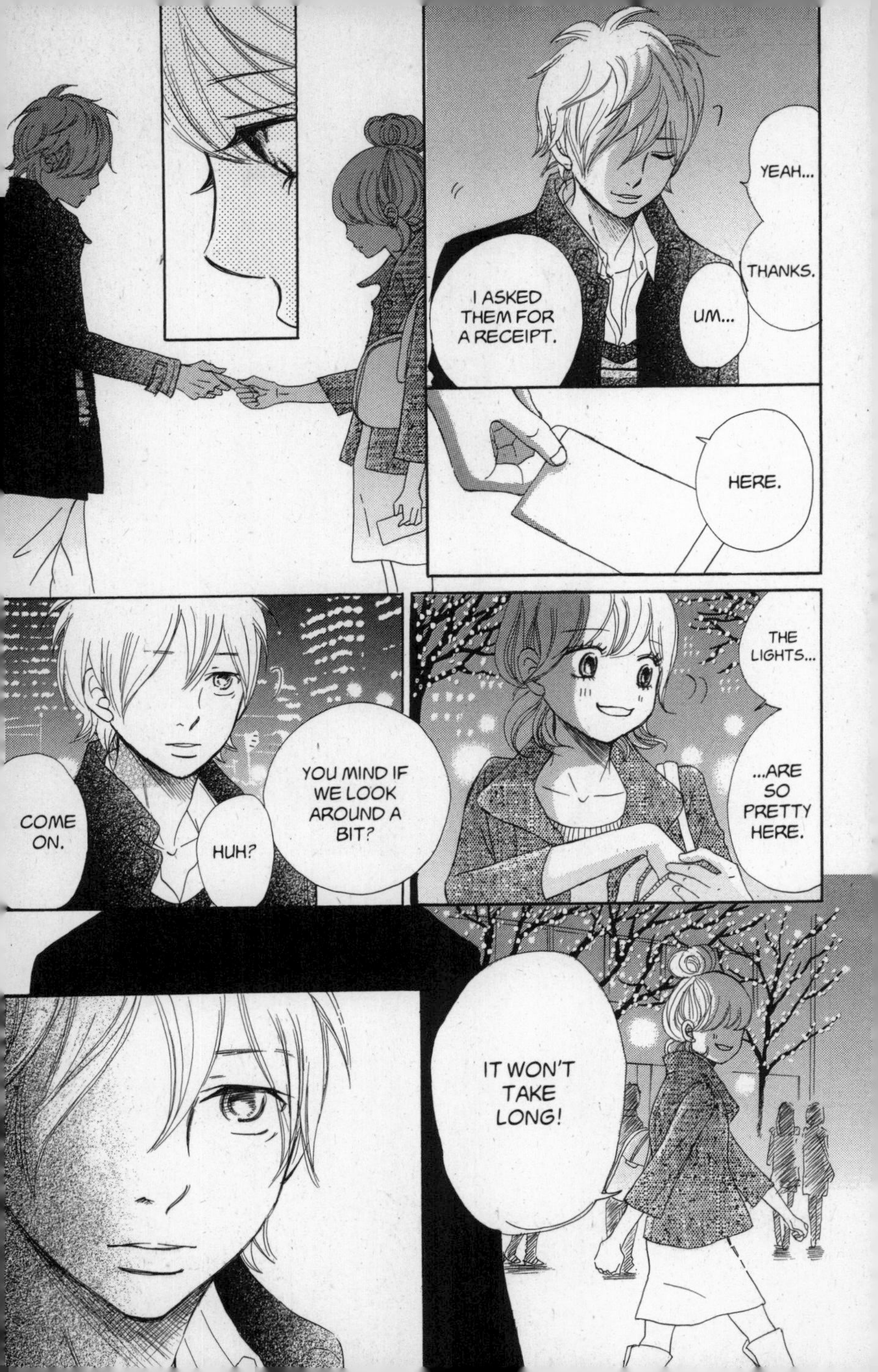
YEAH...
THANKS.
UM...
I ASKED THEM FOR A RECEIPT.
HERE.
THE LIGHTS...
...ARE SO PRETTY HERE.
YOU MIND IF WE LOOK AROUND A BIT?
HUH?
COME ON.
IT WON'T TAKE LONG!

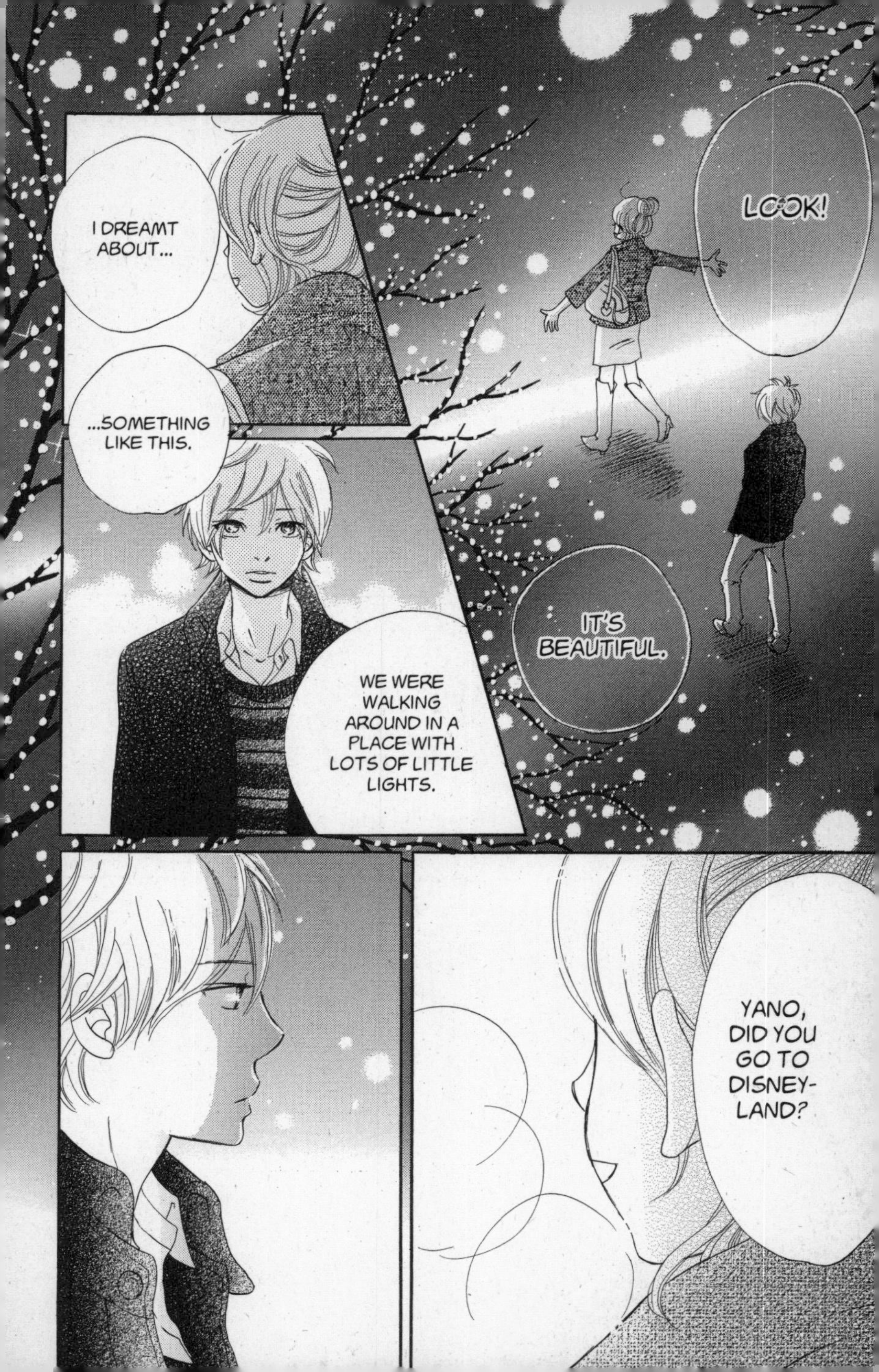
LOOK!
IT'S BEAUTIFUL.
I DREAMT ABOUT...
...SOMETHING LIKE THIS.
WE WERE WALKING AROUND IN A PLACE WITH LOTS OF LITTLE LIGHTS.
YANO, DID YOU GO TO DISNEY-LAND?

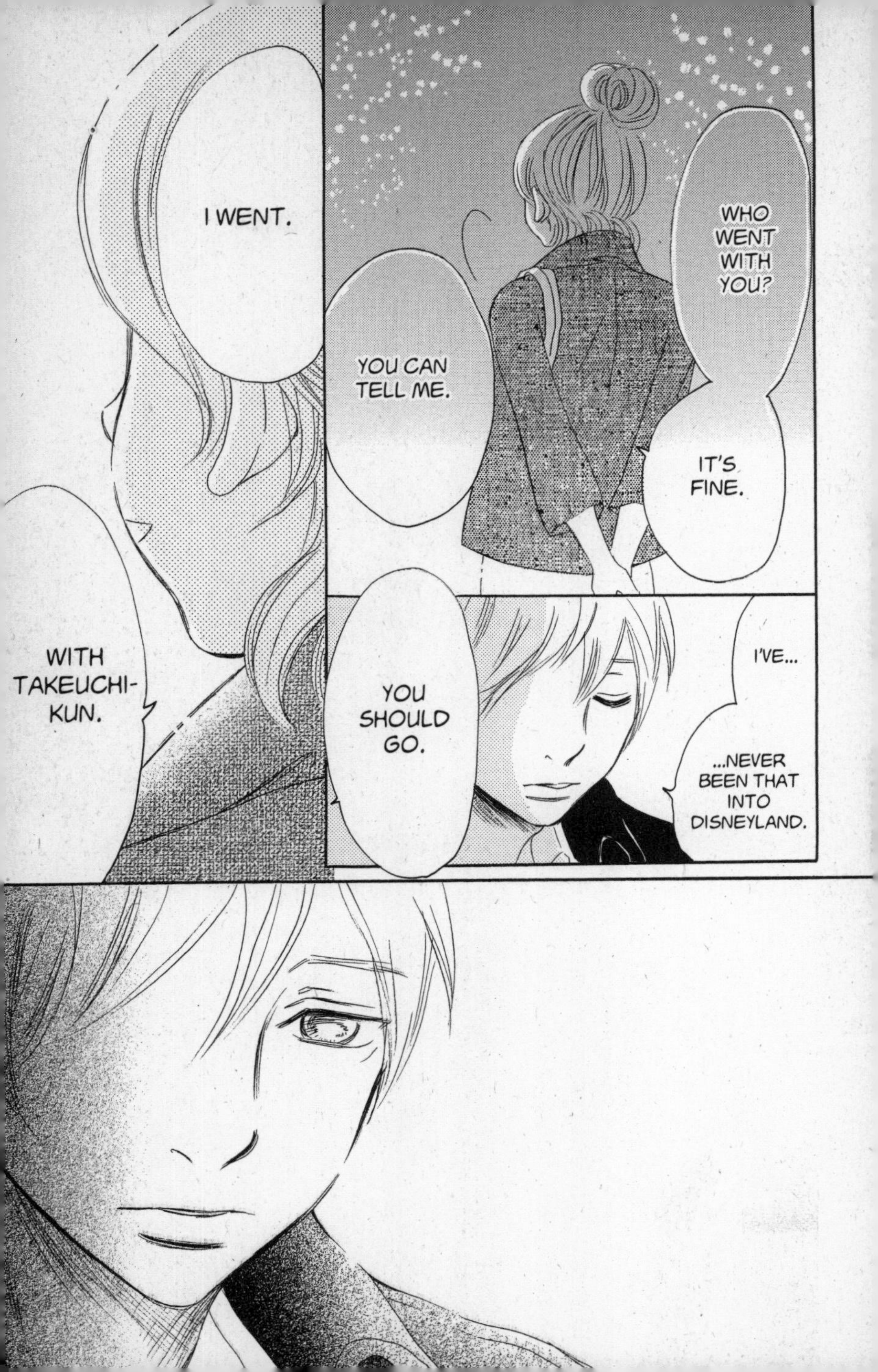
WHO WENT WITH YOU?
IT'S FINE.
YOU CAN TELL ME.
I'VE...
...NEVER BEEN THAT INTO DISNEYLAND.
YOU SHOULD GO.
I WENT.
WITH TAKEUCHI-KUN.

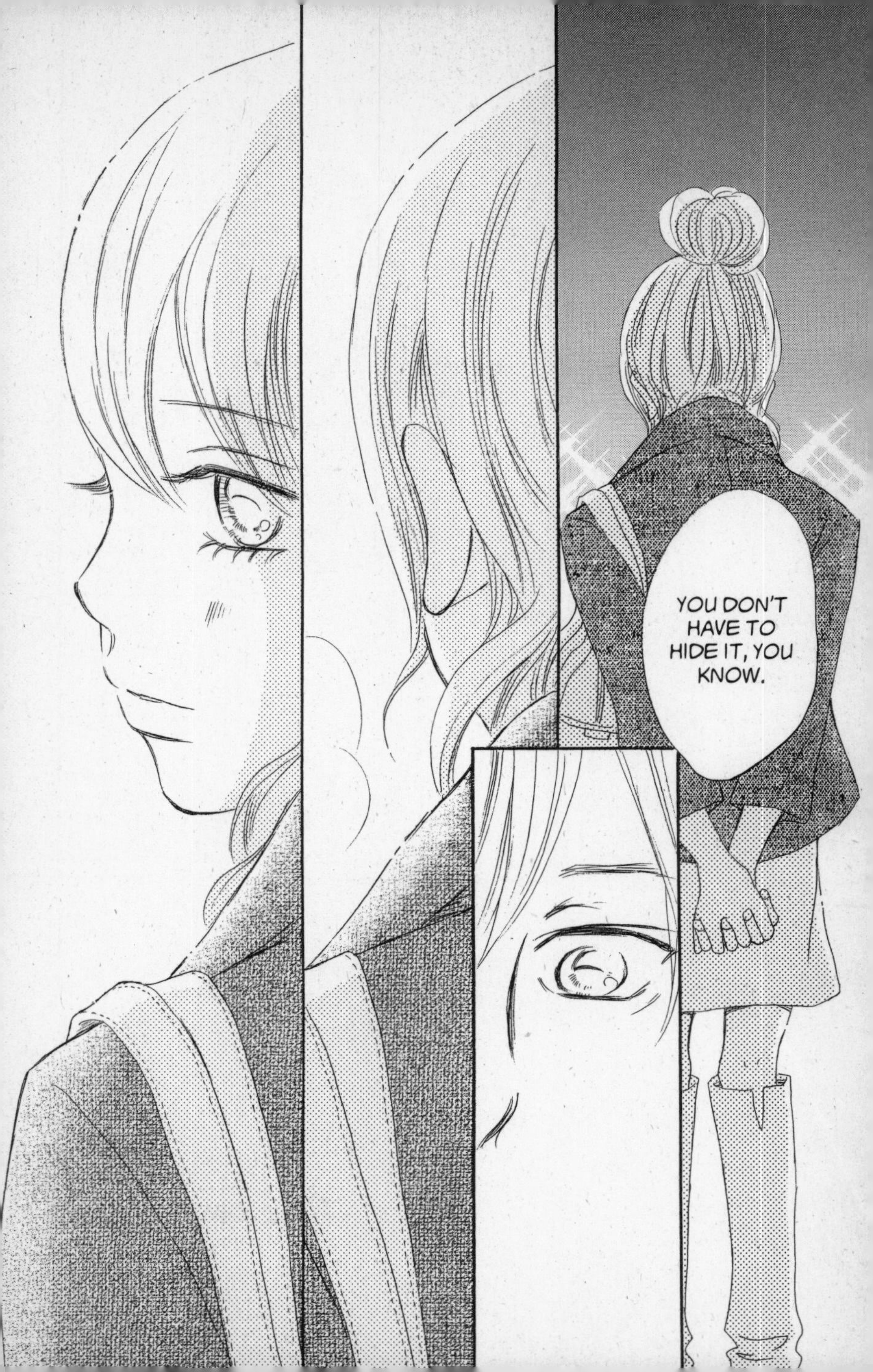
YOU DON'T HAVE TO HIDE IT, YOU KNOW.

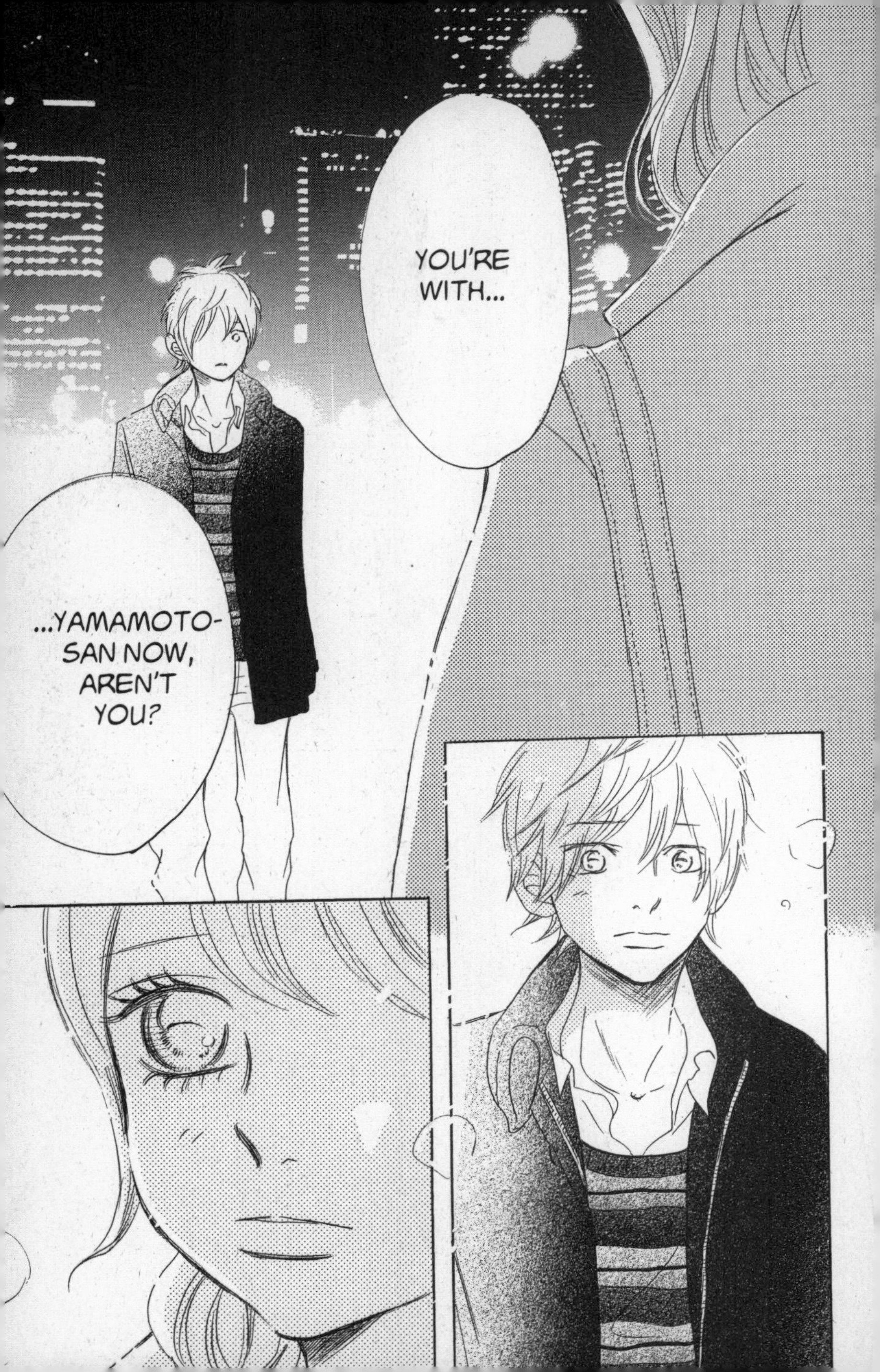
YOU'RE WITH...
...YAMAMOTO-SAN NOW, AREN'T YOU?

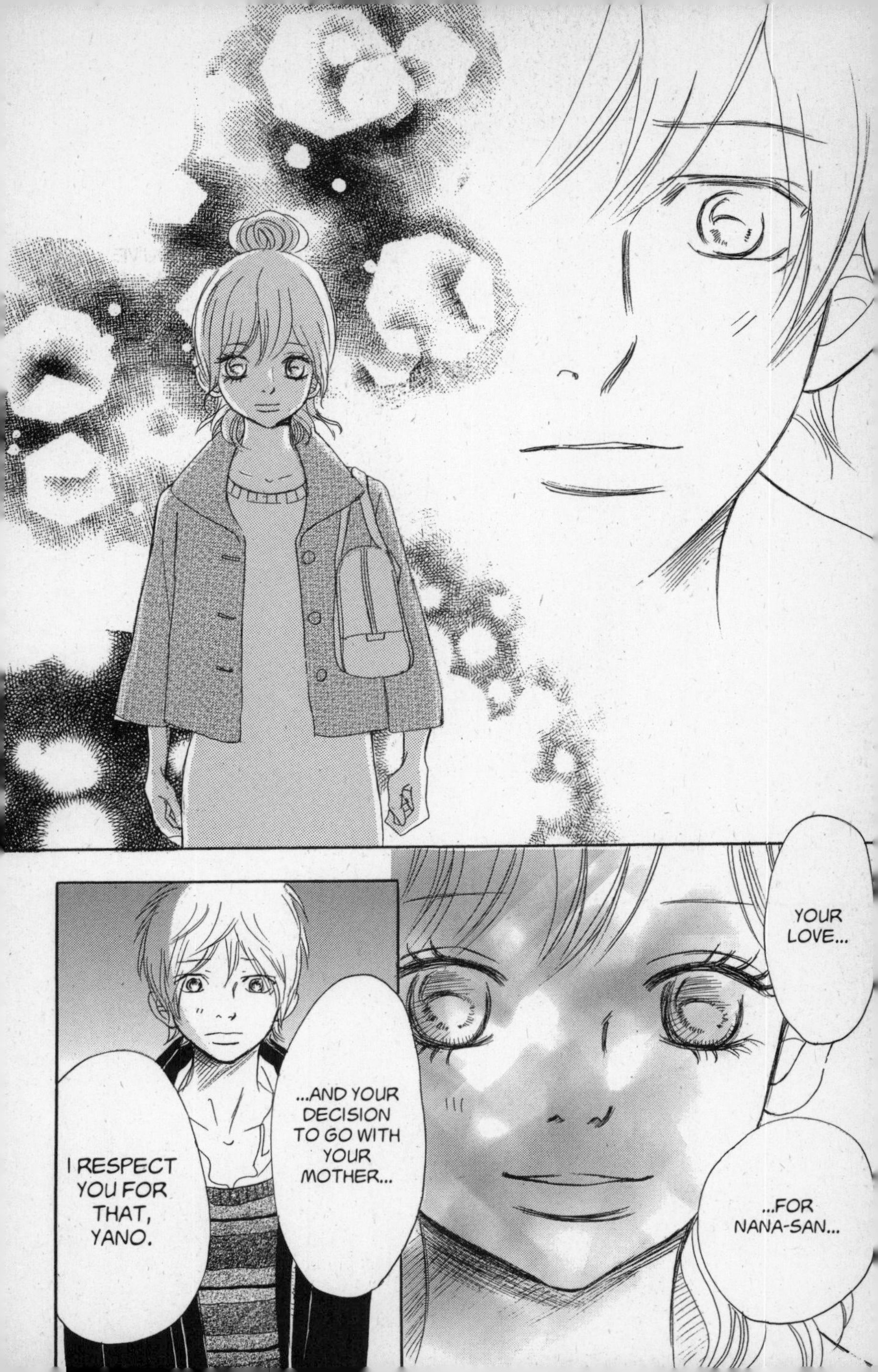
YOUR LOVE...
...FOR NANA-SAN...
...AND YOUR DECISION TO GO WITH YOUR MOTHER...
I RESPECT YOU FOR THAT, YANO.

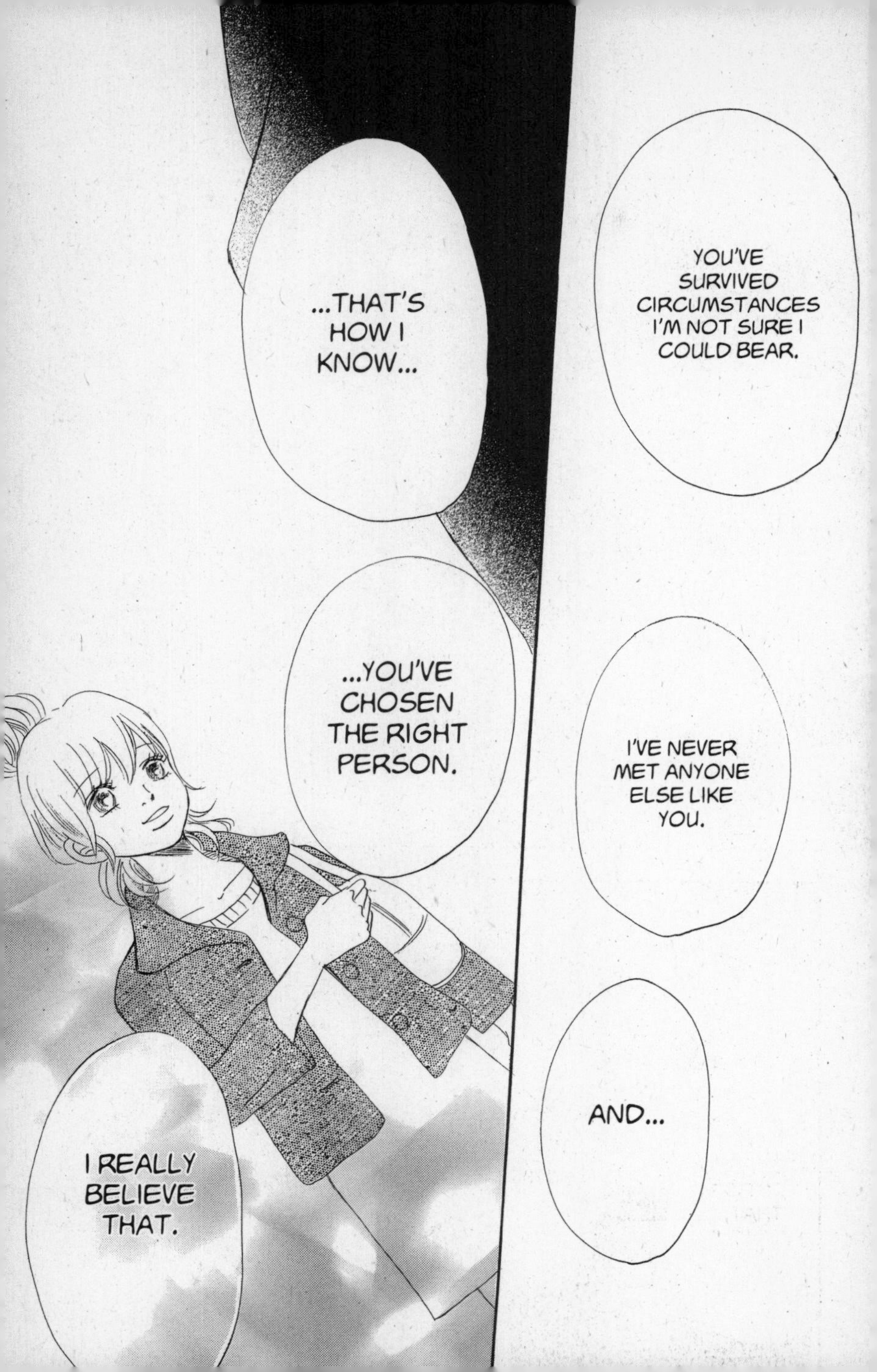
YOU'VE SURVIVED CIRCUMSTANCES I'M NOT SURE I COULD BEAR.
I'VE NEVER MET ANYONE ELSE LIKE YOU.
AND...
...THAT'S HOW I KNOW...
...YOU'VE CHOSEN THE RIGHT PERSON.
I REALLY BELIEVE THAT.

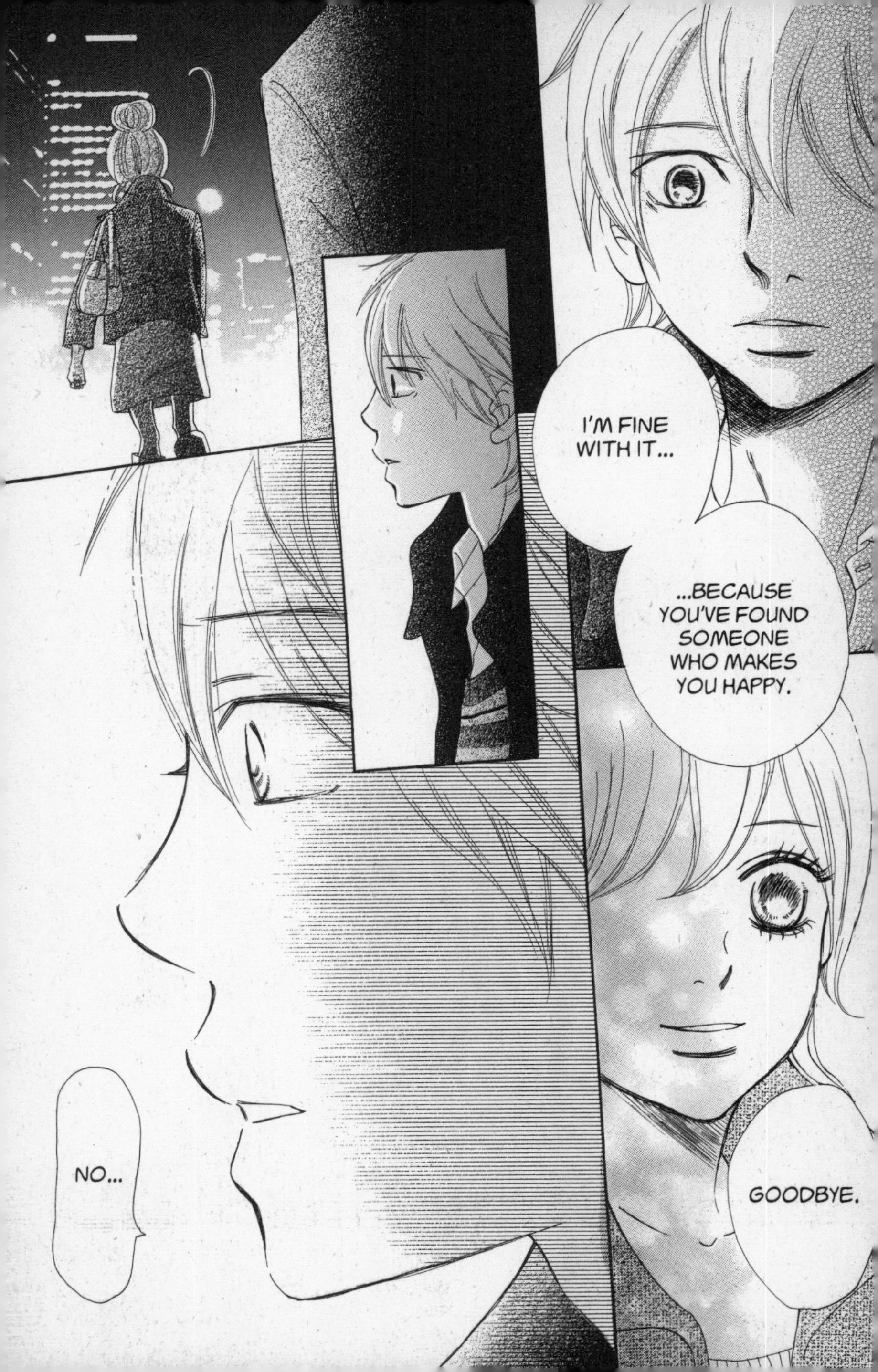
I'M FINE WITH IT...
...BECAUSE YOU'VE FOUND SOMEONE WHO MAKES YOU HAPPY.
GOODBYE.
NO...

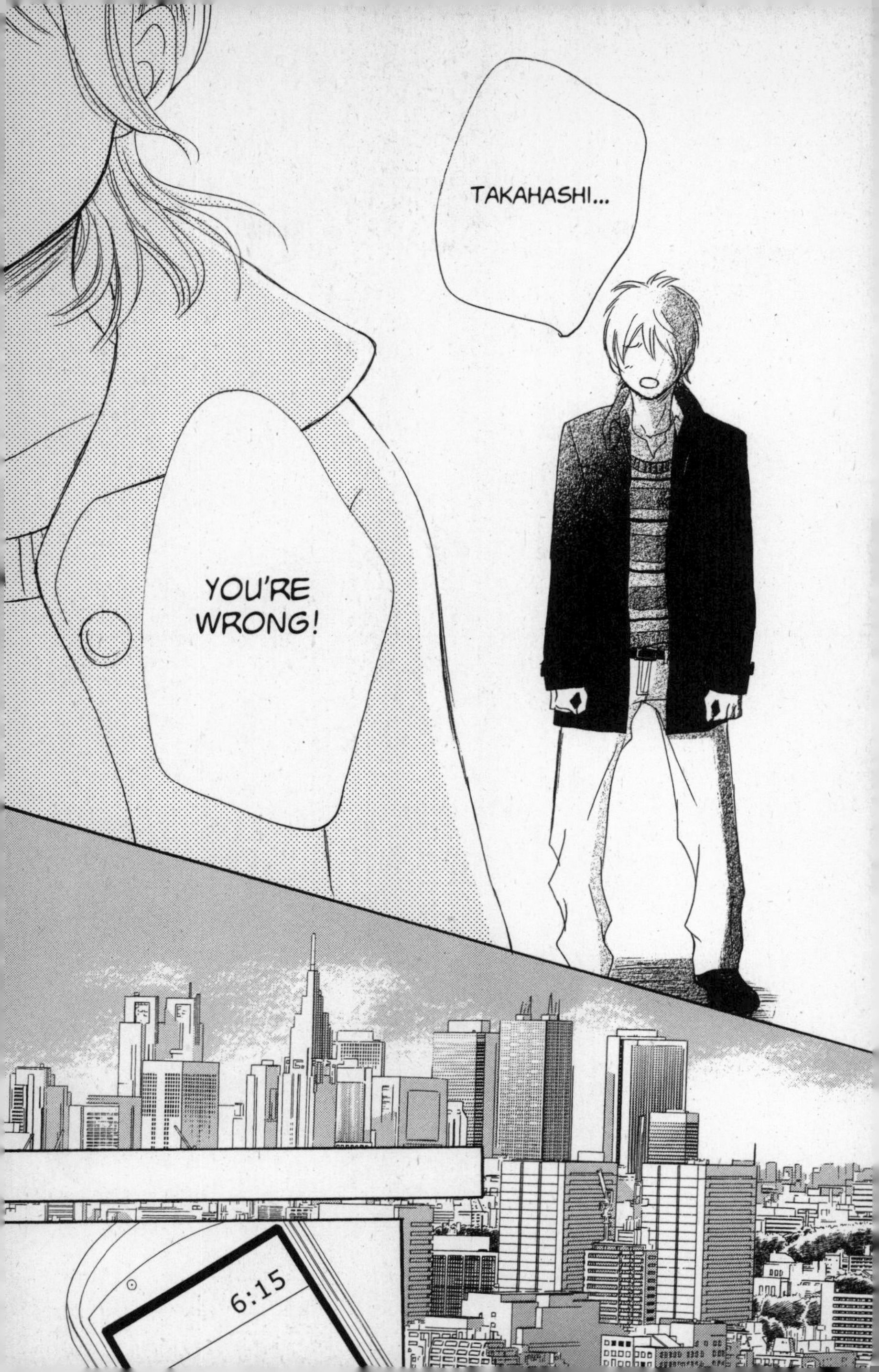
TAKAHASHI...
YOU'RE WRONG!
6:15

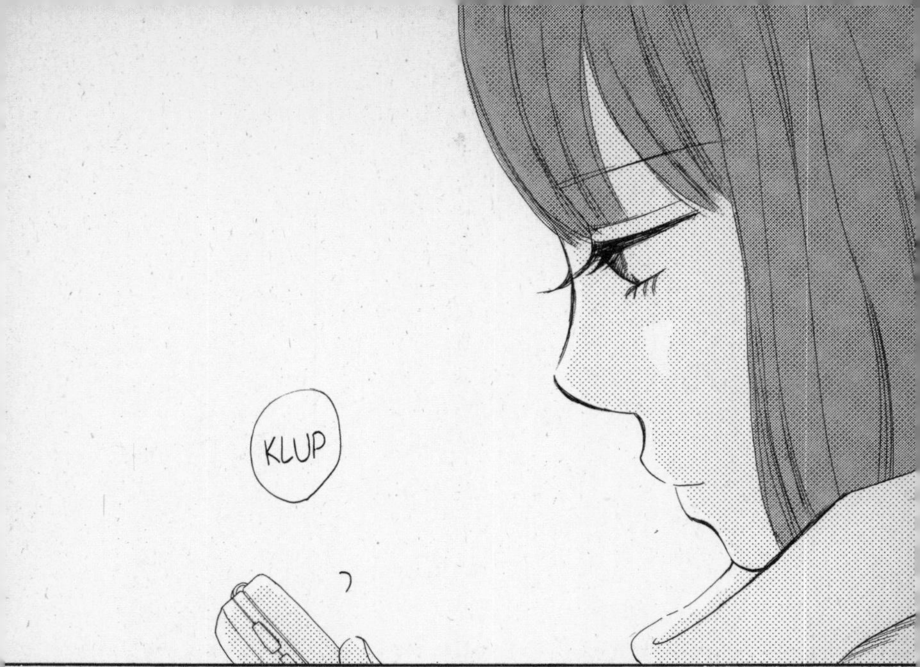
KLUP
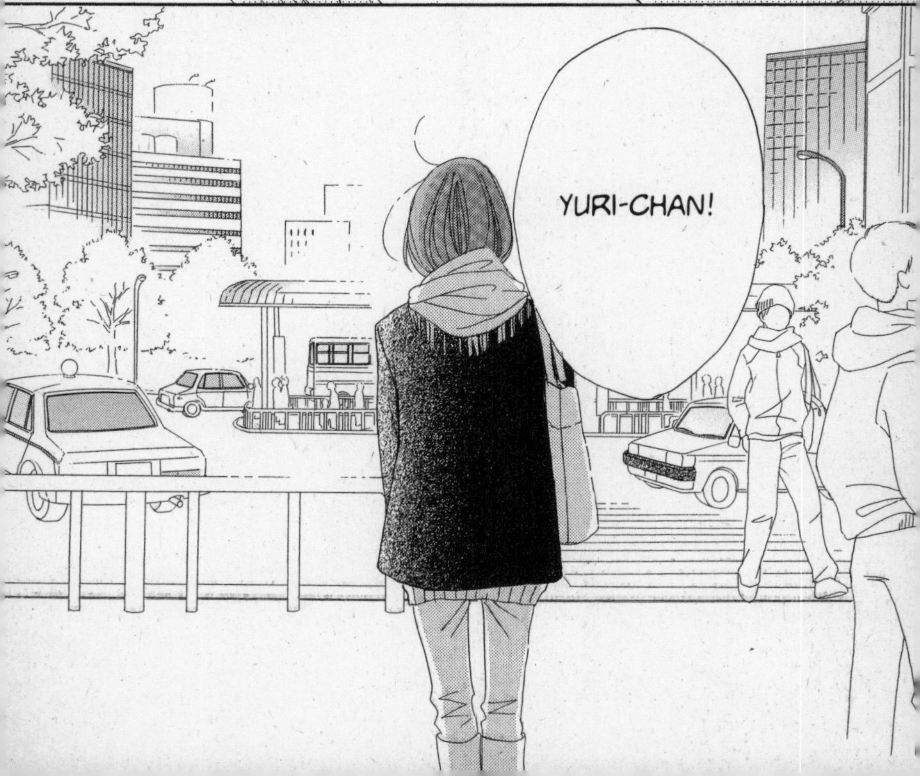
YURI-CHAN!

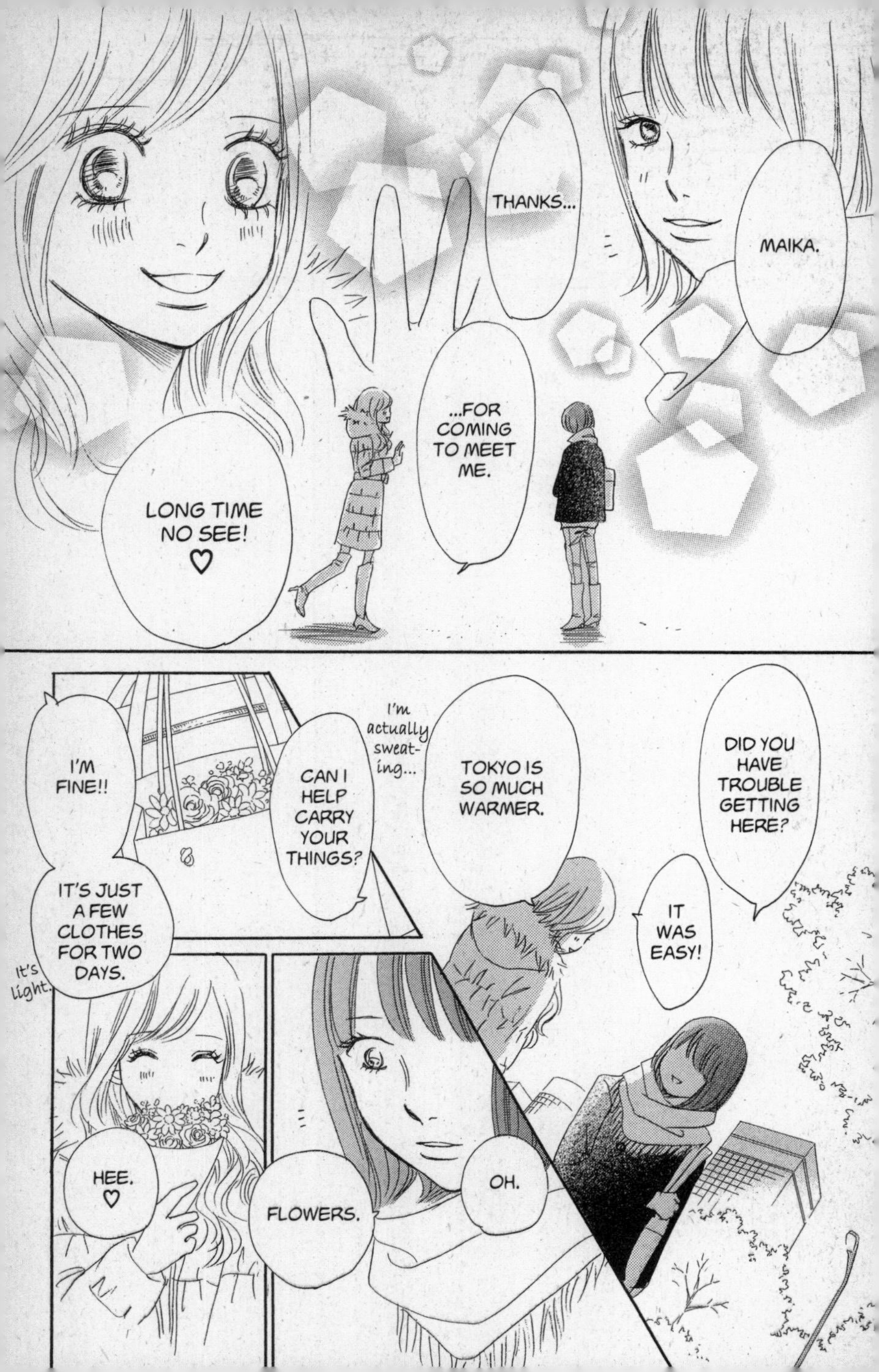
MAIKA.
THANKS...
...FOR COMING TO MEET ME.
LONG TIME NO SEE! ♡
DID YOU HAVE TROUBLE GETTING HERE?
IT WAS EASY!
TOKYO IS SO MUCH WARMER.
I'm actually sweating...
CAN I HELP CARRY YOUR THINGS?
I'M FINE!!
IT'S JUST A FEW CLOTHES FOR TWO DAYS.
It's light.
OH.
FLOWERS.
HEE. ♡

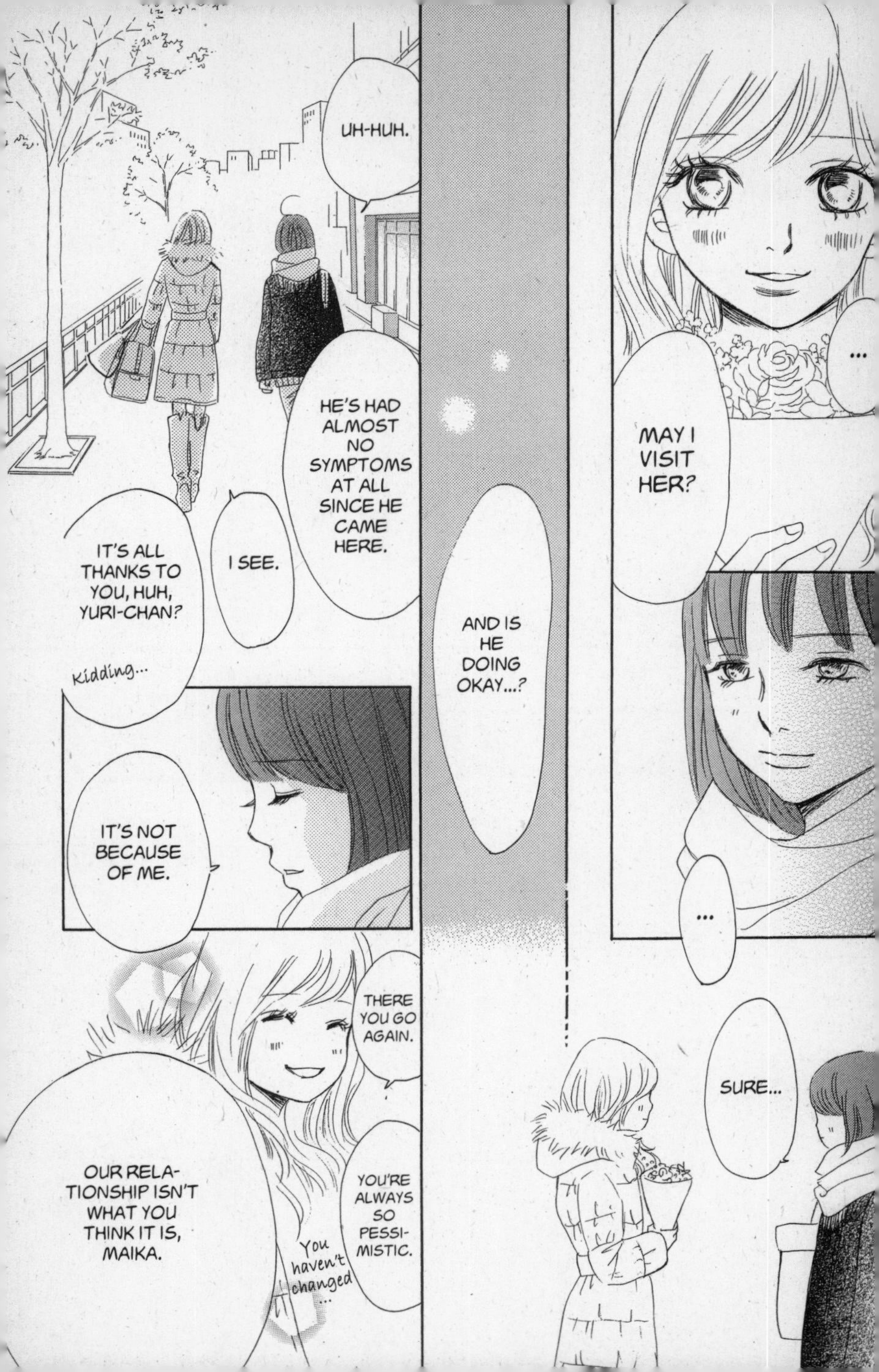

...
MAY I VISIT HER?
...
SURE...
AND IS HE DOING OKAY...?
UH-HUH.
HE'S HAD ALMOST NO SYMPTOMS AT ALL SINCE HE CAME HERE.
I SEE.
IT'S ALL THANKS TO YOU, HUH, YURI-CHAN?
Kidding...
IT'S NOT BECAUSE OF ME.
THERE YOU GO AGAIN.
YOU'RE ALWAYS SO PESSIMISTIC.
You haven't changed...
OUR RELATIONSHIP ISN'T WHAT YOU THINK IT IS, MAIKA.

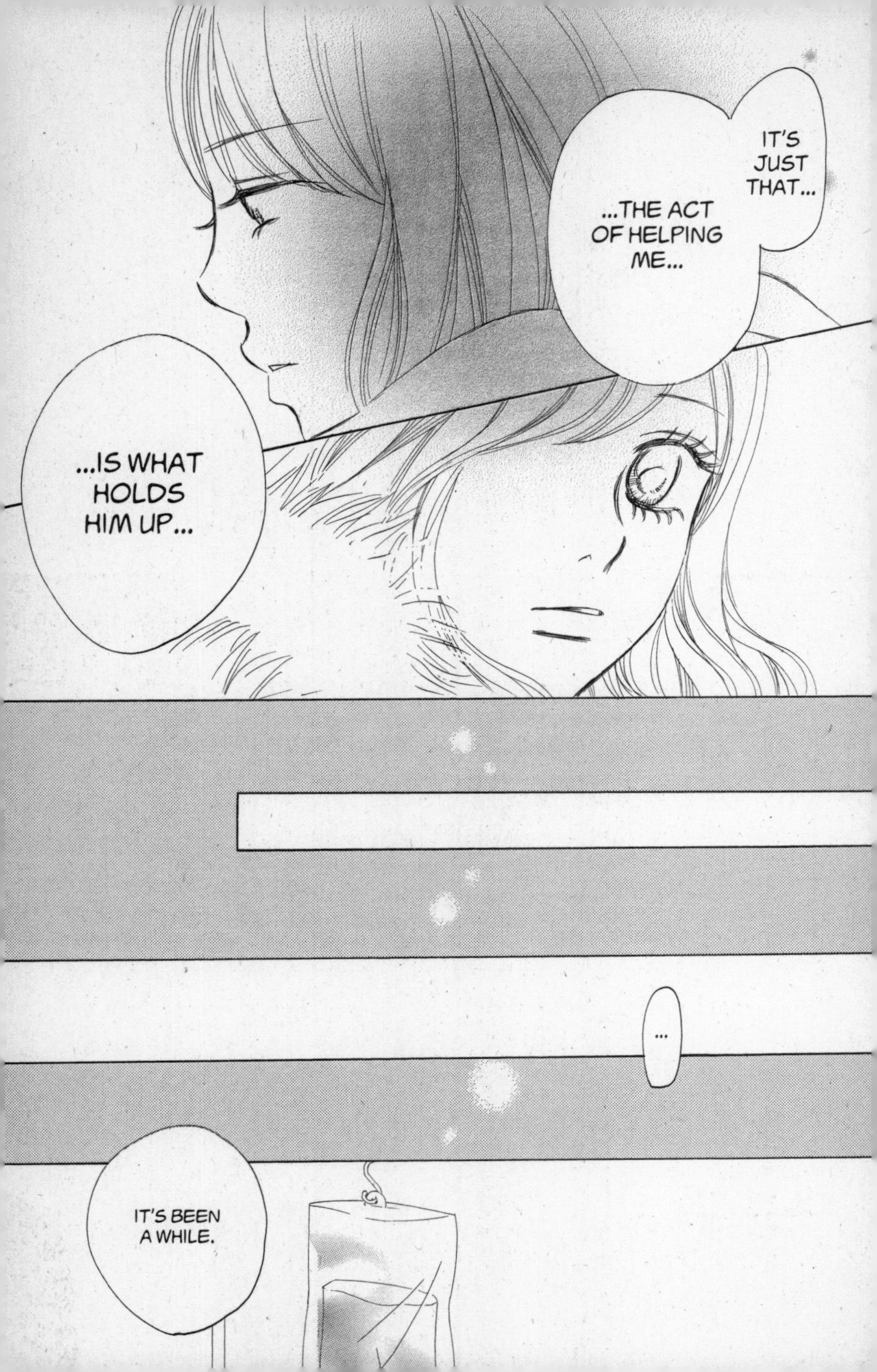
IT'S JUST THAT...
...THE ACT OF HELPING ME...
...IS WHAT HOLDS HIM UP...
...
IT'S BEEN A WHILE.

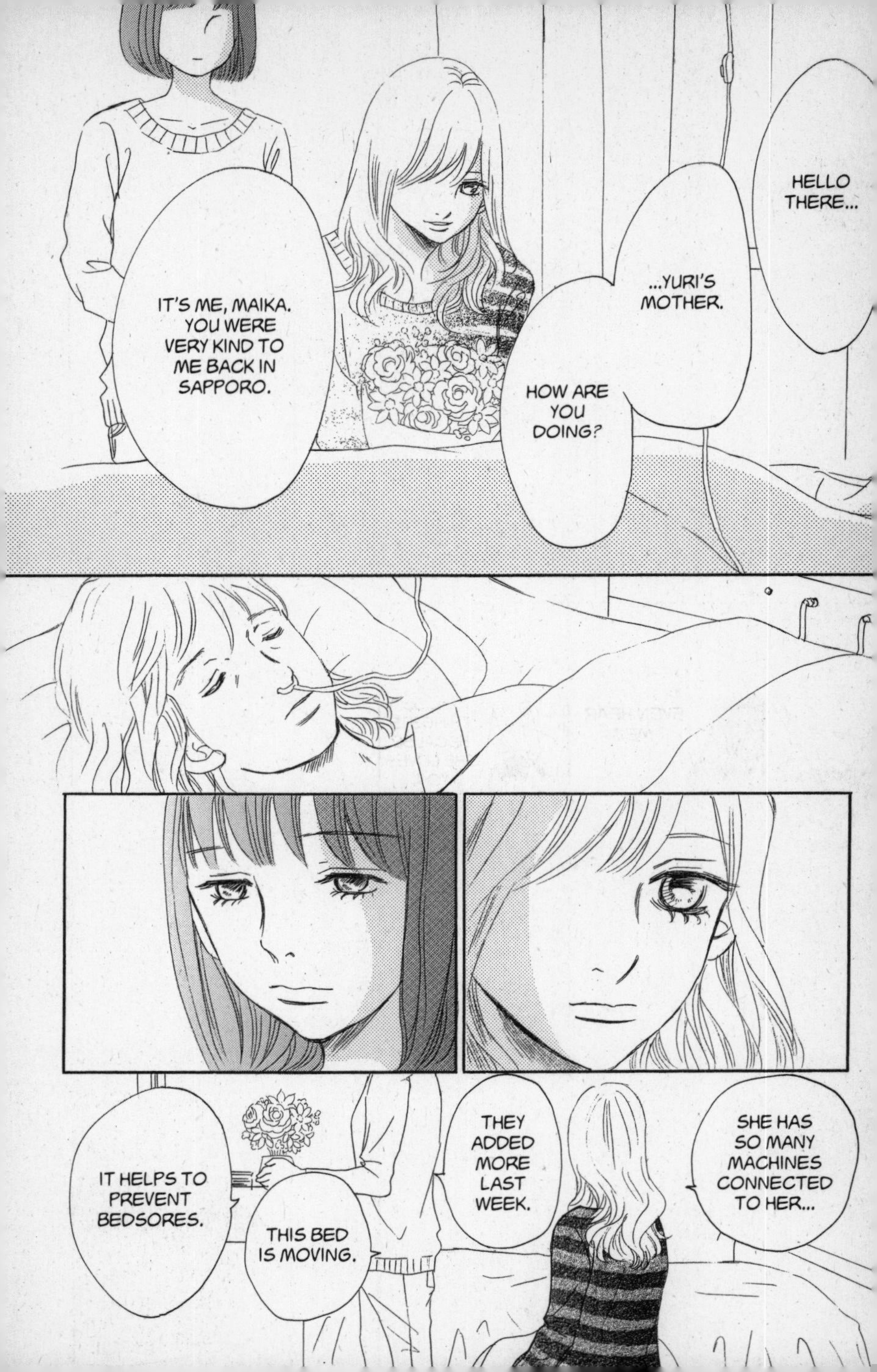
HELLO THERE...
...YURI'S MOTHER.
HOW ARE YOU DOING?
IT'S ME, MAIKA. YOU WERE VERY KIND TO ME BACK IN SAPPORO.
SHE HAS SO MANY MACHINES CONNECTED TO HER...
THEY ADDED MORE LAST WEEK.
THIS BED IS MOVING.
IT HELPS TO PREVENT BEDSORES.

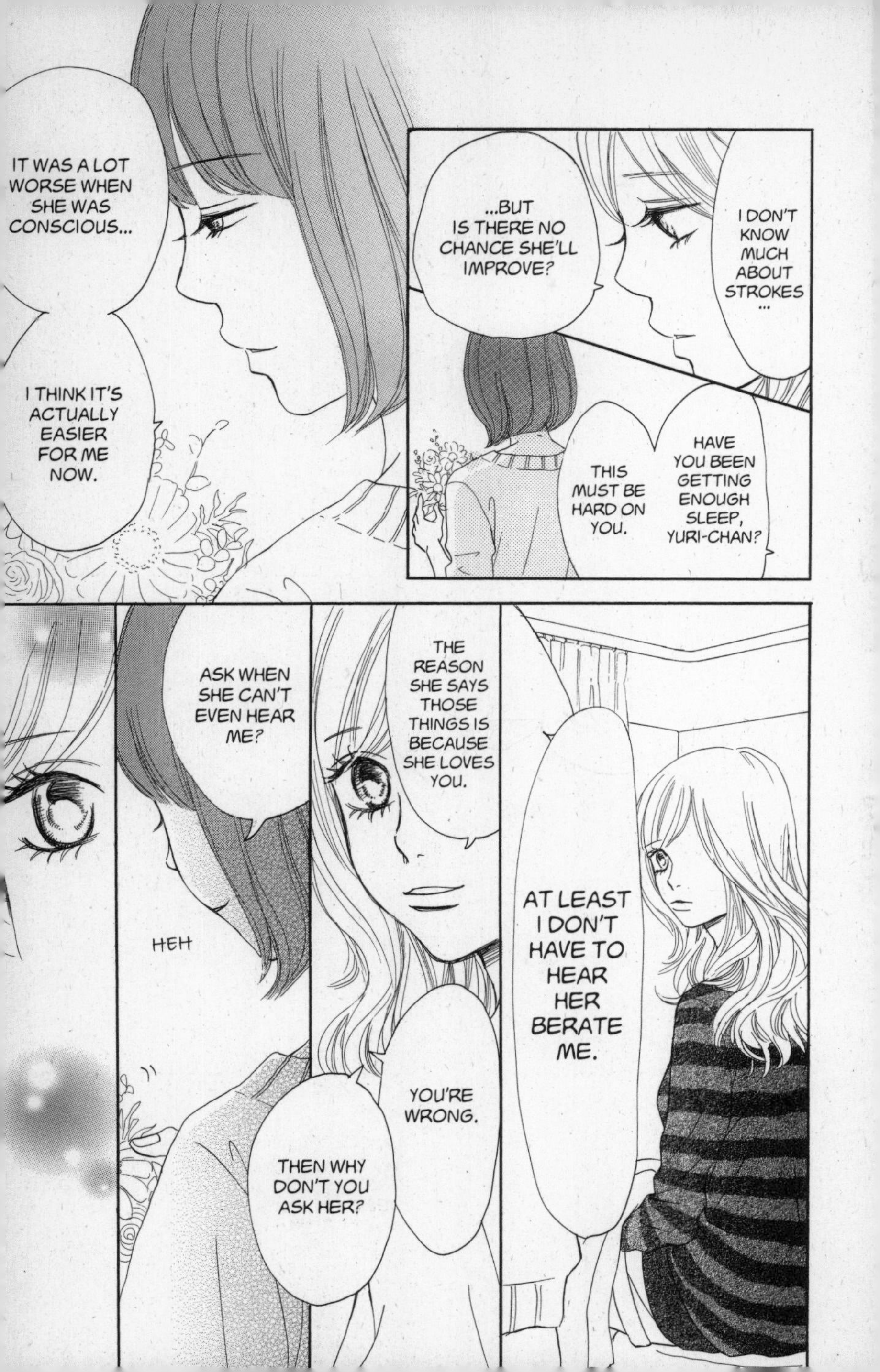
I DON'T KNOW MUCH ABOUT STROKES...
...BUT IS THERE NO CHANCE SHE'LL IMPROVE?
HAVE YOU BEEN GETTING ENOUGH SLEEP, YURI-CHAN?
THIS MUST BE HARD ON YOU.
IT WAS A LOT WORSE WHEN SHE WAS CONSCIOUS...
I THINK IT'S ACTUALLY EASIER FOR ME NOW.
AT LEAST I DON'T HAVE TO HEAR HER BERATE ME.
THE REASON SHE SAYS THOSE THINGS IS BECAUSE SHE LOVES YOU.
YOU'RE WRONG.
THEN WHY DON'T YOU ASK HER?
ASK WHEN SHE CAN'T EVEN HEAR ME?
HEH

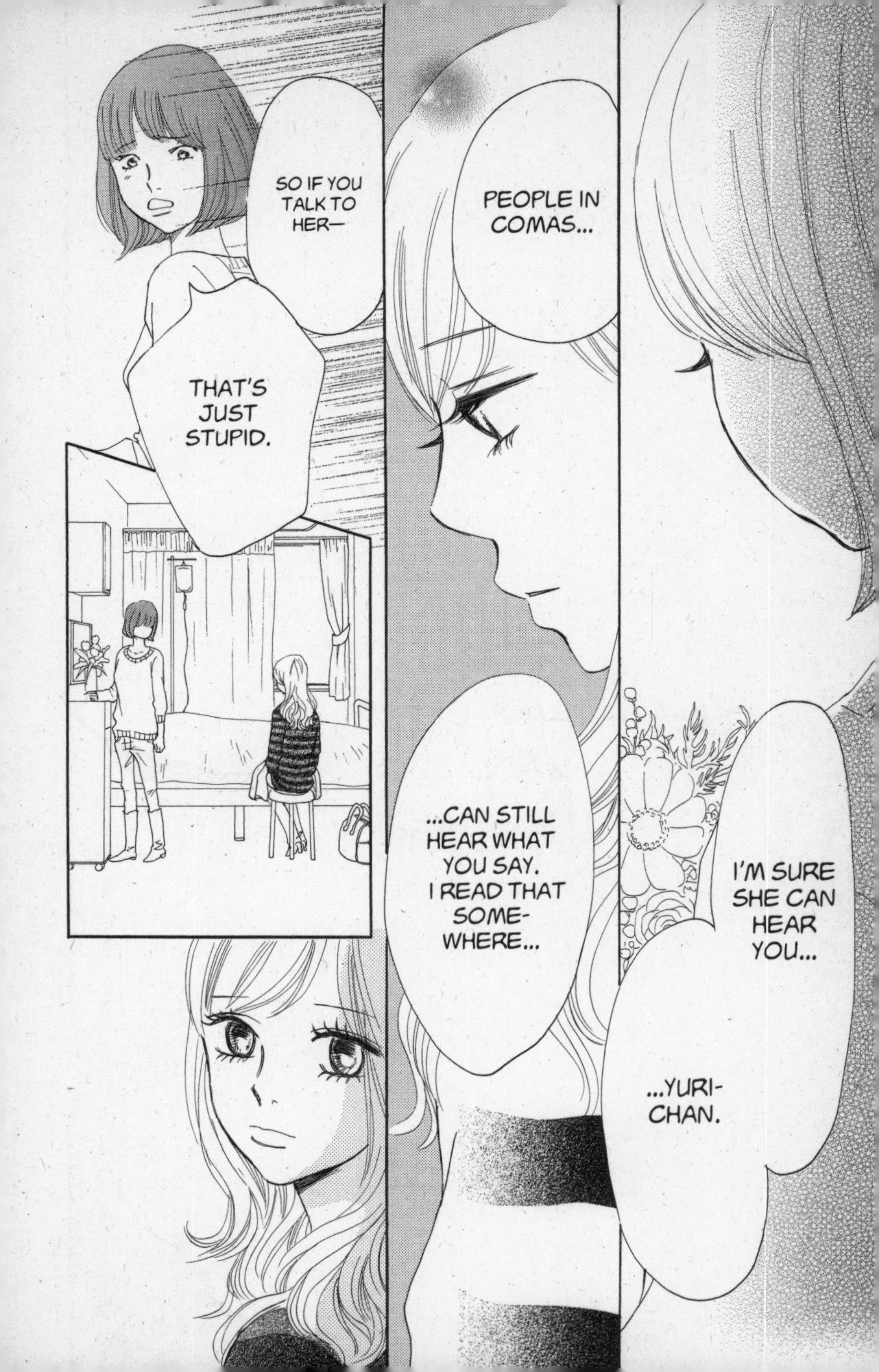
I'M SURE SHE CAN HEAR YOU...
...YURI-CHAN.
PEOPLE IN COMAS...
...CAN STILL HEAR WHAT YOU SAY. I READ THAT SOME-WHERE...
SO IF YOU TALK TO HER—
THAT'S JUST STUPID.

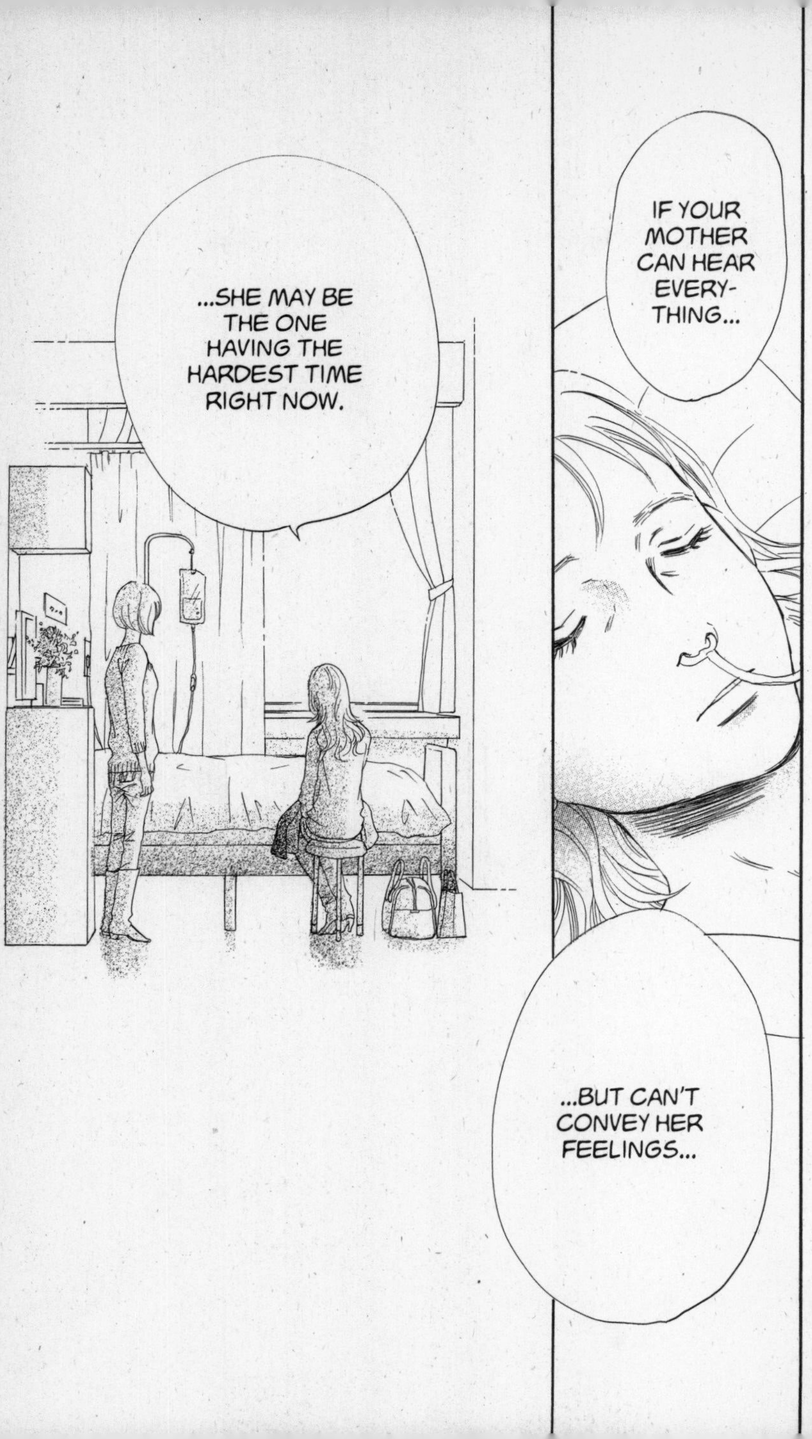
IF YOUR MOTHER CAN HEAR EVERY-THING...
...BUT CAN'T CONVEY HER FEELINGS...
...SHE MAY BE THE ONE HAVING THE HARDEST TIME RIGHT NOW.

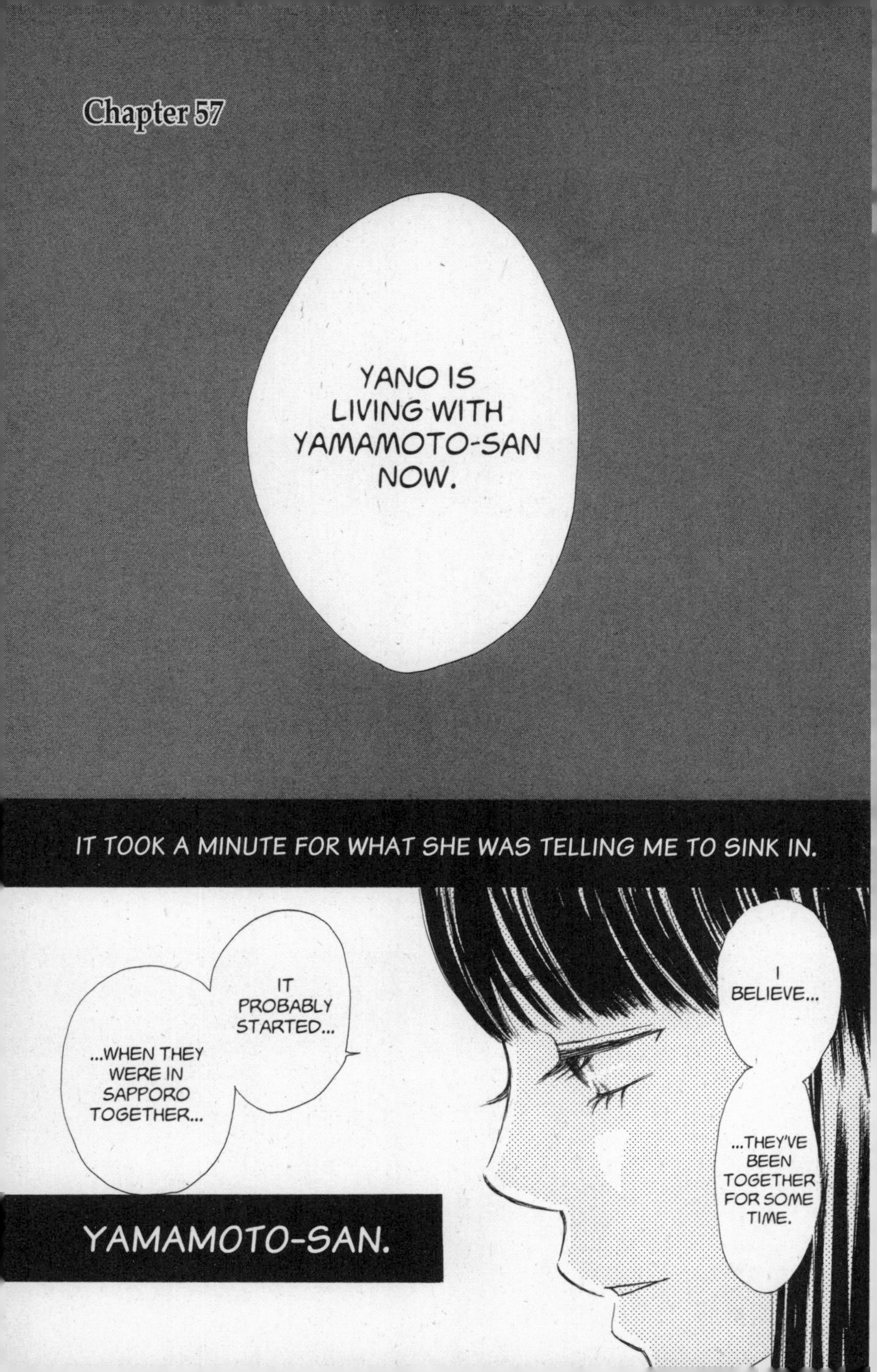
Chapter 57
YANO IS LIVING WITH YAMAMOTO-SAN NOW.
IT TOOK A MINUTE FOR WHAT SHE WAS TELLING ME TO SINK IN.
I BELIEVE...
...THEY'VE BEEN TOGETHER FOR SOME TIME.
IT PROBABLY STARTED...
...WHEN THEY WERE IN SAPPORO TOGETHER...
YAMAMOTO-SAN.

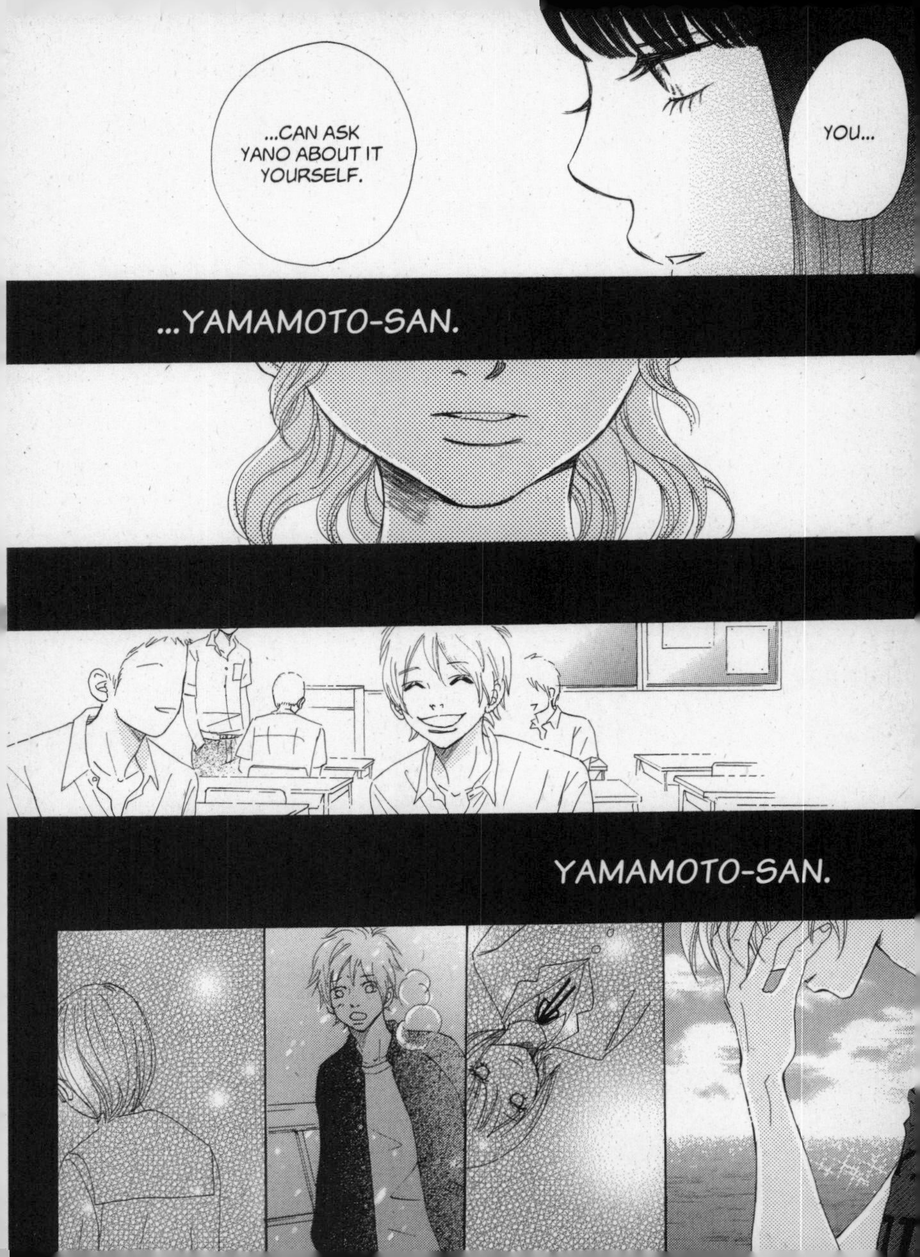
YOU...
...CAN ASK YANO ABOUT IT YOURSELF.
...YAMAMOTO-SAN.
YAMAMOTO-SAN.

Chapter 57

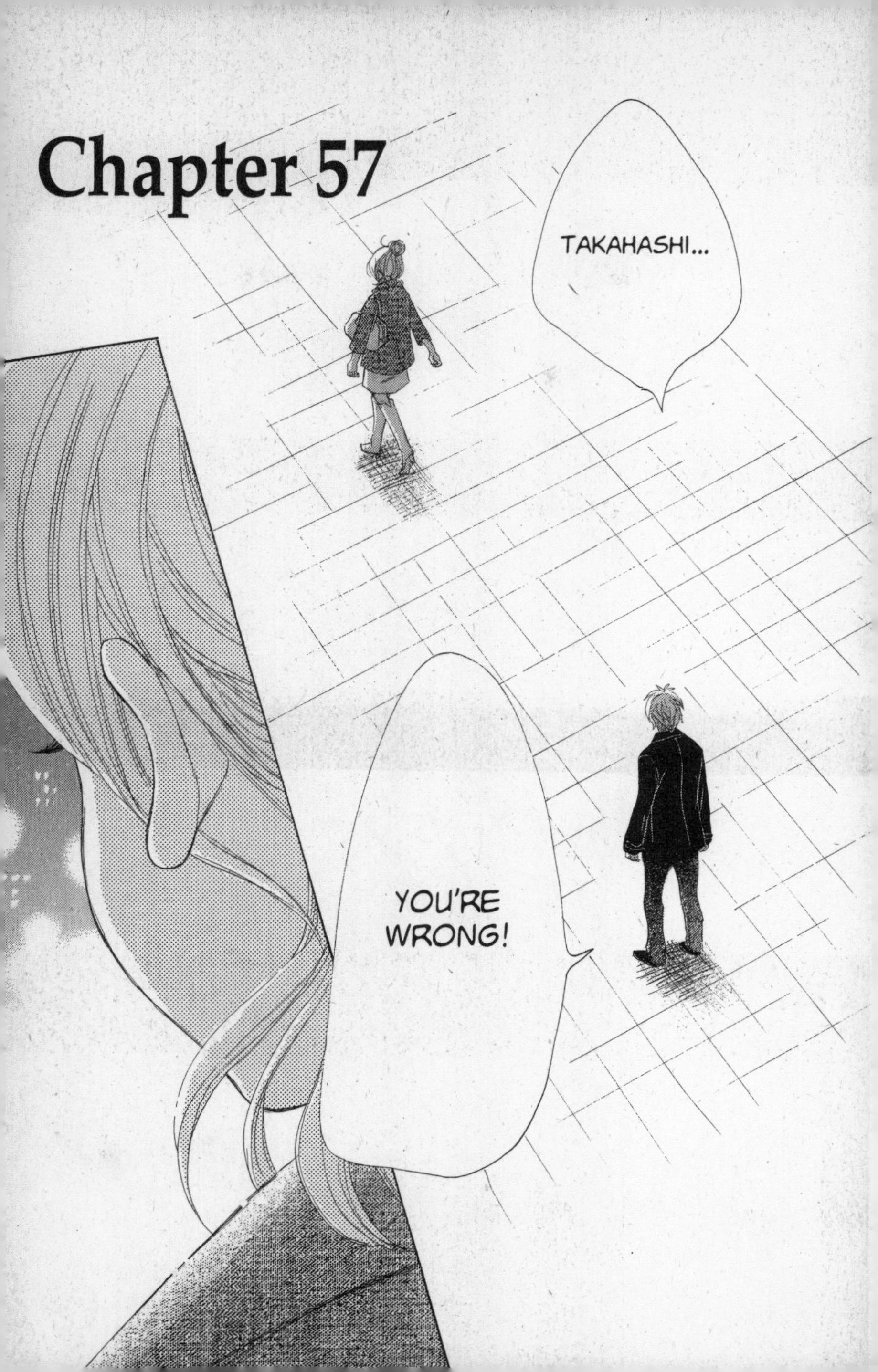
TAKAHASHI...
YOU'RE WRONG!

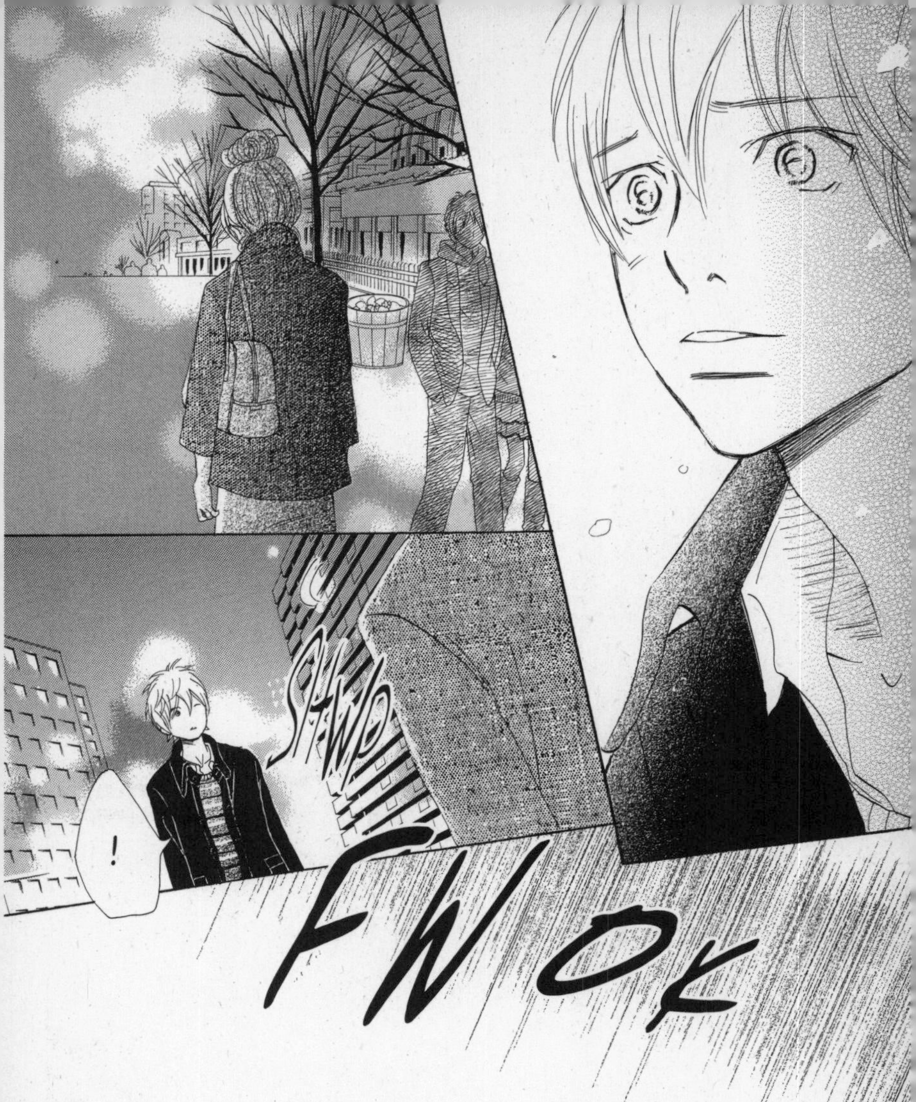
SHWP
!
FWOK

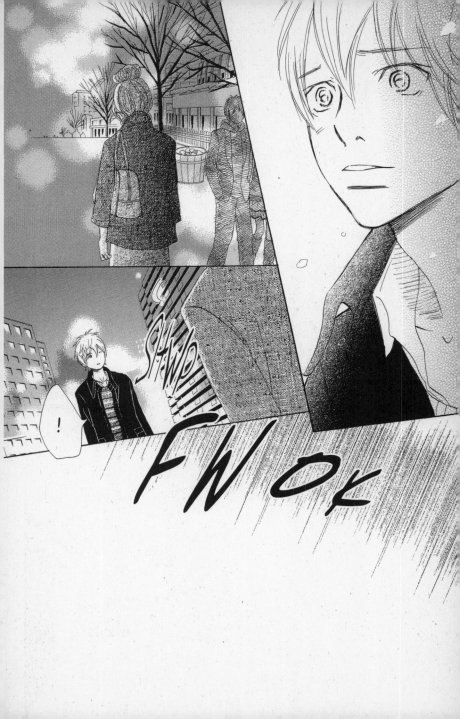

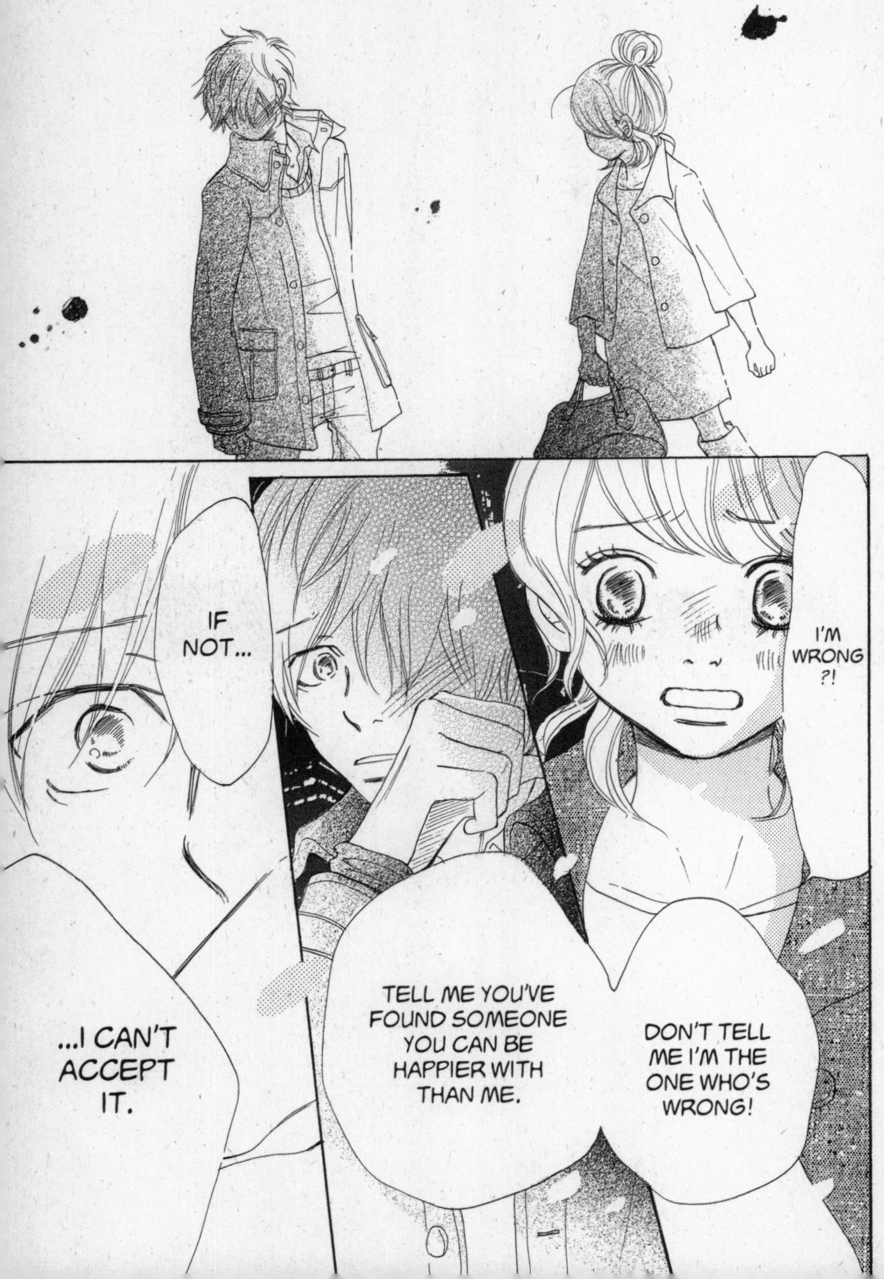
I'M WRONG?!
DON'T TELL ME I'M THE ONE WHO'S WRONG!
TELL ME YOU'VE FOUND SOMEONE YOU CAN BE HAPPIER WITH THAN ME.
IF NOT...
...I CAN'T ACCEPT IT.

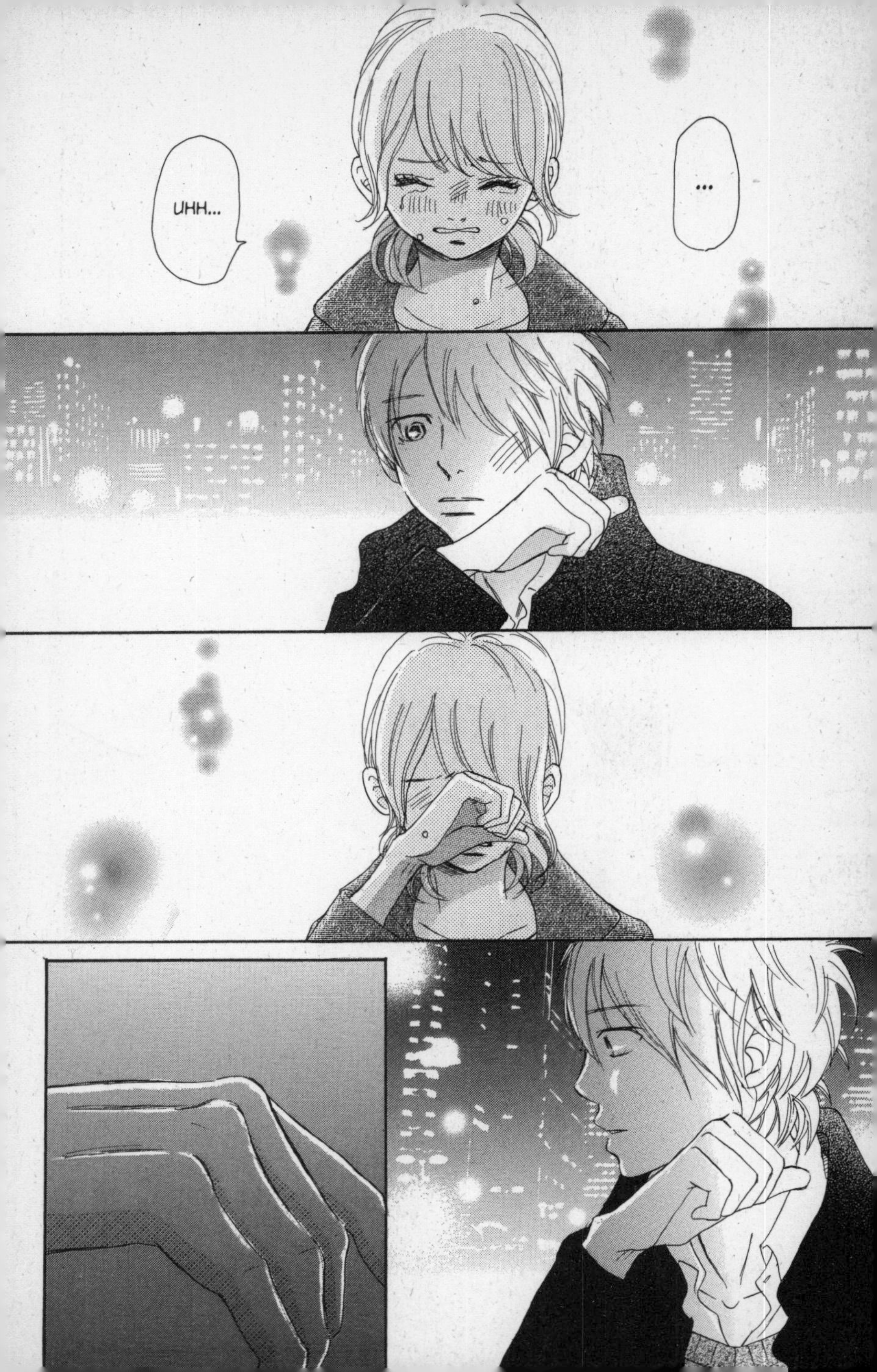
...
UHH...

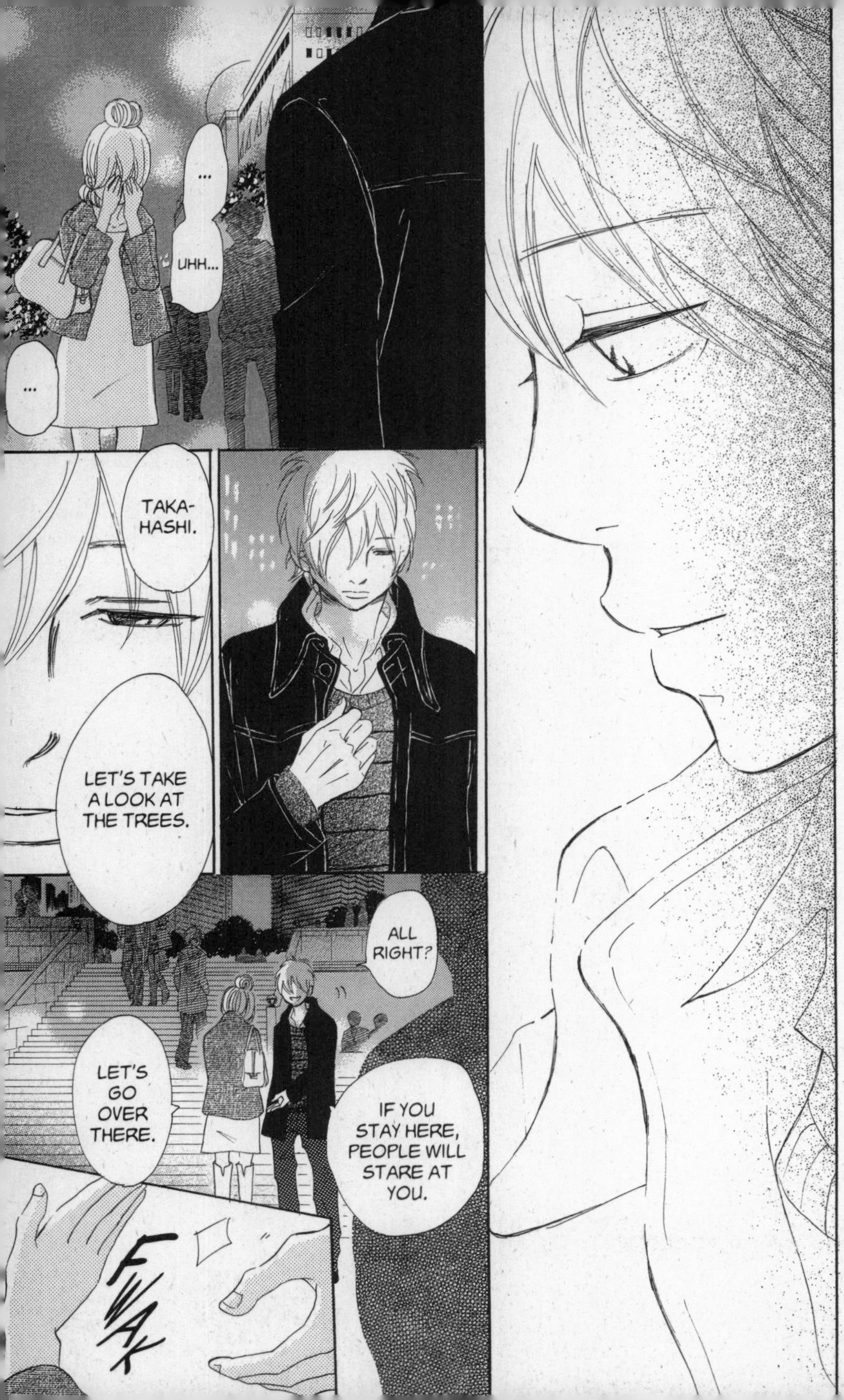
...
UHH...
...
TAKA-HASHI.
LET'S TAKE A LOOK AT THE TREES.
ALL RIGHT?
IF YOU STAY HERE, PEOPLE WILL STARE AT YOU.
LET'S GO OVER THERE.
FWAK

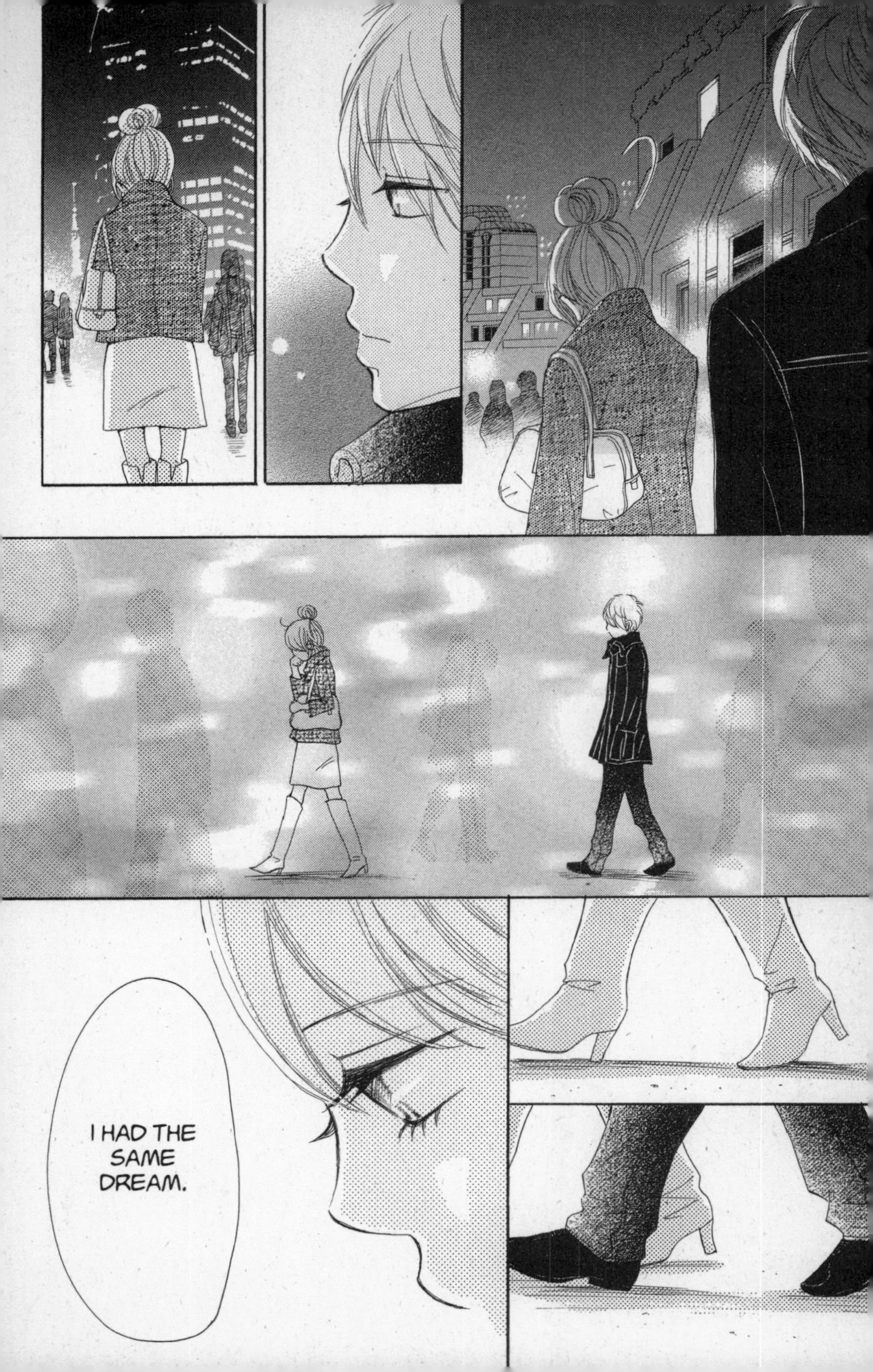
I HAD THE SAME DREAM.

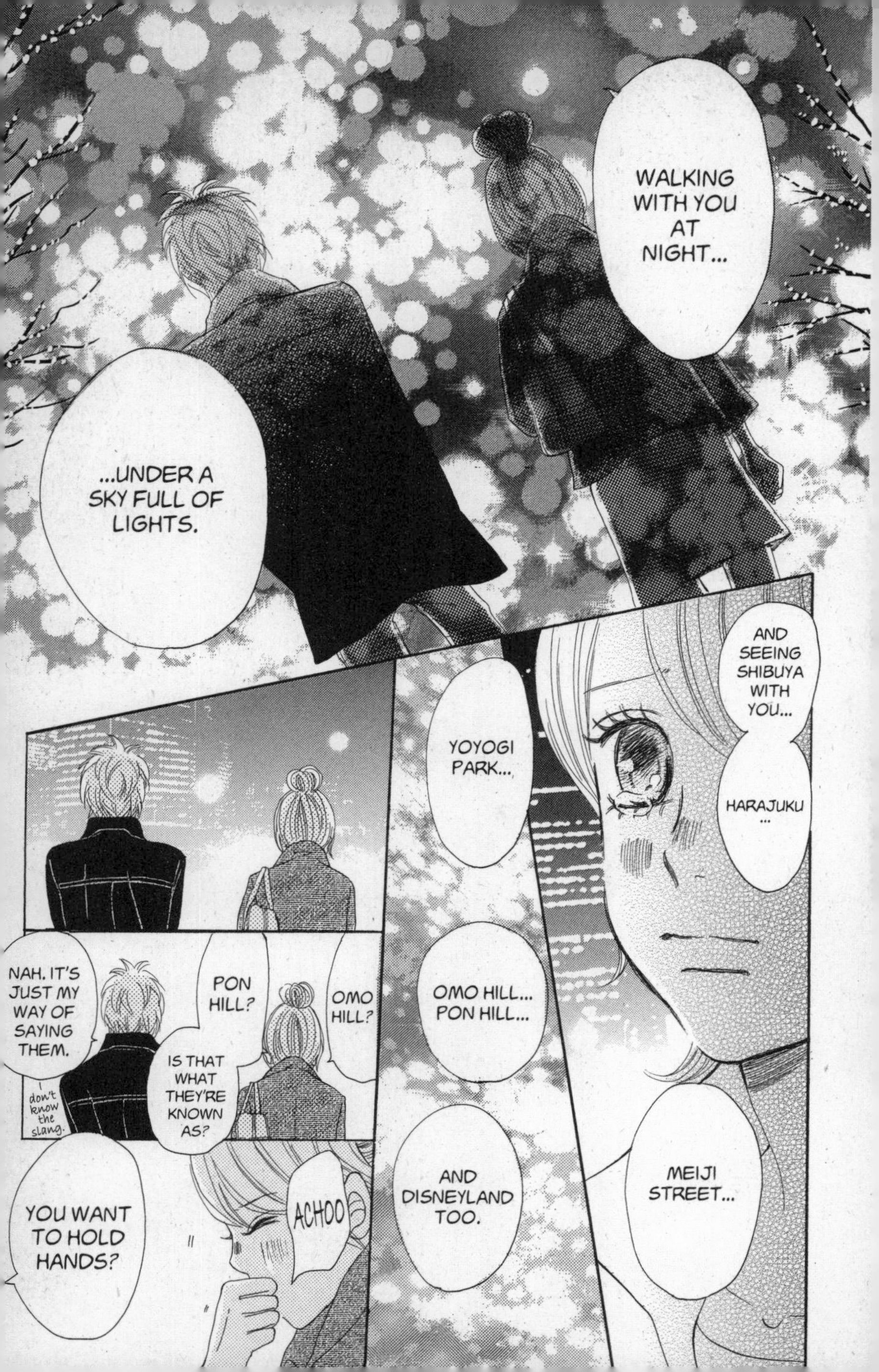
WALKING WITH YOU AT NIGHT...
...UNDER A SKY FULL OF LIGHTS.
AND SEEING SHIBUYA WITH YOU...
HARAJUKU ...
YOYOGI PARK...
OMO HILL... PON HILL...
MEIJI STREET...
AND DISNEYLAND TOO.
OMO HILL?
PON HILL?
IS THAT WHAT THEY'RE KNOWN AS?
NAH. IT'S JUST MY WAY OF SAYING THEM.
I don't know the slang.
ACHOO
YOU WANT TO HOLD HANDS?

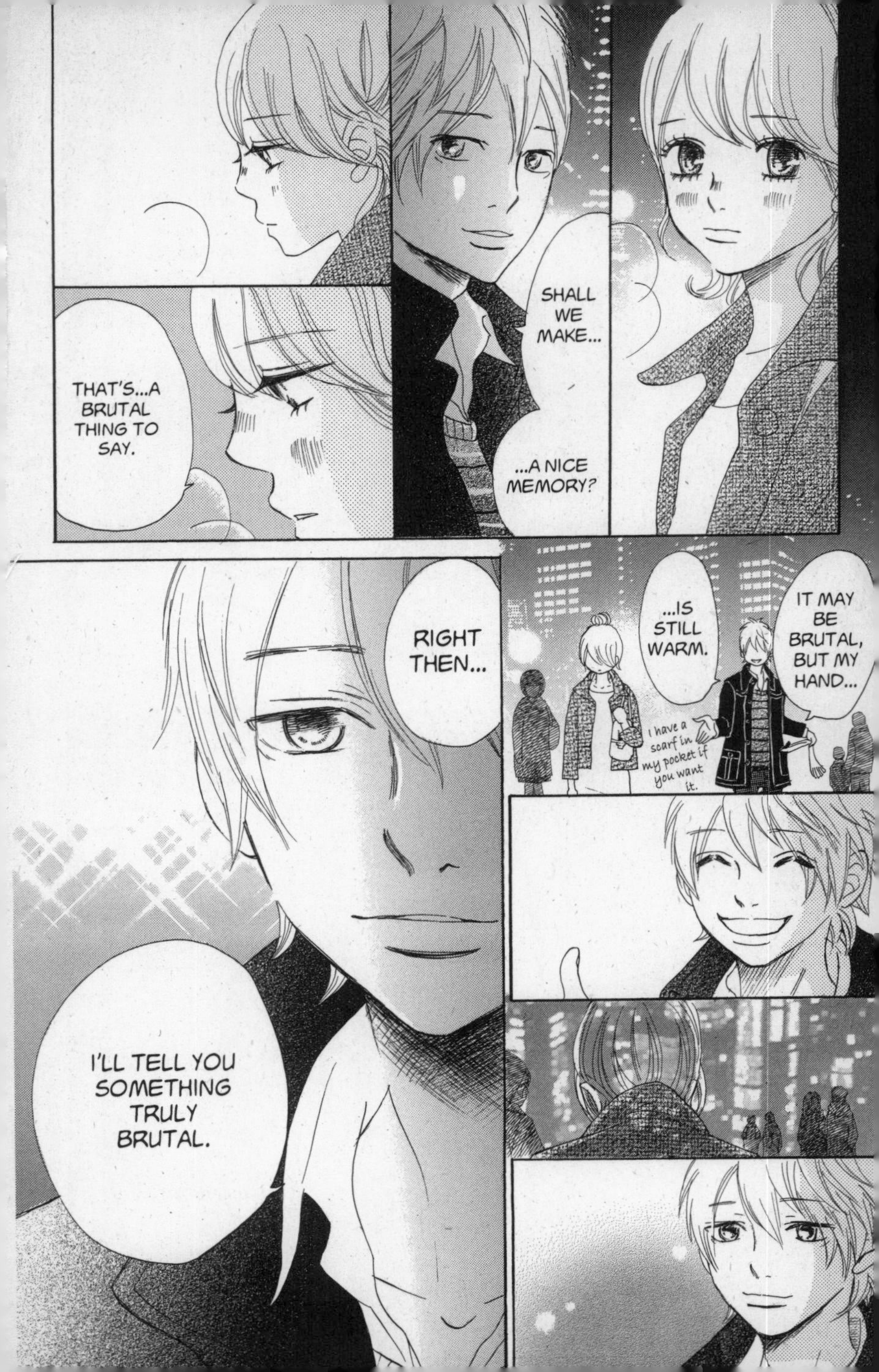
SHALL WE MAKE...
...A NICE MEMORY?
THAT'S...A BRUTAL THING TO SAY.
IT MAY BE BRUTAL, BUT MY HAND...
...IS STILL WARM.
I have a scarf in my pocket if you want it.
RIGHT THEN...
I'LL TELL YOU SOMETHING TRULY BRUTAL.

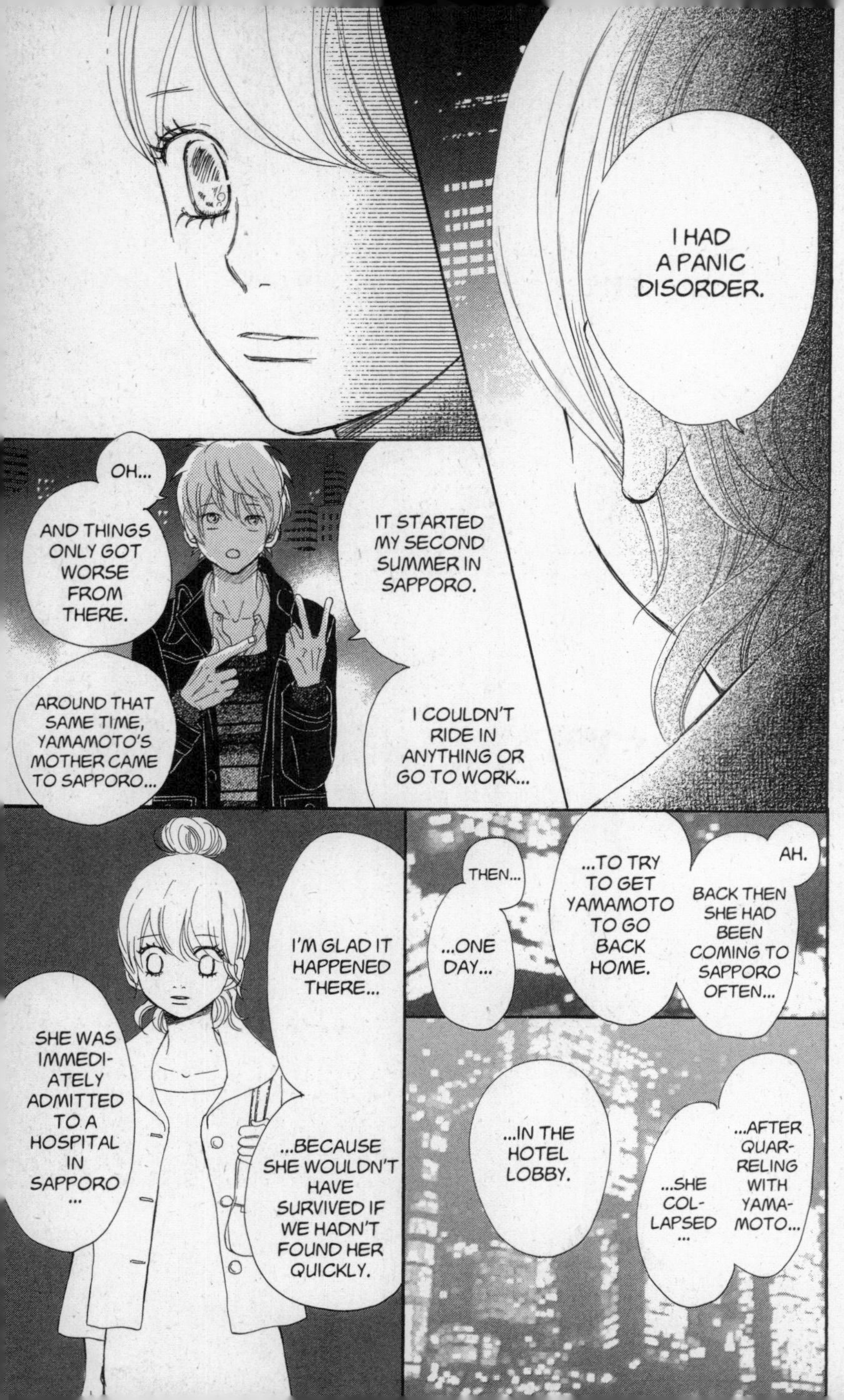
I HAD A PANIC DISORDER.
IT STARTED MY SECOND SUMMER IN SAPPORO.
I COULDN'T RIDE IN ANYTHING OR GO TO WORK...
OH...
AND THINGS ONLY GOT WORSE FROM THERE.
AROUND THAT SAME TIME, YAMAMOTO'S MOTHER CAME TO SAPPORO...
AH.
BACK THEN SHE HAD BEEN COMING TO SAPPORO OFTEN...
...TO TRY TO GET YAMAMOTO TO GO BACK HOME.
THEN...
...ONE DAY...
...AFTER QUARRELING WITH YAMAMOTO...
...SHE COLLAPSED...
...IN THE HOTEL LOBBY.
SHE WAS IMMEDIATELY ADMITTED TO A HOSPITAL IN SAPPORO...
I'M GLAD IT HAPPENED THERE...
...BECAUSE SHE WOULDN'T HAVE SURVIVED IF WE HADN'T FOUND HER QUICKLY.

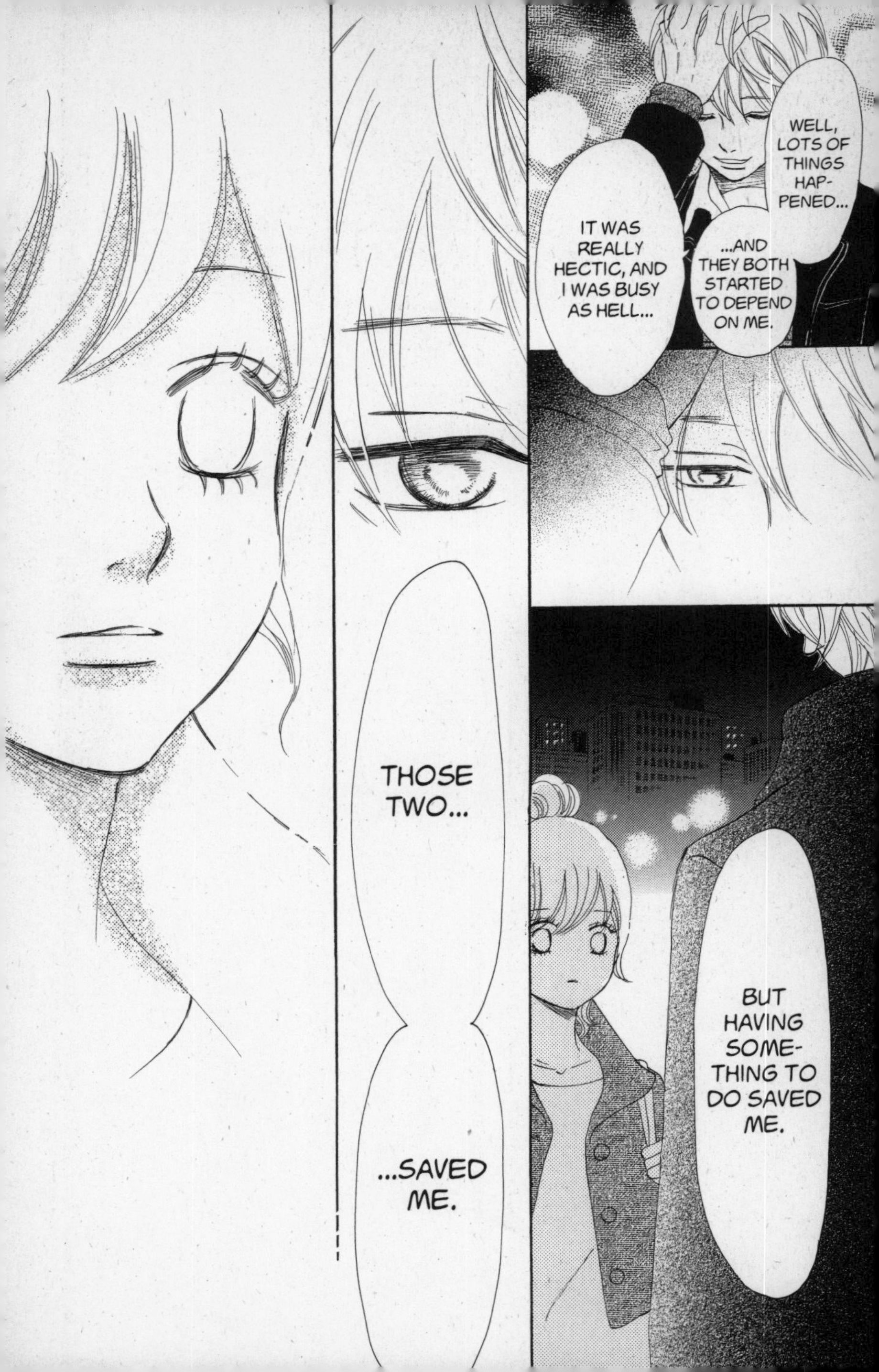
WELL, LOTS OF THINGS HAP-PENED...
IT WAS REALLY HECTIC, AND I WAS BUSY AS HELL...
...AND THEY BOTH STARTED TO DEPEND ON ME.
BUT HAVING SOME-THING TO DO SAVED ME.
THOSE TWO...
...SAVED ME.

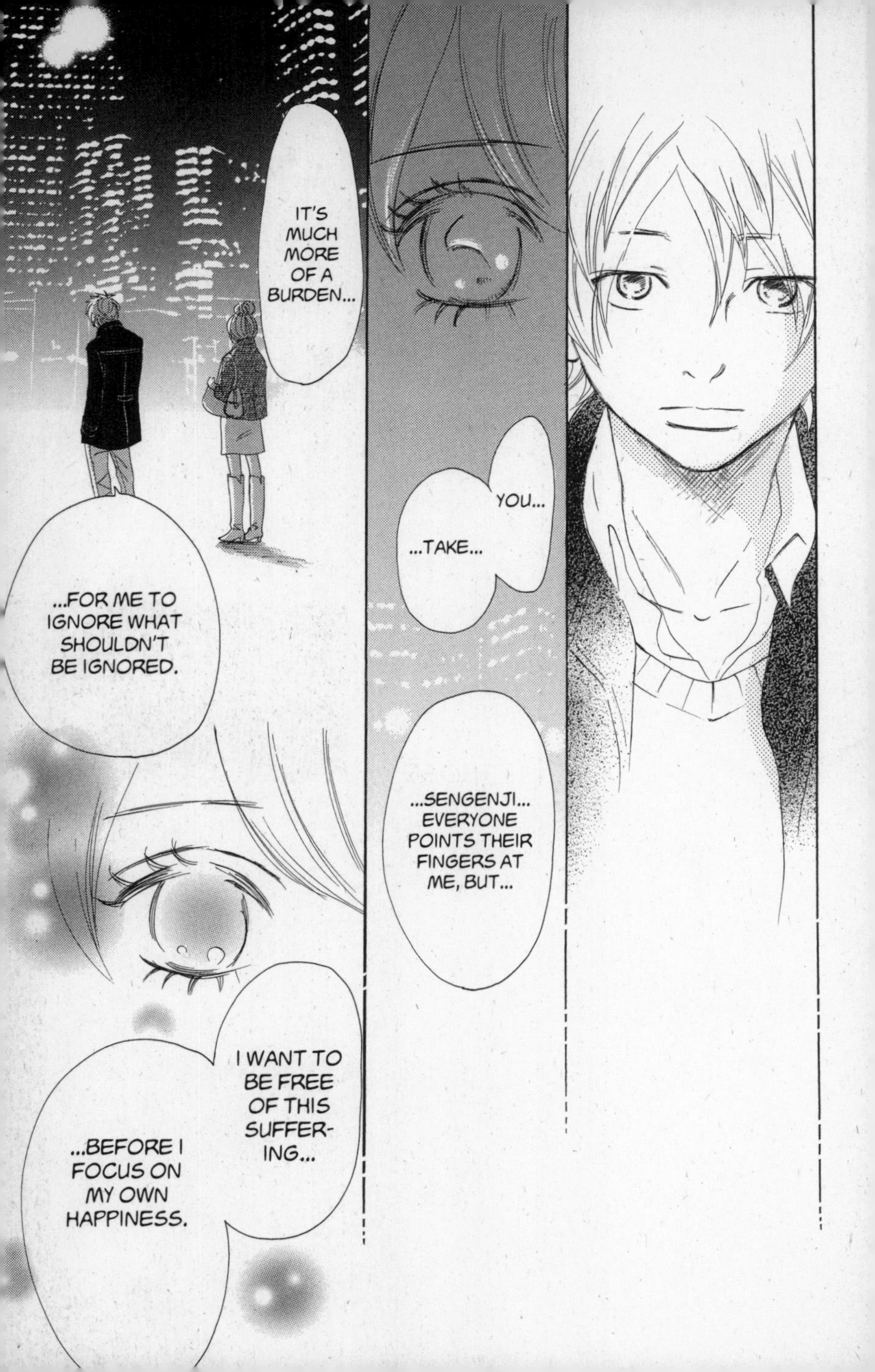
YOU...
...TAKE...
...SENGENJI... EVERYONE POINTS THEIR FINGERS AT ME, BUT...
IT'S MUCH MORE OF A BURDEN...
...FOR ME TO IGNORE WHAT SHOULDN'T BE IGNORED.
I WANT TO BE FREE OF THIS SUFFER-ING...
...BEFORE I FOCUS ON MY OWN HAPPINESS.

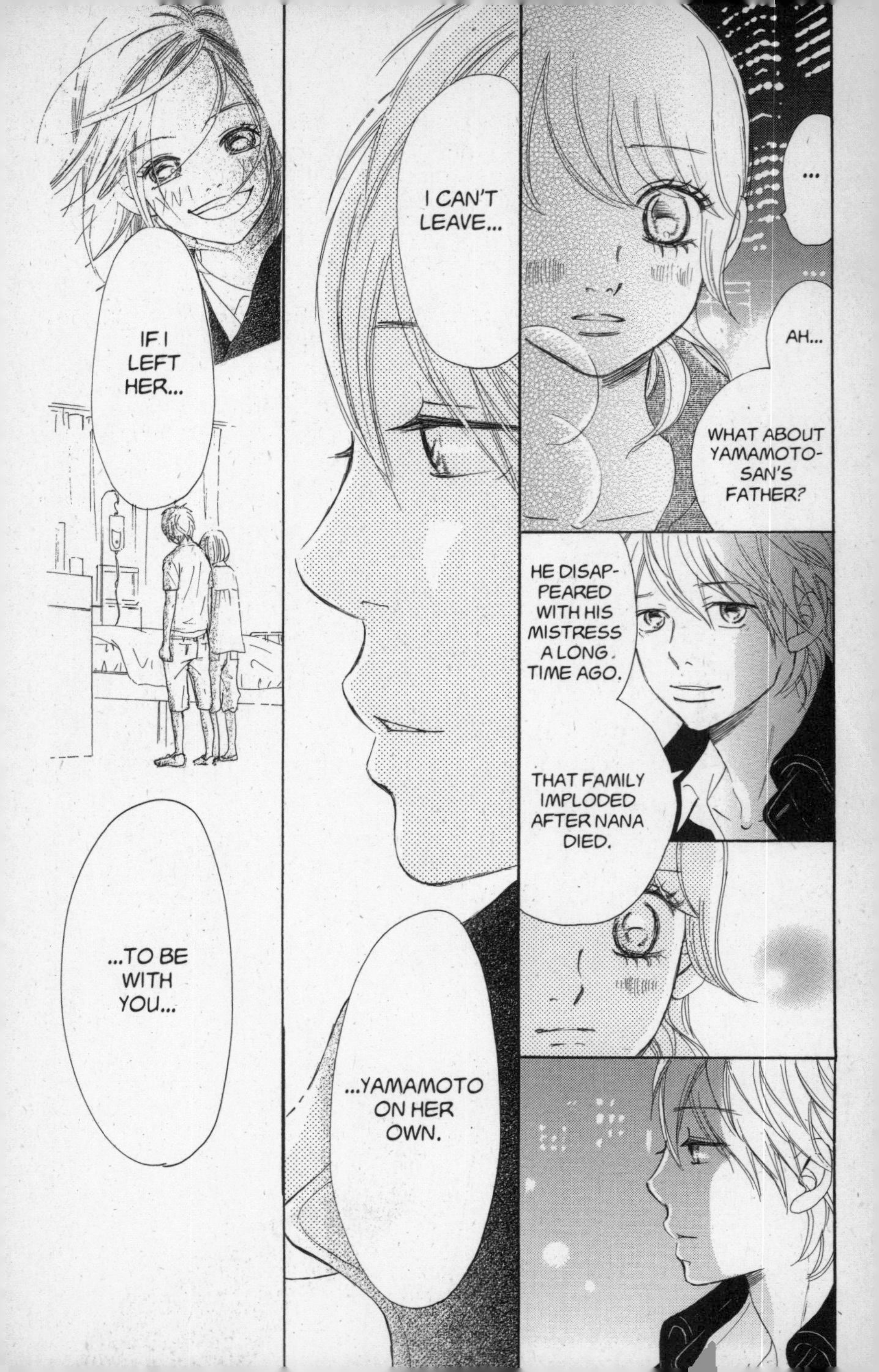
...
AH...
WHAT ABOUT YAMAMOTO-SAN'S FATHER?
HE DISAPPEARED WITH HIS MISTRESS A LONG TIME AGO.
THAT FAMILY IMPLODED AFTER NANA DIED.
I CAN'T LEAVE...
...YAMAMOTO ON HER OWN.
IF I LEFT HER...
...TO BE WITH YOU...

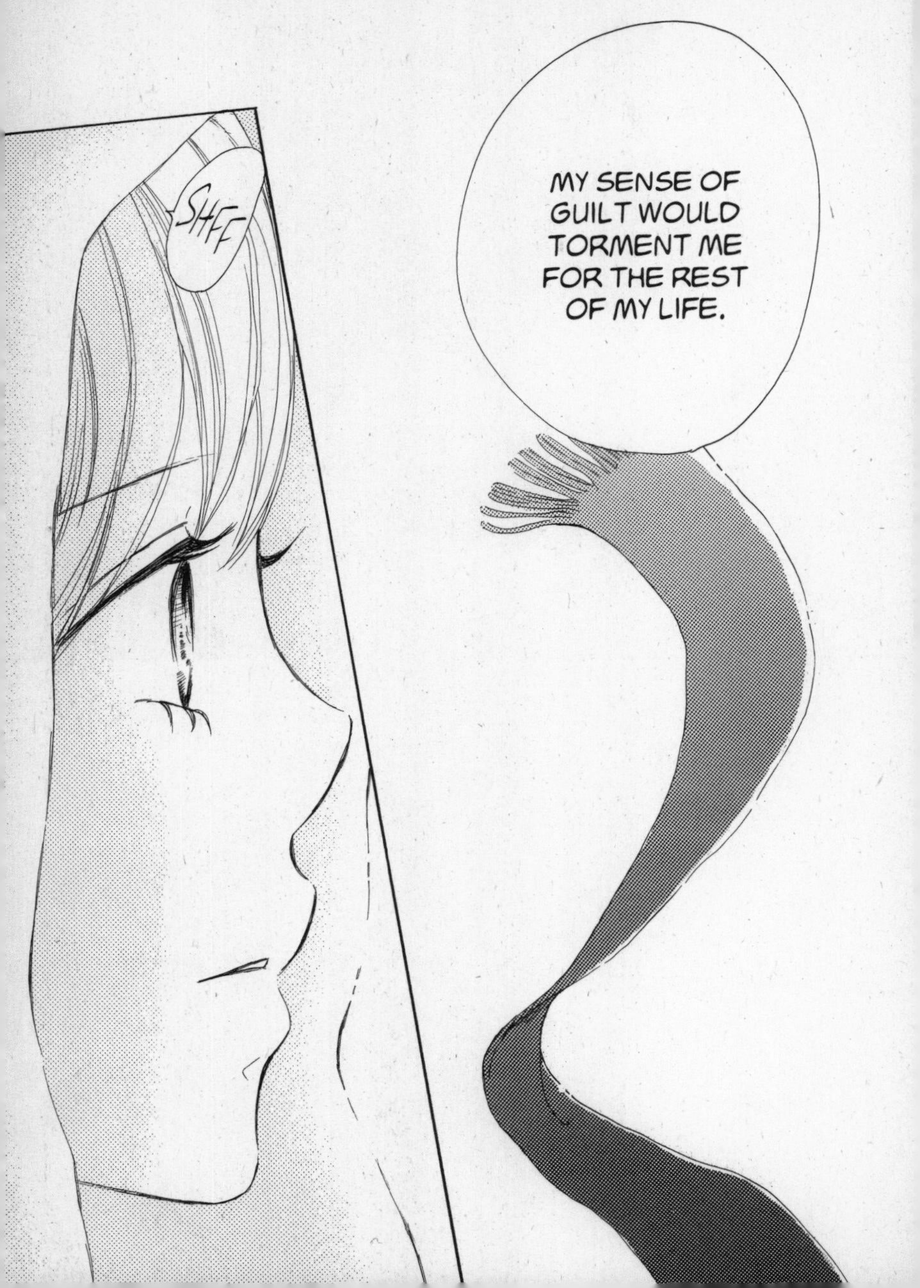
MY SENSE OF GUILT WOULD TORMENT ME FOR THE REST OF MY LIFE.
SHFF

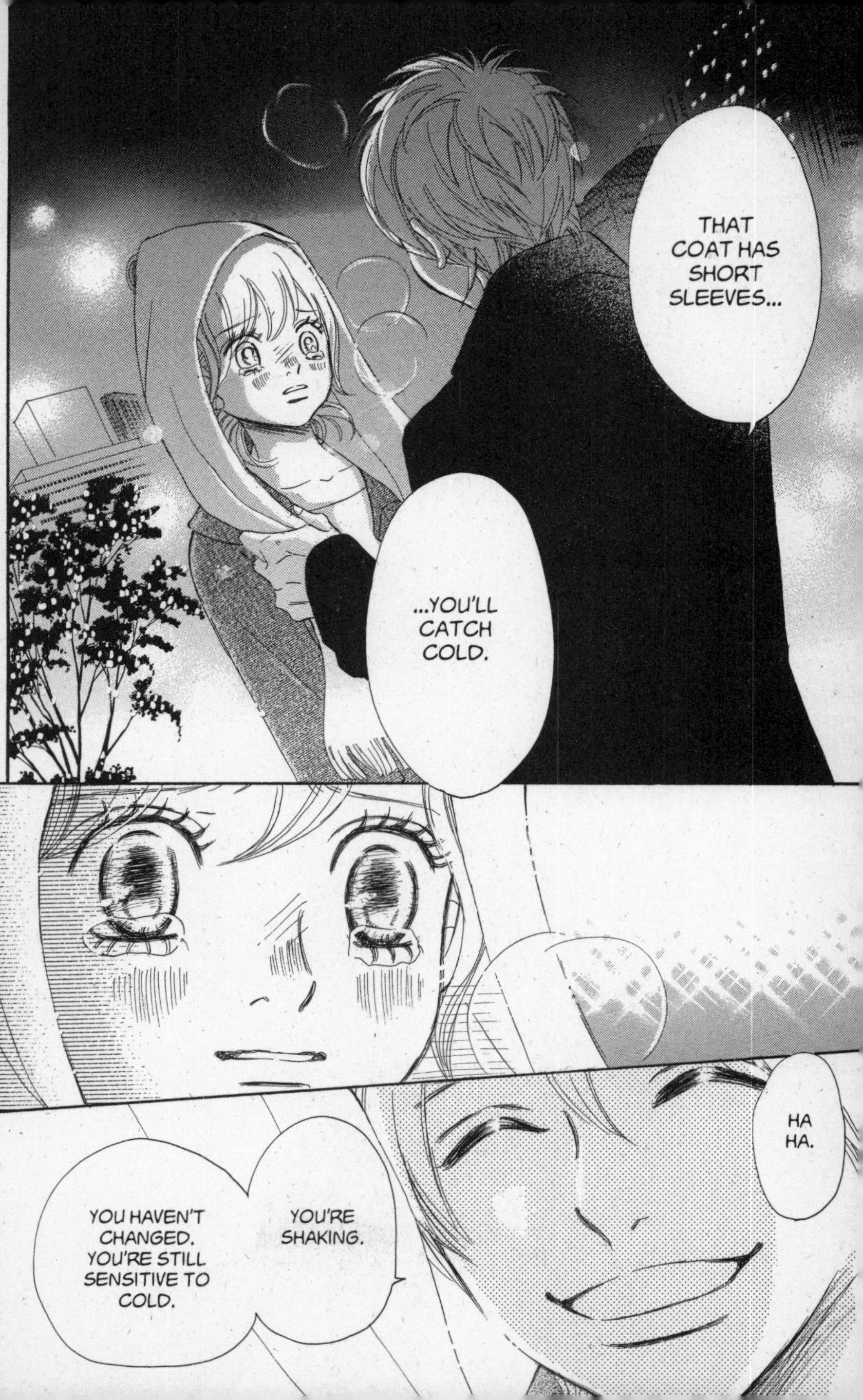
THAT COAT HAS SHORT SLEEVES...
...YOU'LL CATCH COLD.
HA HA.
YOU'RE SHAKING.
YOU HAVEN'T CHANGED. YOU'RE STILL SENSITIVE TO COLD.

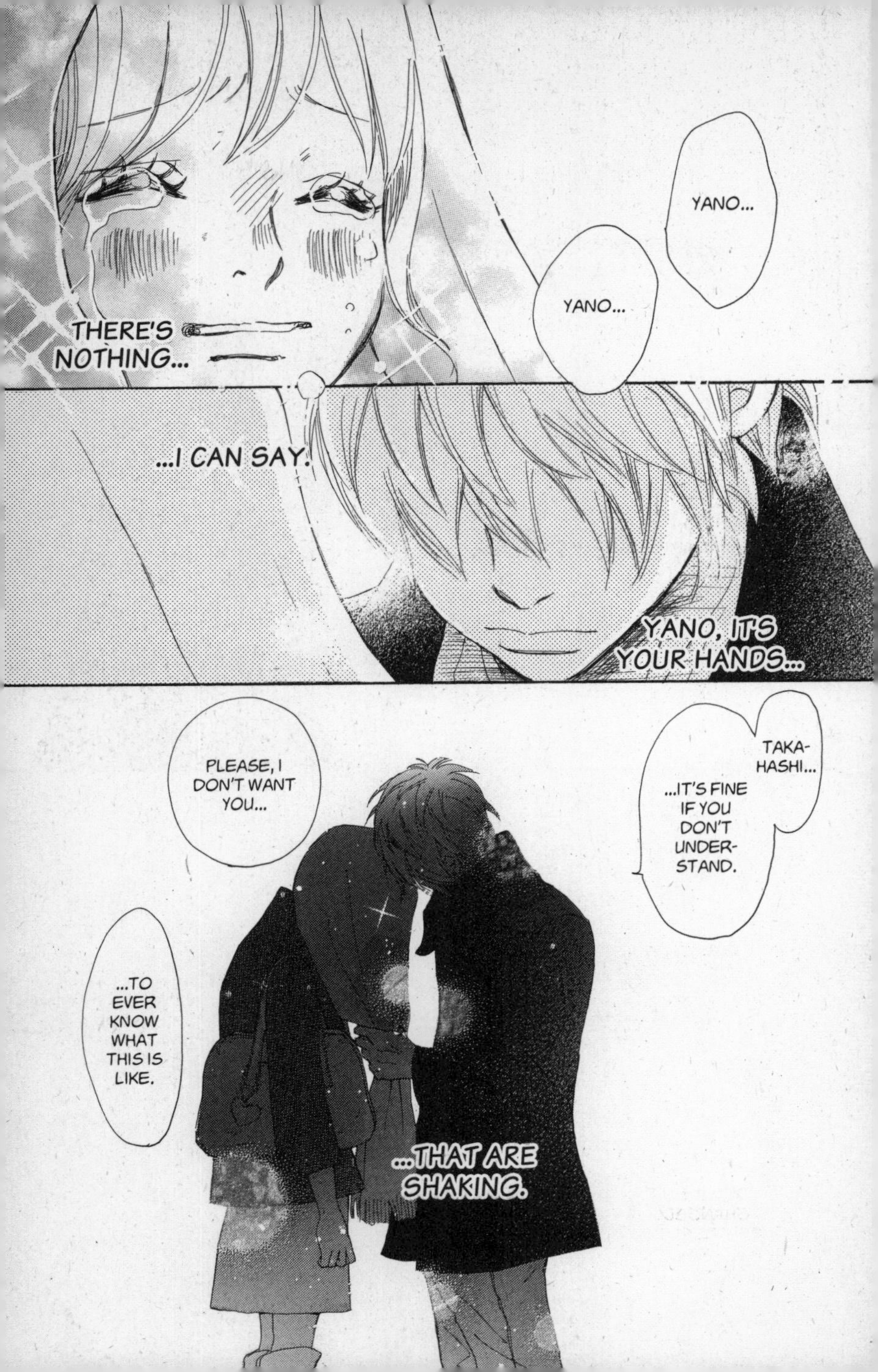
YANO...
YANO...
THERE'S NOTHING...
...I CAN SAY.
YANO, IT'S YOUR HANDS...
TAKA-HASHI... ...IT'S FINE IF YOU DON'T UNDER-STAND.
PLEASE, I DON'T WANT YOU...
...TO EVER KNOW WHAT THIS IS LIKE.
...THAT ARE SHAKING.

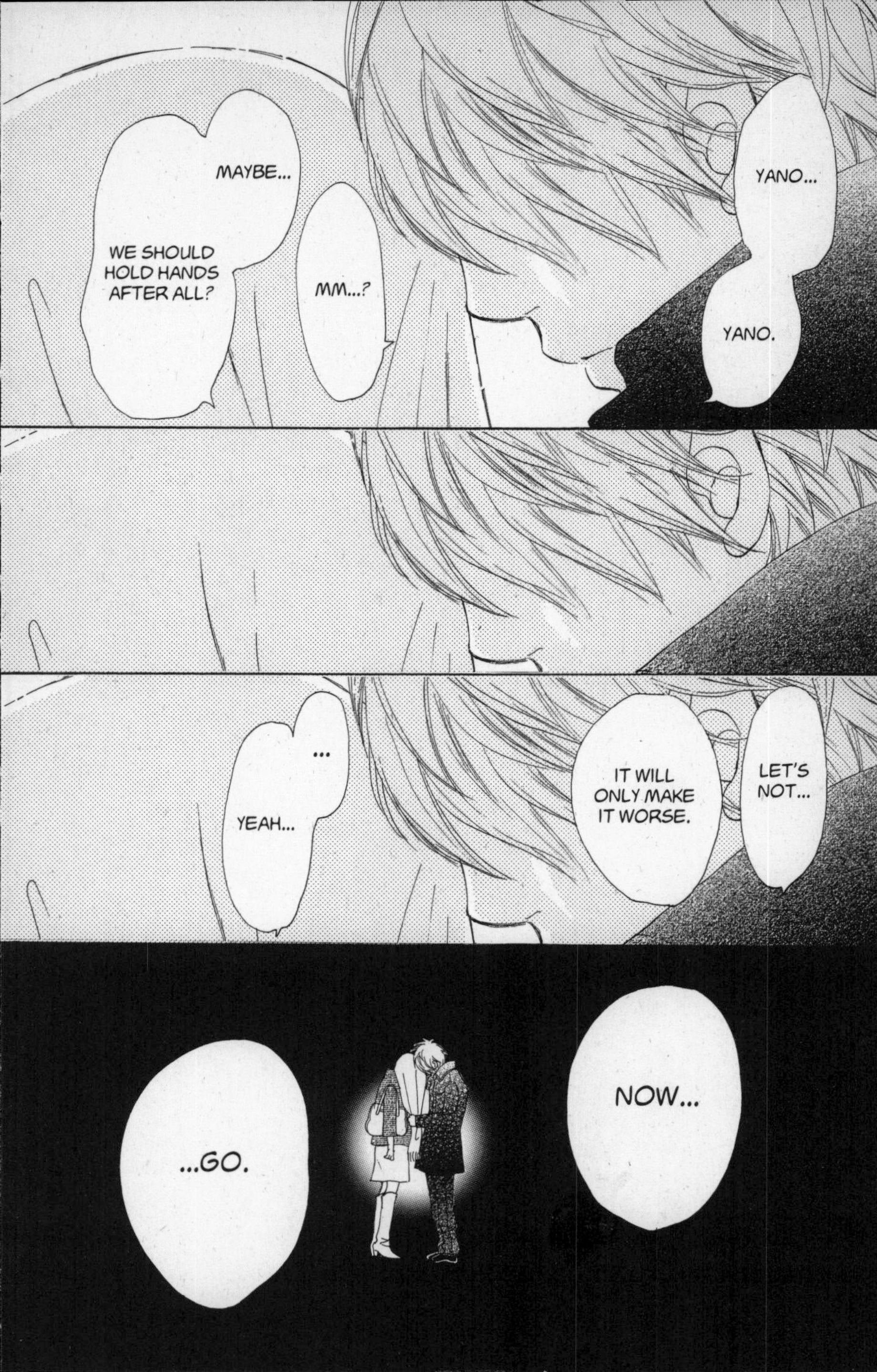
YANO...
YANO.
MM...?
MAYBE...
WE SHOULD HOLD HANDS AFTER ALL?
LET'S NOT...
IT WILL ONLY MAKE IT WORSE.
...
YEAH...
NOW...
...GO.

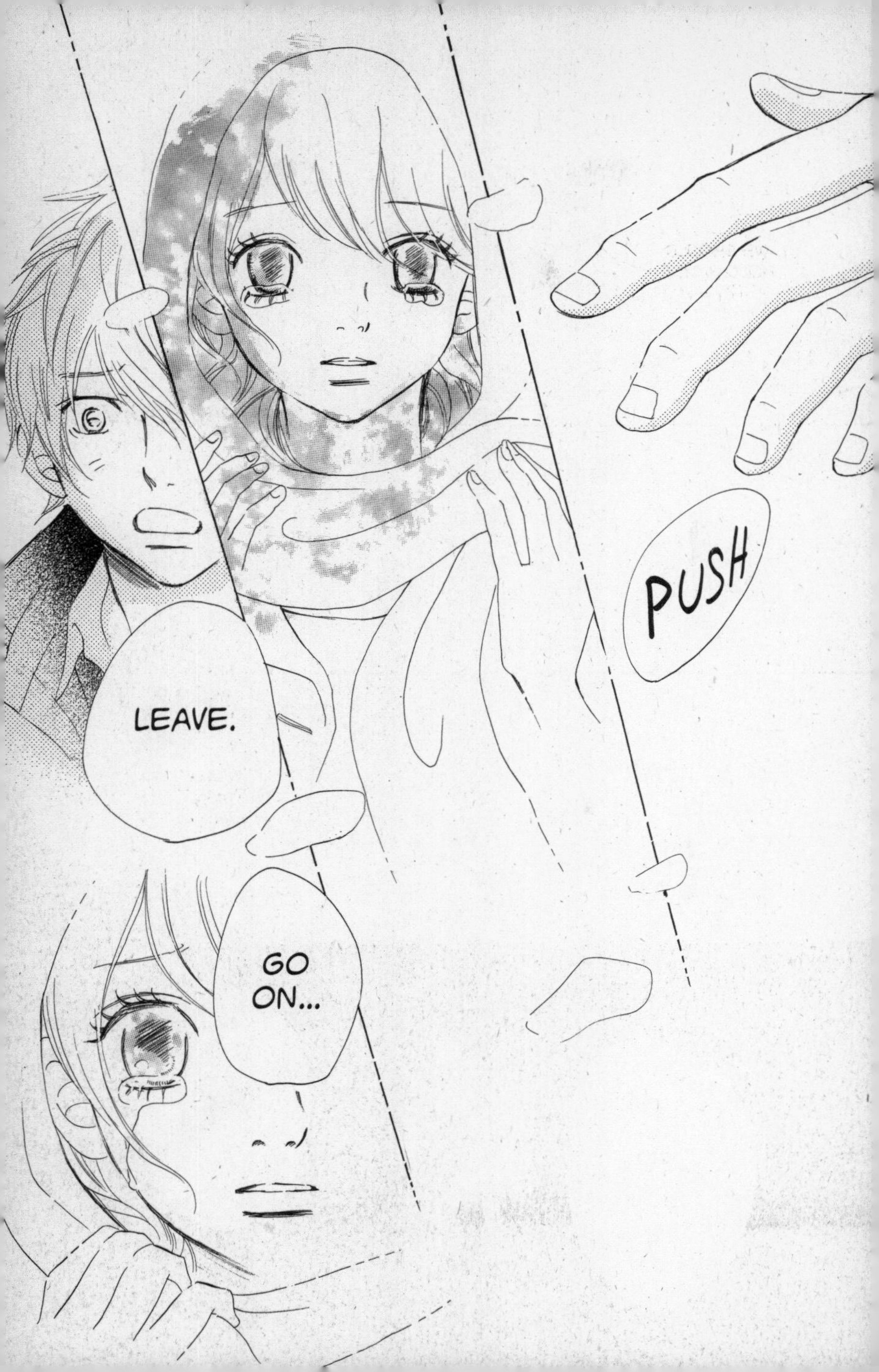
PUSH
LEAVE.
GO ON...

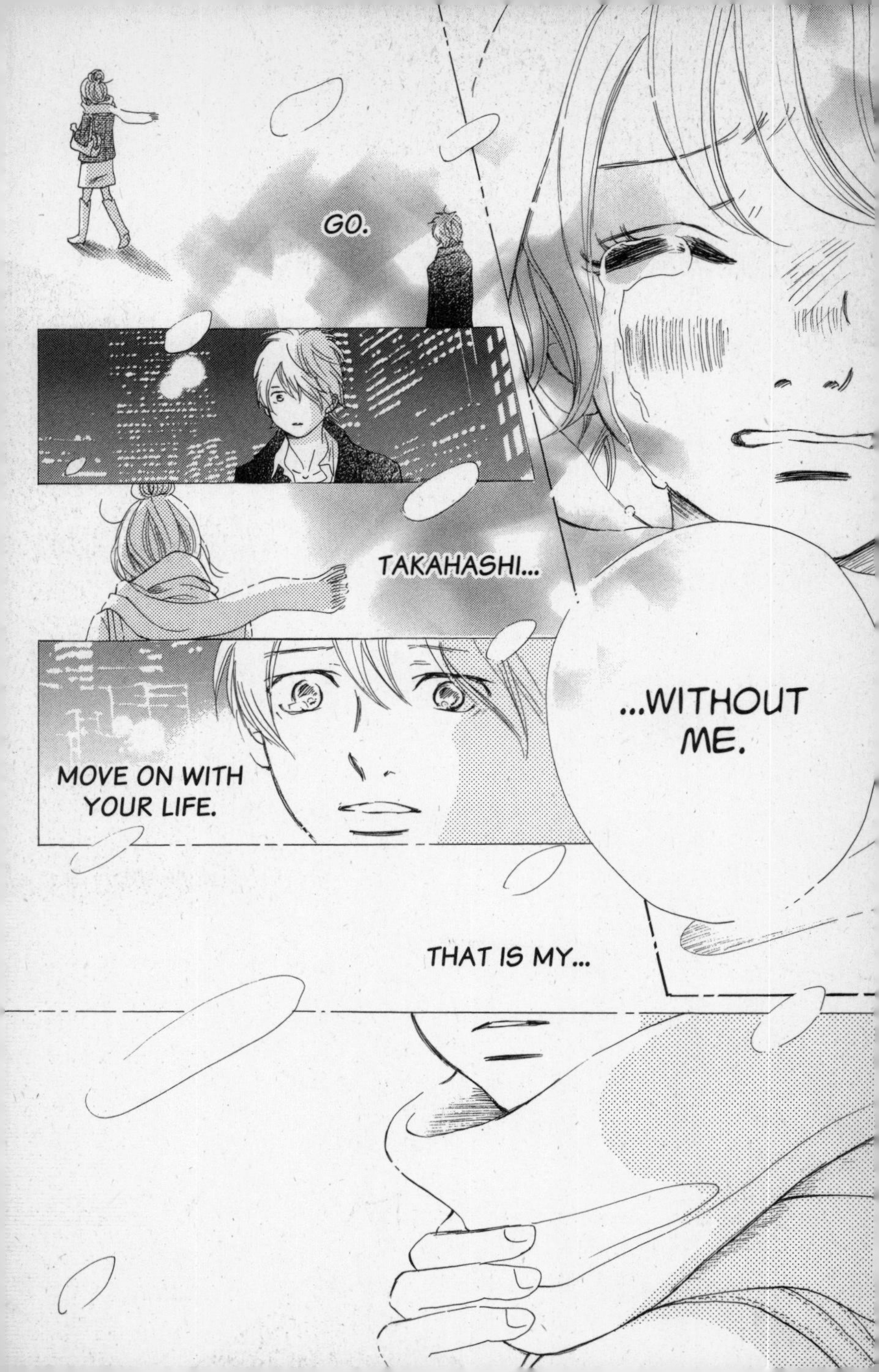
GO.
TAKAHASHI...
MOVE ON WITH YOUR LIFE.
...WITHOUT ME.
THAT IS MY...

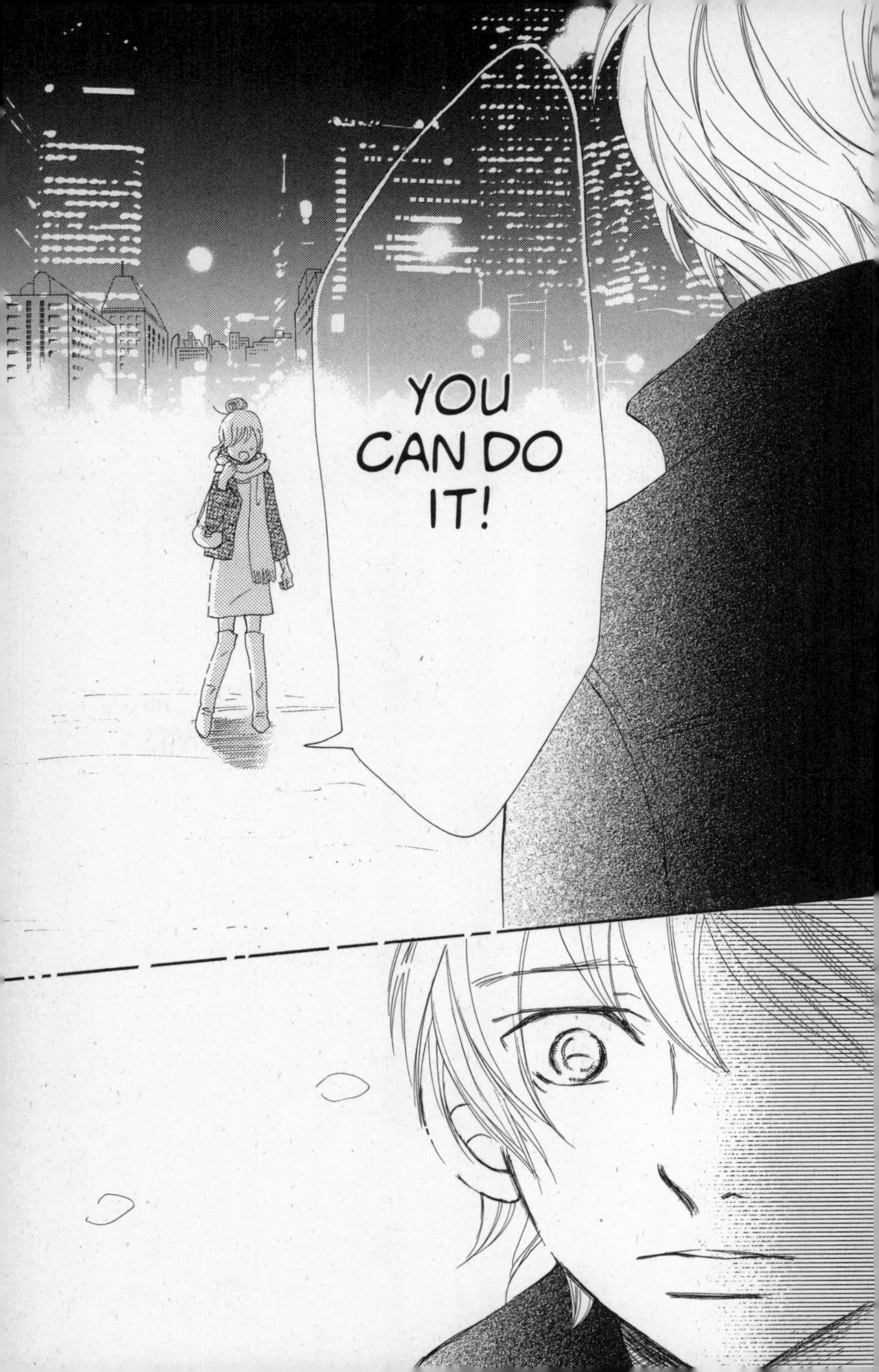
YOU CAN DO IT!

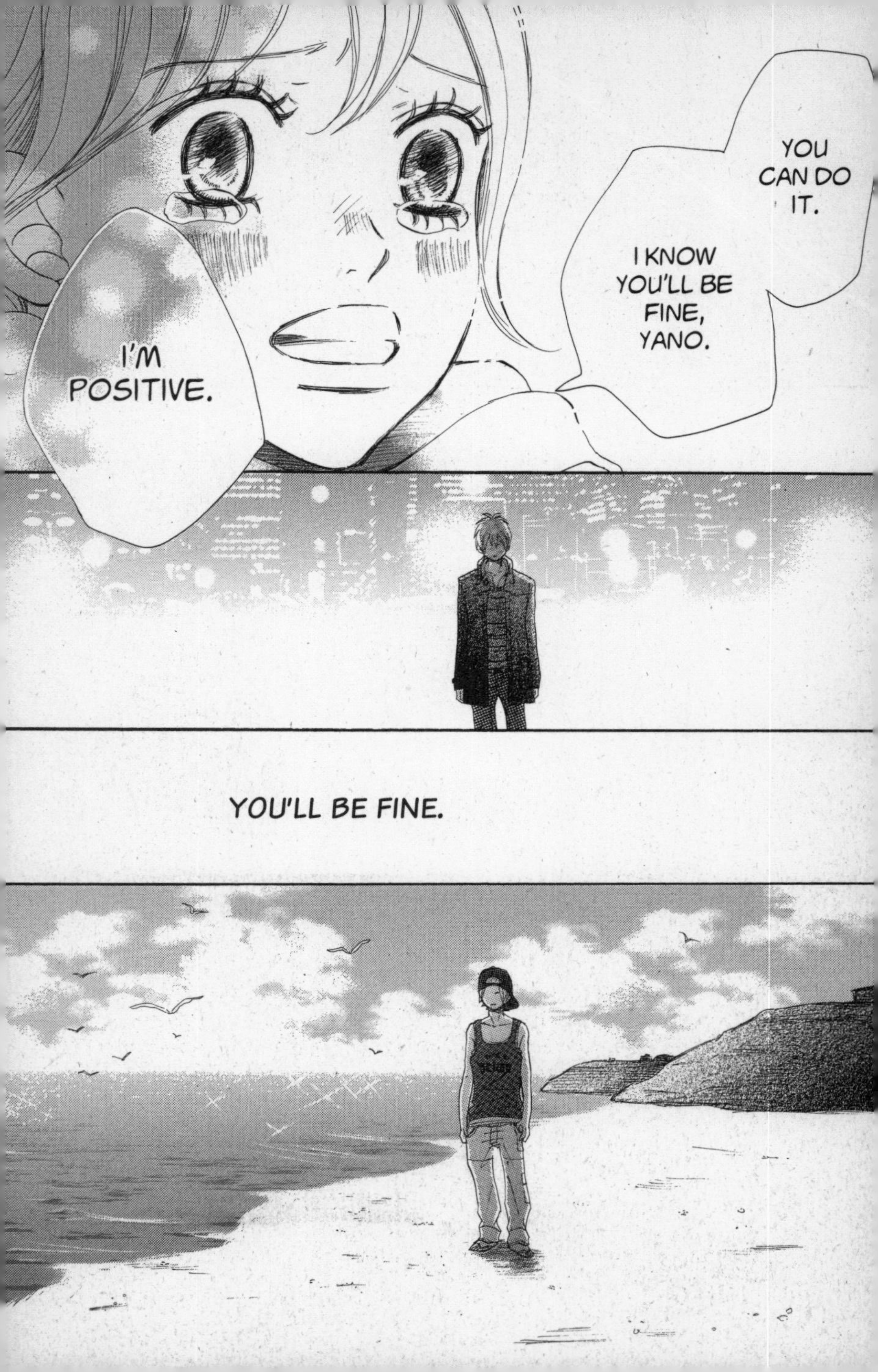
YOU CAN DO IT.
I KNOW YOU'LL BE FINE, YANO.
I'M POSITIVE.
YOU'LL BE FINE.

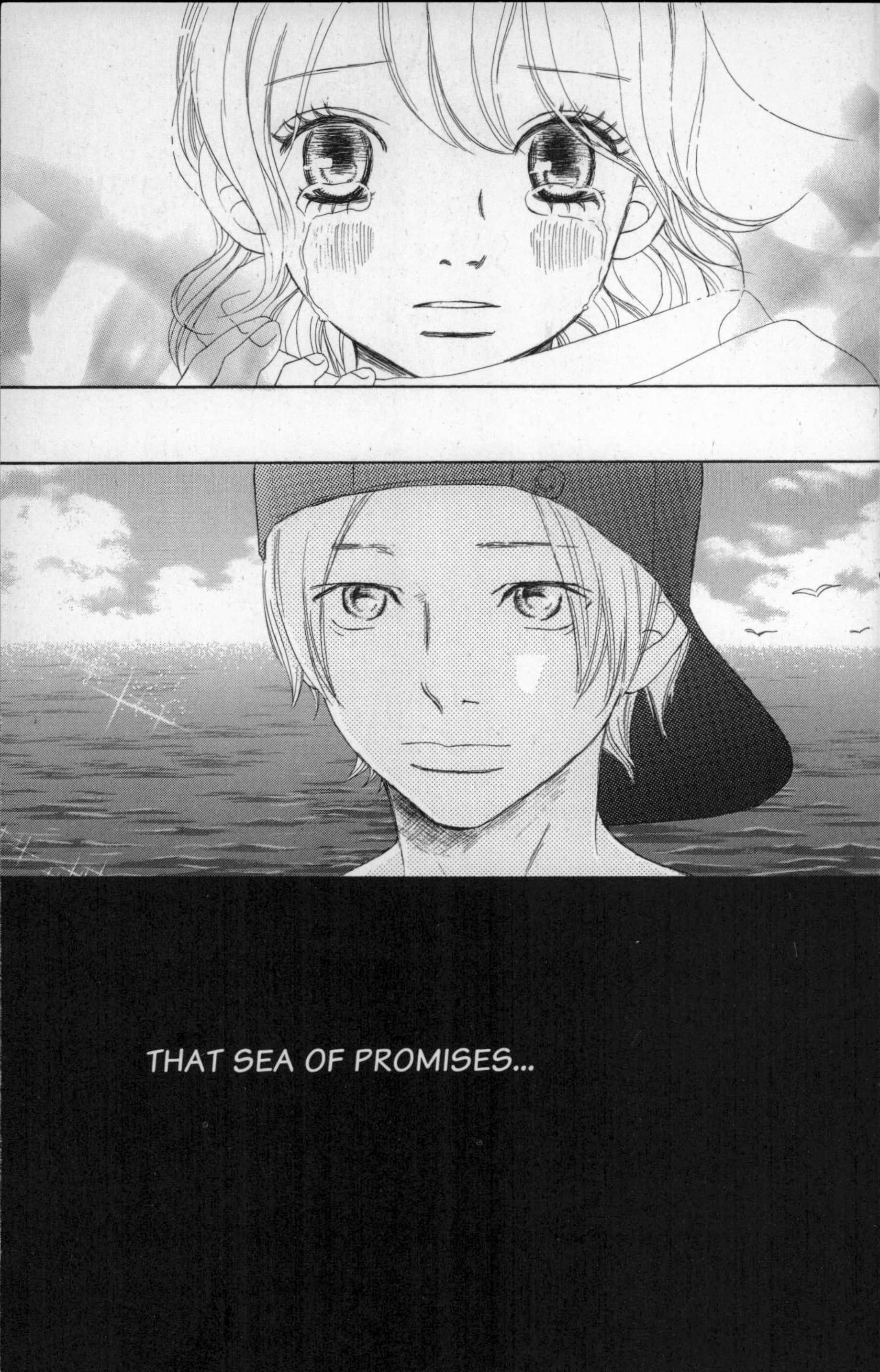
THAT SEA OF PROMISES...

YOU'RE RETURNING
THERE, AREN'T YOU?

NONE WILL BLAME YOU.

WE ALL LOVE YOU.

Chapter 58

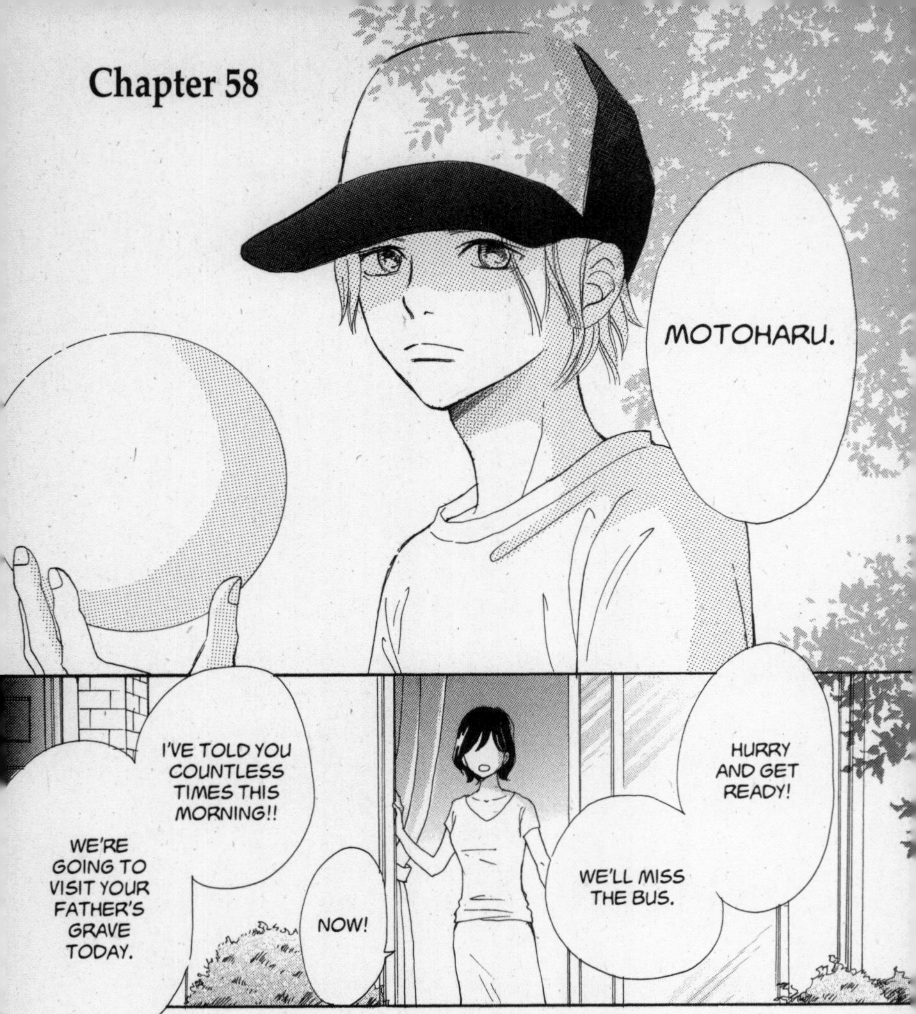
MOTOHARU.
HURRY AND GET READY!
WE'LL MISS THE BUS.
NOW!
I'VE TOLD YOU COUNTLESS TIMES THIS MORNING!!
WE'RE GOING TO VISIT YOUR FATHER'S GRAVE TODAY.

Chapter 58

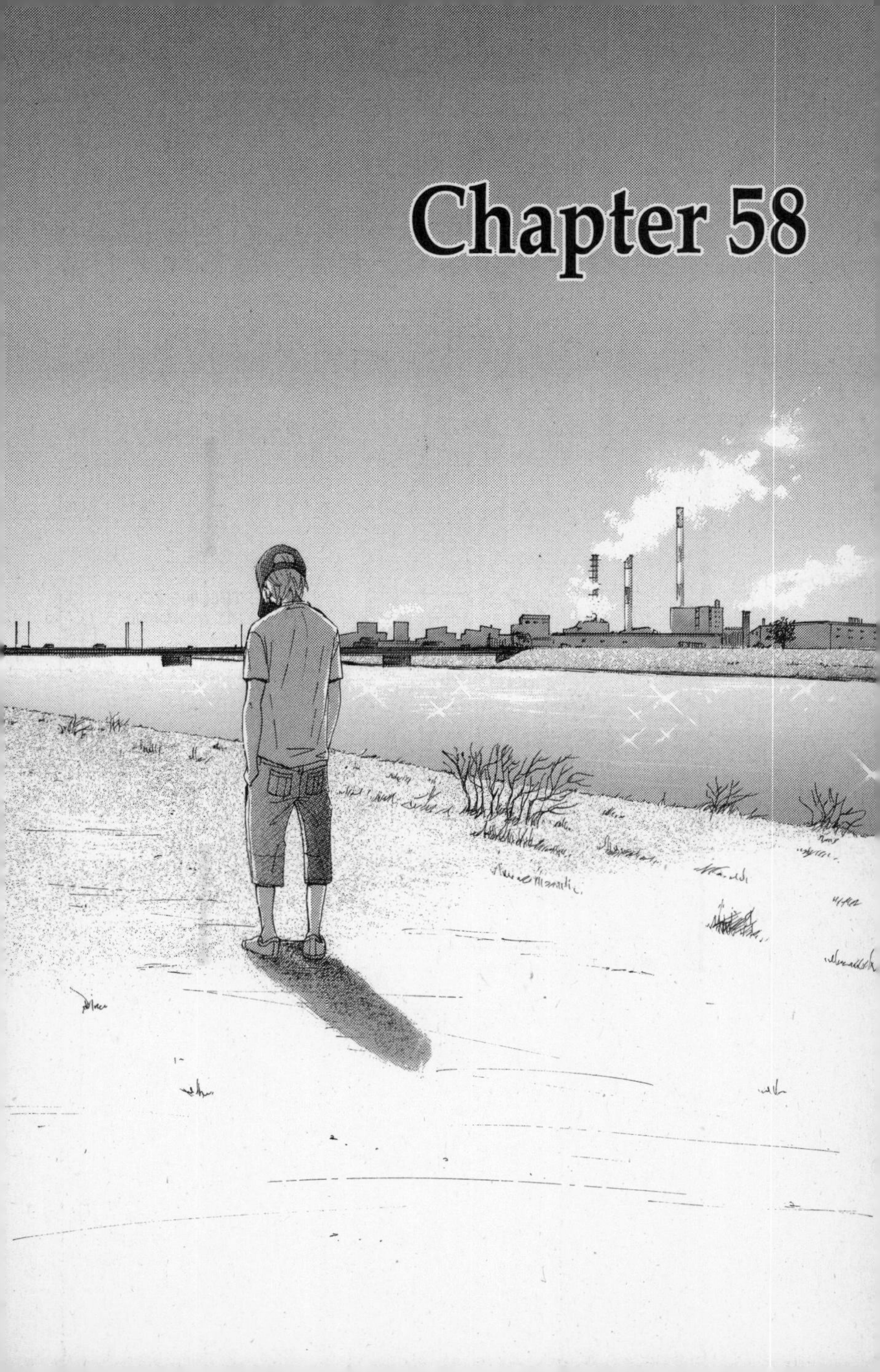

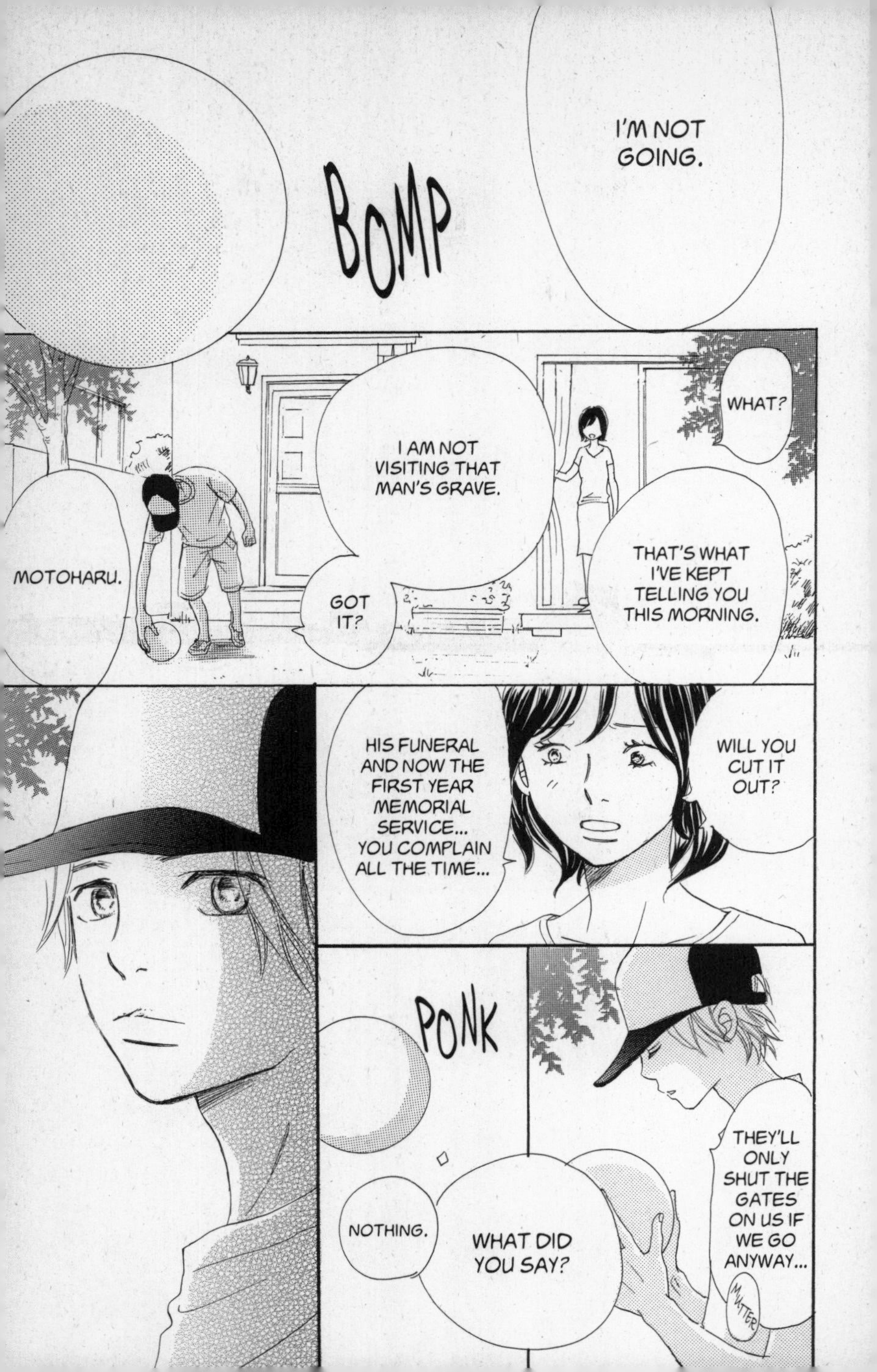
I'M NOT GOING.
BOMP
WHAT?
THAT'S WHAT I'VE KEPT TELLING YOU THIS MORNING.
I AM NOT VISITING THAT MAN'S GRAVE.
GOT IT?
MOTOHARU.
WILL YOU CUT IT OUT?
HIS FUNERAL AND NOW THE FIRST YEAR MEMORIAL SERVICE... YOU COMPLAIN ALL THE TIME...
THEY'LL ONLY SHUT THE GATES ON US IF WE GO ANYWAY...
MUTTER
WHAT DID YOU SAY?
PONK
NOTHING.

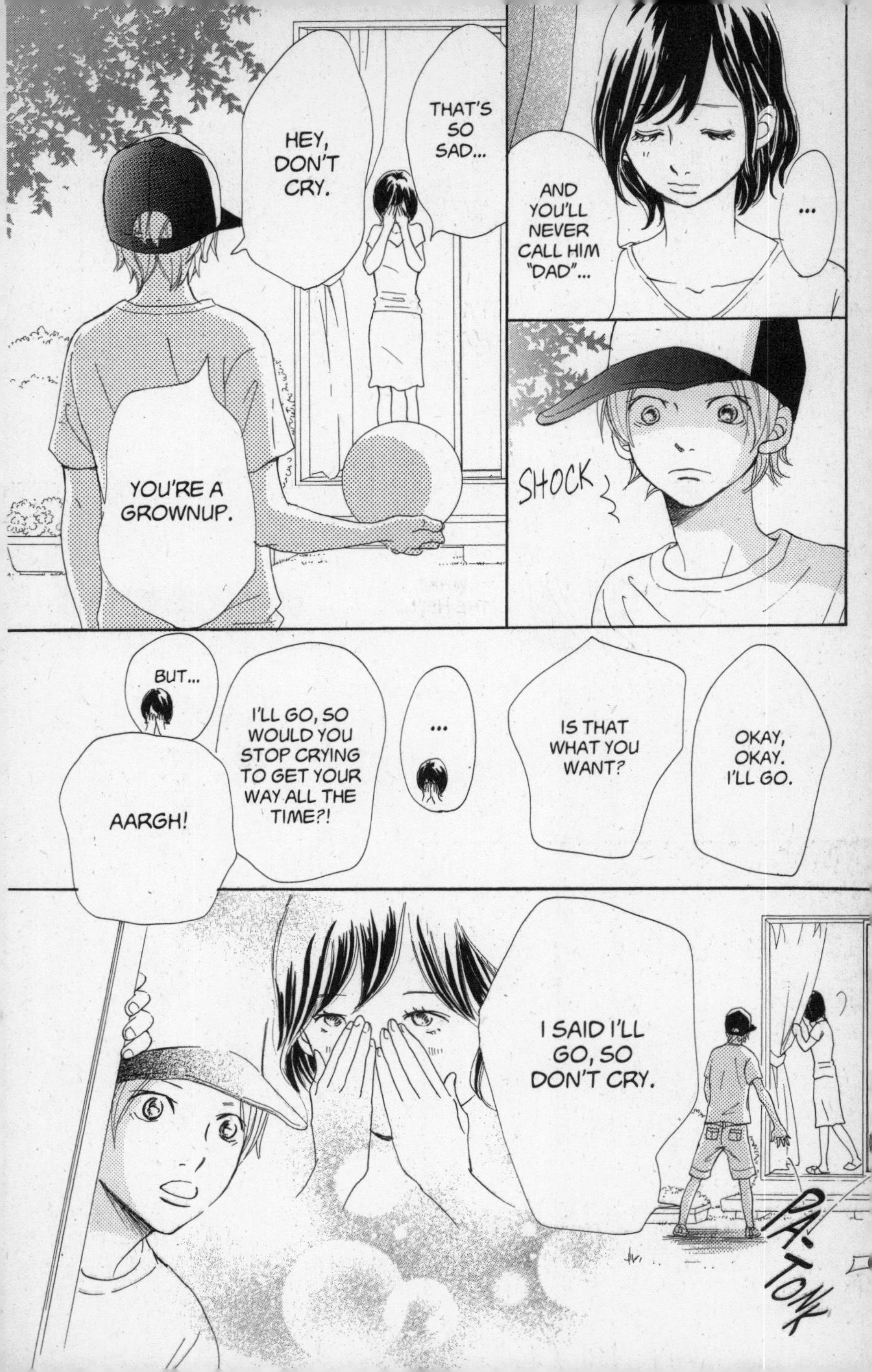
...
AND YOU'LL NEVER CALL HIM "DAD"...
SHOCK
THAT'S SO SAD...
HEY, DON'T CRY.
YOU'RE A GROWNUP.
OKAY, OKAY. I'LL GO.
IS THAT WHAT YOU WANT?
...
I'LL GO, SO WOULD YOU STOP CRYING TO GET YOUR WAY ALL THE TIME?!
BUT...
AARGH!
PA-TONK
I SAID I'LL GO, SO DON'T CRY.

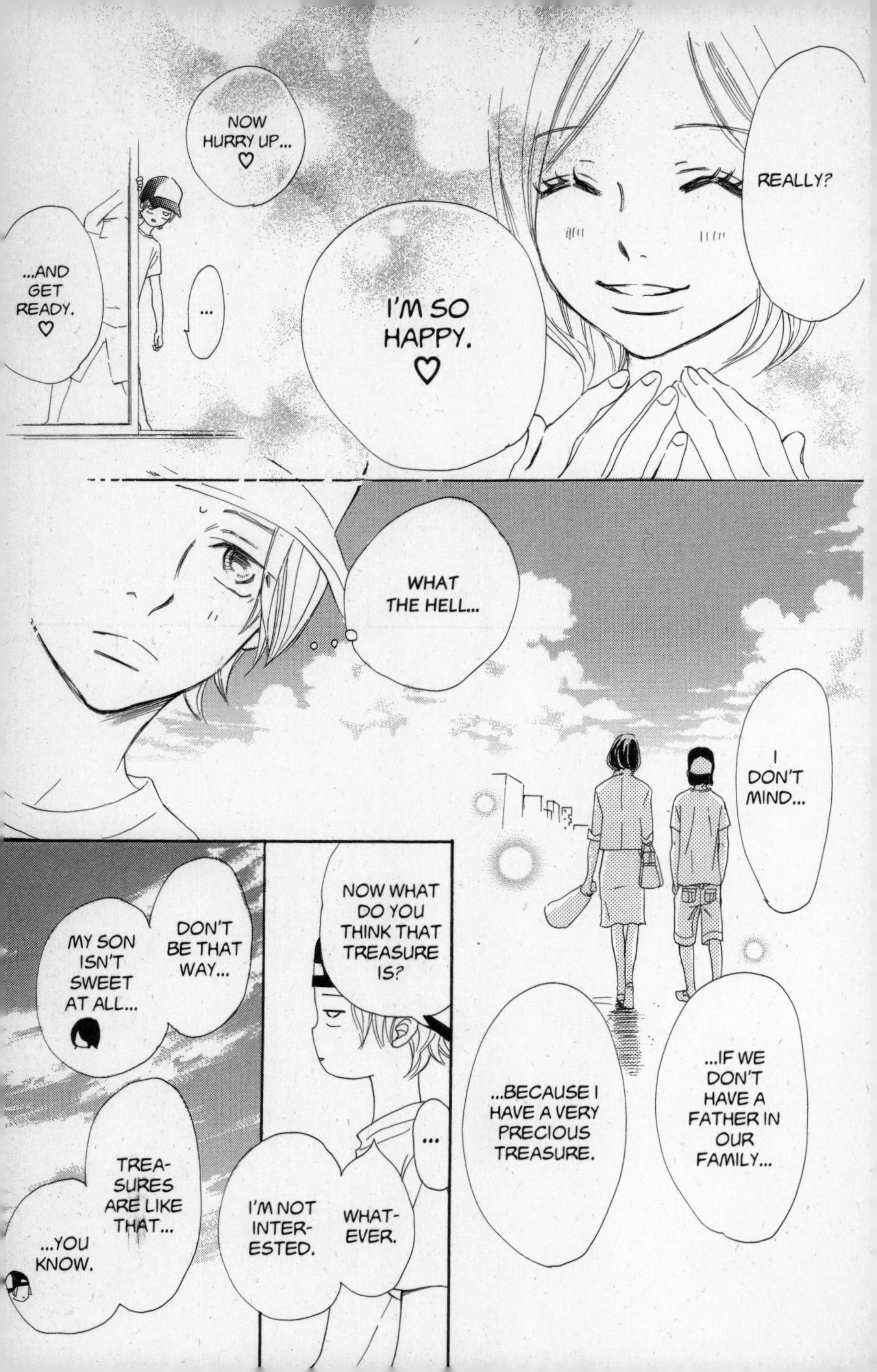
REALLY?
I'M SO HAPPY. ♡
NOW HURRY UP... ♡
...
...AND GET READY. ♡
I DON'T MIND...
...IF WE DON'T HAVE A FATHER IN OUR FAMILY...
...BECAUSE I HAVE A VERY PRECIOUS TREASURE.
WHAT THE HELL...
NOW WHAT DO YOU THINK THAT TREASURE IS?
...
WHAT-EVER.
I'M NOT INTER-ESTED.
DON'T BE THAT WAY...
MY SON ISN'T SWEET AT ALL...
TREA-SURES ARE LIKE THAT...
...YOU KNOW.

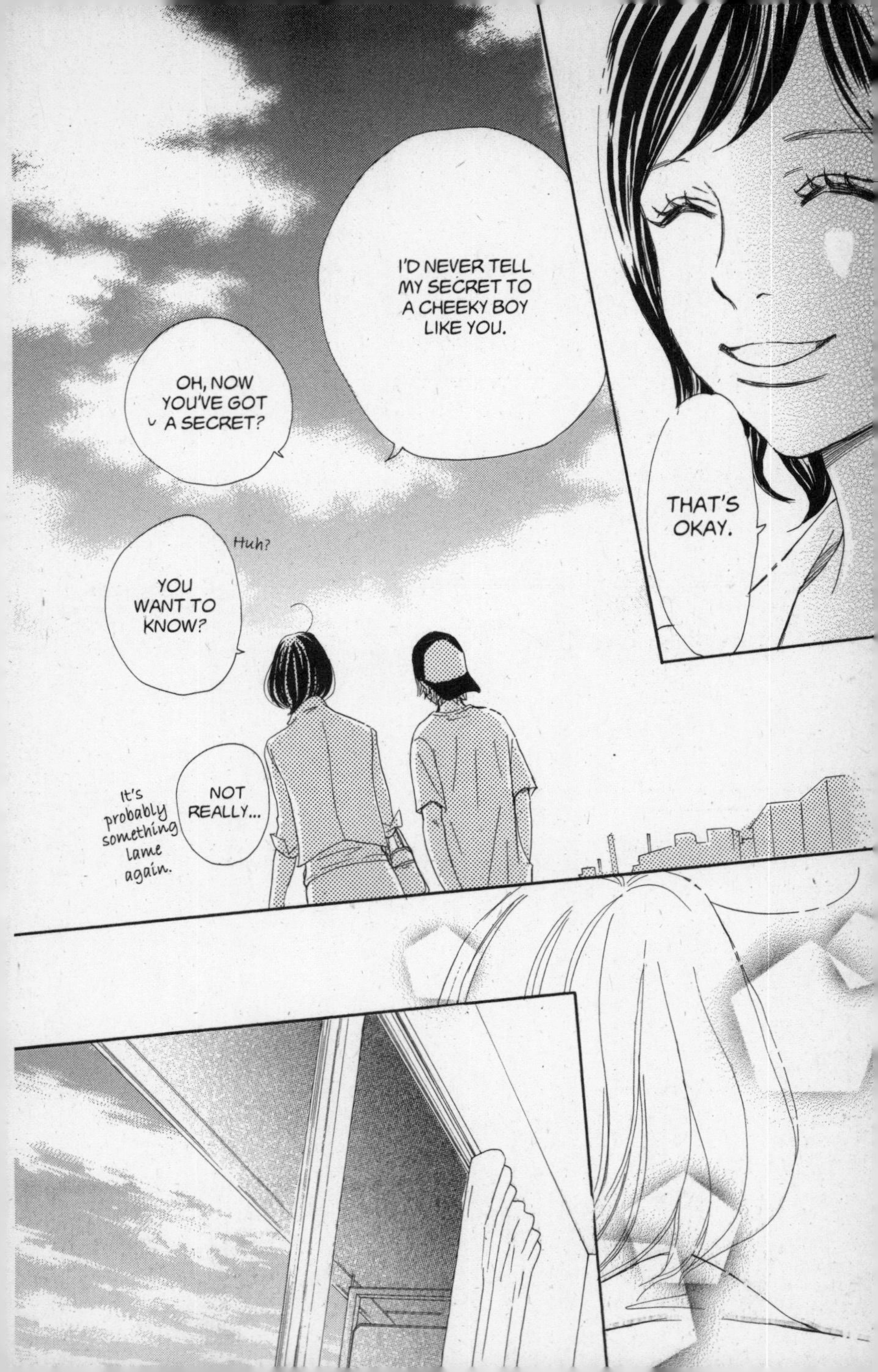
THAT'S OKAY.
I'D NEVER TELL MY SECRET TO A CHEEKY BOY LIKE YOU.
OH, NOW YOU'VE GOT A SECRET?
Huh?
YOU WANT TO KNOW?
NOT REALLY...
It's probably something lame again.

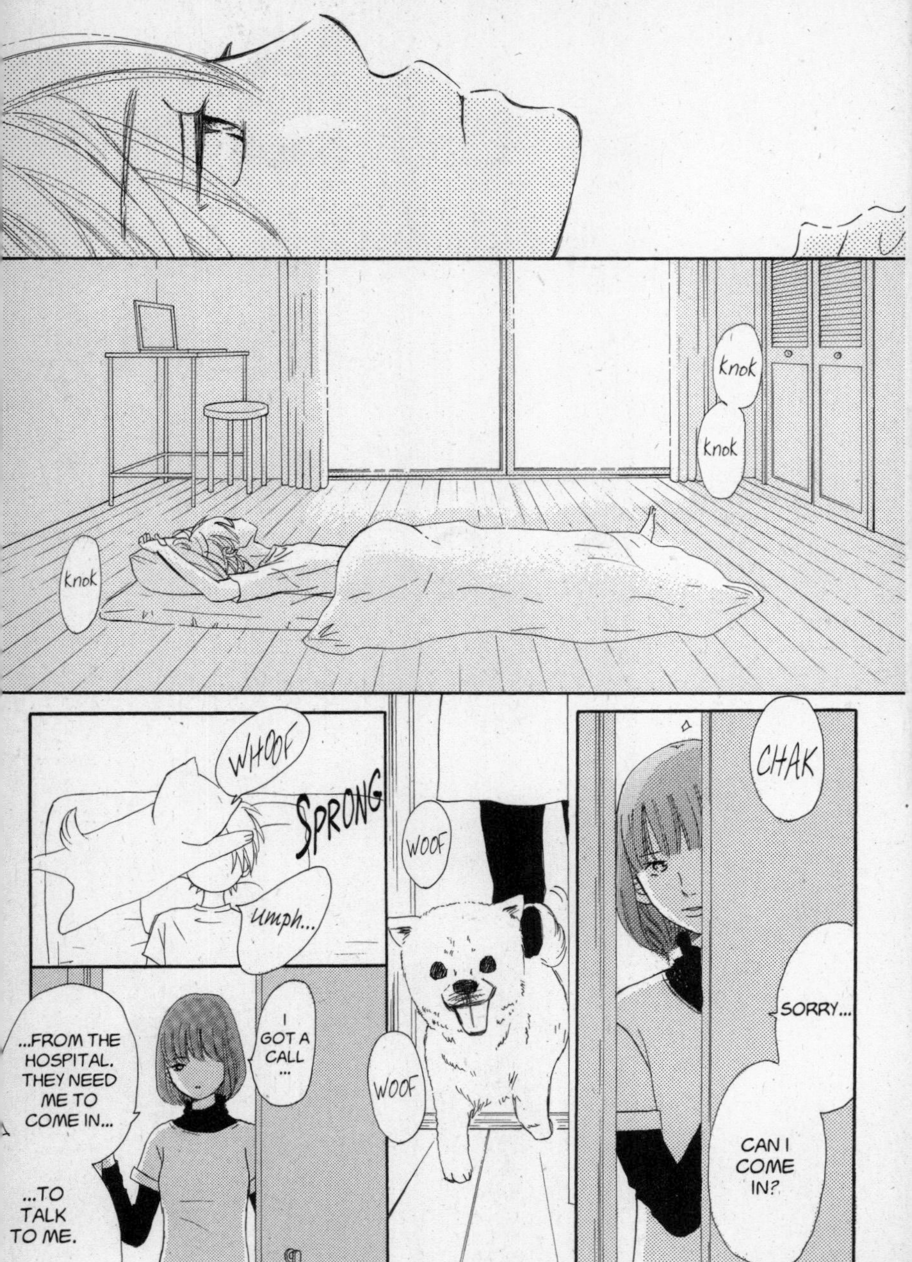
knok
knok
knok
CHAK
SORRY...
CAN I COME IN?
WOOF
WOOF
WHOOF
SPRONG
umph...
I GOT A CALL ...
...FROM THE HOSPITAL. THEY NEED ME TO COME IN...
...TO TALK TO ME.

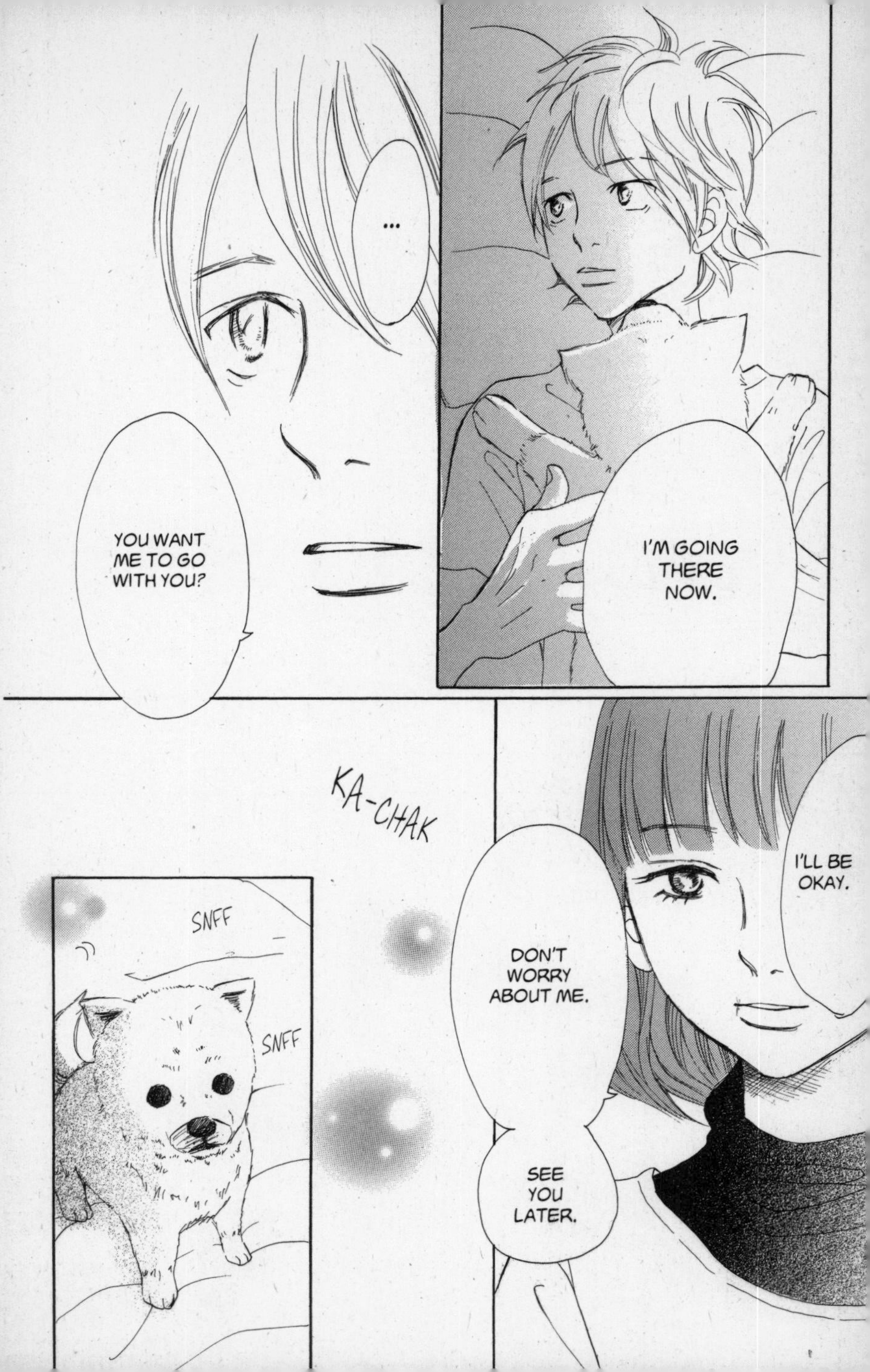
I'M GOING THERE NOW.
...
YOU WANT ME TO GO WITH YOU?
I'LL BE OKAY.
DON'T WORRY ABOUT ME.
SEE YOU LATER.
KA-CHAK
SNFF
SNFF

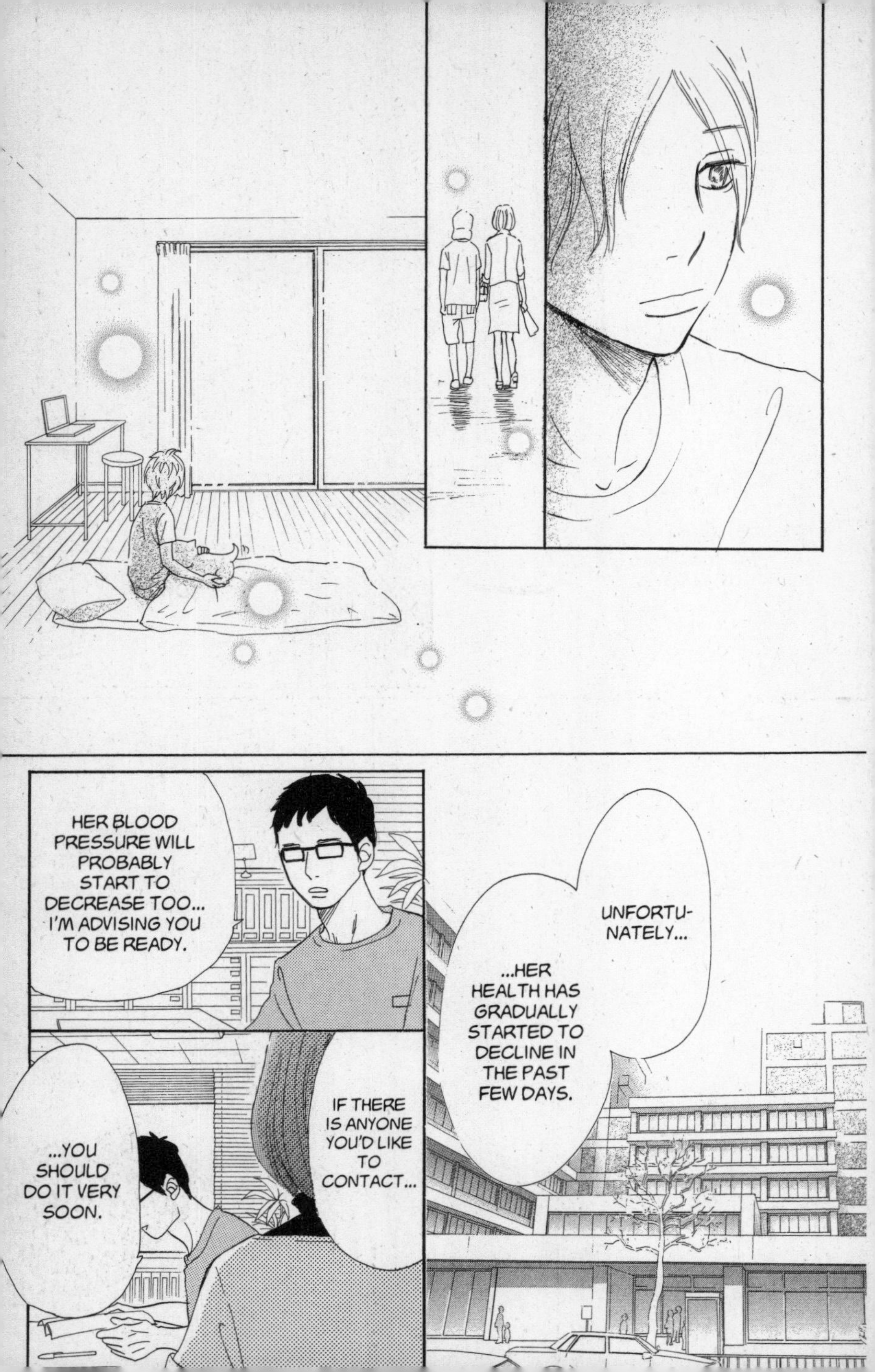
UNFORTU-NATELY...
...HER HEALTH HAS GRADUALLY STARTED TO DECLINE IN THE PAST FEW DAYS.
HER BLOOD PRESSURE WILL PROBABLY START TO DECREASE TOO... I'M ADVISING YOU TO BE READY.
IF THERE IS ANYONE YOU'D LIKE TO CONTACT...
...YOU SHOULD DO IT VERY SOON.

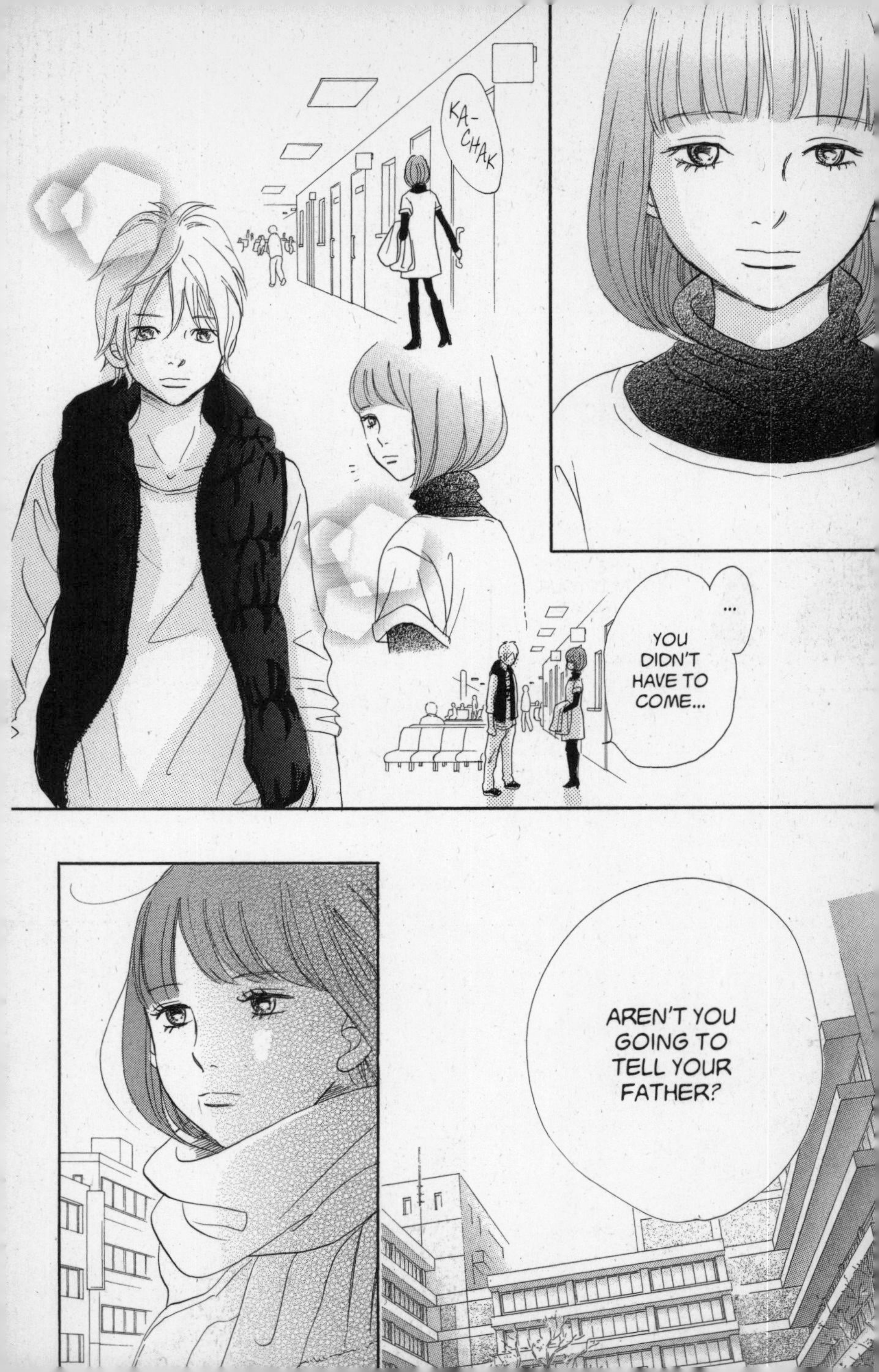
KA-CHAK
...
YOU DIDN'T HAVE TO COME...
AREN'T YOU GOING TO TELL YOUR FATHER?

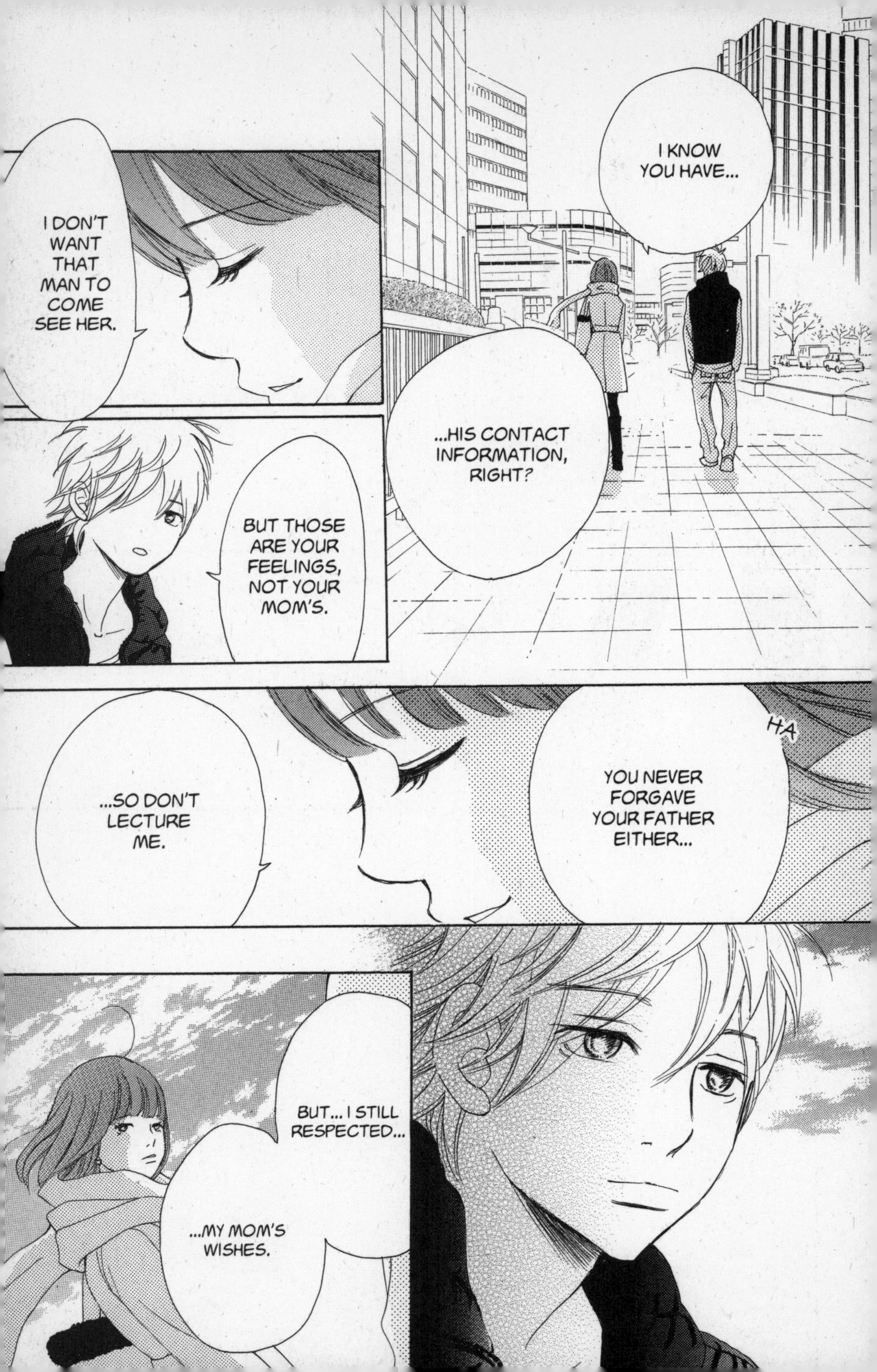
I KNOW YOU HAVE...
...HIS CONTACT INFORMATION, RIGHT?
I DON'T WANT THAT MAN TO COME SEE HER.
BUT THOSE ARE YOUR FEELINGS, NOT YOUR MOM'S.
HA
YOU NEVER FORGAVE YOUR FATHER EITHER...
...SO DON'T LECTURE ME.
BUT... I STILL RESPECTED...
...MY MOM'S WISHES.

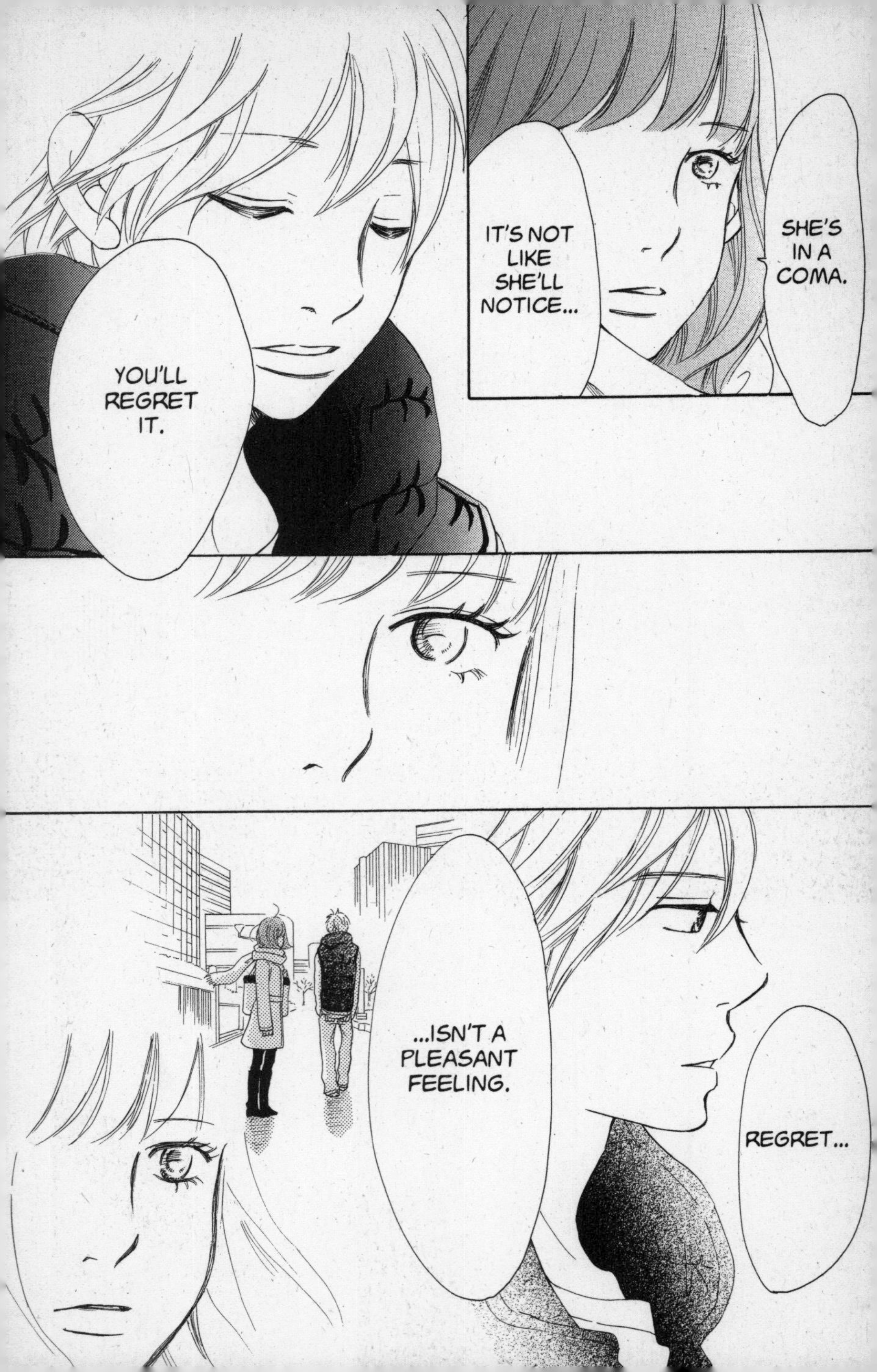
SHE'S IN A COMA.
IT'S NOT LIKE SHE'LL NOTICE...
YOU'LL REGRET IT.
REGRET...
...ISN'T A PLEASANT FEELING.

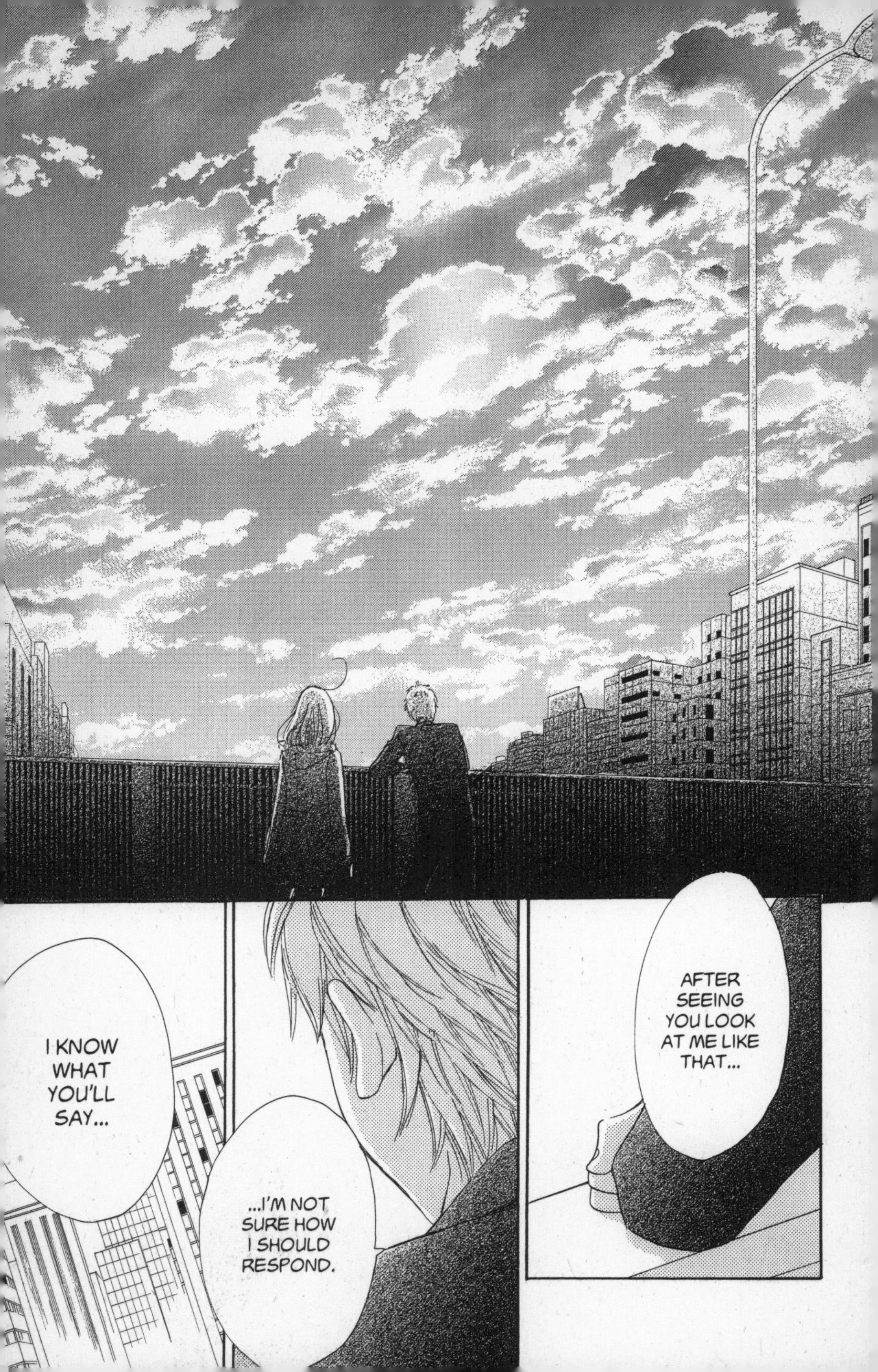
AFTER SEEING YOU LOOK AT ME LIKE THAT...
...I'M NOT SURE HOW I SHOULD RESPOND.
I KNOW WHAT YOU'LL SAY...

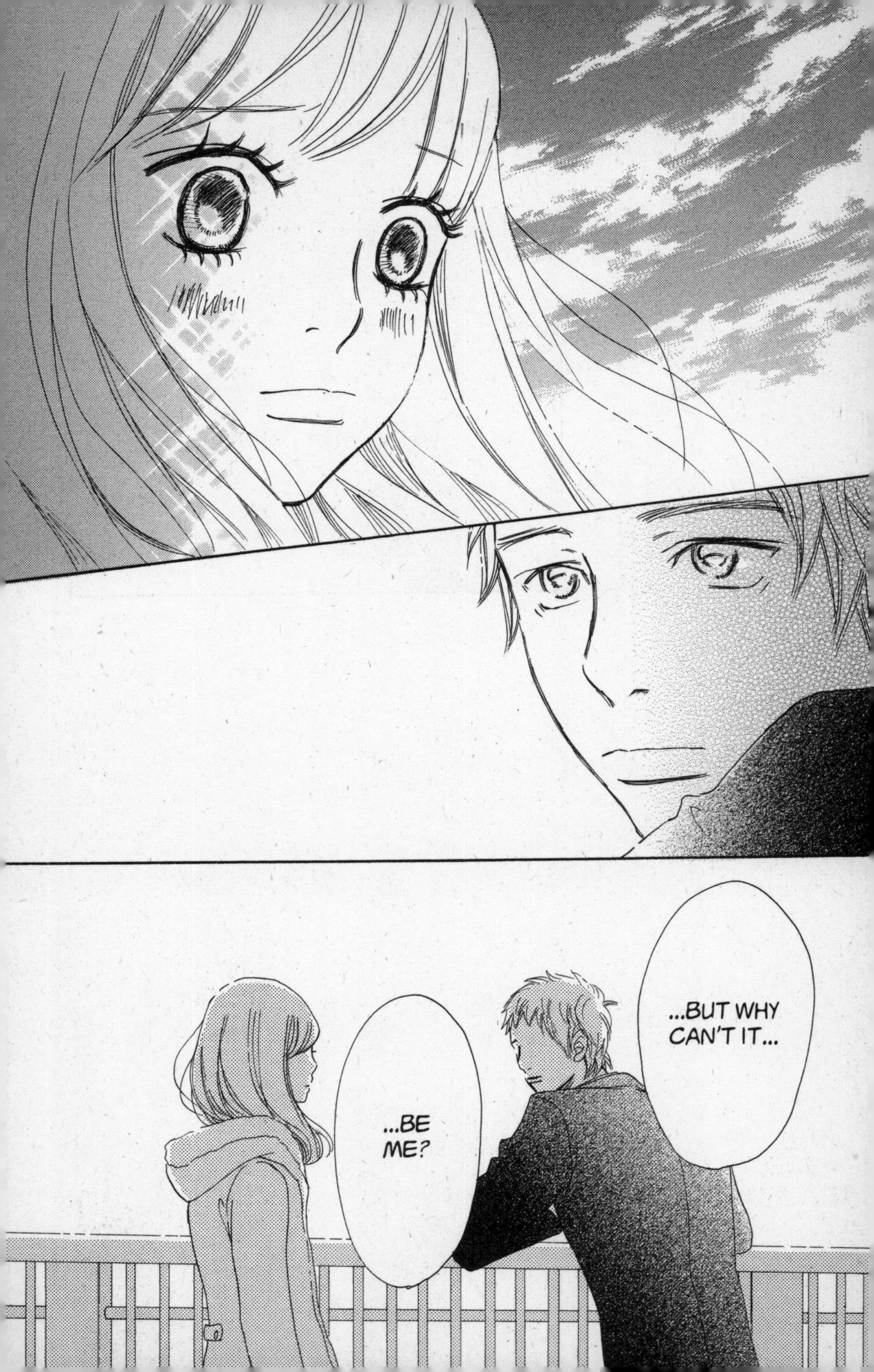
...BUT WHY CAN'T IT...
...BE ME?

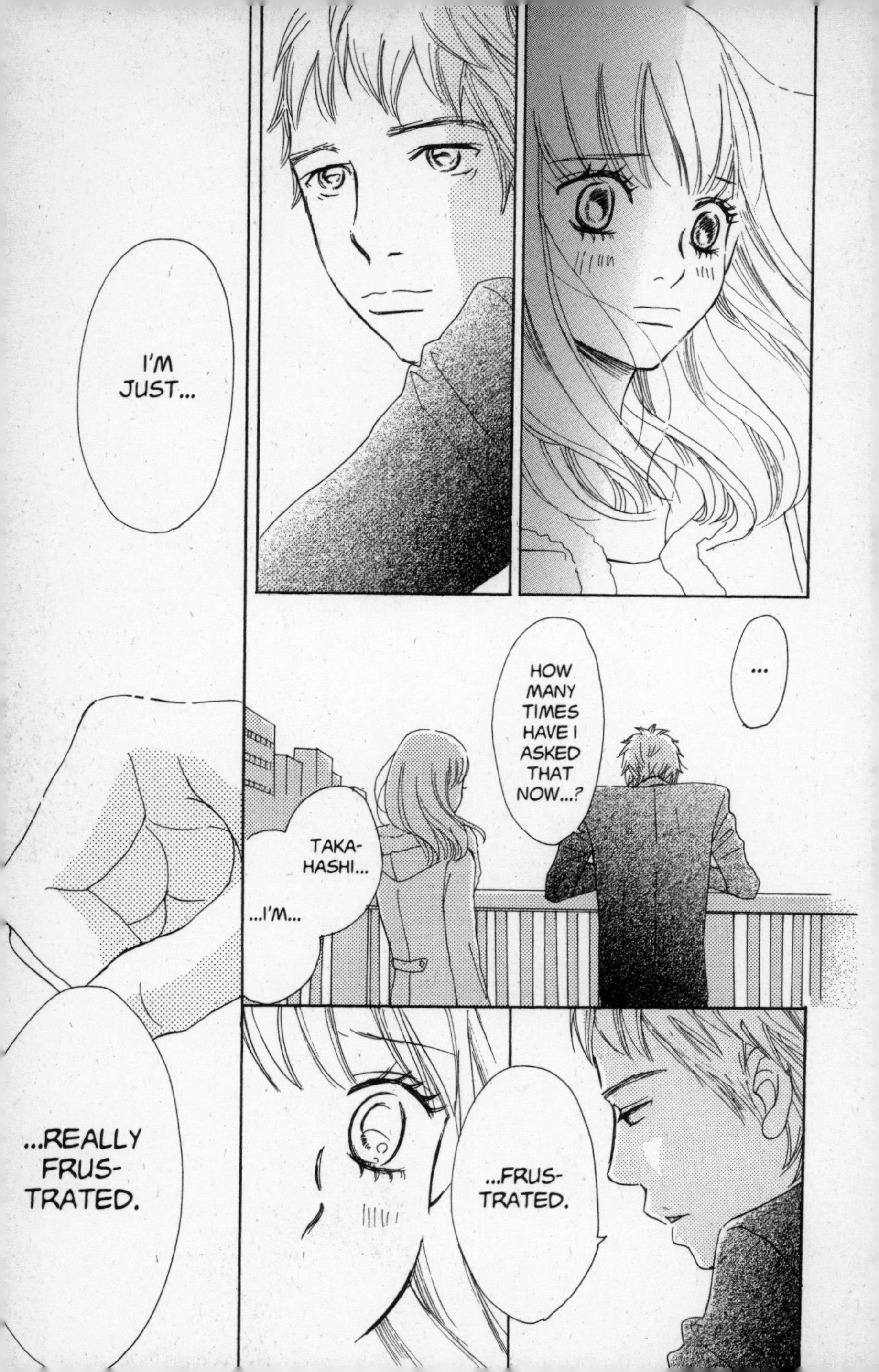
...
HOW MANY TIMES HAVE I ASKED THAT NOW...?
TAKA-HASHI...
...I'M...
...FRUS-TRATED.
I'M JUST...
...REALLY FRUS-TRATED.

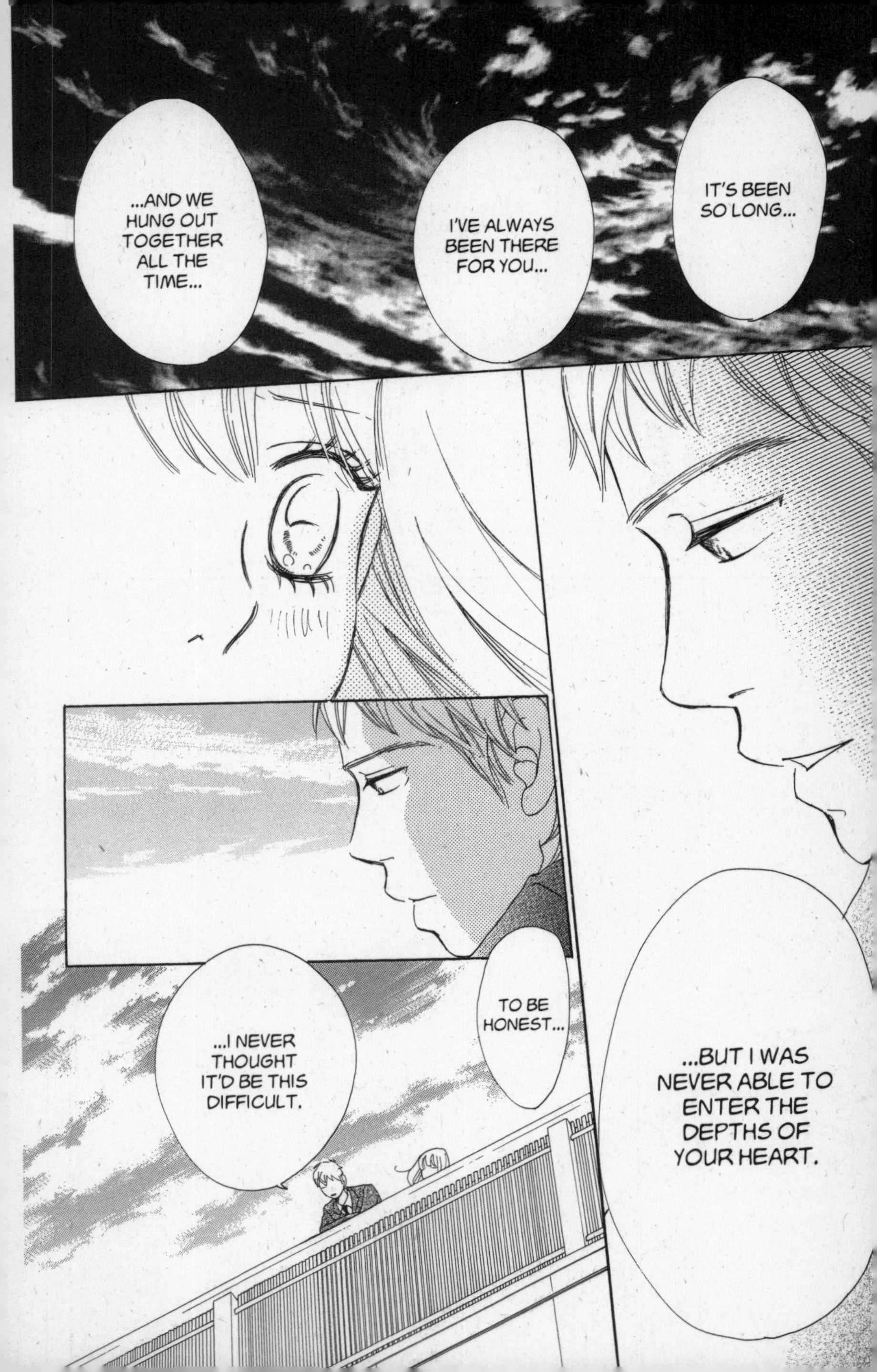
IT'S BEEN SO LONG...
I'VE ALWAYS BEEN THERE FOR YOU...
...AND WE HUNG OUT TOGETHER ALL THE TIME...
...BUT I WAS NEVER ABLE TO ENTER THE DEPTHS OF YOUR HEART.
TO BE HONEST...
...I NEVER THOUGHT IT'D BE THIS DIFFICULT.

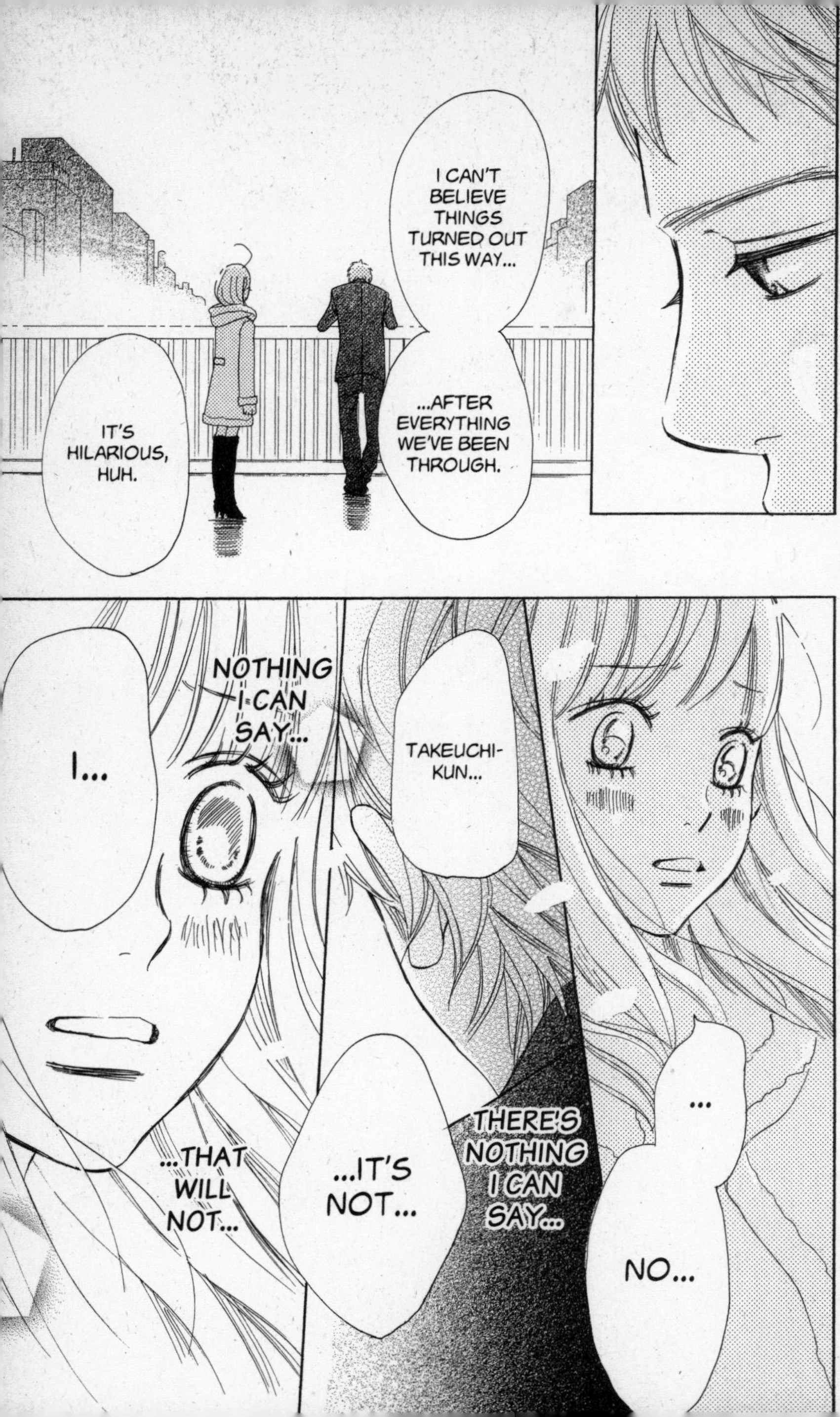
I CAN'T BELIEVE THINGS TURNED OUT THIS WAY...
...AFTER EVERYTHING WE'VE BEEN THROUGH.
IT'S HILARIOUS, HUH.
...
THERE'S NOTHING I CAN SAY...
NO...
TAKEUCHI-KUN...
...IT'S NOT...
NOTHING I CAN SAY...
I...
...THAT WILL NOT...

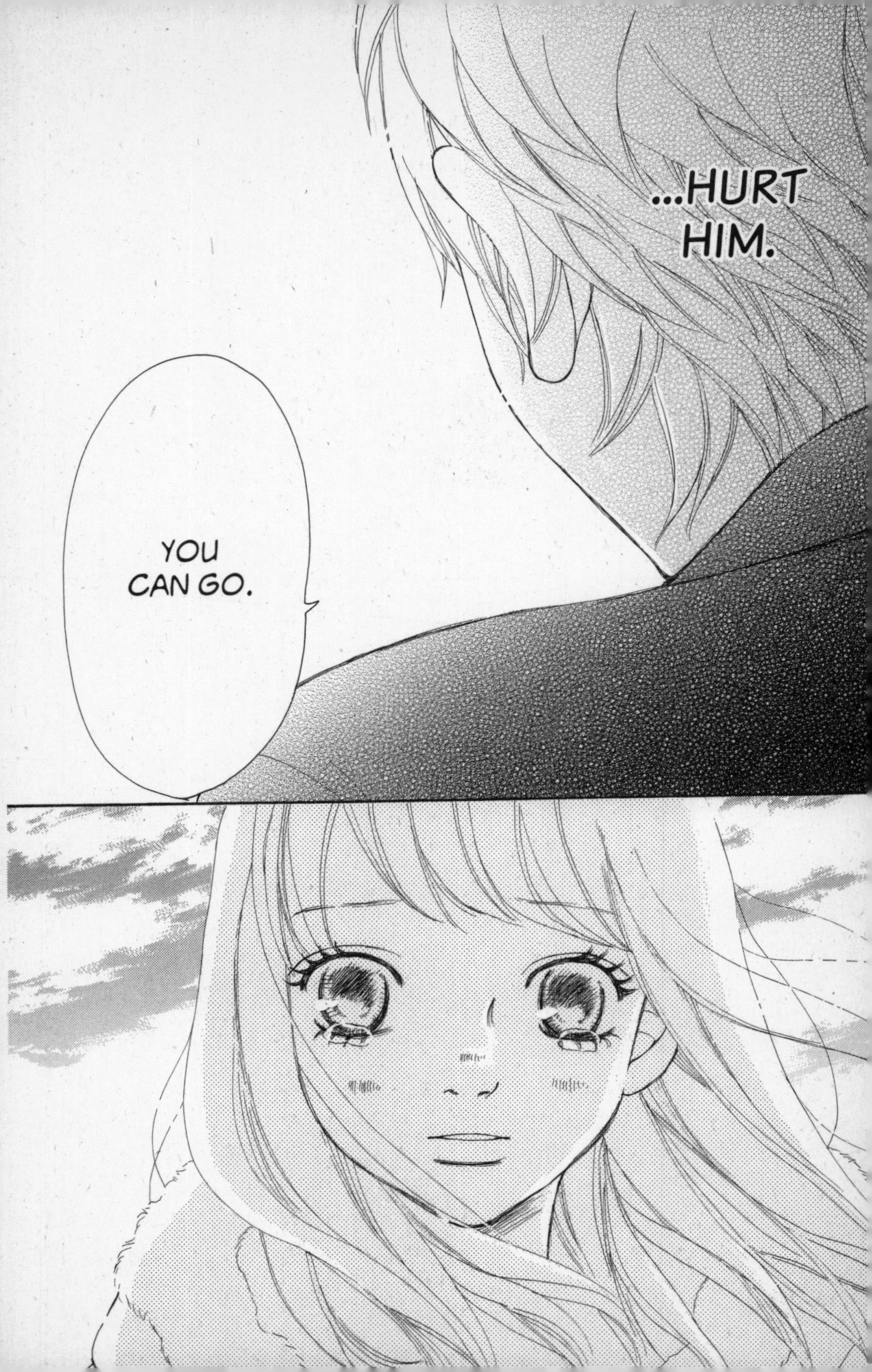
...HURT HIM.
YOU CAN GO.

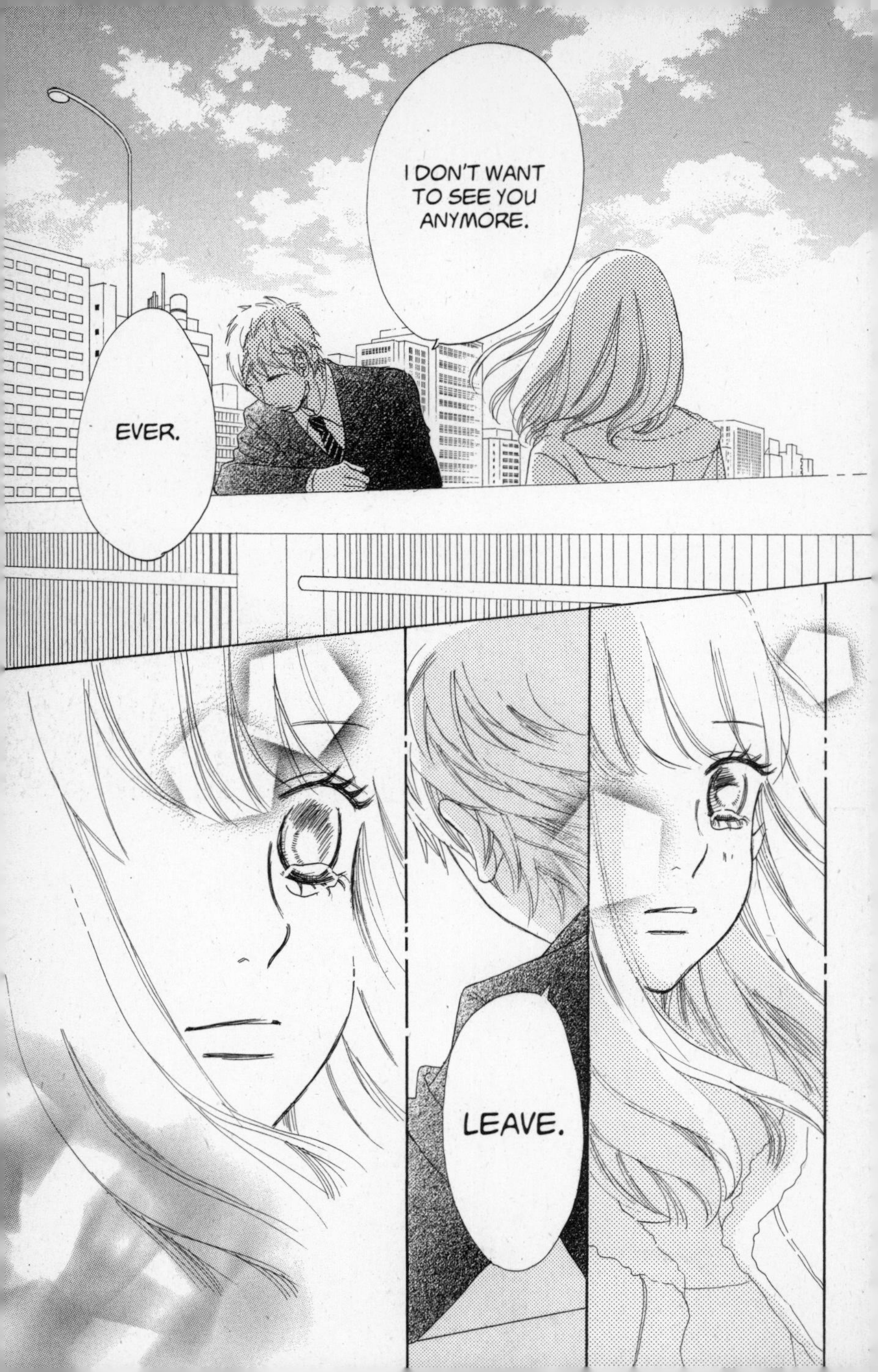
I DON'T WANT TO SEE YOU ANYMORE.
EVER.
LEAVE.

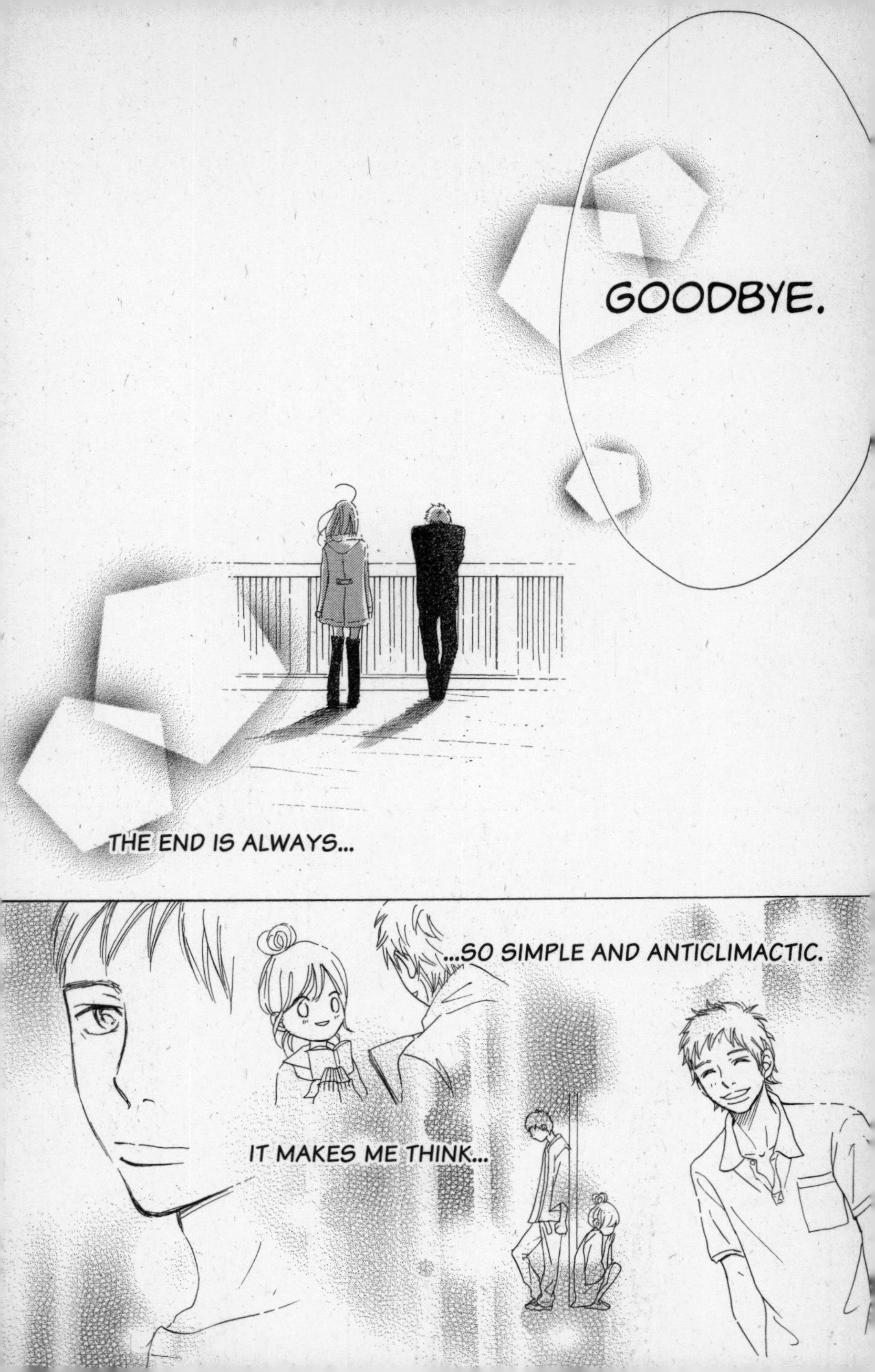
GOODBYE.
THE END IS ALWAYS...
...SO SIMPLE AND ANTICLIMACTIC.
IT MAKES ME THINK...

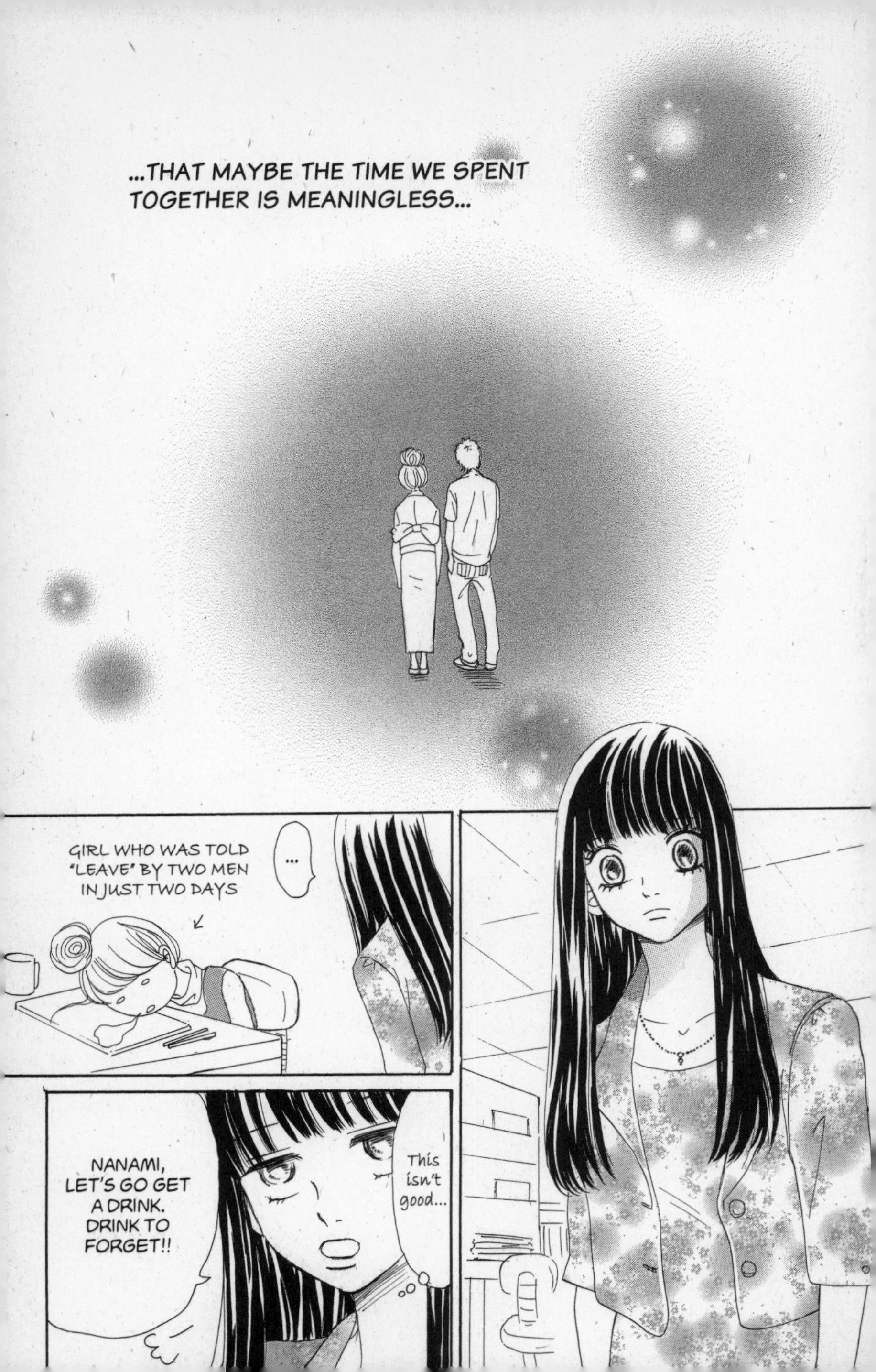
...THAT MAYBE THE TIME WE SPENT TOGETHER IS MEANINGLESS...
...
GIRL WHO WAS TOLD "LEAVE" BY TWO MEN IN JUST TWO DAYS
This isn't good...
NANAMI, LET'S GO GET A DRINK. DRINK TO FORGET!!

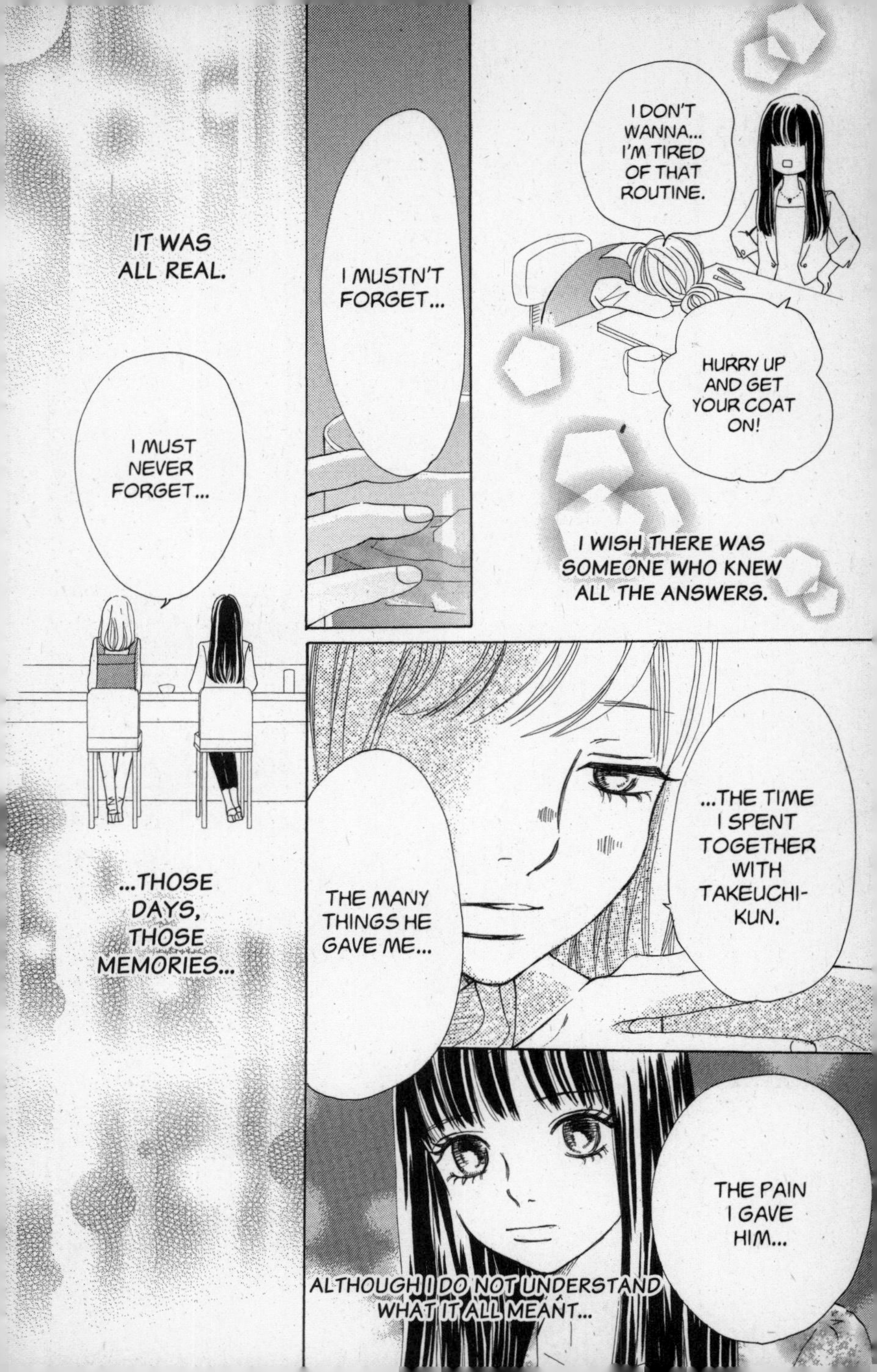
I DON'T WANNA... I'M TIRED OF THAT ROUTINE.
HURRY UP AND GET YOUR COAT ON!
I WISH THERE WAS SOMEONE WHO KNEW ALL THE ANSWERS.
I MUSTN'T FORGET...
...THE TIME I SPENT TOGETHER WITH TAKEUCHI-KUN.
THE MANY THINGS HE GAVE ME...
THE PAIN I GAVE HIM...
ALTHOUGH I DO NOT UNDERSTAND WHAT IT ALL MEANT...
IT WAS ALL REAL.
I MUST NEVER FORGET...
...THOSE DAYS, THOSE MEMORIES...

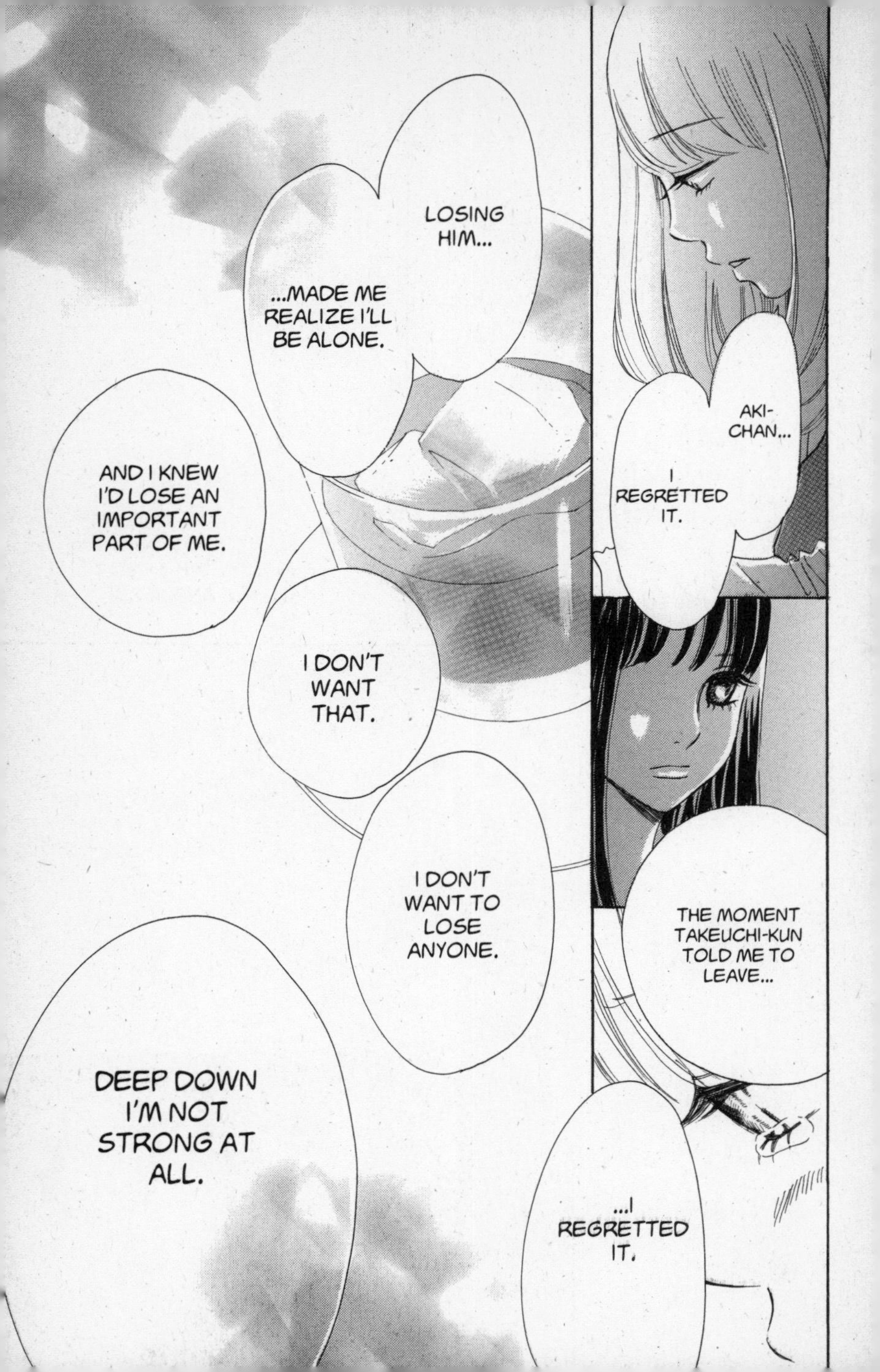
AKI-CHAN...
I REGRETTED IT.
THE MOMENT TAKEUCHI-KUN TOLD ME TO LEAVE...
...I REGRETTED IT.
LOSING HIM...
...MADE ME REALIZE I'LL BE ALONE.
AND I KNEW I'D LOSE AN IMPORTANT PART OF ME.
I DON'T WANT THAT.
I DON'T WANT TO LOSE ANYONE.
DEEP DOWN I'M NOT STRONG AT ALL.

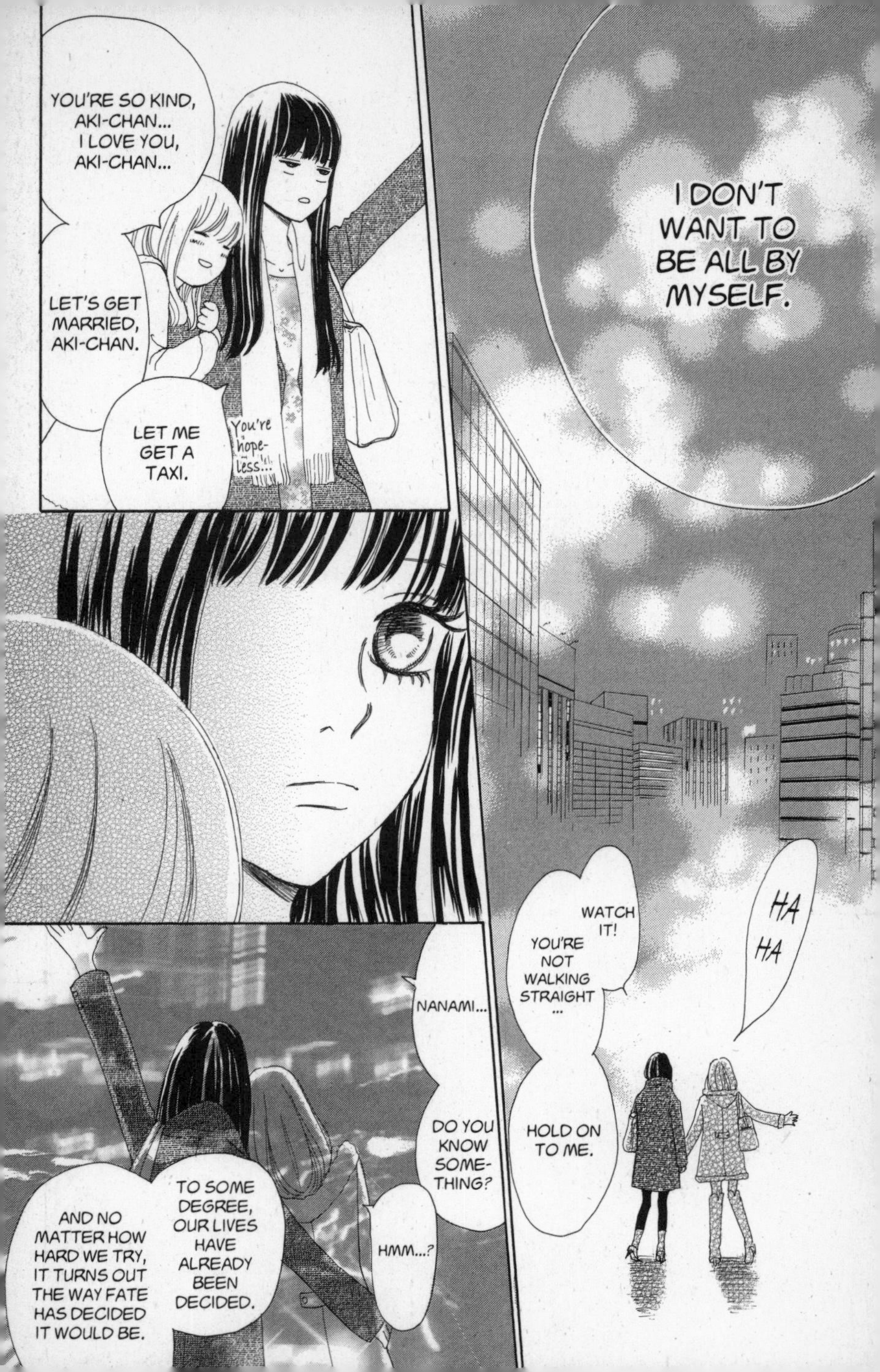
I DON'T WANT TO BE ALL BY MYSELF.
HA HA
WATCH IT! YOU'RE NOT WALKING STRAIGHT ...
HOLD ON TO ME.
YOU'RE SO KIND, AKI-CHAN... I LOVE YOU, AKI-CHAN...
LET'S GET MARRIED, AKI-CHAN.
You're hopeless...
LET ME GET A TAXI.
NANAMI...
DO YOU KNOW SOMETHING?
HMM...?
TO SOME DEGREE, OUR LIVES HAVE ALREADY BEEN DECIDED.
AND NO MATTER HOW HARD WE TRY, IT TURNS OUT THE WAY FATE HAS DECIDED IT WOULD BE.

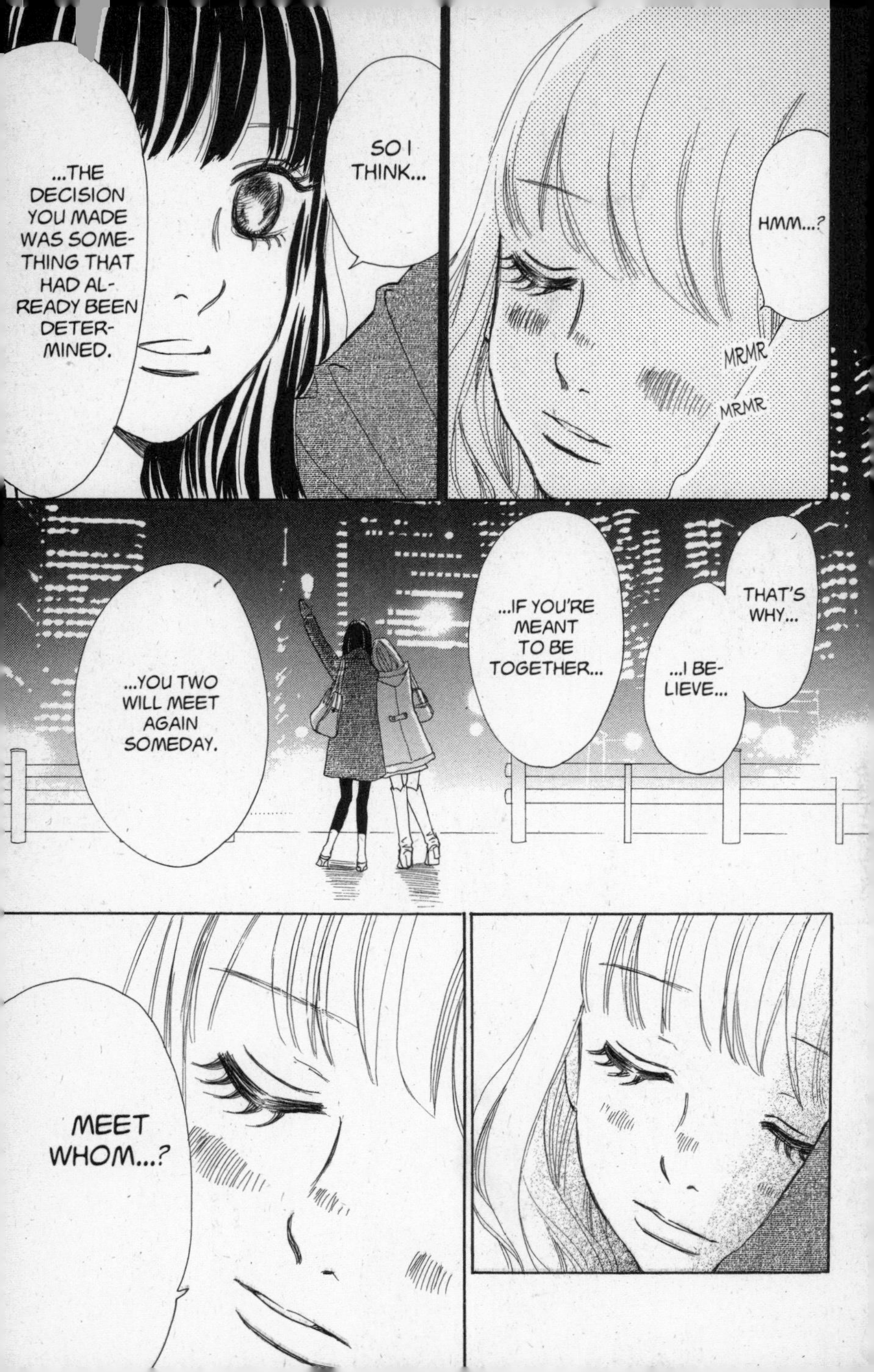
HMM...?
MRMR
MRMR
SO I THINK...
...THE DECISION YOU MADE WAS SOME-THING THAT HAD AL-READY BEEN DETER-MINED.
THAT'S WHY...
...I BE-LIEVE...
...IF YOU'RE MEANT TO BE TOGETHER...
...YOU TWO WILL MEET AGAIN SOMEDAY.
MEET WHOM...?

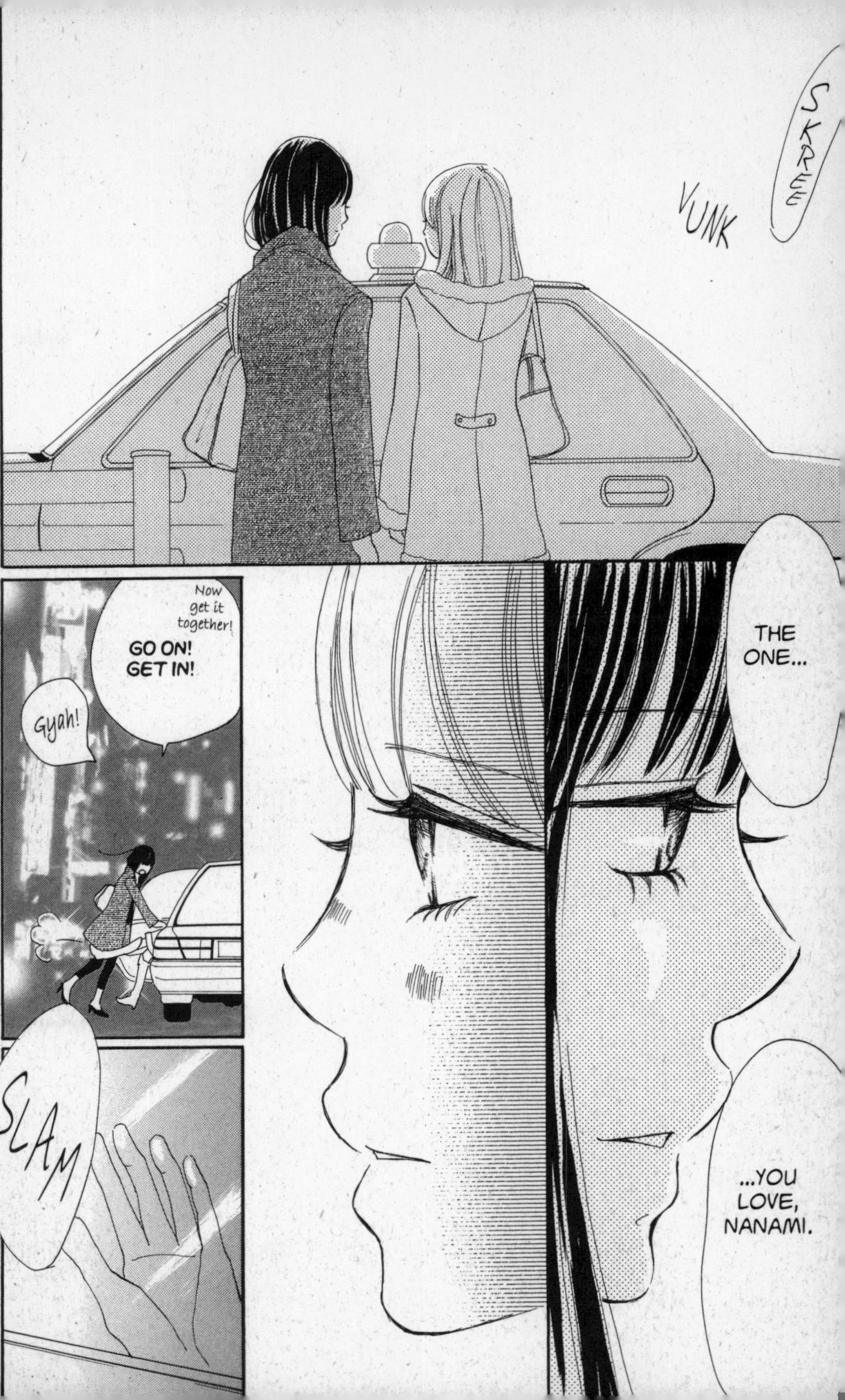
SKREE
VUNK
THE ONE...
...YOU LOVE, NANAMI.
Now get it together!
GO ON! GET IN!
Gyah!
SLAM

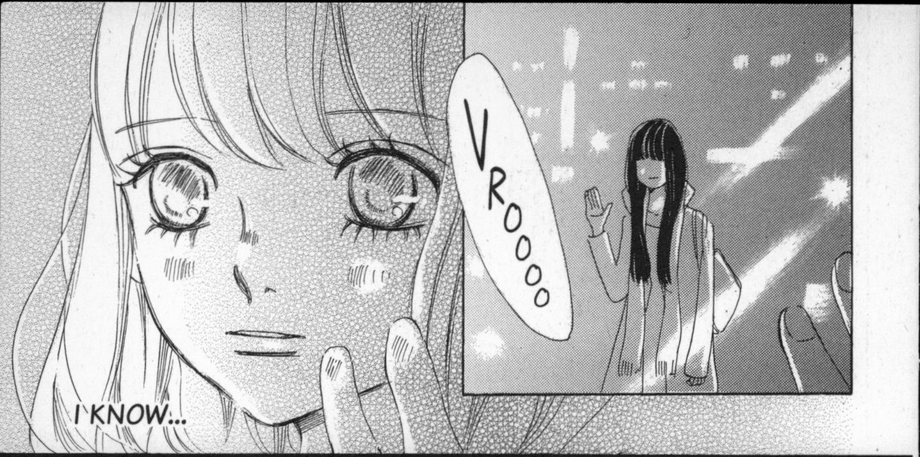
VROOOO
I KNOW...

...THAT EXACT MOMENT WHEN YOUR EXPERIENCES TURN TO MEMORIES.

MEMORIES ARE KIND.

ALWAYS.

I NEED TO SLEEP.
I'LL MAKE MY ENTREATIES IN MY DREAMS.

MAY YOUR

MEMORIES...

...BE KIND TO

YOU TOO.

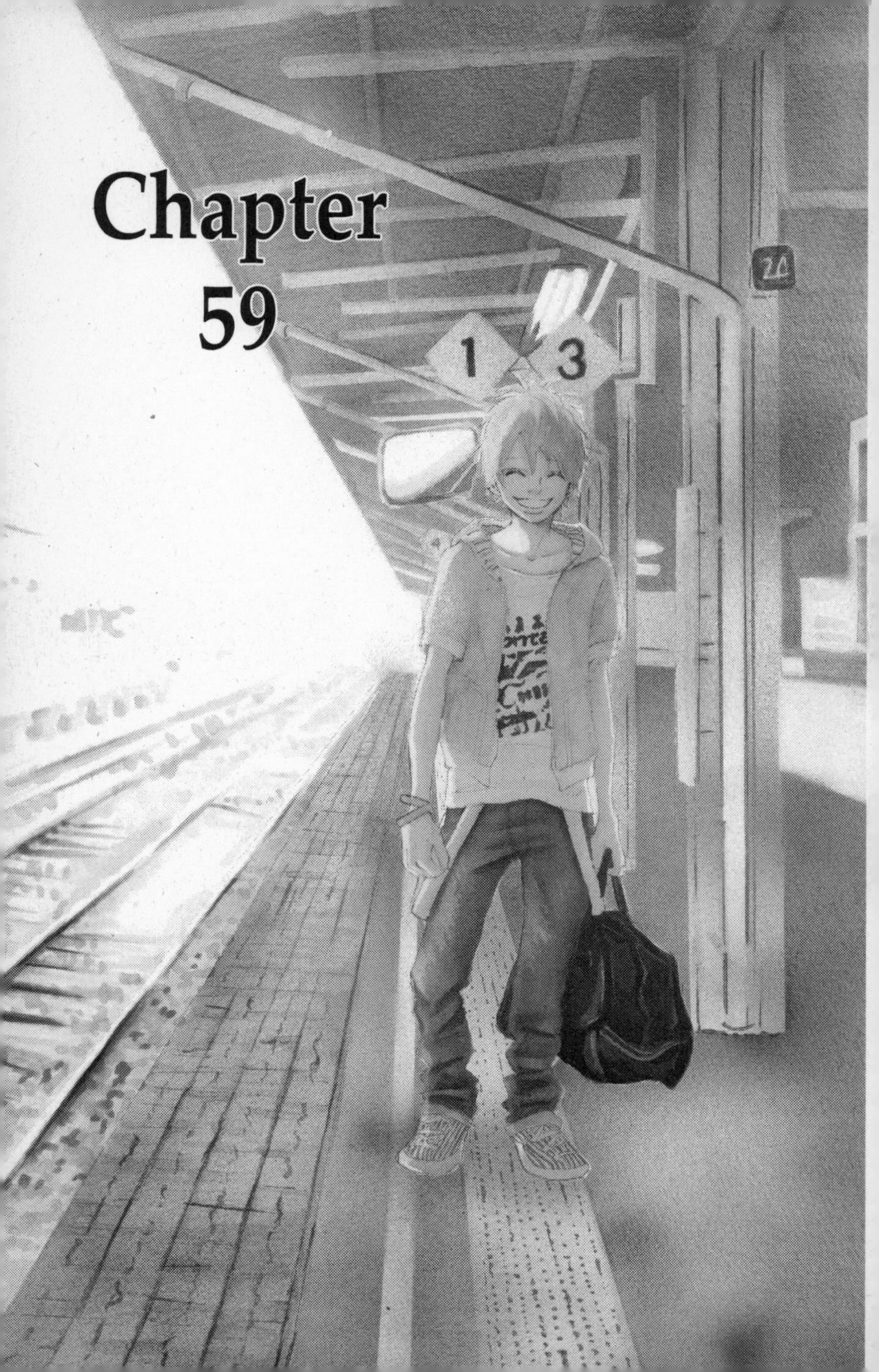
Chapter
59
24
1
3

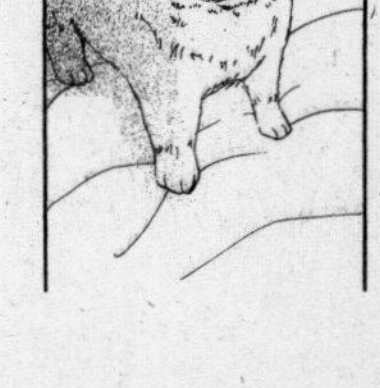
SNFF
SNFF

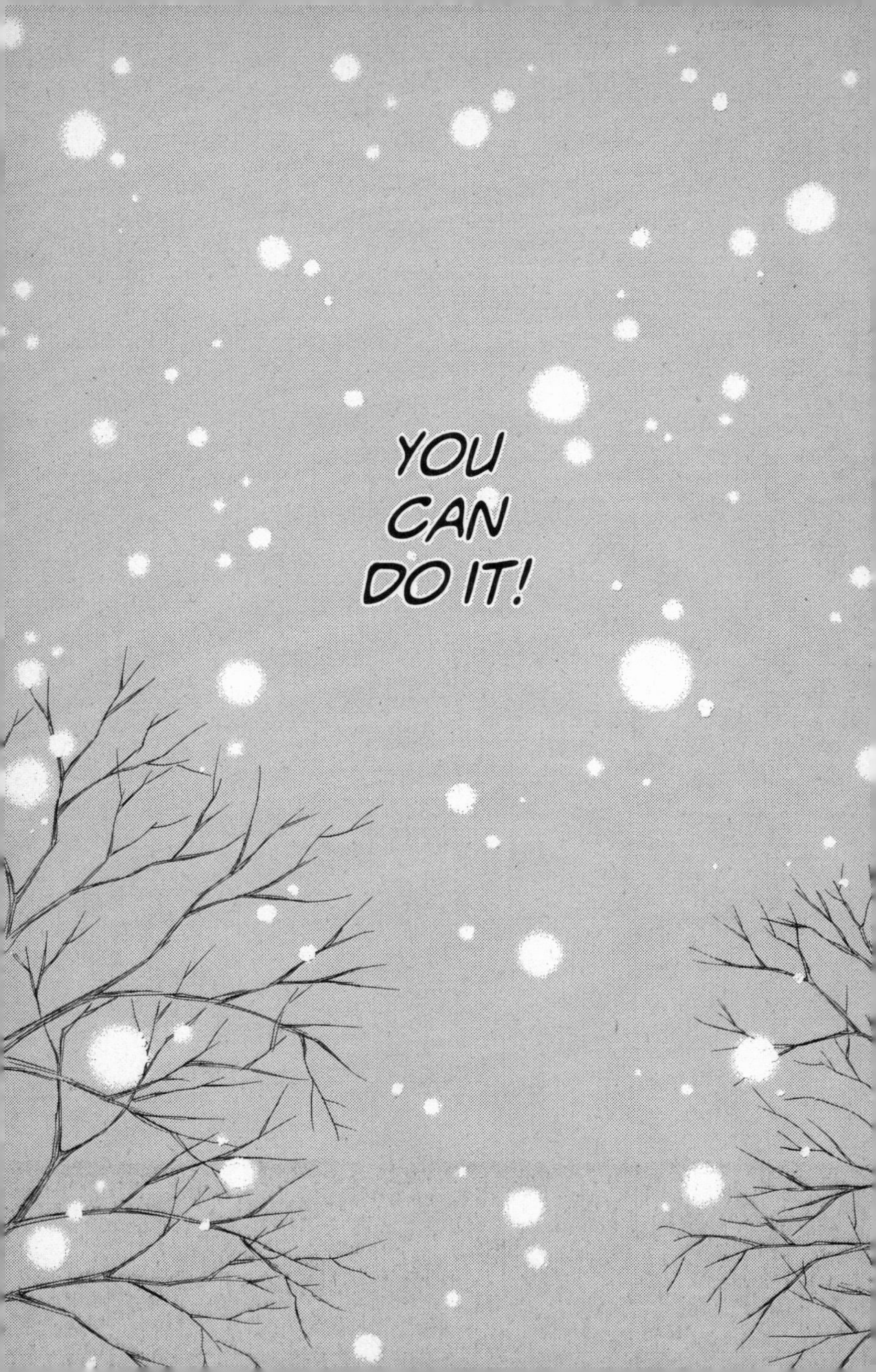
YOU CAN DO IT!

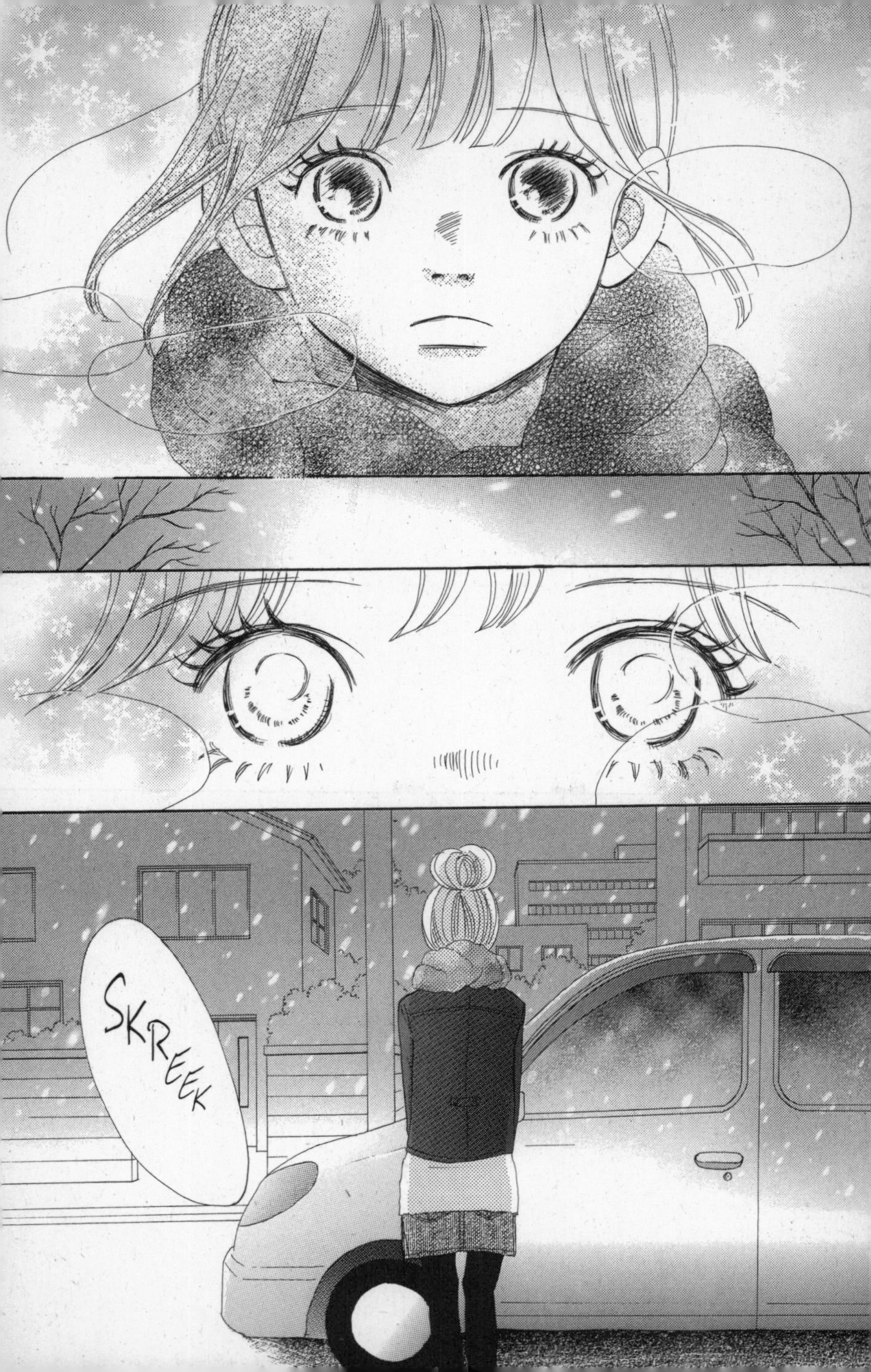
SKREEK

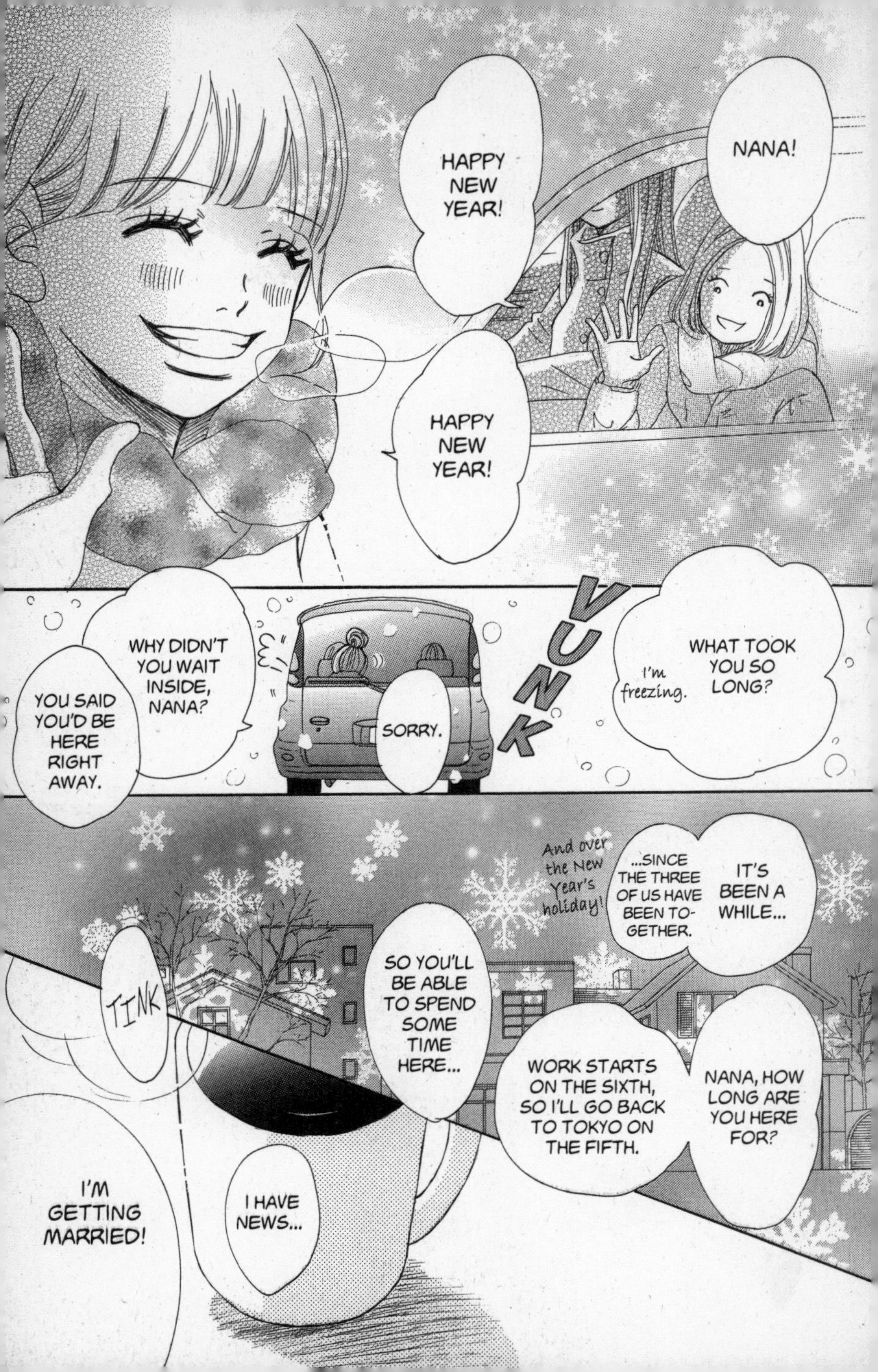
NANA!
HAPPY NEW YEAR!
HAPPY NEW YEAR!
WHAT TOOK YOU SO LONG?
I'm freezing.
VUNK
SORRY.
WHY DIDN'T YOU WAIT INSIDE, NANA?
YOU SAID YOU'D BE HERE RIGHT AWAY.
IT'S BEEN A WHILE...
...SINCE THE THREE OF US HAVE BEEN TO-GETHER.
And over the New Year's holiday!
NANA, HOW LONG ARE YOU HERE FOR?
WORK STARTS ON THE SIXTH, SO I'LL GO BACK TO TOKYO ON THE FIFTH.
SO YOU'LL BE ABLE TO SPEND SOME TIME HERE...
TINK
I HAVE NEWS...
I'M GETTING MARRIED!

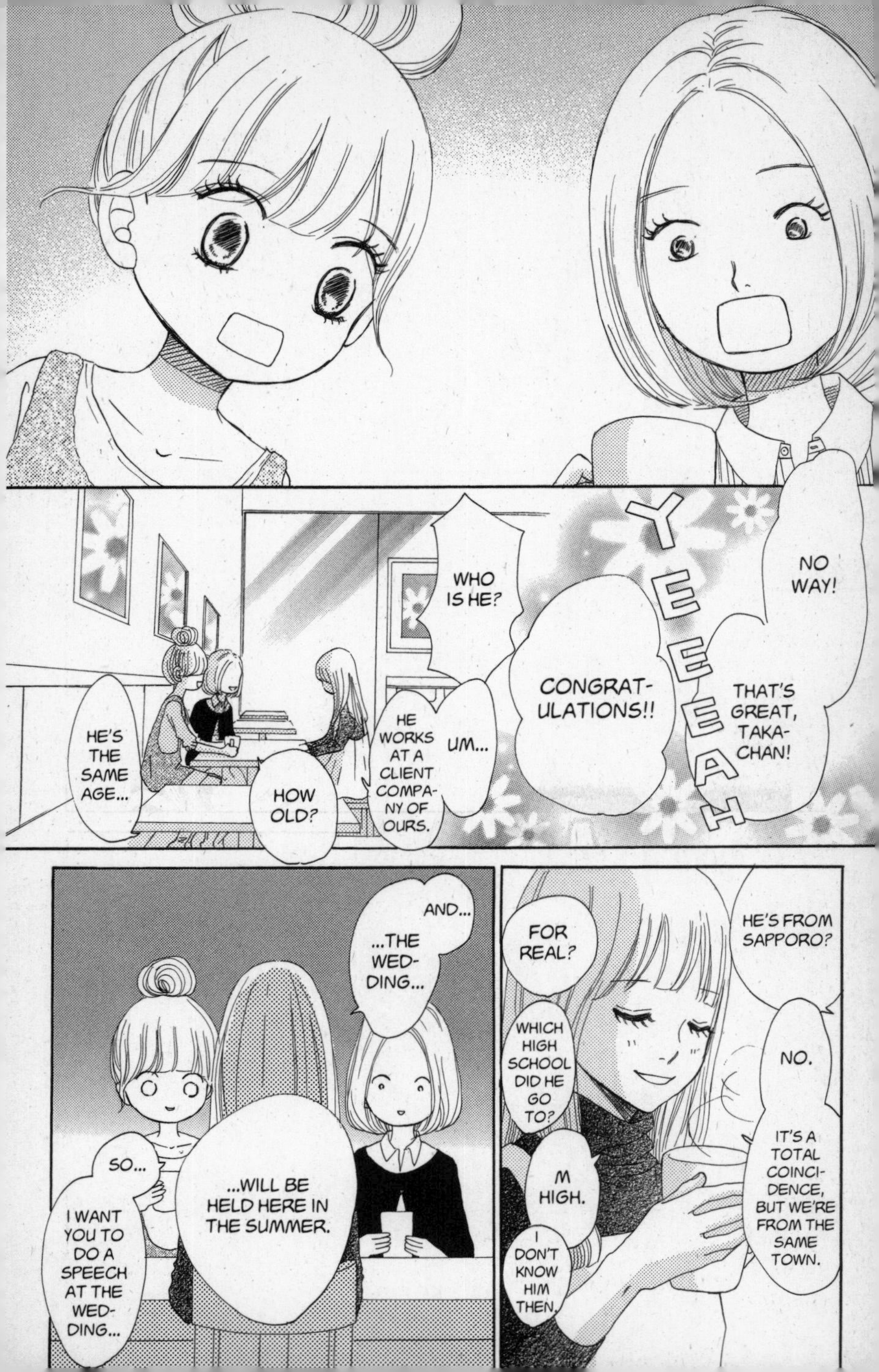
NO WAY!
THAT'S GREAT, TAKA-CHAN!
YEEEAH
CONGRAT-ULATIONS!!
WHO IS HE?
UM...
HE WORKS AT A CLIENT COMPA-NY OF OURS.
HOW OLD?
HE'S THE SAME AGE...
HE'S FROM SAPPORO?
FOR REAL?
NO.
IT'S A TOTAL COINCI-DENCE, BUT WE'RE FROM THE SAME TOWN.
WHICH HIGH SCHOOL DID HE GO TO?
M HIGH.
I DON'T KNOW HIM THEN.
AND...
...THE WED-DING...
...WILL BE HELD HERE IN THE SUMMER.
SO...
I WANT YOU TO DO A SPEECH AT THE WED-DING...

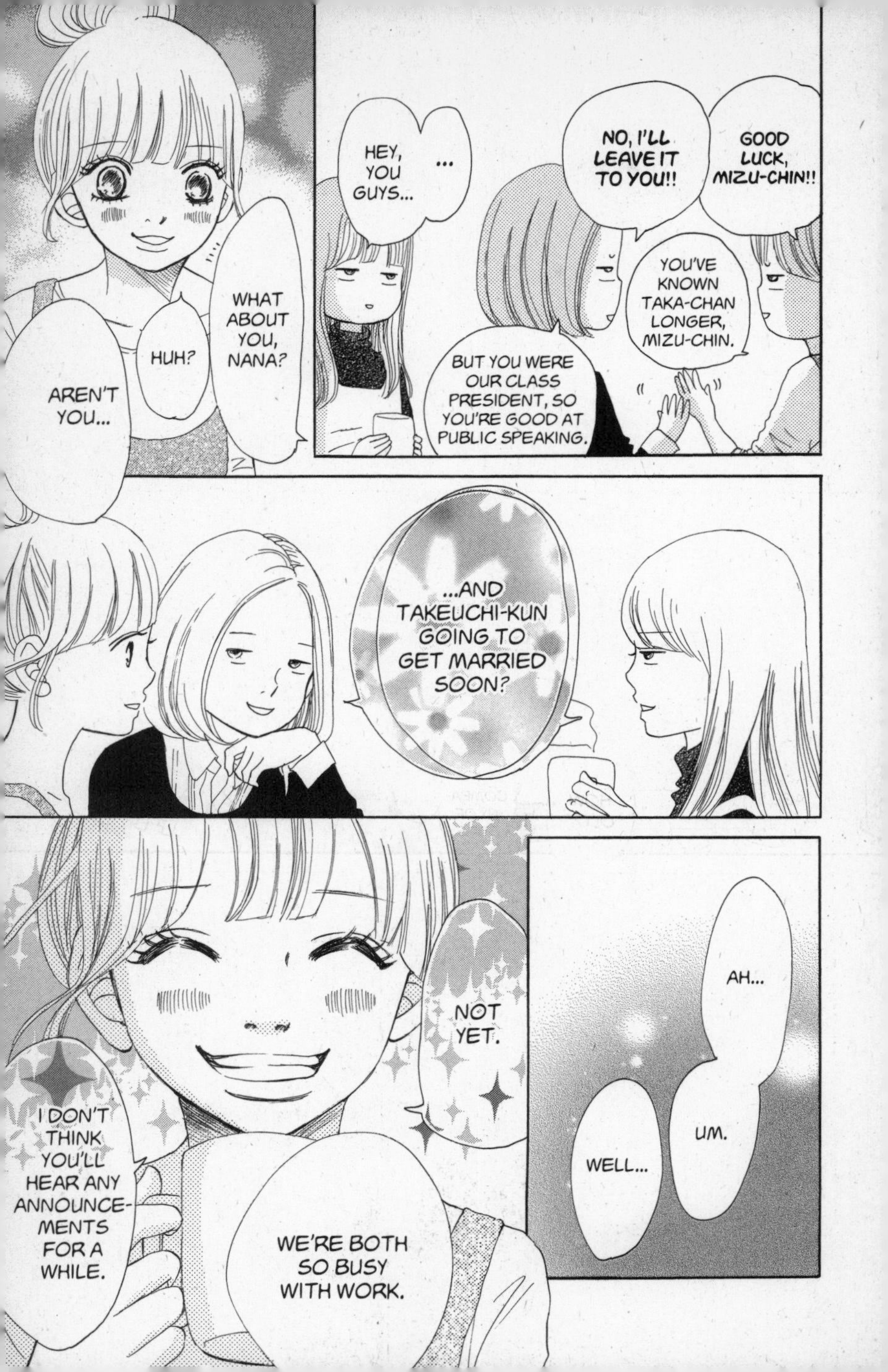
GOOD LUCK, MIZU-CHIN!!
NO, I'LL LEAVE IT TO YOU!!
YOU'VE KNOWN TAKA-CHAN LONGER, MIZU-CHIN.
BUT YOU WERE OUR CLASS PRESIDENT, SO YOU'RE GOOD AT PUBLIC SPEAKING.
...
HEY, YOU GUYS...
WHAT ABOUT YOU, NANA?
HUH?
AREN'T YOU...
...AND TAKEUCHI-KUN GOING TO GET MARRIED SOON?
AH...
UM.
WELL...
NOT YET.
WE'RE BOTH SO BUSY WITH WORK.
I DON'T THINK YOU'LL HEAR ANY ANNOUNCEMENTS FOR A WHILE.

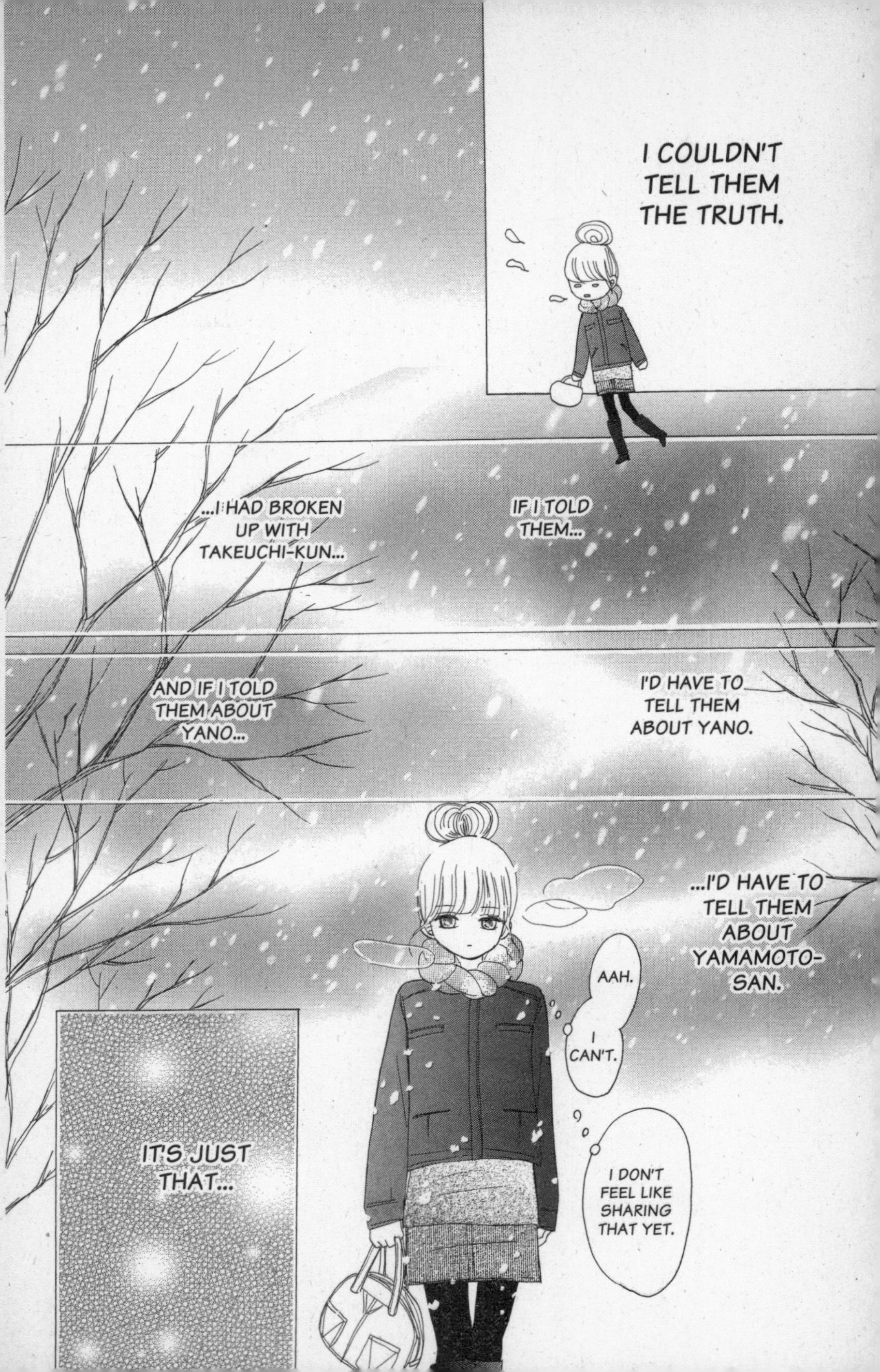
I COULDN'T TELL THEM THE TRUTH.
IF I TOLD THEM...
...I HAD BROKEN UP WITH TAKEUCHI-KUN...
I'D HAVE TO TELL THEM ABOUT YANO.
AND IF I TOLD THEM ABOUT YANO...
...I'D HAVE TO TELL THEM ABOUT YAMAMOTO-SAN.
AAH.
I CAN'T.
I DON'T FEEL LIKE SHARING THAT YET.
IT'S JUST THAT...

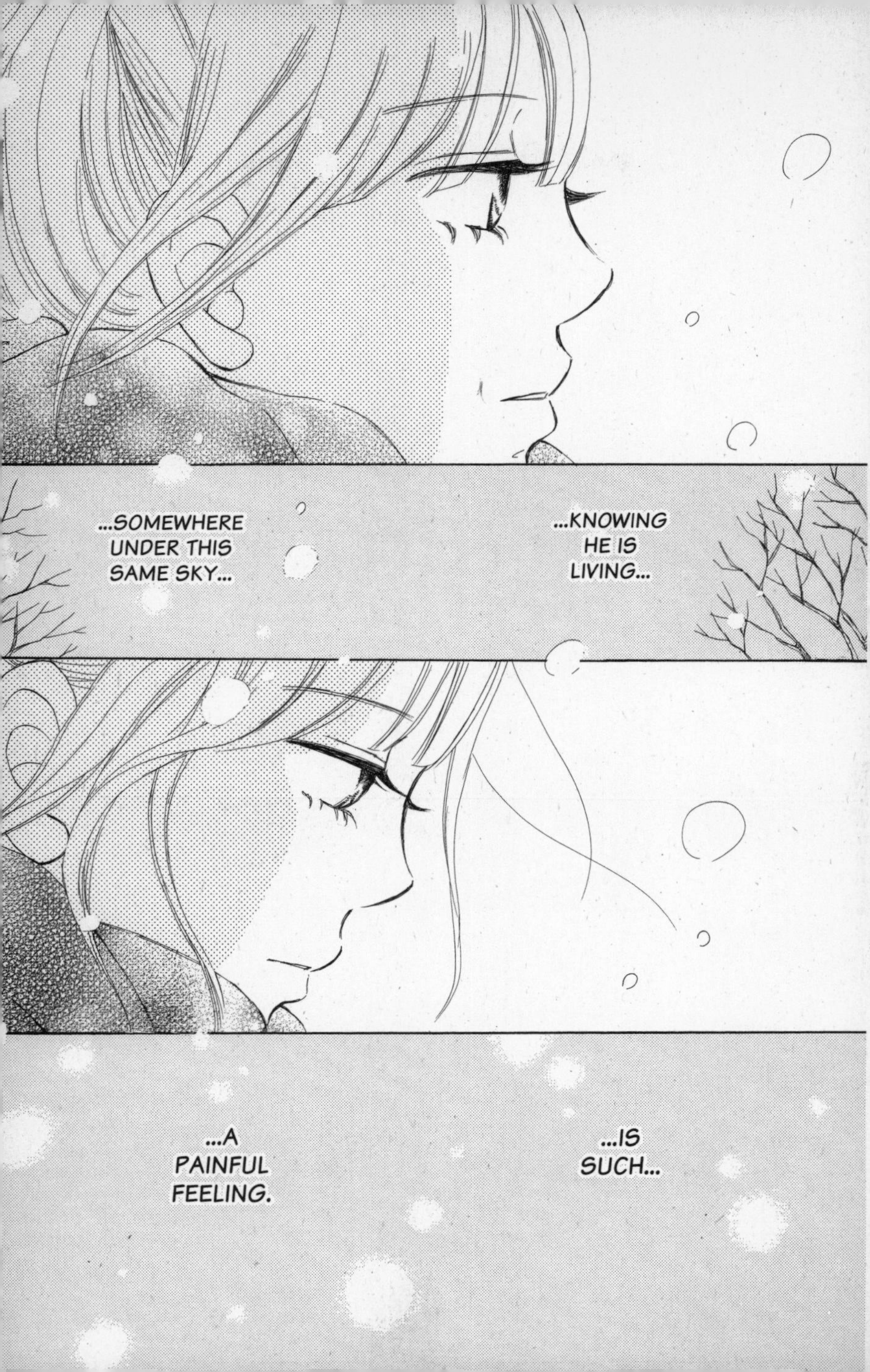
...KNOWING HE IS LIVING...
...SOMEWHERE UNDER THIS SAME SKY...
...IS SUCH...
...A PAINFUL FEELING.

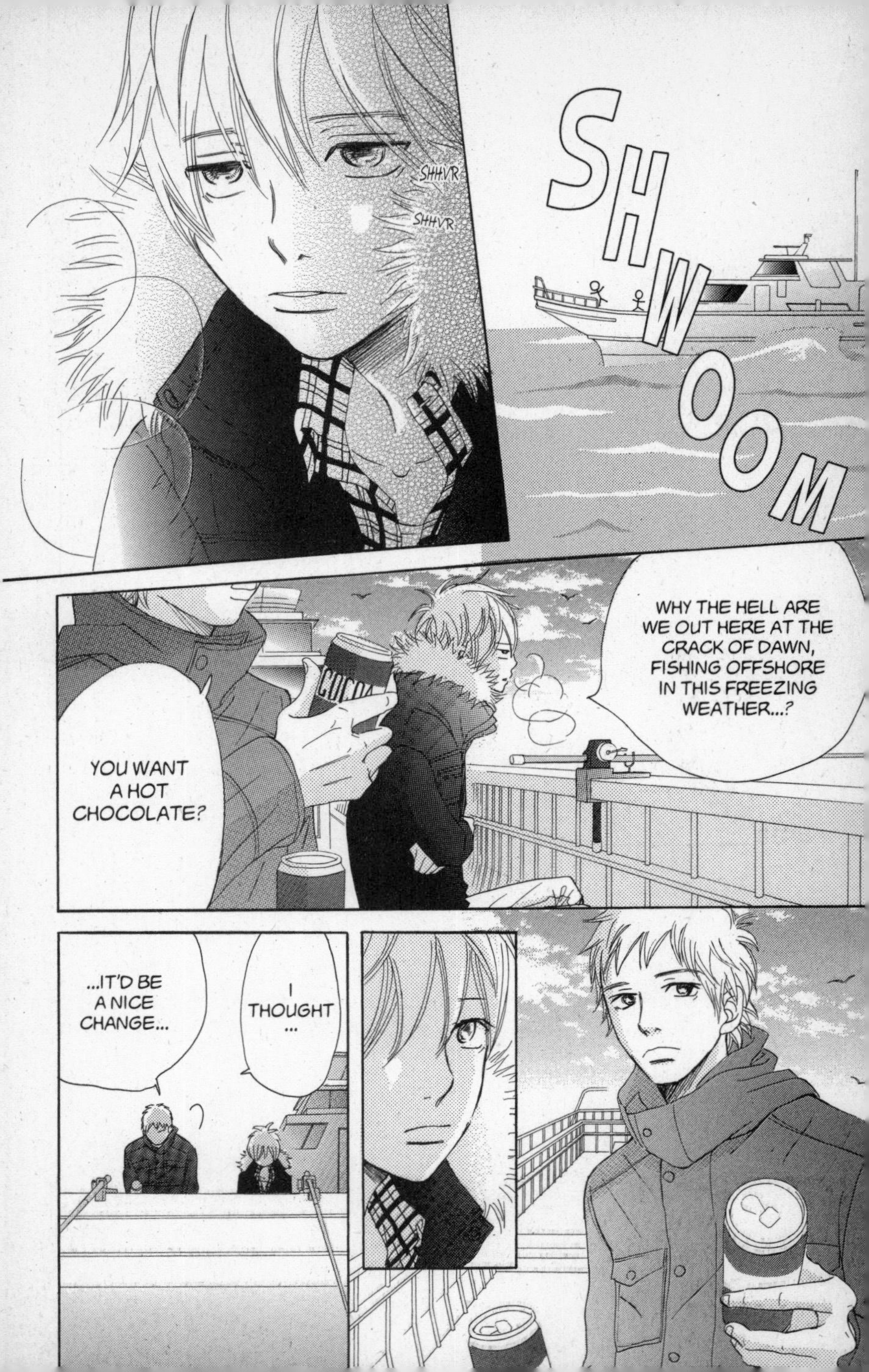
SHWOOM
SHHVR
SHHVR
WHY THE HELL ARE WE OUT HERE AT THE CRACK OF DAWN, FISHING OFFSHORE IN THIS FREEZING WEATHER...?
YOU WANT A HOT CHOCOLATE?
I THOUGHT ...
...IT'D BE A NICE CHANGE...

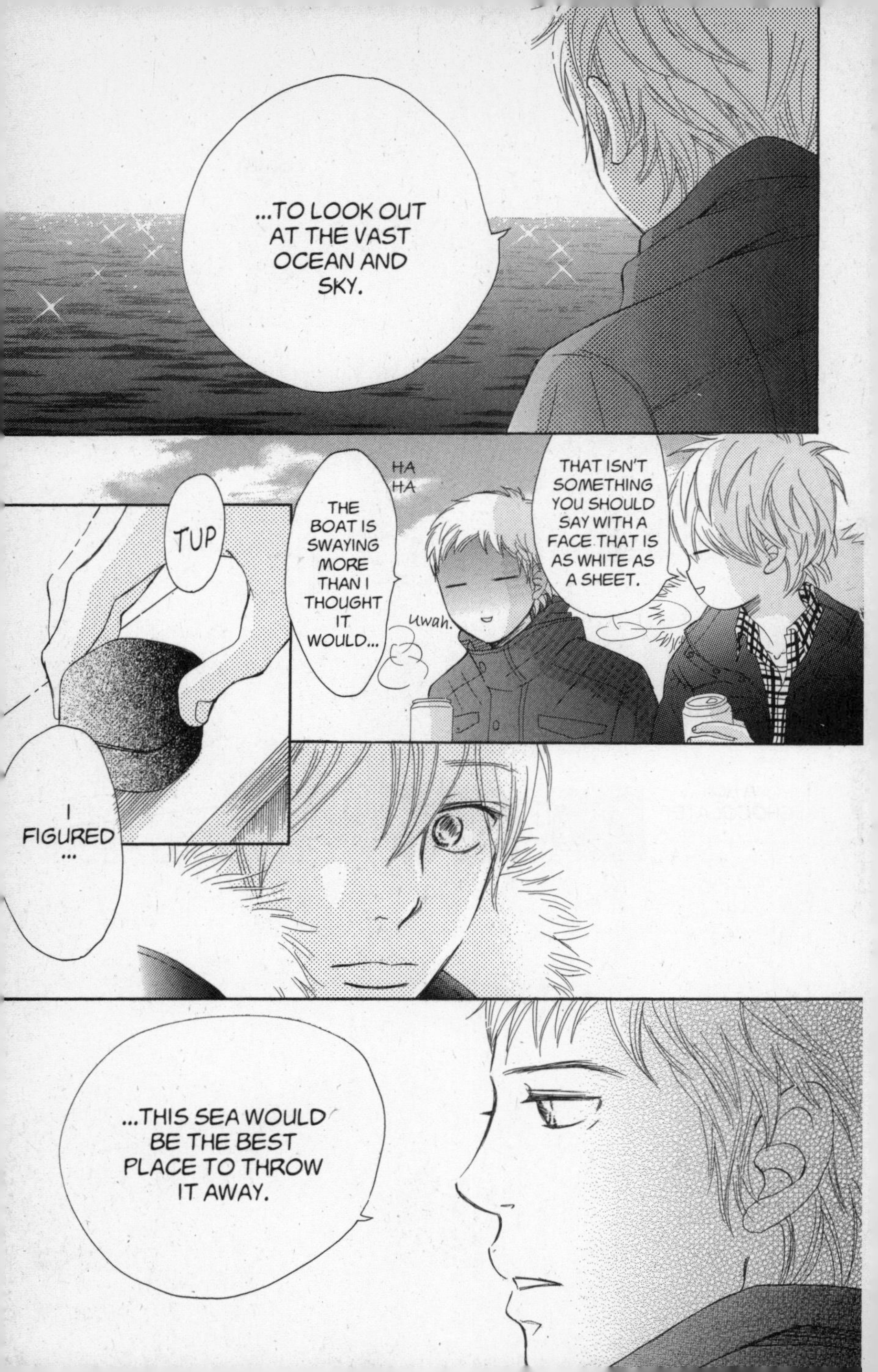
...TO LOOK OUT AT THE VAST OCEAN AND SKY.
HA HA
THE BOAT IS SWAYING MORE THAN I THOUGHT IT WOULD...
uwah.
THAT ISN'T SOMETHING YOU SHOULD SAY WITH A FACE THAT IS AS WHITE AS A SHEET.
TUP
I FIGURED ...
...THIS SEA WOULD BE THE BEST PLACE TO THROW IT AWAY.

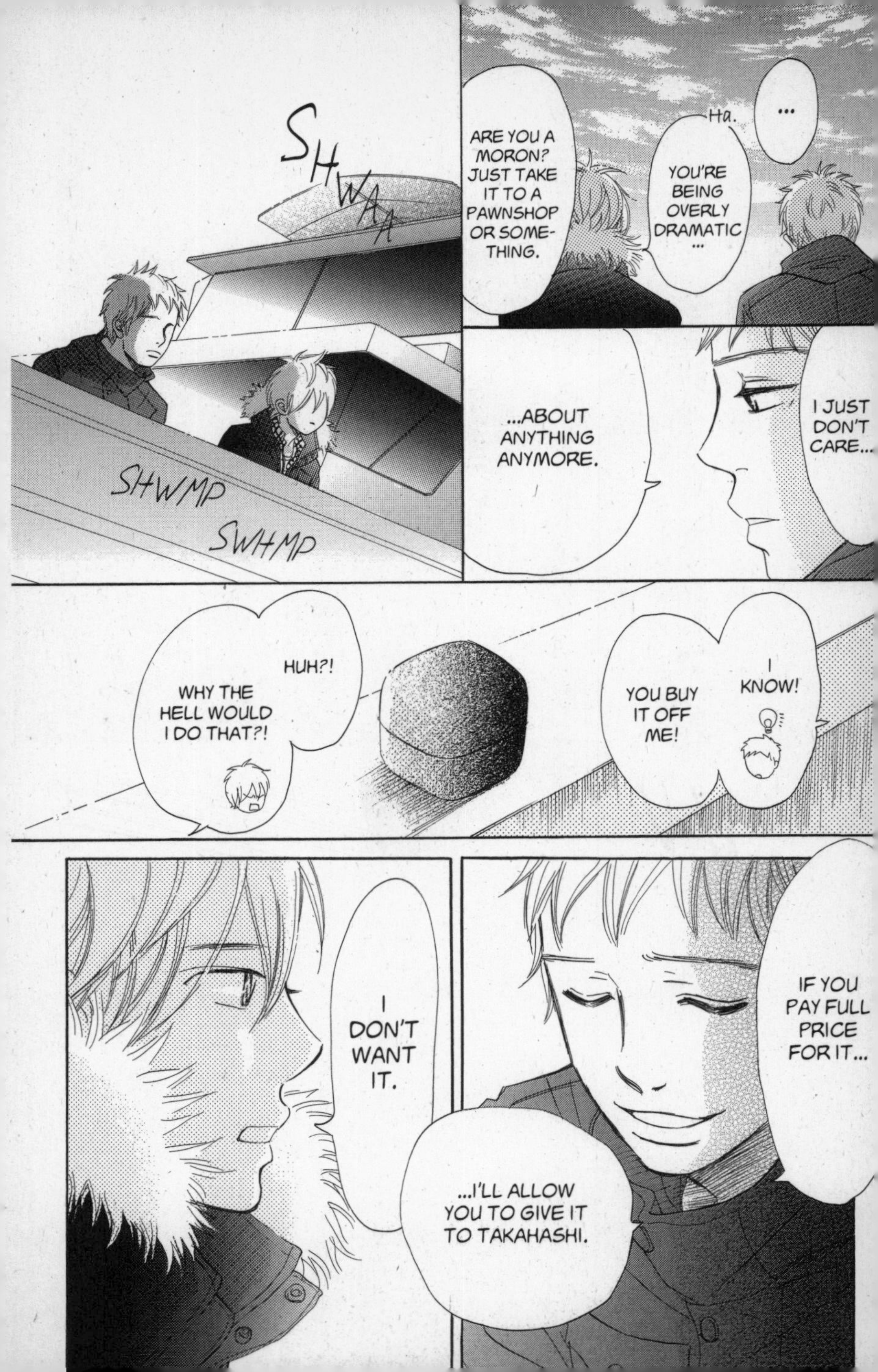
...
Ha.
YOU'RE BEING OVERLY DRAMATIC...
ARE YOU A MORON? JUST TAKE IT TO A PAWNSHOP OR SOME-THING.
I JUST DON'T CARE...
...ABOUT ANYTHING ANYMORE.
SHWAA
SHWMP
SWHMP
I KNOW!
YOU BUY IT OFF ME!
HUH?!
WHY THE HELL WOULD I DO THAT?!
IF YOU PAY FULL PRICE FOR IT...
...I'LL ALLOW YOU TO GIVE IT TO TAKAHASHI.
I DON'T WANT IT.

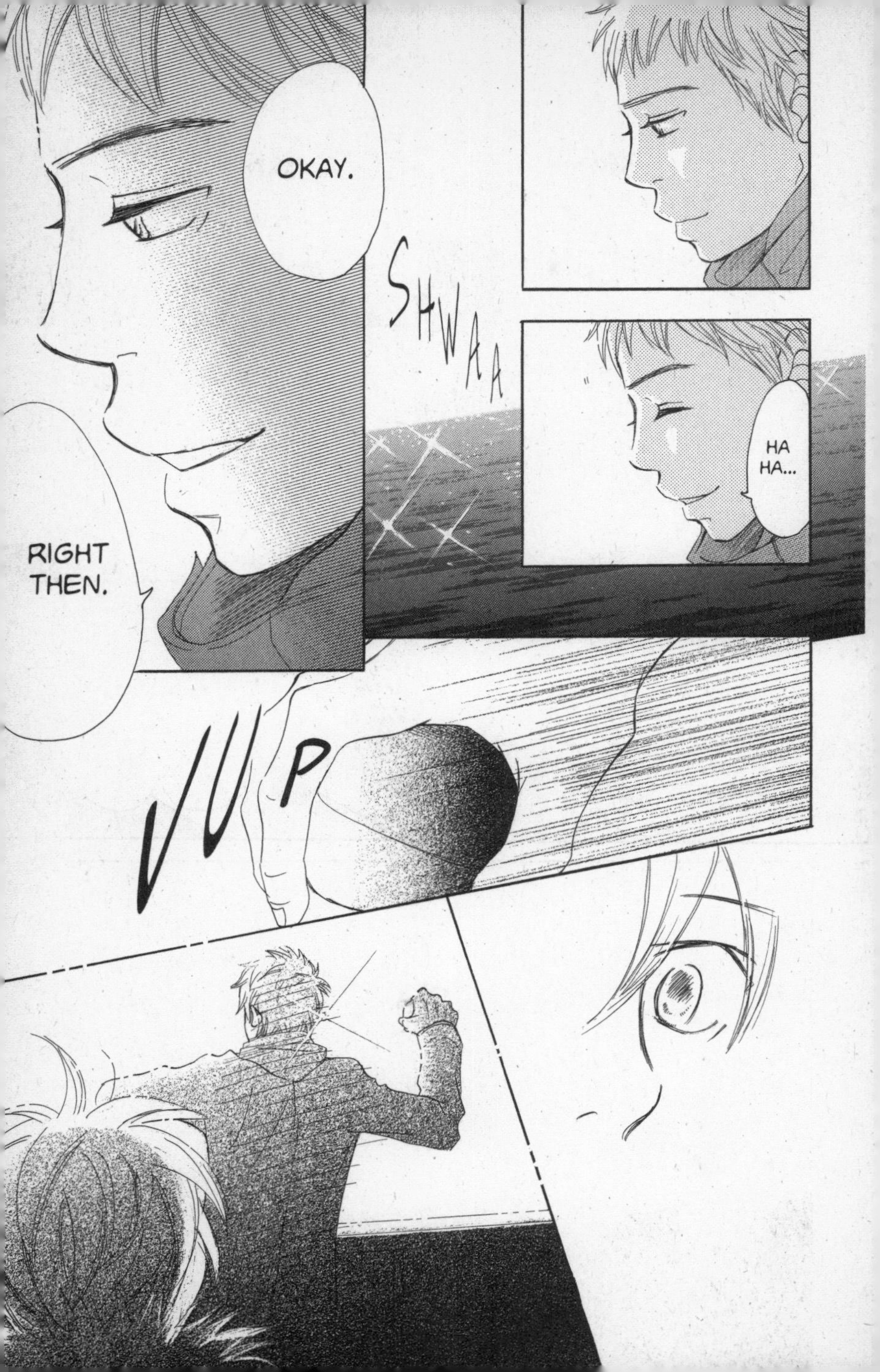
SHWAA
HA HA...
OKAY.
RIGHT THEN.
VUP

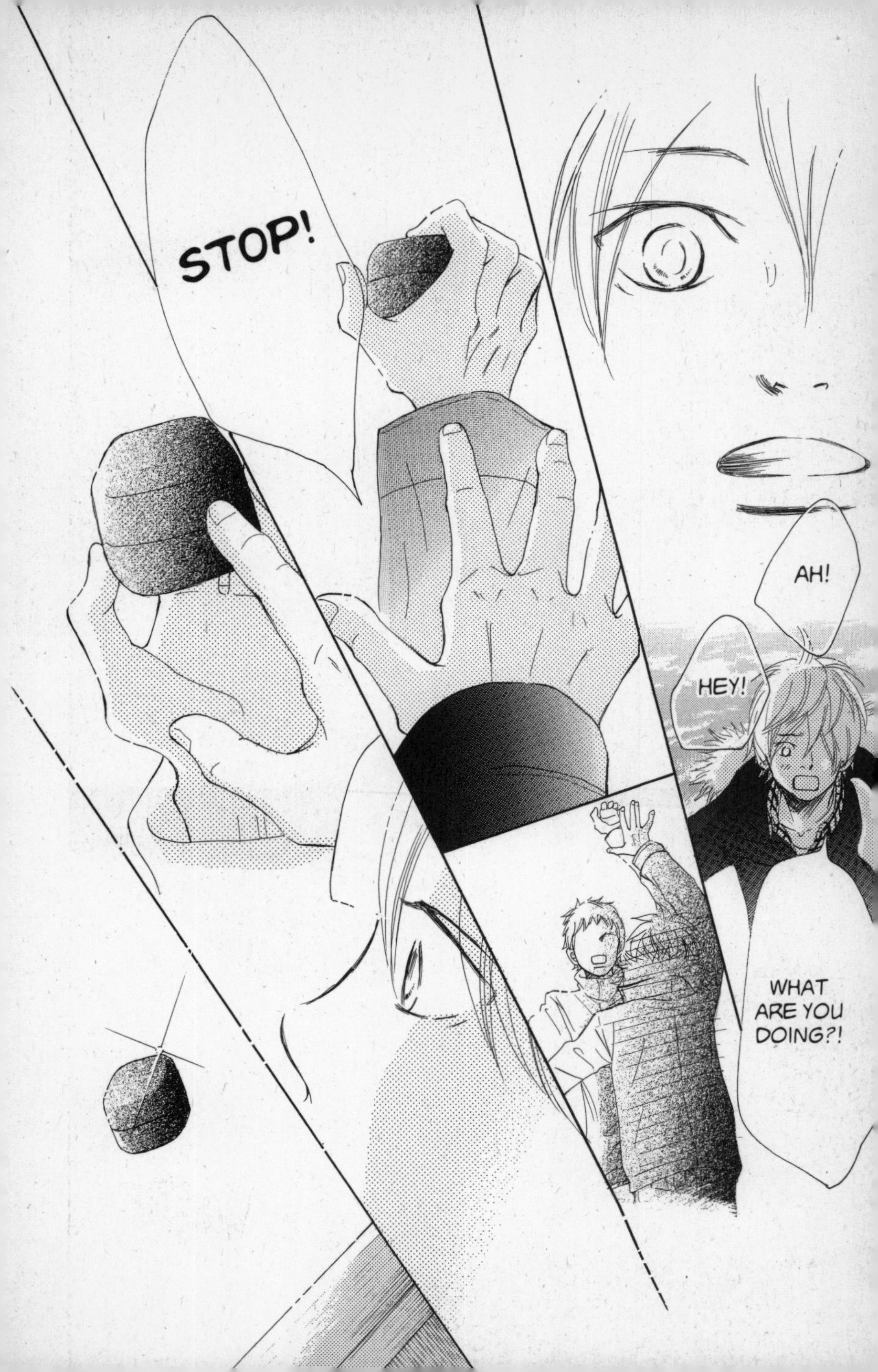
AH!
HEY!
WHAT ARE YOU DOING?!
STOP!

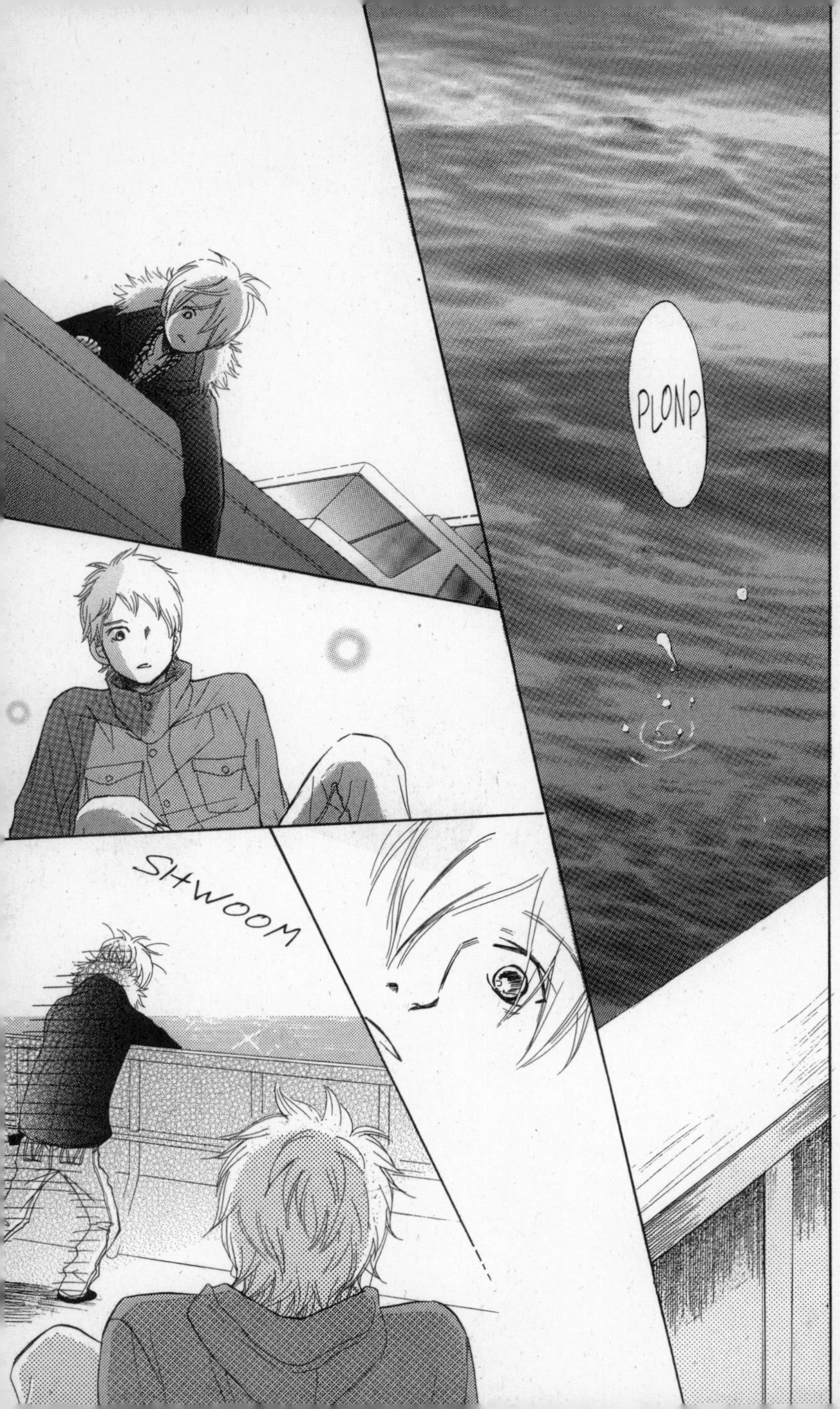
PLONP
SHWOOM

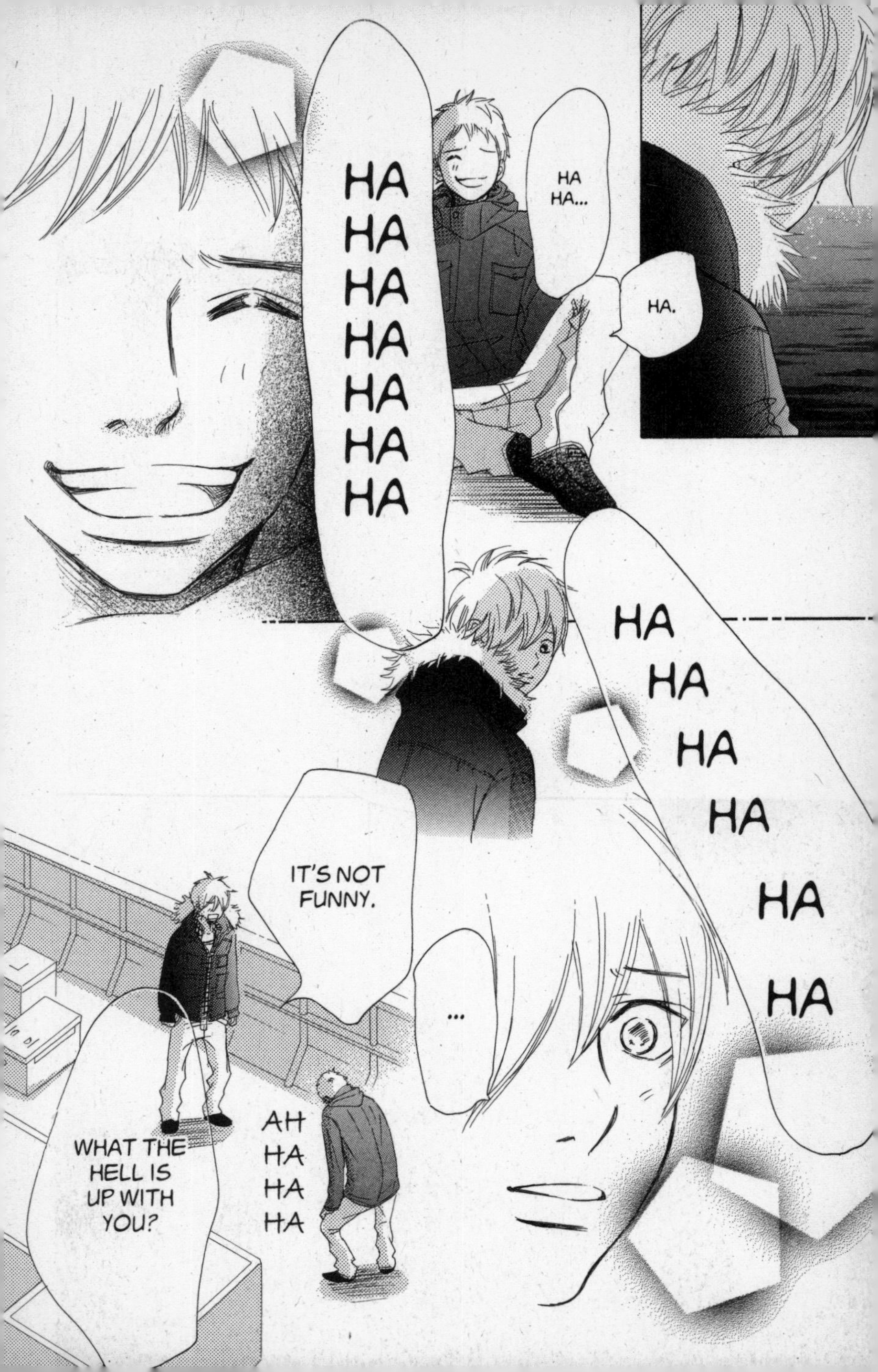
HA.
HA HA...
HA HA HA HA HA HA HA
HA HA HA HA HA HA
IT'S NOT FUNNY.
...
AH HA HA HA
WHAT THE HELL IS UP WITH YOU?

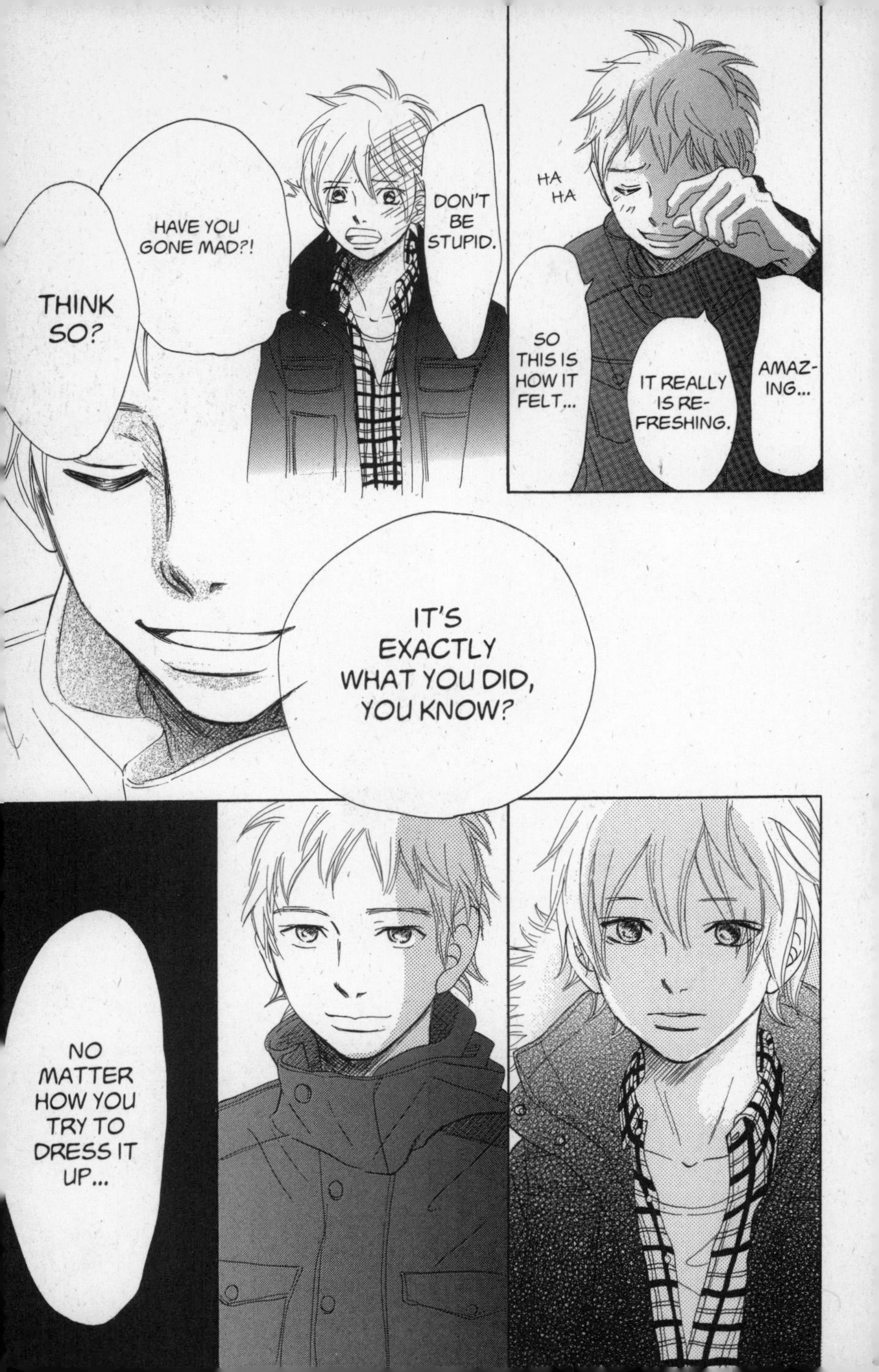
HA HA
AMAZ-ING...
IT REALLY IS RE-FRESHING.
SO THIS IS HOW IT FELT...
DON'T BE STUPID.
HAVE YOU GONE MAD?!
THINK SO?
IT'S EXACTLY WHAT YOU DID, YOU KNOW?
NO MATTER HOW YOU TRY TO DRESS IT UP...

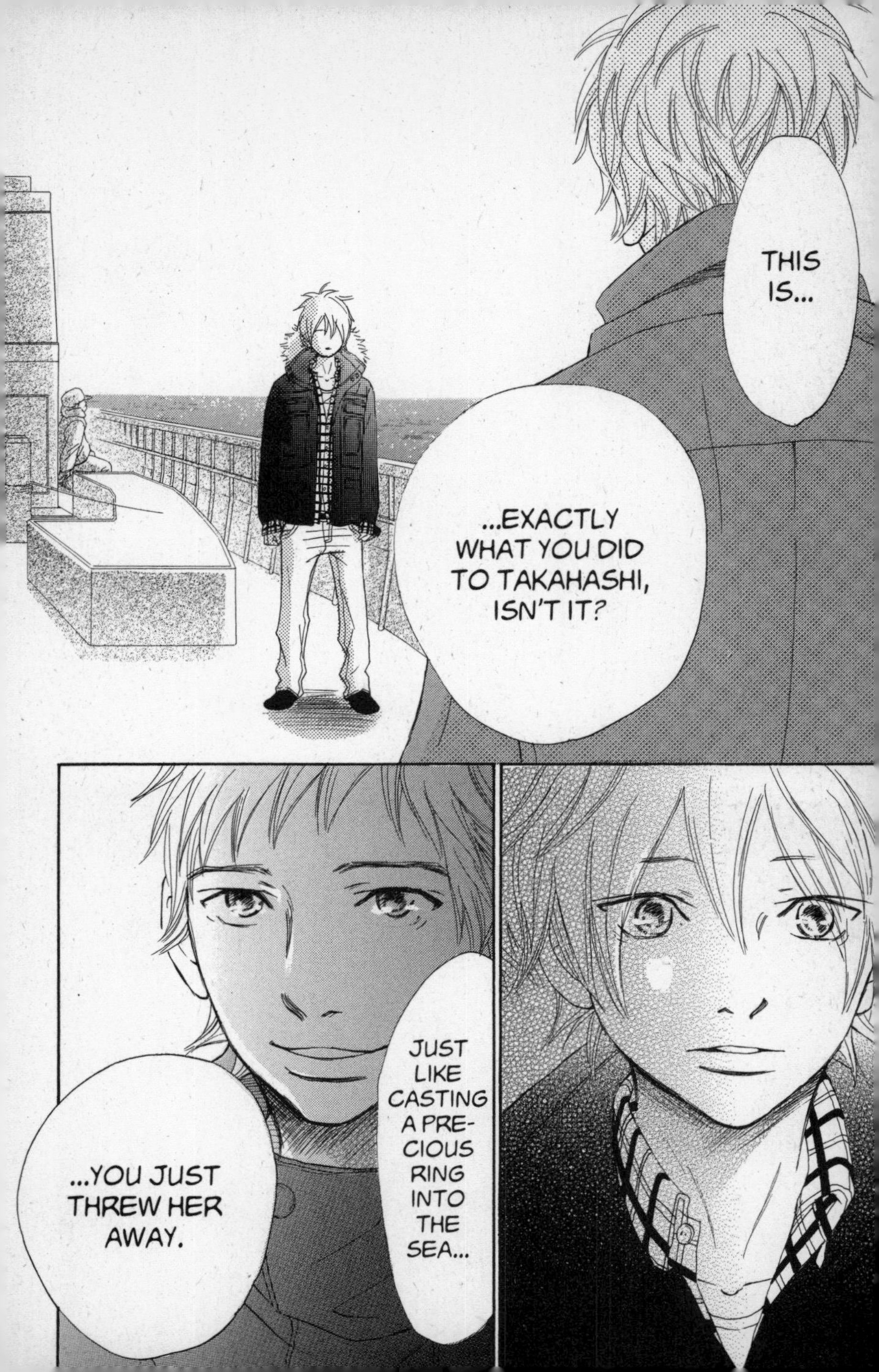
THIS IS...
...EXACTLY WHAT YOU DID TO TAKAHASHI, ISN'T IT?
JUST LIKE CASTING A PRE-CIOUS RING INTO THE SEA...
...YOU JUST THREW HER AWAY.

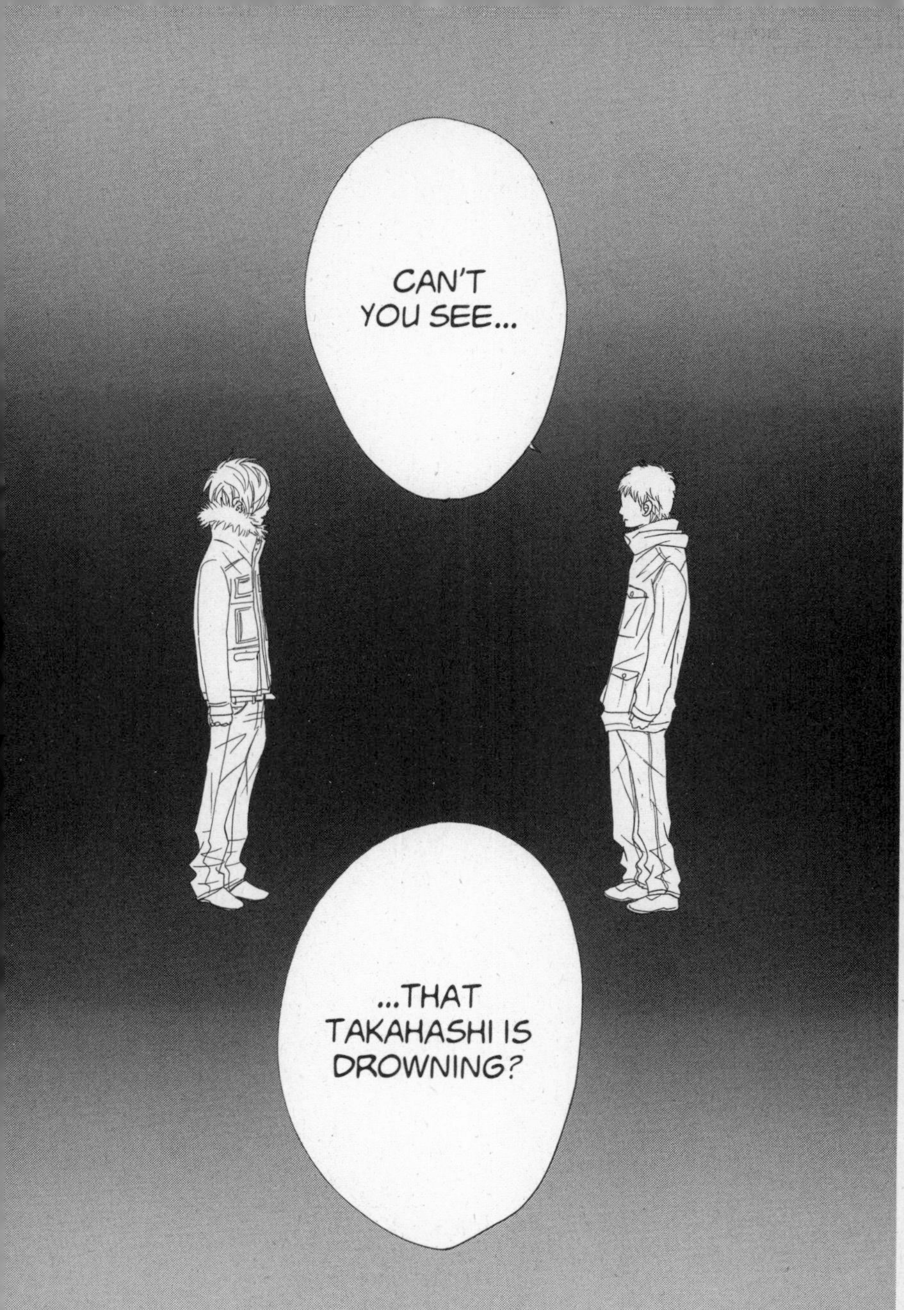
CAN'T YOU SEE...
...THAT TAKAHASHI IS DROWNING?

WE WERE THERE VOL. 14/END

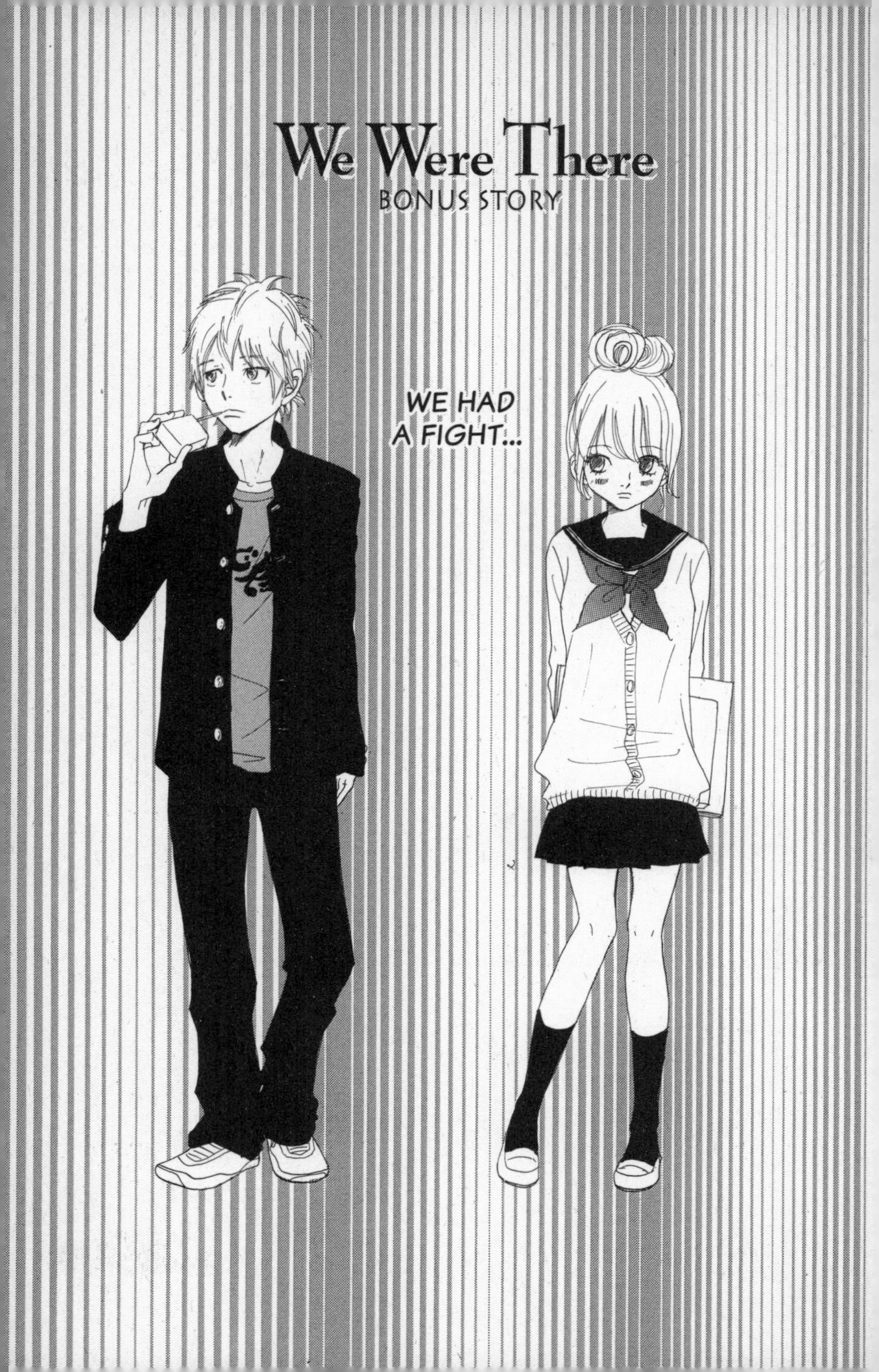
We Were There
BONUS STORY
WE HAD A FIGHT...

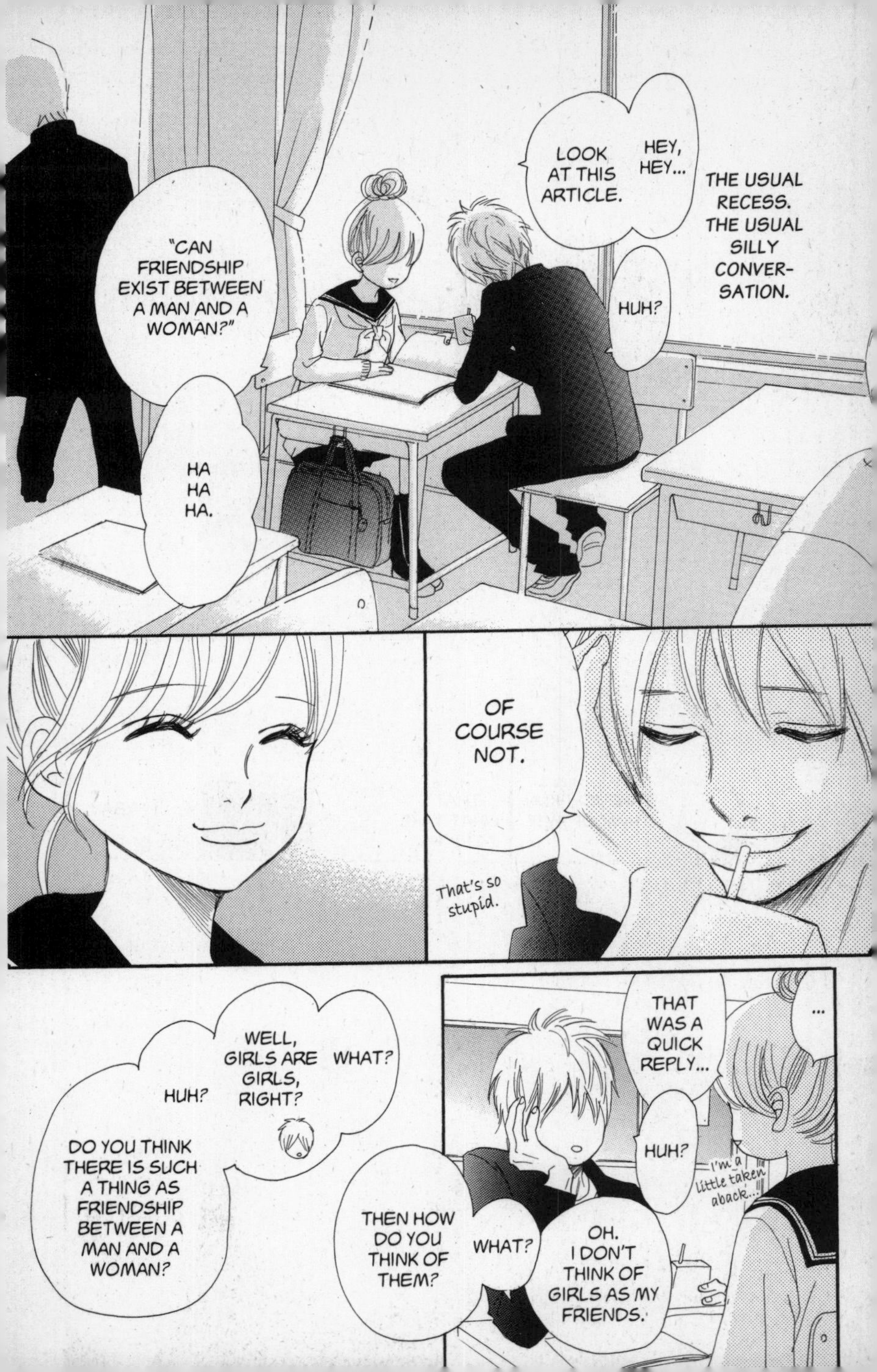
THE USUAL RECESS. THE USUAL SILLY CONVERSATION.
HEY, HEY... LOOK AT THIS ARTICLE.
HUH?
"CAN FRIENDSHIP EXIST BETWEEN A MAN AND A WOMAN?"
HA HA HA.
OF COURSE NOT.
That's so stupid.
...
THAT WAS A QUICK REPLY...
HUH?
I'm a little taken aback...!!
OH. I DON'T THINK OF GIRLS AS MY FRIENDS.
WHAT?
THEN HOW DO YOU THINK OF THEM?
WHAT?
WELL, GIRLS ARE GIRLS, RIGHT?
HUH?
DO YOU THINK THERE IS SUCH A THING AS FRIENDSHIP BETWEEN A MAN AND A WOMAN?

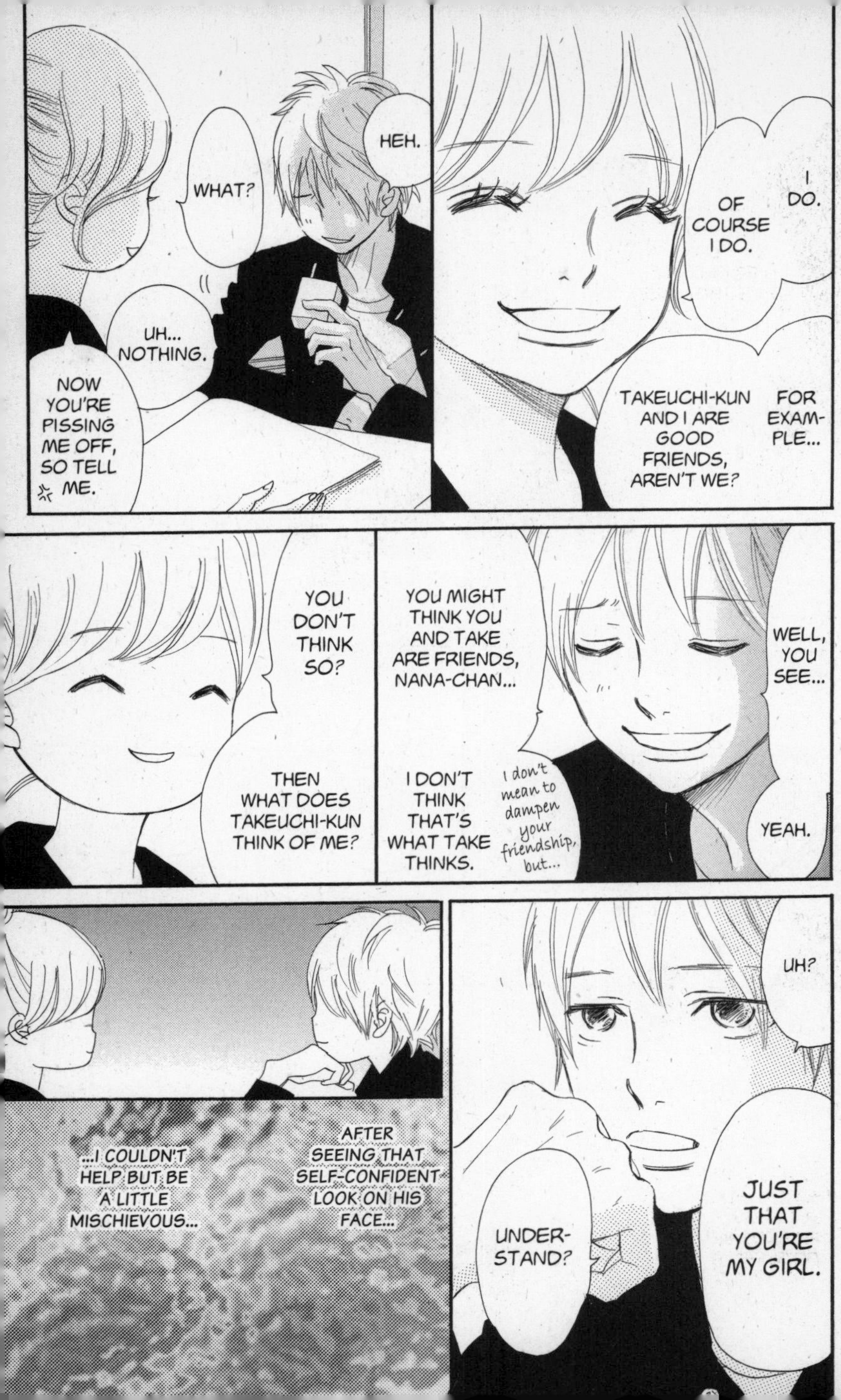
I DO.
OF COURSE I DO.
FOR EXAMPLE...
TAKEUCHI-KUN AND I ARE GOOD FRIENDS, AREN'T WE?
HEH.
WHAT?
UH... NOTHING.
NOW YOU'RE PISSING ME OFF, SO TELL ME.
WELL, YOU SEE...
YOU MIGHT THINK YOU AND TAKE ARE FRIENDS, NANA-CHAN...
YEAH.
I don't mean to dampen your friendship, but...
I DON'T THINK THAT'S WHAT TAKE THINKS.
YOU DON'T THINK SO?
THEN WHAT DOES TAKEUCHI-KUN THINK OF ME?
UH?
JUST THAT YOU'RE MY GIRL.
UNDER-STAND?
AFTER SEEING THAT SELF-CONFIDENT LOOK ON HIS FACE...
...I COULDN'T HELP BUT BE A LITTLE MISCHIEVOUS...

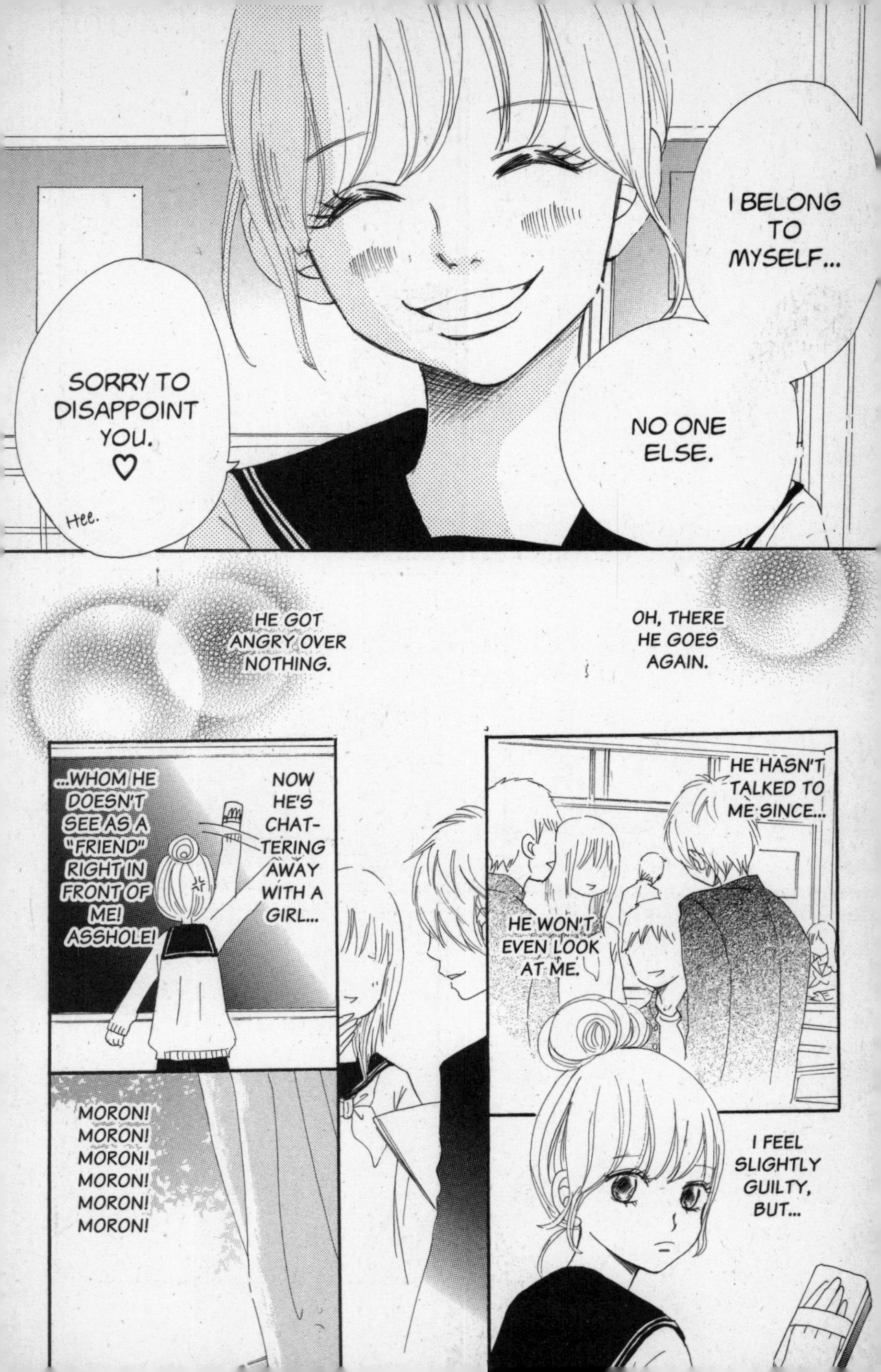
I BELONG TO MYSELF...
NO ONE ELSE.
SORRY TO DISAPPOINT YOU. ♡
Hee.
OH, THERE HE GOES AGAIN.
HE GOT ANGRY OVER NOTHING.
HE HASN'T TALKED TO ME SINCE...
HE WON'T EVEN LOOK AT ME.
I FEEL SLIGHTLY GUILTY, BUT...
NOW HE'S CHAT-TERING AWAY WITH A GIRL...
...WHOM HE DOESN'T SEE AS A "FRIEND" RIGHT IN FRONT OF ME! ASSHOLE!
MORON! MORON! MORON! MORON! MORON! MORON!

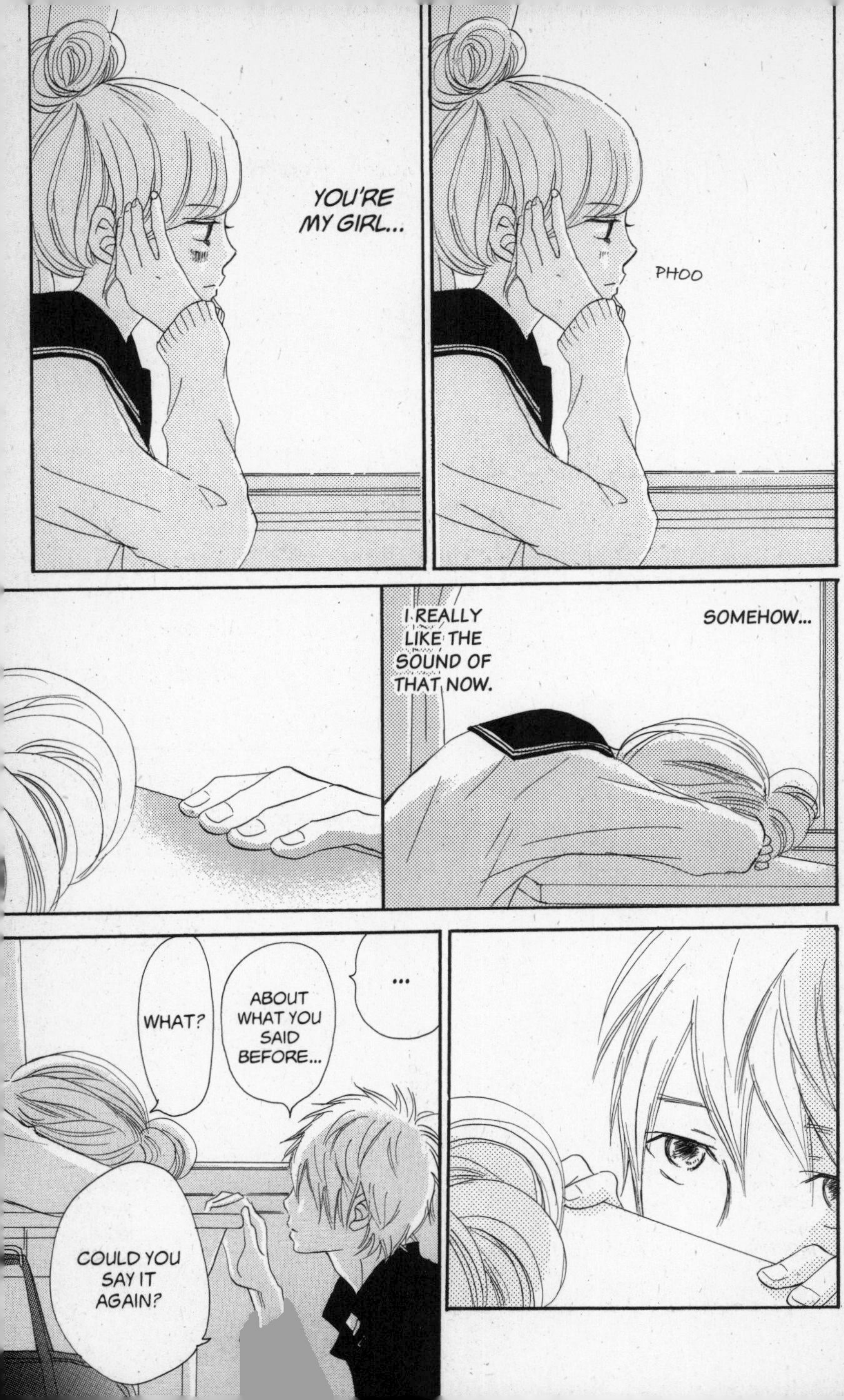
PHOO
YOU'RE MY GIRL...
SOMEHOW...
I REALLY LIKE THE SOUND OF THAT NOW.
...
ABOUT WHAT YOU SAID BEFORE...
WHAT?
COULD YOU SAY IT AGAIN?

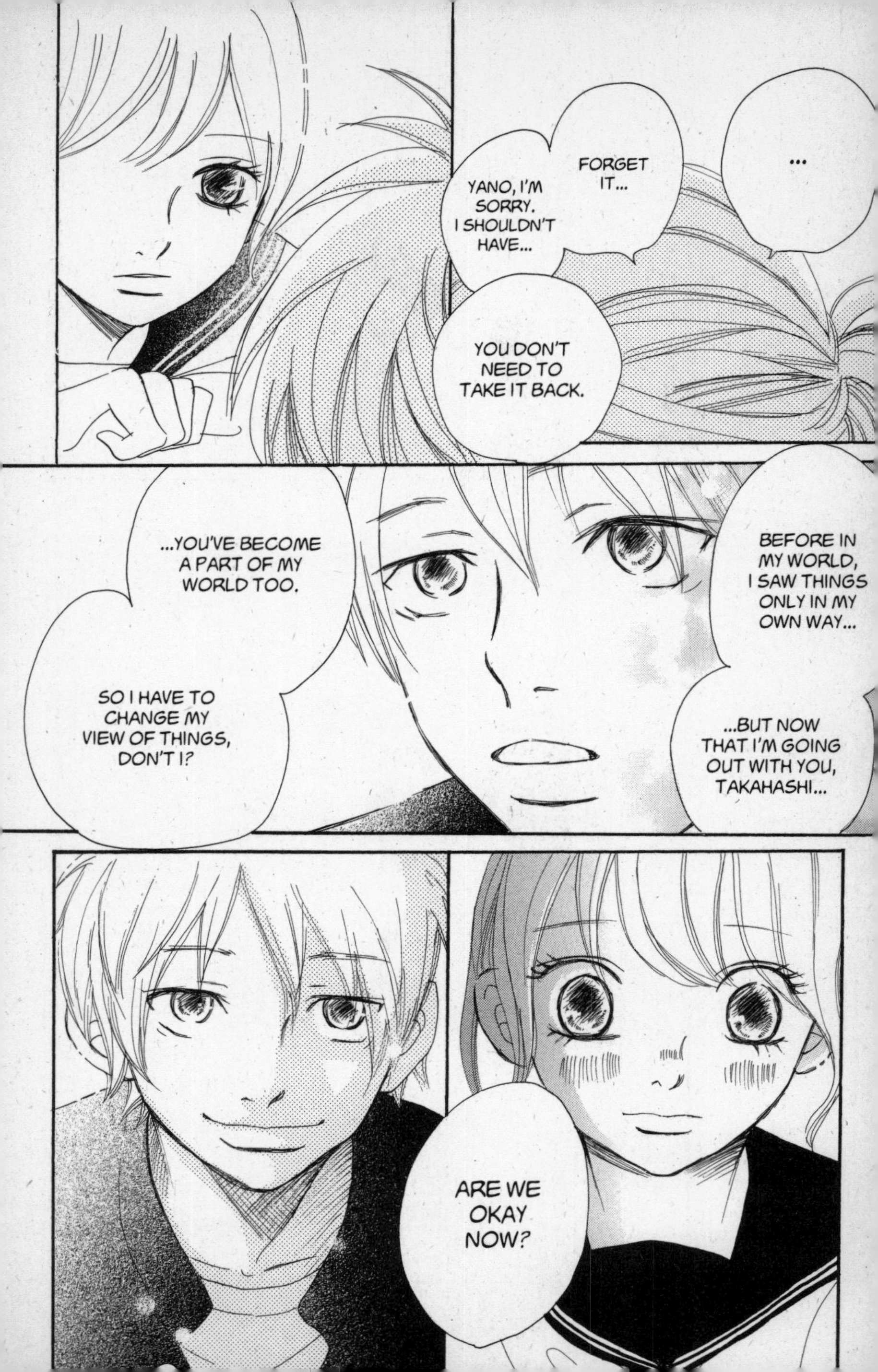
...
FORGET IT...
YANO, I'M SORRY. I SHOULDN'T HAVE...
YOU DON'T NEED TO TAKE IT BACK.
BEFORE IN MY WORLD, I SAW THINGS ONLY IN MY OWN WAY...
...BUT NOW THAT I'M GOING OUT WITH YOU, TAKAHASHI...
...YOU'VE BECOME A PART OF MY WORLD TOO.
SO I HAVE TO CHANGE MY VIEW OF THINGS, DON'T I?
ARE WE OKAY NOW?

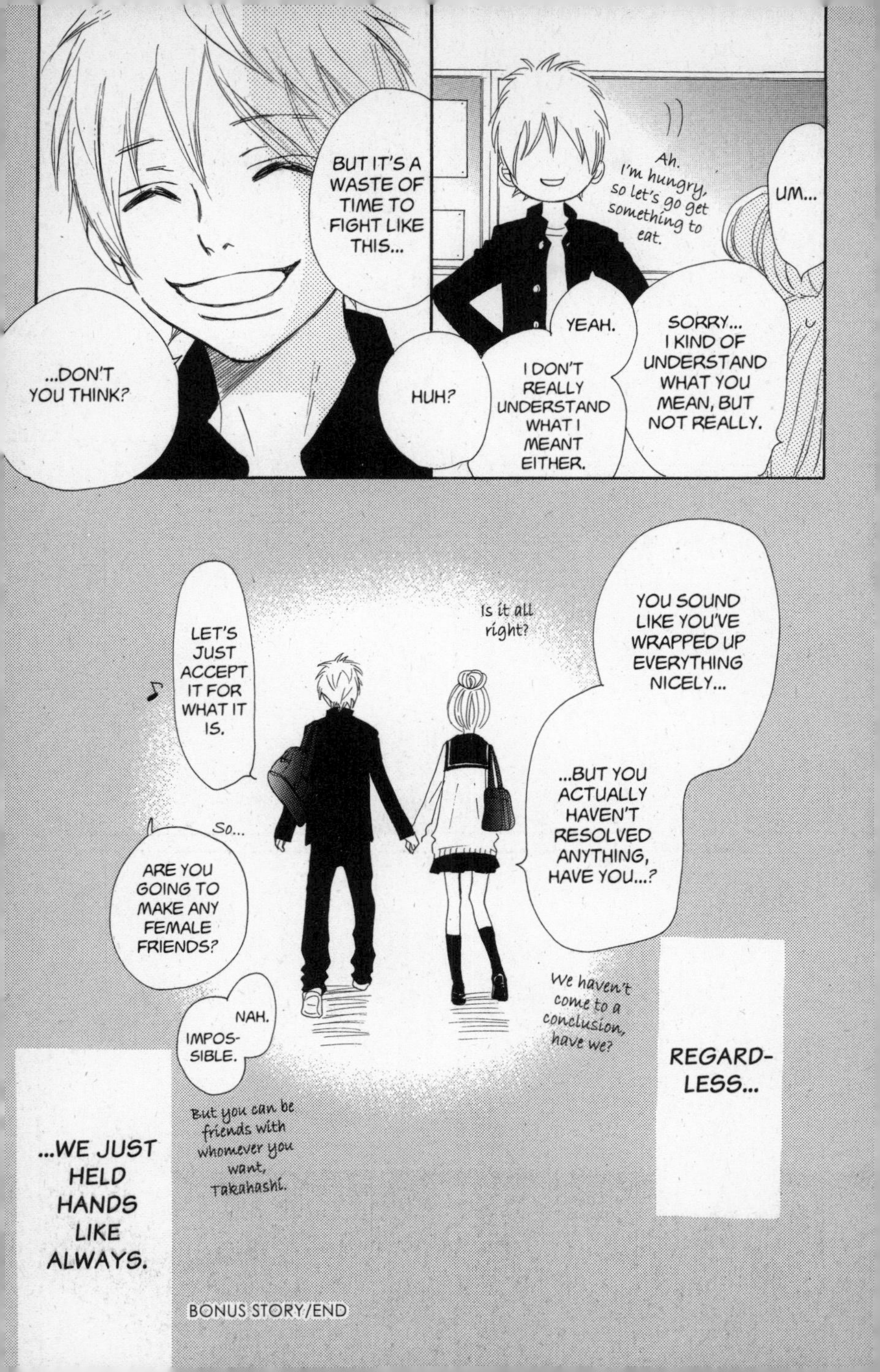
UM...
Ah. I'm hungry, so let's go get something to eat.
SORRY... I KIND OF UNDERSTAND WHAT YOU MEAN, BUT NOT REALLY.
YEAH.
I DON'T REALLY UNDERSTAND WHAT I MEANT EITHER.
HUH?
BUT IT'S A WASTE OF TIME TO FIGHT LIKE THIS...
...DON'T YOU THINK?
REGARDLESS...
YOU SOUND LIKE YOU'VE WRAPPED UP EVERYTHING NICELY...
...BUT YOU ACTUALLY HAVEN'T RESOLVED ANYTHING, HAVE YOU...?
Is it all right?
LET'S JUST ACCEPT IT FOR WHAT IT IS.
We haven't come to a conclusion, have we?
So...
ARE YOU GOING TO MAKE ANY FEMALE FRIENDS?
NAH. IMPOSSIBLE.
But you can be friends with whomever you want, Takahashi.
...WE JUST HELD HANDS LIKE ALWAYS.
BONUS STORY/END

I'm sorry it took longer than usual for volume 14 to come out.
I'd like to try to get volume 15 to you during the winter...
But then again, the winter in Hokkaido is very long.
I remember saying this back in volume 10, but I never
thought this series would go beyond fifteen volumes.
—Yuuki Obata

Yuuki Obata's birthday is January 9. Her debut manga, *Raindrops*, won
the Shogakukan Shinjin Comics Taisho Kasaku Award in 1998. Her
current series, *We Were There* (*Bokura ga Ita*), won the 50th Shogakukan
Manga Award and was adapted into an animated television series. She
likes sweets, coffee, drinking with friends, and scary stories. Her hobby
is browsing in bookshops.

WE WERE THERE
Vol. 14
Shojo Beat Edition

STORY & ART BY
YUUKI OBATA

© 2002 Yuuki OBATA/Shogakukan
All rights reserved.
Original Japanese edition "BOKURA GA ITA"
published by SHOGAKUKAN Inc.

Adaptation/Nancy Thistlethwaite
Translation/Tetsuichiro Miyaki
Touch-up Art & Lettering/Inori Fukuda Trant
Design/Jodie Yoshioka, Genki Hagata
Editor/Nancy Thistlethwaite

Printed in Canada

Published by VIZ Media, LLC
P.O. Box 77010
San Francisco, CA 94107

10 9 8 7 6 5 4 3 2 1
First printing, May 2012

The VIZ Manga App has some new friends...

The world's best manga is now on the iPad,™ iPhone™ and iPod™ touch

To learn more, visit viz.com

From legendary manga like *Death Note* to *Absolute Boyfriend*, the best manga in the world is now available on multiple devices through the official VIZ Manga app.

- **Hundreds of volumes available**
- **Free App**
- **New content weekly**
- **Free chapter 1 previews**

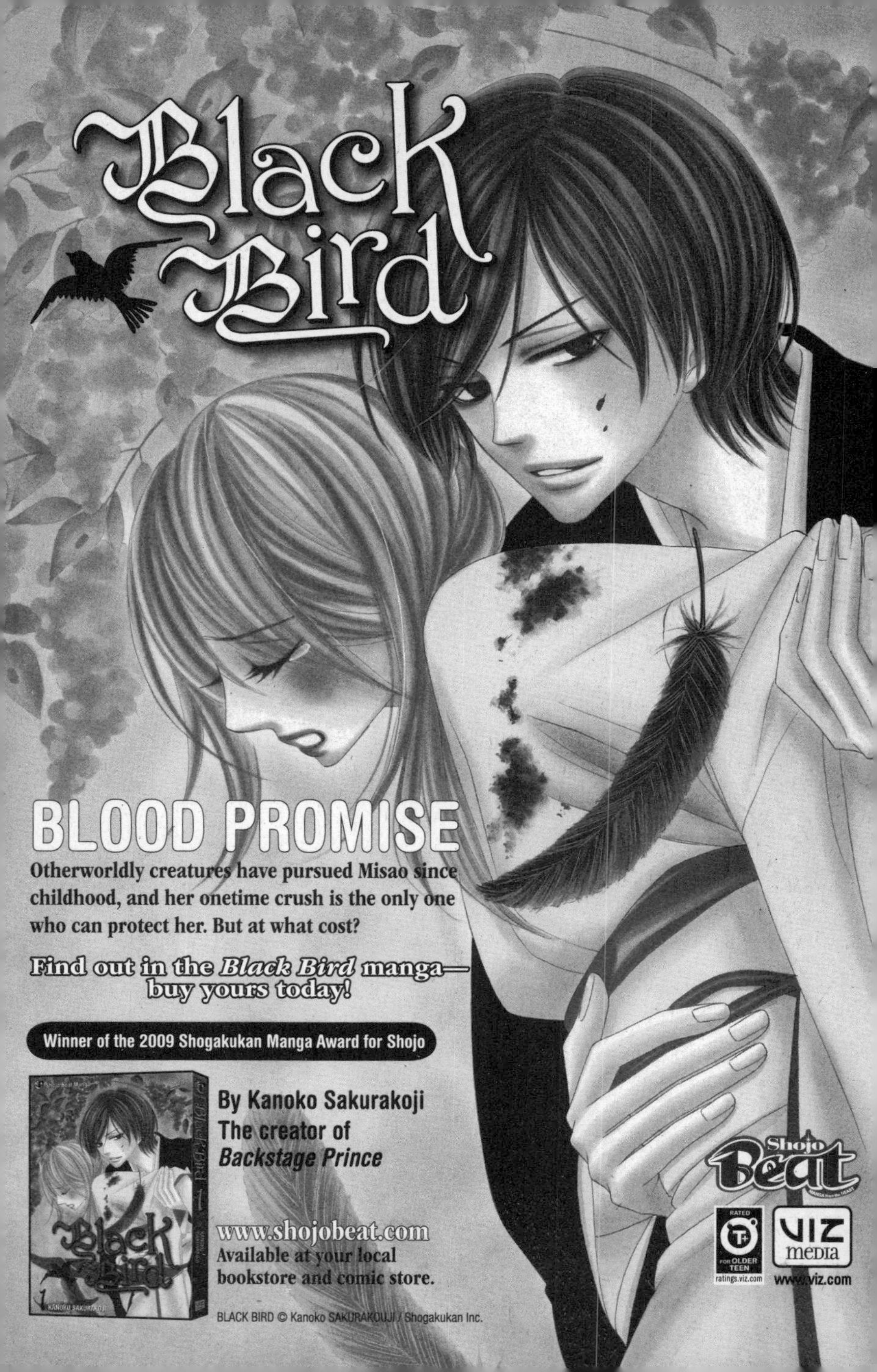
Black Bird
BLOOD PROMISE
Otherworldly creatures have pursued Misao since childhood, and her onetime crush is the only one who can protect her. But at what cost?
Find out in the *Black Bird* manga—
buy yours today!
Winner of the 2009 Shogakukan Manga Award for Shojo
By Kanoko Sakurakoji
The creator of
Backstage Prince
www.shojobeat.com
Available at your local bookstore and comic store.
BLACK BIRD © Kanoko SAKURAKOUJI / Shogakukan Inc.
Shojo Beat
RATED T+ FOR OLDER TEEN
ratings.viz.com
VIZ media
www.viz.com

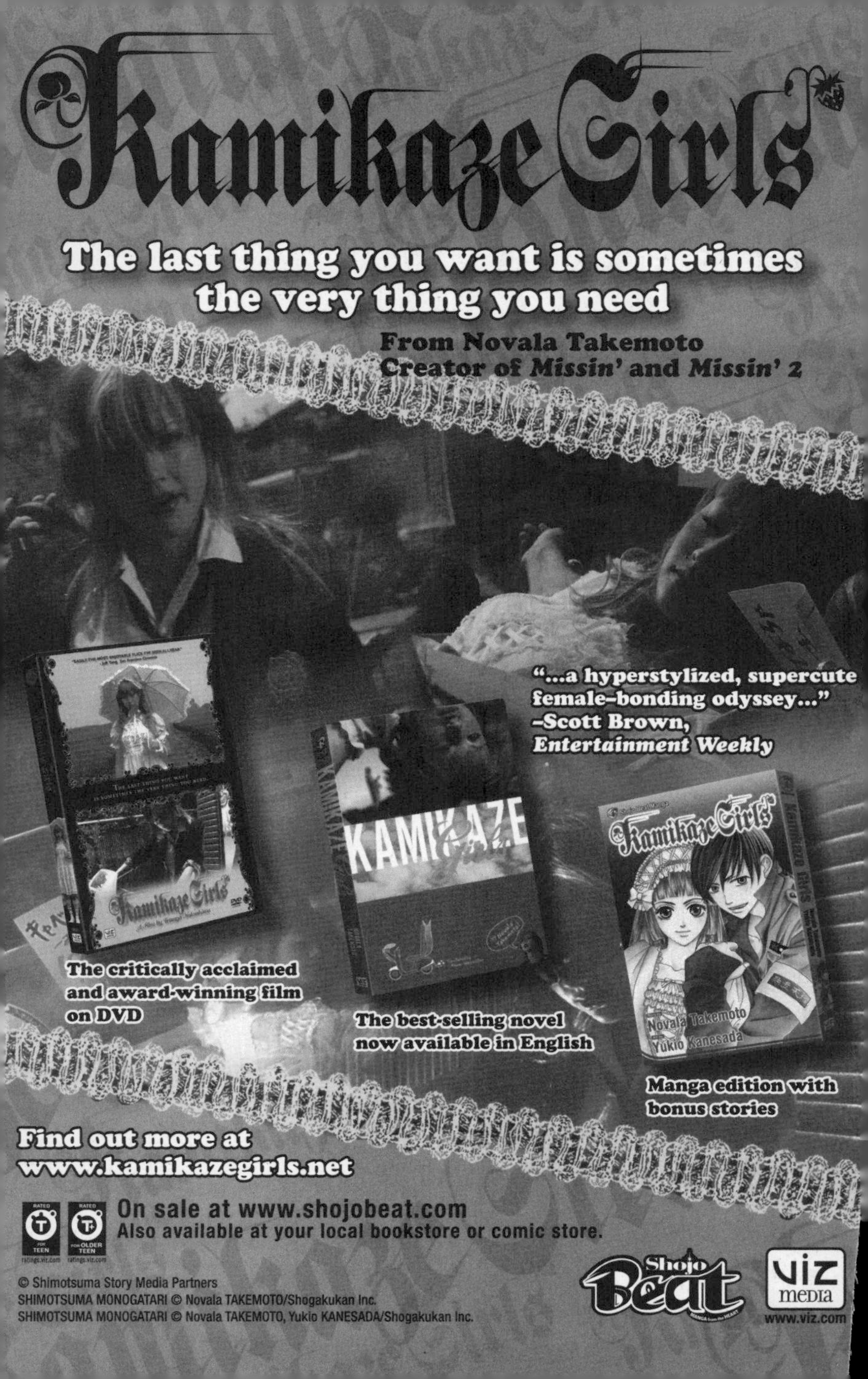
Kamikaze Girls
The last thing you want is sometimes the very thing you need
From Novala Takemoto
Creator of Missin' and Missin' 2
"...a hyperstylized, supercute female-bonding odyssey..."
–Scott Brown, Entertainment Weekly
KAMIKAZE
Kamikaze Girls
Novala Takemoto
Yukio Kanesada
The critically acclaimed and award-winning film on DVD
The best-selling novel now available in English
Manga edition with bonus stories
Find out more at www.kamikazegirls.net
On sale at www.shojobeat.com
Also available at your local bookstore or comic store.
RATED T FOR TEEN ratings.viz.com
RATED T+ FOR OLDER TEEN ratings.viz.com
Shojo Beat
VIZ media
www.viz.com
© Shimotsuma Story Media Partners
SHIMOTSUMA MONOGATARI © Novala TAKEMOTO/Shogakukan Inc.
SHIMOTSUMA MONOGATARI © Novala TAKEMOTO, Yukio KANESADA/Shogakukan Inc.

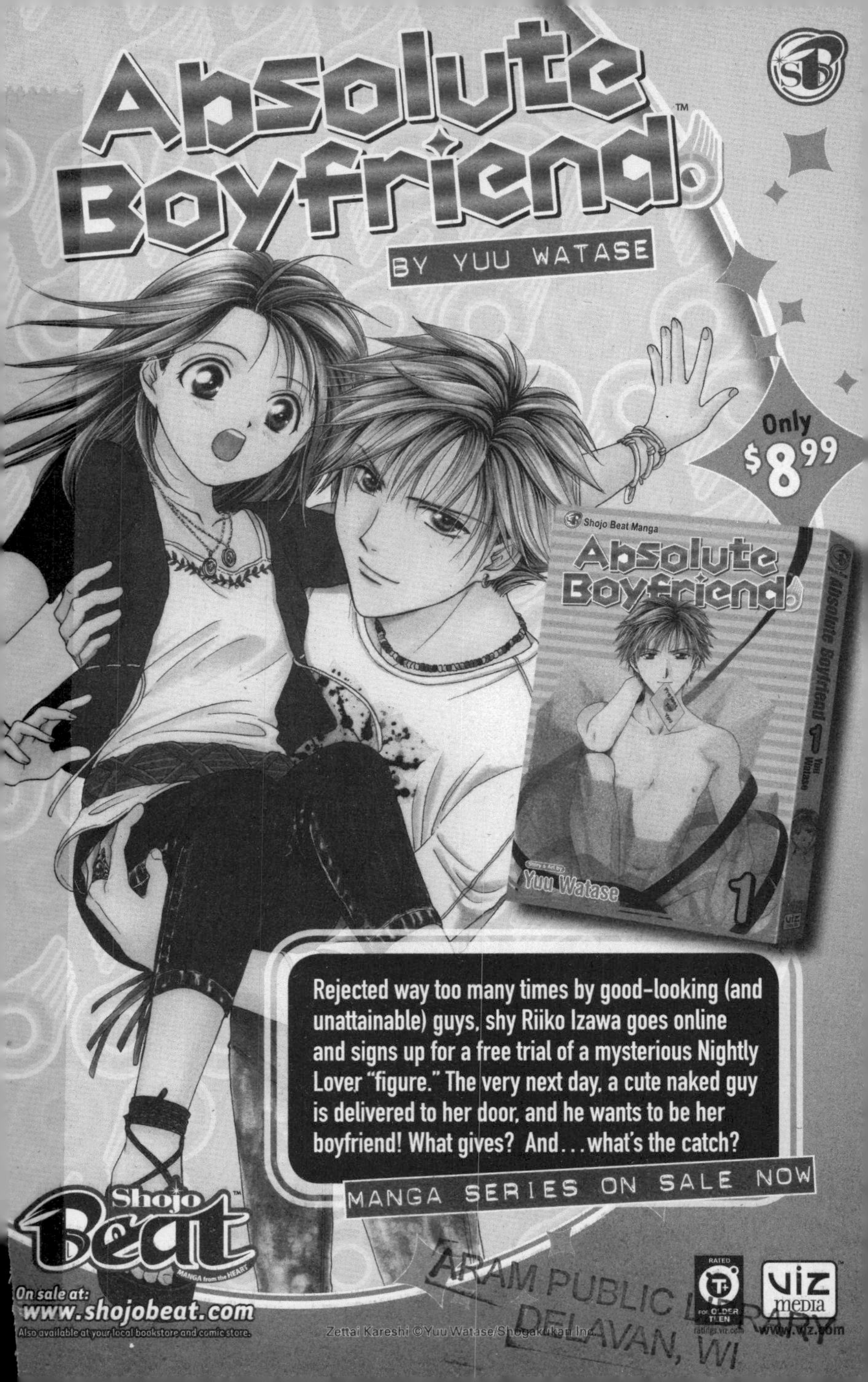

Absolute Boyfriend™
BY YUU WATASE
Only $8.99
Shojo Beat Manga
Absolute Boyfriend
Yuu Watase
1
Rejected way too many times by good-looking (and unattainable) guys, shy Riiko Izawa goes online and signs up for a free trial of a mysterious Nightly Lover "figure." The very next day, a cute naked guy is delivered to her door, and he wants to be her boyfriend! What gives? And...what's the catch?
MANGA SERIES ON SALE NOW
Shojo Beat™
MANGA from the HEART
On sale at:
www.shojobeat.com
Also available at your local bookstore and comic store.
Zettai Kareshi © Yuu Watase/Shogakukan Inc.
RATED T+ FOR OLDER TEEN
ratings.viz.com
viz media
www.viz.com
ARAM PUBLIC LIBRARY
DELAVAN, WI